Cherishing Life

love is for eternity

JOEL PATCHEN

Love Is For Eternity © 2010 Joel Patchen

All rights reserved. No portion of this book may be reproduced, stored in a retrieval system, or transmitted in any form or by any means—electronic, mechanical, photocopy, recording, or any other—except for brief quotations in printed reviews, without the prior permission of the publisher.

Published by Anna's Choice, LLC
Colorado Springs, Colorado, and printed in the United States of America.
www.annaschoice.org

ISBN 978-0-9818870-4-3

Cover and Interior Design: Granite Creative, inc.

Editorial assistance: Leonard G. Goss, GoodEditors.com

Scripture taken from the HOLY BIBLE, NEW INTERNATIONAL VERSION. Copyright © 1973, 1978, 1984 by International Bible Society. Used by permission of Zondervan. All rights reserved.

Scripture taken from the Holy Bible, New King James Version (NKJV) © 1979, 1980, 1982, 1991, Thomas Nelson, Inc., Publishers.

Scripture taken from the NEW AMERICAN STANDARD BIBLE®, copyright © 1960, 1962, 1963, 1968, 1971, 1972, 1973, 1975, 1977, 1995, by The Lockman Foundation. Used by permission.

Scripture quotations are from The Holy Bible, English Standard Version® (ESV®), copyright © 2001 by Crossway Bibles, a publishing ministry of Good News Publishers. Used by permission. All rights reserved.

Scripture quotations marked HCSB have been taken from the Holman Christian Standard Bible®, Copyright © 1999, 2000, 2002, 2003 by Holman Bible Publishers. Used by permission. Holman Christian Standard Bible®, Holman CSB®, and HCSB® are federally registered trademarks of Holman Bible Publishers.

Graphite illustration for January: Robin Coran
Photographic image for February: ZINQ Stock / Shutterstock Images LLC
Graphite illustrations for the months of March, April, and June depicting the preborn child were drawn using the photography of Andrzej Zachwieja and Jan Walczewski as featured in "Windows to the Womb," by Life Issues Institute: Robin Coran (April's image actually 11 weeks)
Photographic image for May: "Windows to the Womb," Life Issues Institute
Ultrasound image for July: provided by Joel Patchen (taken between 22 and 24 weeks)
Photographic image for August: Carl Stewart / Shutterstock Images LLC
Graphite illustration for September of newborn's feet: Robin Coran, with acknowledgment of Lee Robinson Photography for providing original image.
Photographic image for October: Monkey Business Images / Shutterstock Images LLC
Photographic image for November: Dgrilla / Shutterstock Images LLC
Photographic images for December (in order from left to right): Carlos E. Santa Maria; Pakhnyushcha; Wong Sze Yuen; OLJ Studio / Shutterstock Images LLC

Acknowledgments

I would like to thank the Creator for fearfully and wonderfully making me, for guiding my steps, and for directing my paths on this mission for life. Lord, your works are wonderful, and I am especially blessed and humbled to be one of them. I pray you are pleased with what is written here and that it adds to your glory and honor. Explode your truth through these pages and diminish those things derived from the flesh.

Thank you, Mom and Dad, for your faith, love, generosity, and encouragement. There is no doubt I am a reflection of you both in many ways. I love you and can never repay you for the myriad of sacrifices you've made or the things you've done for me. Thanks for loving and caring for me from the womb right up to the present.

To Michelle, my love. Without your support, hard work, and friendship this work might never have been accomplished. Thank you for partnering with me on behalf of the weak, broken, needy, fatherless, and oppressed among us. May God richly reward you for the role you've played in this mission for life.

To my children, thank you for your daily reminder of the preciousness of life and the sacrifices you've made as I labored on this project. I love you more than words can express, and I look forward to seeing how each of you will add to this beautiful tapestry of life.

To my family, friends, and fellow believers, it truly is a blessing to live life with you. Your prayers, support, and fellowship have beautified my existence and brought me joy and flavor.

As a layman, I would like to express my gratitude to my father and the many men and women of God who have mentored, equipped, and encouraged me over the years in my faith. I would also like to thank those pastors, teachers, authors, commentators, theologians, apologists, pro-life advocates, and others who have been used by the Holy Spirit to instruct me. Whether in person or through their works, their insights have aided my understanding of the truth. It should go without saying that many of the applications, observations, and insights shared in this book are not exclusive to me. My instruction has come from their words and the Word (Gal. 6:6).

Finally, I thank David Moore for his friendship and help with editing. Your time and efforts spent cleaning up my spelling and grammatical errors have been most helpful and substantial. Writing is only profitable when it is effectively communicated and easily understood, so thank you. Additional thanks belong to Leonard G. Goss of GoodEditors.com for his editorial insight, assistance, and refinement.

Preface

The ideas in this book are not new, but they are important. What is more important than life and its source? The writer of Ecclesiastes was right in that "what has been will be again, what has been done will be done again; there is nothing new under the sun" (1:9 NIV). From time to time, however, we need a refresher. We need to be reminded of profound truths and the biblical exhortation to love our neighbor, especially those neighbors we don't readily see. The Holy Scriptures are the cornerstone of this devotional and undoubtedly the most important part. God's Word will not return void when it is read, spoken, or heard (Isa. 55:10-11). Furthermore, God watches over his Word to perform it (Jer. 1:12). Therefore, it is my contention that the Word of God is plain to anyone who earnestly searches the Bible while seeking the Lord of the Bible. For believers, God has and will continue to write his Word on the tablet of our hearts (Jer. 31:31-34; Heb. 8:6-13; 10:14-24). God's Word is not time sensitive, being understood only from a certain time period or context. Instead, it is eternal and ageless. The Bible has been applicable to every past generation with access to it and, I believe, it will continue astounding and overwhelming future generations with its relevance to their particular times.

This devotional is constructed around the Bible and what it teaches about dignity and the sanctity of human life. It offers readers a biblical foundation for defending life, addressing abortion, and understanding life's beginning, value, and purpose. Sadly, some of my readers will have already experienced one or more abortions in their past. Let me assure everyone that God's love for us never wanes, and his forgiveness is available and sufficient to atone for all sins. He offers rest for our souls (Matt. 11:28-30). God loves us and wants to set us free. But since this resource aims to inform the body of Christ about the clear biblical merits for the abolition of abortion, it does not focus primarily on recovery and healing for the post-abortive believer. For those who have already been through the process of recovery and healing, this material may be well worth reading. If not, I suggest seeking help from a local church or pregnancy resource center that can direct one to resources that might be more appropriate. If the contents of this devotional cause any distress or pain, seek help from a professional post-abortion counselor.

I once heard a Japanese pastor say, "Tell me your dream and I will prophesy your future." Well, my dream is to abolish abortion in America and the world! Will you dream with me over the next 365 days? Let's see just how far God takes our dreams and uses them for his glory. Only God can accomplish this work, but like so many times before, he is excited about using the efforts of his human instruments to bring it about. Looking ahead to the day when abortion ends, I present this work with great expectation. May it bless, motivate, encourage, equip, and change the church forever.

Finally, any errors or inconsistencies found in this devotional belong solely to me. For questions about how a particular word or verse is rendered in its context, please refer to the Bible verse or passage in question. I hope readers find this effort both life-giving and life-changing. Above all, be encouraged and challenged about life and the God who created it!

Dedication

To my daughter Brooke, who taught me more about life's beauty, frailty, preciousness, and value during her brief time here on earth, from conception to death, than I had learned in the thirty-two years prior to her creation by God.

January

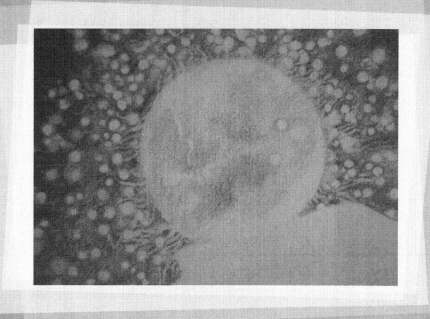

CONCEPTION: THE ZYGOTE

JANUARY 1

Isaiah 46:3-4 NIV

Listen to me, O house of Jacob, all you who remain of the house of Israel, you whom I have upheld since you were conceived, and have carried since your birth. Even to your old age and gray hairs I am he, I am he who will sustain you. I have made you and I will carry you; I will sustain you and I will rescue you.

∞

God values every part of our life journey from conception to earthly death. He has promised to take care of our present, as well as our eternity, when we place our trust in him. God has numbered our hairs, written our names on his hands, and died a criminal's death to secure our redemption (Luke 12:6-7; Isa. 49:15-16; Luke 23:33-34). We are God's treasure, the work of his hands, fashioned in the very image of God Almighty!

PRAYER FOCUS: God, increase my reverence and gratitude for all life. Holy Spirit, transform the hearts and minds of people locally, nationally, and globally to respect what the Father has made. Lord, help me treat my family, friends, and neighbors with dignity and grace.

DID YOU KNOW? From the moment of conception the zygote (the cell formed by the union of the male sperm and the female egg) contains the entire genetic code, mapping out everything about a person before the single cell divides for the first time. As Randy Alcorn stated, "The newly fertilized egg contains a staggering amount of genetic information, sufficient to control the individual's growth and development for his entire lifetime. A single thread of DNA from a human cell contains information equivalent to a library of one thousand volumes."[1]

REFLECTIONS

JANUARY 2

Psalm 139:13-16 NIV

For you created my inmost being; you knit me together in my mother's womb. I praise you because I am fearfully and wonderfully made; your works are wonderful, I know that full well. My frame was not hidden from you when I was made in the secret place. When I was woven together in the depths of the earth, your eyes saw my unformed body. All the days ordained for me were written in your book before one of them came to be.

Have you ever thought about how wonderful you are simply because God made you? The awesome truth is that the same hands that made the universe, all the creatures on the earth, and the Amazon rainforest made you. God fashioned you as an unequaled and entirely distinct being, unique from every other work of creation. You are not just a part of God's masterpiece; you are a masterpiece, God's priceless piece of art. Don't wait for the rocks to cry out—lift your voice today and praise the One who gave you life!

PRAYER FOCUS: Thank you, God, for giving me life. Lord, use my uniqueness to bring you glory. Help me see my value and the value of others from your perspective rather than the world's.

DID YOU KNOW? The reason we like to travel and stay in nice hotels is because we all began life in the nicest place we will ever stay besides heaven. That's right. Our first stop was at the comfort womb inn. During the beginning of our second week of life, we all checked in to the luxurious accommodations of our mother's womb for the next nine months.

REFLECTIONS

JANUARY 3

2 Timothy 3:16-17 ESV

All Scripture is breathed out by God and profitable for teaching, for reproof, for correction, and for training in righteousness, that the man of God may be competent, equipped for every good work.

We can trust God's Word to be the absolute authority in all matters of life because it is the very words of Almighty God written through human vessels inspired by the Holy Spirit. In every season of life, in all personal, social, political, moral, and ethical decisions, the Bible should be our source for truth and the answer to our questions. God's Word is flawless, trustworthy, enduring, pure, righteous, sure, radiant, wise, and altogether lovely (Ps. 19). We can take our questions, doubts, needs, dreams, and circumstances to the Lord in prayer, asking him to reveal the answers in Scripture. If we are persistent in reading God's Word, we will discover all truth. As the gospel of Matthew tells us, "Ask, and it will be given to you; seek, and you will find; knock, and it will be opened to you" (Matt. 7:7 ESV).

PRAYER FOCUS: God, give me a hunger and a thirst for your Word. Jesus, saturate my life with the wisdom of the Bible and allow it to dwell richly in me. As I pray the words of Scripture, make them become a spring of life-giving truth inside of me.

DID YOU KNOW? The Bible was written over a fifteen-hundred-year time span by more than forty different people. The human authors were very different from each other in vocation, education, experience, personality, and ability. Yet this diverse group from kings to fishermen wrote the most cohesive, enduring, and cherished piece of literature the world has ever known.[2] It was Jesus who said, "With God all things are possible" (Matt. 19:26 ESV).

REFLECTIONS

JANUARY 4

Hebrews 3:4 NASB

For every house is built by someone, but the builder of all things is God.

My children and I often play the "Who Made It" game in the car while we are driving to various places in town or visiting relatives. The game goes something like, "John, who made the street?" "Man," he will answer. "That's correct," I will say. "Elijah, who made the stars?" "God," he will answer. "Right." "Elijah, who made Mom and Peter and Esther?" Elijah answers, "God," and I tell him, "You're getting pretty good at this." In fact, my children are getting so good at the game that they now realize the deeper truth affirmed in today's Scripture, that the builder of all things is God. This has made me sophisticate things just a little: "John, who made the fence?" "Man," John will say. "Elijah, who made the wood that the fence is made out of?" "God," he will reply. Every raw material and element on earth, including our ability to think and create, came from the Creator and his spoken word.

PRAYER FOCUS: Thank you, God, for making me and everyone I love. Lord, you created all my talent, intellect, and abilities, so how can I use them for the glory of your Kingdom? Jesus, help me pursue the things you birth in my heart.

DID YOU KNOW? The Empire State Building is currently New York City's tallest building. According to *Firefly's World of Facts*, the building was erected on the site of the Waldorf-Astoria Hotel, taking a total of 410 days at a completion rate of four-and-a-half floors a week.[3] As amazing and ingenious as this construction project was, absolutely nothing compares to the things God has made. Consider the lilies of the field, the mass of the mountains, the heat of the sun, the brightness of the stars, the size of the universe, the speed of a cheetah, the flight of a bird, the amazing properties of water, and the wonder and complexities of the human body. God reveals himself every day in the things he has made. All we have to do is look around to discover the great eternal God!

REFLECTIONS

JANUARY 5

Genesis 1:27-28 ESV

So God created man in his own image, in the image of God he created him; male and female he created them. And God blessed them. And God said to them, "Be fruitful and multiply and fill the earth and subdue it and have dominion over the fish of the sea and over the birds of the heavens and over every living thing that moves on the earth."

The only thing in all creation made in the image of God is people! Every member of the human family has the distinct privilege of being fashioned by the hands of the Almighty in his very own likeness. God singled us out from the rest of his creation by granting us dominion over all other living things. From the beginning God asked us to be good stewards of the planet and its people, filling the earth with our offspring. God desires to have a world full of people so that he can woo each heart to share in an intimate relationship with him. This is why we were created—so the Creator of the universe could have a personal relationship with us, to know us, to love us, and to fellowship with us on an individual level. The Father has also prepared many rooms in his house because in eternity he wants heaven to be full of people as well (John 14:2).

PRAYER FOCUS: God, I'm glad you love, want, and value me, and I ask you to continue giving me a sense of how precious I am to you. Lord, deepen our relationship and invigorate our intimate times together. Help me value and respect every human life regardless of its race, shape, size, ability, health, age, or development.

DID YOU KNOW? "Unraveled and stretched end to end, the DNA molecules in a human cell would be more than six feet long."[4] Every cell in the human body is incredibly complex, and the human body contains trillions of them.

REFLECTIONS

JANUARY 6

Psalm 127:3 NKJV

Behold, children are a heritage from the LORD, the fruit of the womb is a reward.

My children can be difficult, trying, and exhausting, but they are without a doubt one of God's greatest blessings in my life. They bring joy and laughter to our home and a future hope for all they might accomplish. They give my life purpose and meaning, and they fill each day with adventure and discovery. Whether they rise or fall, succeed or fail, I love being their father and having a privileged relationship with them. My children are a rich reward from God and I am thankful he entrusted them to me. I understand that they are first and foremost God's children and that he expects me to protect, love, and mentor them. It is a shameful thing to talk of unwanted children because it reveals our lack of understanding about God and who his children are. God made all of us, and he wants to adopt all who are willing into his loving family. The Creator never makes mistakes or people he doesn't love and want. Regardless of our conception, circumstance, or family experience, God wants us! There is no such thing as an unwanted child because we are all wanted by our Creator.

PRAYER FOCUS: God, show me your fatherly love and allow me to see that I'm your child. Reveal to me my worth and the worth of others. Help me to know you better, and help every person to ask you to come into their hearts and adopt them through saving faith in your Son, the Lord Jesus. May they confess him with their mouths and call upon his name to be saved (Rom. 10:9-13).

DID YOU KNOW? According to *The Boston Globe*, 250,000 adoptions take place each year on earth, and nearly half of these adoptions involve homes in the United States.[5] Every child without a home longs to be adopted into a loving family that will meet their needs. For those who haven't yet come home to their heavenly Father, Jesus can adopt them and bring them home.

REFLECTIONS

JANUARY 7

Romans 1:19-20 ESV

For what can be known about God is plain to them, because God has shown it to them. For his invisible attributes, namely, his eternal power and divine nature, have been clearly perceived, ever since the creation of the world, in the things that have been made. So they are without excuse.

How can we pay attention to the size of the ocean, or regard the number of species it contains, and not feel God's power? How can we take a walk in the wilderness and hear the wind whistle through the trees, and not feel the divine presence? How can we study the complexity of the human body and the cells of which it is made, and not marvel at its Designer? How can we hold a newborn baby and not perceive God's breath of life? The answer is that we cannot. The evidence for God is all around us—in everything he has made.

PRAYER FOCUS: Thank you, God, for giving me life and for putting me on a planet so marvelously designed that it supports and sustains all things together in perfect harmony.

DID YOU KNOW? Darwin's suspected transitional fossils or "missing links" to prove his theory of evolution are still missing! Michael Denton has written, "Despite the tremendous increase in geological activity in every corner of the globe and despite the discovery of many strange and hitherto unknown forms, the infinitude of connecting links has still not been discovered and the fossil record is about as discontinuous as it was when Darwin was writing the *Origin*."[6] Currently, molecular biology is exposing Darwin's limited knowledge of the single-celled organism and its complexity. We must never believe the erroneous notion that human life came from nothing, has no purpose, and is an accident of time and space. We were made by God to fulfill his purposes and to love and serve his kingdom and his people. He molded us, loves us, and this life we are living is one of his greatest gifts to us.

REFLECTIONS

JANUARY 8

Colossians 1:15-20 NIV

He is the image of the invisible God, the firstborn over all creation. For by him all things were created: things in heaven and on earth, visible and invisible, whether thrones or powers or rulers or authorities; all things were created by him and for him. He is before all things, and in him all things hold together. And he is the head of the body, the church; he is the beginning and the firstborn from among the dead, so that in everything he might have the supremacy. For God was pleased to have all his fullness dwell in him, and through him to reconcile to himself all things, whether things on earth or things in heaven, by making peace through his blood, shed on the cross.

∞

Jesus is the creator of all things and truly deserves the title Immanuel, which means "God with us." He is God in the flesh. Jesus shared in our humanity from his conception to his death on the cross. He bore all our shame and iniquity so we might be reconciled to a just and holy God who required sacrifice for our sins. His sacrifice qualified us for adoption as sons and daughters of God. Through Jesus' work, we can all become adopted sons and daughters of God (Gal. 4:4-7). This means we are not only made by God, but we are made for God, in order that we might have fellowship and intimacy with him. We can place our faith in Jesus Christ—we can do it today—and we can let his sacrifice on the cross for our sins wipe away our slate of sin and restore us to a right relationship with the Father.

PRAYER FOCUS: God, I'm overwhelmed that you loved me enough to die for me on the cross and pay for all my sins. I trust your Word that says, "As far as the east is from the west, so far does he remove our transgressions from us" (Ps. 103:12 ESV). Thank you, Lord, for your love and graciousness. Give all who confess Christ a sense of your redeeming power to deliver them from all sin. Lord, move upon the hearts of all to surrender their lives to you and invite you to become their Savior and Lord. Let us confess our belief in you and your resurrection from the dead, and let us ask you to cleanse us from our sins (John 3:16-21; Acts 4:10-12; 16:30-34; Rom. 1:16-17; 5:6-11; 10:9-13; Eph. 1:13-14; 2:8-9; 1 John 3:23-24).

DID YOU KNOW? Jesus of Nazareth fulfilled all Old Testament prophecies about the coming Messiah. Check out the following prophecies and their fulfillment in Scripture:

The Messiah would be born of a virgin—Isaiah 7:14 and Luke 1:26-35

The Messiah would be born in Bethlehem—Micah 5:2 and Matthew 2:1

The Messiah would enter Jerusalem on a donkey—Zechariah 9:9 and Luke 19:35-37

The Messiah would be resurrected after death—Psalm 16:10 and Acts 2:31

The Messiah would be betrayed—Psalm 41:9 and Matthew 10:4

The Messiah would be pierced in his side—Zechariah 12:10 and John 19:34

The Messiah's death would cause darkness during the day—Amos 8:9 and Matthew 27:45

The Messiah would be buried in a rich man's tomb—Isaiah 53:9 and Matthew 27:57-60

The Messiah's crucifixion events would be unique—Psalm 22:1-18 and Mark 15:34; Luke 23:33-37; John 19:36-37.[7]

JANUARY 9

Hebrews 2:14-17 NIV

Since the children have flesh and blood, he too shared in their humanity so that by his death he might destroy him who holds the power of death—that is, the devil—and free those who all their lives were held in slavery by their fear of death. For surely it is not angels he helps, but Abraham's descendants. For this reason he had to be made like his brothers in every way, in order that he might become a merciful and faithful high priest in service to God, and that he might make atonement for the sins of the people.

Jesus is the perfect advocate to the Father because he shared fully in our humanity, and was subject to all the trials and temptations that we experience in this earthly life. God loved us enough to walk in our shoes and become one of us, even to the point of suffering, persecution, and unjust punishment. Jesus defeated spiritual death through his sacrifice on the cross. He is holding out the free gift of life for all eternity to anyone who believes he died for their sins. Just like Jesus, we owe it to the people we are helping to listen to their needs and walk in their shoes as we offer them assistance.

PRAYER FOCUS: God, help me become more aware of the needs of the people around me. Holy Spirit, give me the time, ability, and resources to meet their needs. Lord, I want to become focused on others instead of focused on myself.

DID YOU KNOW? Every human being on earth was created through the biological process of fertilization, with the exception of those created at the beginning and Jesus: Adam was fashioned from the dust of the ground, and Eve was formed from the rib of Adam. Jesus was conceived by God's Holy Spirit.

REFLECTIONS

JANUARY 10

Ecclesiastes 11:5 ESV

As you do not know the way the spirit comes to the bones in the womb of a woman with child, so you do not know the work of God who makes everything.

God is beyond our comprehension and mysterious in many ways, but he has not left us without truth. The truth in God's Word is rich and vast enough to engage any subject or answer any question we might have. With all the knowledge and insight the human race has gained through medicine, science, experimentation, and technology, we still don't have all the answers, and we frequently discover that the answers we do have are inaccurate or incomplete. While it is true that we have made many significant discoveries about life in the womb, we will probably never understand it all. Only God knows the intimate and minute details of life. Therefore, God's Word is the best source for separating out his wisdom as to the origin and value of human life in the womb and beyond. The Scriptures make it very clear that God is the creator of everything, including children in the womb, who are full human persons from the moment he conceives them.

PRAYER FOCUS: Thank you, God, for your mystery, your truth, and a faith that can reconcile them together. Father, transform my heart and mind through this daily study of your counsel on life and its value, purpose, and preciousness. Lord, awaken me to what your Word says about the dignity and value of every human life from conception forward. Jesus, arrest my heart by what is contained in these pages and use it for your glory and good pleasure.

DID YOU KNOW? By the end of the eighth week in the womb, a baby's bones begin to form, and by the sixteenth week those bones have hardened enough to be seen in ultrasound scans.[8]

REFLECTIONS

JANUARY 11

Micah 7:18-19 NIV

Who is a God like you, who pardons sin and forgives the transgression of the remnant of his inheritance? You do not stay angry forever but delight to show mercy. You will again have compassion on us; you will tread our sins underfoot and hurl all our iniquities into the depths of the sea.

∞

The Bible teaches that we are all sinners who have fallen short of the glory of God. But it also teaches that God has atoned for our sins through the perfect life and sacrifice of his only Son. It is an awesome, life-giving moment when we decide to allow Jesus to pay our debt and erase our sin, to realize that all our sins are covered upon faith in Jesus Christ through God's grace and that we are now forever his adopted child, part of his glorious inheritance. As we pursue what God's Word says about the preciousness of life, we will discover the sinful, ugly reality of abortion. Thankfully abortion, like all sin, has been dealt with by Jesus on the cross in his mercy, compassion, and forgiveness. God is willing and able to forgive us for any sin if we confess it to him. If we are haunted by abortion or any other sin, we can give it to Jesus, ask his forgiveness, and allow him to mend our broken heart and cast our sin into the depths of the ocean.

PRAYER FOCUS: Holy Spirit, search my heart and reveal to me the sins I need to address. Jesus, I give my sins to you and repent of them. Thank you for your super-abundant mercy and for the fact that you delight to shower your mercy upon me!

DID YOU KNOW? The ocean's deepest point is the Marianas Trench in the Pacific Ocean, having a depth of 35,837 feet, which is deeper than Mount Everest is tall. The Pacific Ocean is 64,185,629 square miles, easily big enough to hold all your sins and mine.[9]

REFLECTIONS

JANUARY 12

2 Samuel 22:31 NKJV

As for God, His way is perfect; the word of the Lord is proven; He is a shield to all who trust in Him.

God's Word is proven. The Bible has stood the test of time and survived countless attacks from critics who deny it is from divine origins. We can trust God's Word and take refuge in it. Never be ashamed of the Gospel. Hold on to the words of Scripture and let them become a fortress against any storm as we cling to the promises of God. I think about Jesus when I read this verse because he is called the Way, the Word, and the Lord in Scripture. In the sixth chapter of Ephesians the apostle Paul tells us to put on the full armor of God as we journey through the Christian life. He wrote, "be strong in the Lord and in the power of His might. Put on the whole armor of God, that you may be able to stand against the wiles of the devil. For we do not wrestle against flesh and blood, but against principalities, against powers, against the rulers of the darkness of this age, against spiritual *hosts* of wickedness in the heavenly *places*. Therefore take up the whole armor of God, that you may be able to withstand in the evil day, and having done all, to stand" (Eph. 6:10-13 NKJV). How appropriate that the shield protecting us from the Enemy is called the shield of faith. There is no greater protection than when we place our faith in Jesus.

PRAYER FOCUS: Thank you, heavenly Father, for the beauty, perfection, and timelessness of your eternal and unerring Word. Holy Spirit, give me a desire to read and memorize the Bible, and give me the courage and opportunity to share your Word with others and those I love. Lord Jesus, honor my faith by granting me the protection and provision that comes from being hidden in you.

DID YOU KNOW? There are hundreds of names and titles used for Jesus in the Bible. Some of my favorites are the Prince of Peace (Isa. 9:6), the Prince of life (Acts 3:15), the Branch (Zech. 3:8), I Am (John 8:58), Wonderful Counselor (Isa. 9:6), the way, the truth, and the life (John 14:6), and the Lamb (Rev. 17:14).[10]

REFLECTIONS

JANUARY 13

Isaiah 9:6-7 ESV

For to us a child is born, to us a son is given; and the government shall be upon his shoulder, and his name shall be called Wonderful Counselor, Mighty God, Everlasting Father, Prince of Peace. Of the increase of his government and of peace there will be no end, on the throne of David and over his kingdom, to establish it and to uphold it with justice and with righteousness from this time forth and forevermore. The zeal of the Lord of hosts will do this.

If God did not have reverence for the process of human development in the womb, then why did he choose to come to earth through the womb? He did it to share in our humanity and life experience, so that he could be a faithful and merciful High Priest. Jesus Christ entered life as a zygote to show us that every part of our life is sacred and valuable, even the very first moment of our existence. God gave us the gift of himself; for to us a child is born, to us the Son was given. He came to counsel, to bring peace and justice, and to govern. God loves us all so much that he became human by wrapping himself in human flesh and sharing every part of our human journey in order to rescue us from our sin and satisfy his justice through his own righteousness. Hallelujah!

PRAYER FOCUS: Jesus, knowing you shared in my humanity frees me to tell you anything. I know you walked in my shoes and know precisely what I need before I even ask. Thank you, Lord, for your mighty compassion, care, and love for me throughout my life. Jesus, I'm amazed that you left your heavenly throne to become a single-celled zygote in the body of a humble woman, in order to purchase my redemption and grant me fellowship with you through new life.

DID YOU KNOW? The title *Christ* is the Greek translation of the Hebrew word *Messiah*, which means "anointed."[11] The Incarnation was when God took on human form in the person of Jesus. St. Augustine wrote of the incarnation of Christ: "He so loved us that, for our sake, He was made man in time, although through him all times were made. He was made man, who made man. He was created of a mother whom he created. He was carried by hands that he formed. He cried in the manger in wordless infancy, he the Word, without whom all human eloquence is mute."[12]

REFLECTIONS

JANUARY 14

Zechariah 8:16-17 NIV

"These are the things you are to do: Speak the truth to each other, and render true and sound judgment in your courts; do not plot evil against your neighbor, and do not love to swear falsely. I hate all this," declares the LORD.

Regrettably, we live in a culture that willingly violates what God has told us to do in today's Scripture by allowing abortion on demand. The lie that the preborn are not persons is cut from the same cloth that reduced the Jews in Nazi Germany to rats and the African slaves to property in America. We have not spoken the obvious truth that embryology and ultrasound technology clearly display about the developing baby. Nor have we rendered true and sound judgments in our courts. Think, for example, of the *Dred Scott* decision in 1857, which proclaimed that slaves were property and not protected by the U.S. Constitution. Or the *Roe v. Wade* and *Doe v. Bolton* decisions in 1973, stating that a woman has a right to abortion at virtually any time during a pregnancy. Abortion clearly seeks to harm our neighbor and is one of the greatest forms of evil the world has ever known.

PRAYER FOCUS: Lord, I pray that all Christians will rise up and defend the helpless children in the womb. Jesus, these children cannot defend themselves as they are daily being led to the slaughter. Please have mercy on our nation for the slaughter of your innocents, and give us time to repent of our wickedness. Father God, I plead with you to use your people and your supernatural power to end abortion in America and the world!

DID YOU KNOW? Since 1973, the United States has aborted almost fifty million children and is currently supporting the killing of around 3,300 human beings per day. Lord, have mercy on us! Please allow us to see this hidden holocaust for what it is and how it harms your human creation.

REFLECTIONS

JANUARY 15

Micah 6:8 NASB

He has told you, O man, what is good; and what does the Lord require of you but to do justice, to love kindness, and to walk humbly with your God?

If every believer practiced doing justice, loving kindness, and walking humbly with God, what kind of an impact would we make in the world for Christ? I can think of no better description of Jesus than that he is truly a man who embodies all three principles. This Scripture speaks to every aspect of the Christian life and gives us a strategy for ending abortion in America. We need to be tireless in our efforts to secure justice for all children in the womb. At the same time, we need to extend kindness to mothers and fathers experiencing unexpected pregnancies, and we need to extend forgiveness to post-abortive parents. Whenever possible, we can assist the post-abortive person in the healing process by providing them with prayer, support, availability, and referrals to professional post-abortive care. The first step, however, is walking humbly with our God and seeking his wisdom, guidance, and timing.

PRAYER FOCUS: Lord, teach us to walk in humility and to revere the things you have made. Help us to have the courage and the wisdom to make a difference in the lives of our fellow men and women. Jesus, help me make an impact on my culture.

DID YOU KNOW? The great pastor and civil rights leader Martin Luther King, Jr. was born on this day in 1929. God in his providence raised up a great deliverer from the womb during the Great Depression. King received the Nobel Peace Prize in 1964 for his work on behalf of civil rights, justice, and peace.

REFLECTIONS

JANUARY 16

Luke 12:6-7 NIV

Are not five sparrows sold for two pennies? Yet not one of them is forgotten by God. Indeed, the very hairs of your head are all numbered. Don't be afraid; you are worth more than many sparrows.

Many of the arguments for legalized abortion center on the question of value. One of the most common arguments goes something like this: If you don't agree with abortion, don't have one, but don't impose your morality on others. The obvious lie in this argument is that people determine morality and value. But that is just not true. The truth is that God is the sole determiner of morality and value because he alone is the Creator of all things and the determiner of truth. Humanity has tremendous value to God because we are made in his image, and we are the work of his own hands. It is not up to any of us to end innocent human life on our own terms. We must stop asking the world to assess our value and start listening to what the Creator says it is.

PRAYER FOCUS: Father, I'm glad you alone set my worth. Help me see that you value me and all human beings more than anything else in all creation. Thank you for specifically making me to fulfill your purposes. Jesus, transform our culture into a culture that values and protects all human life.

DID YOU KNOW? Alex Rodriguez, the New York Yankees baseball player, earns approximately $1,131 per minute, or $203,703 per game.[13] Bill Gates, the founder of Microsoft, has amassed a personal fortune in excess of $50 billion. While we marvel at this kind of wealth and achievement, these things matter very little in God's economy. God is interested in what is inside the human heart, not in fame, fortune, or worldly achievements.

REFLECTIONS

JANUARY 17

Job 24:12 NIV

The groans of the dying rise from the city, and the souls of the wounded cry out for help. But God charges no one with wrongdoing.

Like so many of us, Job struggled with God's apparent lack of involvement in the midst of his suffering and the suffering of others around him. Scripture teaches that God is slow to anger and desires for all to come to repentance (Exod. 34:6; 2 Pet. 3:9). God is patient with the wicked and gracious to all, which explains to some degree why it appears that he allows bad things to happen. But God will render justice for those who are suffering and judgment upon the wicked in his timing, even though we are slow to perceive it (Exod. 34:7; Ps. 73). Trust that God has a plan even in difficult times, and that ultimately he will use it for good. I believe this verse accurately describes abortion as it is today in our culture. The aborted groan from our cities and their parents are left with wounded souls crying out for help. God is giving us time to repent and urging us to hear their cry and stop the slaughter.

PRAYER FOCUS: Lord, give me a heart for the needy and oppressed, and reveal to me some things I can do to help them in their distress. Thank you, God, for giving us free will; help me use mine for good.

DID YOU KNOW? The womb is the most dangerous place in America for a child. Each day, in the United States, a baby is aborted every twenty-six seconds. Stated another way, approximately 137 babies die every hour, 3,300 per day, 100,000 per month, or 1.2 million babies per year![14]

REFLECTIONS

JANUARY
18

Psalm 142:1-2 NIV

I cry aloud to the Lord; I lift up my voice to the Lord for mercy. I pour out my complaint before him; before him I tell my trouble.

This psalm was written by David when he was in a cave, possibly hiding from Saul, who was trying to kill him. It illuminates the modern-day cry of the preborn in that the nation's most vulnerable children are crying out to God for mercy and rescue as they develop under the constant threat of abortion. Like David, they are hidden in the cave of the womb and are every bit as deserving to be protected from their enemies. Is it not possible to hear the voice of the preborn in today's verses?

PRAYER FOCUS: Lord, I pray that our nation would begin to recognize through science, technology, biology, education, and the Scriptures that the preborn are part of the human family from the moment of conception (fertilization).

DID YOU KNOW? Twenty-two days from conception the new baby's heart begins to beat, and by the week's end the heart is propelling blood through vessels no thicker than a hair.[15]

REFLECTIONS

JANUARY 19

Psalm 142:3-5 NIV

When my spirit grows faint within me, it is you who know my way. In the path where I walk men have hidden a snare for me. Look to my right and see; no one is concerned for me. I have no refuge; no one cares for my life. I cry to you, O LORD; I say, "You are my refuge, my portion in the land of the living."

It is hard to face the horror of abortion and the brutal truth that the child faces great agony as it is literally ripped to pieces in the womb. This atrocity is so ugly and so evil that our natural reaction is to turn away and put it out of our minds. But turning away is a terrible mistake because it allows the evil to continue and even to flourish. Our inability to identify with the preborn and cope with the tragedy of abortion has led to their cry to God, like the cry of the psalmist, "I have no refuge; no one cares for my life." It should grieve all Christians to know that their nation has hidden a snare for many of our brothers and sisters in the womb through legalized killing of the preborn. God is their refuge, and he will rescue them and care for them for all eternity, yet for many, their portion in the land of the living will be shrouded in darkness and their lives will be snuffed out in less than three months.

PRAYER FOCUS: Lord, awaken me to the cry of the preborn babies who are facing abortion, and give me the courage to speak up for them and save their lives!

DID YOU KNOW? Eighty-eight percent of all U.S. abortions occur during the first three months of pregnancy.[16] A human life amendment to the constitution granting equal protection under the law to all people from conception to natural death would overturn all state abortion laws and the Supreme Court decisions allowing abortion on demand in *Roe* and *Doe*. This amendment can be achieved by a two-thirds majority vote in both the U. S. House of Representatives and the U.S. Senate or by a constitutional convention requested by at least thirty-four states.[17]

REFLECTIONS

JANUARY 20

Psalm 142:6-7 NIV

Listen to my cry, for I am in desperate need; rescue me from those who pursue me, for they are too strong for me. Set me free from my prison, that I may praise your name. Then the righteous will gather about me because of your goodness to me.

God is always concerned with the needs of his people. As his children here on earth, we need to be available vessels for heaven's use in meeting those needs. If we haven't taken action already, it is time for everyone in the body of Christ to stand against abortion using every peaceful means necessary or, as Hamlet would say, "To take arms against a sea of troubles, and by opposing end them (*Hamlet*, III, i)."[18] The psalmist tells us that "From the lips of children and infants you have ordained praise because of your enemies, to silence the foe and the avenger" (Ps. 8:2 NIV). I want to hear the praise of the preborn, and I want that praise to establish a stronghold against those who would attack babies in the womb. When will the righteous gather about God's children?

PRAYER FOCUS: God, show me what I can do to take action against abortion. Give me a passion to see all babies in the womb receive justice. Lord, bless all those who labor in pro-life work with protection, provision, and wisdom.

DID YOU KNOW? In 1969, twenty-five percent of births outside of marriage were adopted, but by 1999 that percentage had dropped to a mere two percent.[19] This reduction of adoptions is due primarily to legalized abortion. Tragically, since abortion was legalized, around one in four children conceived in the United States has been surgically aborted each year.[20]

REFLECTIONS

JANUARY
21

1 Corinthians 13:4-8 NIV

Love is patient, love is kind. It does not envy, it does not boast, it is not proud. It is not rude, it is not self-seeking, it is not easily angered, it keeps no record of wrongs. Love does not delight in evil but rejoices with the truth. It always protects, always trusts, always hopes, always perseveres. Love never fails.

The Bible teaches us that "whoever does not love does not know God, because God is love" (1 John 4:8 NIV). God displayed his love for us by dying on the cross for our sins. God's love, like our lives, is for all eternity. Jesus is pleading with us to surrender our lives to him so he can forgive our past, shepherd our present, and secure our future. God does not delight in abortion, but rejoices when we tell the truth about it and begin moving toward ending it in our hearts, our lives, and ultimately our society. Reread 1 Corinthians 13:4-8 and insert the word "God" for the words "love" and "it." This will give us a clear sense of the vastness of God's love and concern for all. Let his love for us and all his children bathe over and comfort us.

PRAYER FOCUS: Lord, thank you that your love for me is beyond measure and without limit. Help me feel the depth of your love for me. Jesus, mature me in love and improve my ability to love you with all my heart, soul, mind, and strength. Holy Spirit, teach me how to love others the way Jesus loved.

DID YOU KNOW? According to the WORDsearch 8 Bible software program, the word *love* is used 551 times in the New International Version translation of the Bible. The Old Testament book which uses the word *love* the most is the book of Psalms, which uses it in 143 verses. It is surprising that the book which uses the word the most in the New Testament is the small book of First John, where it is used twenty-four times.[21]

REFLECTIONS

JANUARY 22

Isaiah 45:9-12 HCSB

Woe to the one who argues with his Maker—one clay pot among many. Does clay say to the one forming it, "What are you making?" Or does your work say, "He has no hands"? How absurd is the one who says to his father, "What are you fathering?" or to his mother, "What are you giving birth to?" This is what the LORD, the Holy One of Israel, and its Maker, says: "Ask Me what is to happen to My sons, and instruct Me about the work of My hands. I made the earth, and created man on it. It was My hands that stretched out the heavens, and I commanded all their host."

Webster's Compact Dictionary defines woe as "grief, misery, misfortune."[22] How much grief, misery, and misfortune could have been avoided if the Supreme Court of the United States of America had heeded the LORD's words spoken through Isaiah and valued life on this day in 1973 when instead they ruled in favor of abortion rights? It is the height of arrogance to presume to know more than one's Creator in determining life and death, ultimate right and wrong, and who is or is not a person! The legacy of this atrocity is fifty million dead, millions hurting, and untold future damage.

PRAYER FOCUS: God, forgive us for all the innocent blood shed in our nation over the past thirty-seven years. Please bring forth more men and women in politics, churches, schools, and society who will speak out against abortion and work toward its end. Lord, show me what I can do in the culture to help raise awareness about the mass killing of innocent preborn children and hasten its abolition.

DID YOU KNOW? Norma McCorvey, the "Jane Roe" of the *Roe v Wade* case, never had the abortion she sought and is now actively pro-life. She has also admitted that the story of her rape was fabricated.[23]

REFLECTIONS

JANUARY 23

Proverbs 31:8-9 NKJV

Open your mouth for the speechless, in the cause of all who are appointed to die. Open your mouth, judge righteously, and plead the cause of the poor and needy.

Believers, we must speak up for the preborn babies in our culture and rescue them from the hands of the abortionist and all who profit from their death. We are all called to administer justice and pursue righteousness, but there is a special burden placed on those in positions of authority. This was not lost on King Lemuel's mother, who spoke these words of wisdom to her son. Never underestimate the role a mother plays in the life and maturation of her children. Women today have a critical role to play in promoting a culture of life and renouncing a culture of death. Abortion strips them of the privileges of motherhood and keeps them from becoming an instrument of influence, wisdom, and love to their children.

PRAYER FOCUS: Father, I'm grateful that you appointed Jesus to speak for me and I ask you to give me the courage to speak up for others who are in distress. Thank you for my mother and that she chose to value my life.

DID YOU KNOW? Recent estimates calculating a stay-at-home mom's economic worth, based on all the jobs she performs—like childcare, cleaning, cooking, psychology, nursing, education, and so on—have suggested that a salary of $122,732 a year would be appropriate.[24]

REFLECTIONS

JANUARY 24

Proverbs 17:15 NIV

Acquitting the guilty and condemning the innocent—the LORD detests them both.

I can't think of a more accurate description of abortion than Proverbs 17:15. Legalized abortion allows the perpetrators of unspeakable atrocities not only to remain free of punishment and justice but to enrich themselves during the process, while condemning innocent babies to death without heeding the testimony of the facts about embryonic and fetal life. If our nation wants to return to our founding principles, that "all men are created equal, that they are endowed by their Creator with certain unalienable Rights, that among these are Life, Liberty, and the Pursuit of Happiness," then we must end the travesty of abortion.

PRAYER FOCUS: Lord, wake up your church and our nation to the truth that human life begins at conception. Show us that our responsibility is to protect and preserve all life, regardless of its stage of development.

DID YOU KNOW? The fifty-six signers of the Declaration of Independence were largely affiliated with the Christian faith. *Adherents.com* claims that "57% of the signers were Episcopalian/Anglican, 23% were Congregationalists, 21% were Presbyterian, 3% were Quaker and Unitarian, and 1% was Catholic." In addition, they report that "four of the signers were active or former full-time ministers."[25] A *Patriot's History of the United States* adds, "It goes without saying, of course, that most of these men were steeped in the traditions and teachings of Christianity—almost half the signers of the Declaration of Independence had some form of seminary training or degree."[26] The Christian worldview expressed by several of our nation's founders and their great respect for the Bible helped forge our founding documents. Our republic's prominence and success is directly related to its foundation in biblical truth. For an excellent discussion of our national Christian heritage, I recommend David Barton's DVD series: *The American Heritage Series*, released in 2007. For more information, visit *www.wallbuilders.com* or call 1-800-873-2845.

REFLECTIONS

JANUARY 25

2 Chronicles 7:13-14 NIV

When I shut up the heavens so that there is no rain, or command locusts to devour the land or send a plague among my people, if my people, who are called by my name, will humble themselves and pray and seek my face and turn from their wicked ways, then will I hear from heaven, and will forgive their sin and will heal their land.

I believe God's charge to Solomon and his chosen people Israel still applies today to those of us who have come to faith in Jesus Christ and been grafted into the family of God, the body of Christ (Acts 10:28-36; Rom. 11:11-25; Gal. 3:28). As God's people, we must humble ourselves before the Lord and ask for forgiveness regarding abortion and our toleration or silent acquiescence of it. We must also repent of our own wicked involvement in abortion. If we have had an abortion, encouraged someone to abort, or procured an abortion, we must repent. If we have been hurt by our participation in abortion, we must allow God to forgive us and heal us in our brokenness. The Bible says to "confess your sins to each other and pray for each other so that you may be healed. The prayer of a righteous person is powerful and effective" (James 5:16 NIV). We should never be afraid to get the help and support of a Christian friend, pastor, or counselor in the body of Christ as we seek restoration and healing. God is longing to forgive us, but we must repent and turn to him in order to be healed.

PRAYER FOCUS: Lord, forgive us for our participation in abortion or our lack of effort in helping those who have been hurt by abortion. God, I repent of _____. Wash us clean, God, forgive our sin, hear our cries, and heal our hearts and our land. Lord, show us how to use the damage, hurt, and pain of abortion for the ultimate good of the Kingdom.

DID YOU KNOW? One in six women who have had an abortion identify themselves as born-again Christians.[27] For more information about the state of abortion and who is affected by it, read chapter three in John Ensor's book, *Answering the Call*.

REFLECTIONS

JANUARY 26

Psalm 126:5-6 ESV

Those who sow in tears shall reap with shouts of joy! He who goes out weeping, bearing the seed for sowing, shall come home with shouts of joy, bringing his sheaves with him.

Weeping can play a vital role in deliverance and spiritual warfare. Our tears of repentance bring healing as the Holy Spirit washes over us. David wrote, "The sacrifices of God are a broken spirit; a broken and contrite heart, O God, you will not despise" (Ps. 51:17 ESV). God even records our tears on his scrolls. The psalmist put it this way: "You have kept count of my tossings; put my tears in your bottle. Are they not in your book?" (Ps. 56:8 ESV). Take time today to ask God how he is grieved by abortion. Sorrow will ultimately give way to joy as we taste God's goodness and begin reaping a harvest of forgiveness and life. In his time, God will use our deliverance and joy to minister to others and bear much fruit.

PRAYER FOCUS: Thank you, God, that no matter where you find me or what I have done, you look for me like the prodigal son's father looked for him in the gospel of Luke (15:11-24). Father, I long to return home and celebrate your goodness to me. Jesus, forgive me for my sins! Lord, cleanse me from all unrighteousness and use my brokenness for your glory.

DID YOU KNOW? Carol Everett was a former abortion clinic director in Texas who played a role in 35,000 abortions, as well as her own. She has written a book about her experiences and her journey to redemption in Christ titled *Blood Money*.[28]

REFLECTIONS

27

JANUARY 27

Romans 13:8-11 ESV

Owe no one anything, except to love each other, for the one who loves another has fulfilled the law. For the commandments, "You shall not commit adultery, You shall not murder, You shall not steal, You shall not covet," and any other commandment, are summed up in this word: "You shall love your neighbor as yourself." Love does no wrong to a neighbor; therefore love is the fulfilling of the law. Besides this you know the time, that the hour has come for you to wake from sleep. For salvation is nearer to us now than when we first believed.

∞

Jesus said that love for our neighbor is the second greatest commandment after loving God. Loving our neighbor isn't just suggested; it is commanded. But who is our neighbor?

On one occasion an expert in the law stood up to test Jesus. "Teacher," he asked, "what must I do to inherit eternal life?" "What is written in the Law?" he replied. "How do you read it?" He answered: "'Love the Lord your God with all your heart and with all your soul and with all your strength and with all your mind'; and, 'Love your neighbor as yourself.'" "You have answered correctly," Jesus replied. "Do this and you will live." But he wanted to justify himself, so he asked Jesus, "And who is my neighbor?" In reply Jesus said: "A man was going down from Jerusalem to Jericho, when he fell into the hands of robbers. They stripped him of his clothes, beat him and went away, leaving him half dead. A priest happened to be going down the same road, and when he saw the man, he passed by on the other side. So too, a Levite, when he came to the place and saw him, passed by on the other side. But a Samaritan, as he traveled, came where the man was; and when he saw him, he took pity on him. Which of these three do you think was a neighbor to the man who fell into the hands of robbers?" The expert in the law replied, "The one who had mercy on him." Jesus told him, "Go and do likewise" (Luke 10:25-33, 36-37 NIV).

This parable by Jesus illustrates that our neighbor is anyone in need, including essentially all of humanity. Love does no harm to its neighbor and considers them better than ourselves. Love intervenes on behalf of a neighbor in distress (Luke 10:34-35). True love is unselfish and giving, the complete opposite of abortion. When are the people of God going to reach out and help their neighbors in the womb?

PRAYER FOCUS: Thank you, God, for loving me when I was lost and in need of a Savior. Father, give me a heart for the hurting and the lost. Show me how I can use my talents, finances, and service to fight abortion.

DID YOU KNOW? Webster's defines the word *neighbor* as "a person who lives near another; a person or thing situated next to another; a fellow human being."[29] In order to be a neighbor we must be close to people and their circumstances. Sadly, with hundreds of Planned Parenthood facilities and many more low-profile abortionist groups in our cities and towns, many of our neighbors don't stand a chance.

JANUARY 28

Lamentations 2:19 NKJV

Arise, cry out in the night, at the beginning of the watches; pour out your heart like water before the face of the Lord. Lift your hands toward Him for the life of your young children, who faint from hunger at the head of every street.

Like the prophet Jeremiah, we need to pray earnestly day and night for God's mercy and the deliverance of our nation from the horror of abortion. Jeremiah was deeply distressed by the suffering of the people around him, especially the little children. Today, children are dying at a rate of 3,300 per day in America because of legalized abortion. Additionally, men and women involved in this horrible procedure do not escape unscathed, for many are suffering physically, psychologically, spiritually, and emotionally from this atrocity. Join with me in praying routinely for the abolition of this monstrosity in America and the world.

PRAYER FOCUS: Lord, supernaturally use our intercession on behalf of moms, dads, and preborn babies to break down barriers, facilitate healing, and open doors for the ending of abortion. Holy God, defeat the plans of the Enemy, send forth deliverers, and rescue your children!

DID YOU KNOW? By day twenty-eight from conception, the baby's vital organs are mapped out, the arms and legs begin to bud, and a basic digestive tract possessing a stomach, liver, pancreas, gall bladder, and thyroid is present. It is amazing that all of this activity and growth is taking place in a child that is no bigger than the head of a match.[30]

REFLECTIONS

JANUARY 29

Matthew 5:44-45 ESV

But I say to you, Love your enemies and pray for those who persecute you, so that you may be sons of your Father who is in heaven. For he makes his sun rise on the evil and on the good, and sends rain on the just and on the unjust.

In our efforts to end abortion, it is important to remember that the pro-abortion faction is made up of people God created, loves, and with whom he hopes to have a life-giving relationship. We should always share the truth in love and communicate our message with dignity and grace. We can pray that those who lobby for and support abortion will come to the knowledge of the truth, give their lives to Christ, and live lives pleasing to God before he calls them home or returns. Jesus said, "For God so loved the world, that he gave his only Son, that whoever believes in him should not perish but have eternal life" (John 3:16 ESV). The apostle Peter wrote, "The Lord is not slow to fulfill his promise as some count slowness, but is patient toward you, not wishing that any should perish, but that all should reach repentance" (2 Pet. 3:9 ESV). Our goal concerning abortionists and pro-choice people in general should be to lead them to salvation in Christ and to change their hearts and minds about the despicable killing of babies in the womb.

PRAYER FOCUS: Lord, I pray for the enlightenment and salvation of people who support abortion. Forgive abortionists and their staff, pro-choice advocates, judges, politicians, presidents, counselors, pastors, or anyone who believes abortion is acceptable. Jesus, change their hearts and renew their minds.

DID YOU KNOW? Norma McCorvey (who was the "Jane Roe" in the *Roe v Wade* case), Bernard Nathanson (the former New York City abortionist and author of *The Hand of God*), and Carol Everett (a former Texas abortion clinic director), are all examples of people who have changed their minds about abortion and placed their trust in Jesus Christ.

REFLECTIONS

JANUARY 30

Leviticus 17:11-14 NASB

For the life of the flesh is in the blood, and I have given it to you on the altar to make atonement for your souls; for it is the blood by reason of the life that makes atonement. Therefore I said to the sons of Israel, "No person among you may eat blood, nor may any alien who sojourns among you eat blood." So when any man from the sons of Israel, or from the aliens who sojourn among them, in hunting catches a beast or a bird which may be eaten, he shall pour out its blood and cover it with earth. For as for the life of all flesh, its blood is identified with its life. Therefore I said to the sons of Israel, "You are not to eat the blood of any flesh, for the life of all flesh is its blood; hoever eats it shall be cut off."

The Bible says that life is in the blood, and we are to treat it with great respect. Abortion spills a great deal of blood and clearly takes the life of a tiny human being in the womb by shedding their blood. God establishes covenants with blood and views blood as sacred, so much so that he required the Israelites to be very careful with food preparation and the disposal of animal blood. If the sons of Israel did not obey God and ate meat with the blood still in it, they were dealt with very severely: "You are not to eat the blood of any flesh, for the life of all flesh is its blood; whoever eats it shall be cut off." The life-giving and sustaining nature of blood is what makes Jesus' blood so powerful in redemption. As God's holy, blameless, perfect, pure, and innocent sacrifice for the sins of the world, Jesus' blood has the power to cover all sin and cleanse us from all unrighteousness. In fact, the New Covenant established by Jesus is the only way we can be reconciled to a holy God who demands justice and perfection.

PRAYER FOCUS: Pray this prayer written by Lou Engle (co-founder of The Call solemn assemblies, *www.thecall.com*): "Jesus, I plead your blood over my sins and the sins of my nation. God, end abortion and send revival to America."[31]

DID YOU KNOW? The child in the womb often has a completely different blood type from its mother. Also, the mother's menstrual period is suppressed during pregnancy by a hormone (human chorionic gonadotrophin) that the embryo (baby) produces.[32]

REFLECTIONS

_____

_____

_____

_____

_____

_____

JANUARY 31

Isaiah 48:17-19 NIV

This is what the Lord says—your Redeemer, the Holy One of Israel: "I am the Lord your God, who teaches you what is best for you, who directs you in the way you should go. If only you had paid attention to my commands, your peace would have been like a river, your righteousness like the waves of the sea. Your descendants would have been like the sand, your children like its numberless grains; their name would never be cut off nor destroyed from before me."

∞

God has always desired to bless us and help us, but he will not interfere with his gift of free will, which is our freedom to do as we want. If we will trust his Word and his teachings, we will experience great abundance and peace. Notice how children are a great component of God's blessing to us. They are the source of our posterity, providing us with a name that endures, that will never be cut off. Anyone can ask God to redeem them by inviting Christ into their life. All it takes is praying a simple prayer asking Jesus to take away one's sins and allowing him to become the Lord and director of their life.

PRAYER FOCUS: Thank you, Lord, that you are my Redeemer and the source of my strength. Holy Spirit, teach me your truth and motivate me to spend time in your Word.

DID YOU KNOW? The Bible has more manuscript evidence to support its authenticity than any other ancient work of literature. At 643, Homer's *Iliad* has the second largest number of surviving manuscripts. But the New Testament has well over 24,000 manuscripts dating much closer to the original work.[33]

REFLECTIONS

February

FOUR WEEKS GESTATION

FEBRUARY
1

Psalm 102:18-20 NIV

Let this be written for a future generation, that a people not yet created may praise the LORD: "The LORD looked down from his sanctuary on high, from heaven he viewed the earth, to hear the groans of the prisoners and release those condemned to death."

In his providence and from the beginning of time God has established a plan for our redemption and escape from death. God's plan doesn't just include people living in the past or those currently living in the present. It also includes those people yet to be created in the womb. God created all of us for his glory, praise, and enjoyment, and it is the divine desire for everyone to overcome the second death through salvation in Christ. God is ultimately more concerned about spiritual death than physical death, but I am sure he wants to liberate his children on abortion's death row to save not only the children but their parents as well from the heartache of this regrettable choice.

PRAYER FOCUS: Father, I praise you for Jesus, creation, children, your goodness, and the pleasures of life you have given us to enjoy. Use me and others to rescue hurting people and those condemned to death.

DID YOU KNOW? The average length of time an inmate spends on death row in Florida is twelve years, according to the Florida Department of Corrections.[1] Contrast this with the fact that eighty-eight percent of all abortions take place sometime during the first three months of pregnancy, and all are completed by the ninth.

REFLECTIONS

FEBRUARY 2

Romans 6:23 ESV

For the wages of sin is death, but the free gift of God is eternal life in Christ Jesus our Lord.

The Bible clearly teaches that abortion is a sin, but so is lying, disobeying parents, lust, anger, sexual immorality, theft, idolatry, gossip, and the list goes on. So how then can anyone be free of sin? Only through the blood of Jesus and adopting his righteousness by faith do we have hope and freedom from the law of God. Jesus made the first move and conquered sin. He has already paid for our sins and washed us clean. The next move is up to us. If we have never thanked him or confessed our belief in him, what are we waiting for? Rest in Jesus and let him restore us and fix what we cannot. The free gift of eternal life with God is available to all who believe and call upon Jesus' name.

PRAYER FOCUS: Thank you, God, for casting all my sins into the depths of the sea (Mic. 7:19) and separating them from me as far as the east is from the west (Ps. 103:12). Give me an eternal mindset and a constant sense of the blessed life you have prepared for me in heaven after my death.

DID YOU KNOW? Anne Frank, the famous German diarist, died at the age of fifteen in a concentration camp. John F. Kennedy died in Dallas, Texas, from a gunshot wound at the age of forty-six. Amelia Earhart died at the age of forty from a probable airplane crash. Death can come at any time and under any circumstance. Are we prepared?

REFLECTIONS

FEBRUARY 3

Matthew 12:11-12 NIV

He said to them, "If any of you has a sheep and it falls into a pit on the Sabbath, will you not take hold of it and lift it out? How much more valuable is a person than a sheep! Therefore it is lawful to do good on the Sabbath."

Jesus gave this illustration to the Pharisees in order to point out how skewed and warped their priorities and values were. It greatly upset the Pharisees that Jesus would heal a man on the Sabbath, a day reserved for rest. The Pharisees were caught up in the letter of the law rather than the spirit of the law, and as the apostle Paul wrote, "the letter kills, but the Spirit gives life" (2 Cor. 3:6 NIV). Jesus, however, taught that it is always acceptable to do good and help God's people. Through his actions, Jesus demonstrated the love he has for people and the value of all God's children! With his words the Lord also confirmed the biblical hierarchy of creation and the privileged place humanity holds at the top of the order. All creation is precious and valuable, but God died for people alone, and the worth of each individual is evident in Jesus' sacrifice.

PRAYER FOCUS: God, it lifts my spirit to know how much you value me. I ask you to use me as a source of help and truth to people around me. Lord, present me with opportunities to do good things for others so I can bless their lives.

DID YOU KNOW? By the fourth and fifth week from conception, the baby's heart beats at a regular rhythm, the brain has developed into five areas, and the eyes and ears are beginning to form.[2]

REFLECTIONS

FEBRUARY 4

Ezekiel 16:20-22 NIV

And you took your sons and daughters whom you bore to me and sacrificed them as food to the idols. Was your prostitution not enough? You slaughtered my children and sacrificed them to the idols. In all your detestable practices and your prostitution you did not remember the days of your youth, when you were naked and bare, kicking about in your blood.

Abortion is modern-day child sacrifice. We no longer sacrifice our children for rain or the worship of demonic pagan idols like Baal or Molech. No, we sacrifice them to more subtle idols like convenience, fear, pleasure, reputation, and careers. The prophet Ezekiel points out that in our lack of humility we often forget the commonality we have with our children from conception to death. We all started out the same and progressed through the same stages as a zygote, embryo, fetus, newborn, toddler, child, teenager, adult, and eventually an elder. As one author wrote, "Human life is a continuum beginning at conception and ending at natural death. You did not come from a zygote, you once *were* a zygote. You did not evolve from a fetus, you once *were* a fetus."[3] Notice also to whom God says the children belong. He calls them "my children." They are God's children and we are only stewards of them, privileged to have them and blessed by them.

PRAYER FOCUS: Lord Jesus, forgive me for having an abortion, recommending an abortion, defending abortion, supporting abortion, remaining neutral about abortion, or being silent about abortion. Thank you, Father God, for forgiving me and for being patient with me in my sin. Help me to use what I'm learning to defend, protect, and cherish all life from conception to undetermined death.

DID YOU KNOW? Abortifacients (a device or pill that induces abortion) are being used more frequently today than in the past. The "morning after pill," commonly referred to as "emergency contraception," does not prevent conception in most cases but instead kills the embryo by hardening the lining of the uterus, thus preventing implantation. RU486 blocks the nutrient progesterone and starves the child, thus aborting the newly created life.[4] These two common methods are among the most popular.

REFLECTIONS

FEBRUARY 5

Genesis 4:1 NIV

Adam lay with his wife Eve, and she became pregnant and gave birth to Cain. She said, "With the help of the LORD I have brought forth a man."

Eve had the privilege of walking with God in the Garden of Eden and intimately sharing life with him. She knew better than anyone that God is the Author of life and creation. Notice her acknowledgement that it was only through God's help that she was able to conceive and bear a child. Eve's comment is in stark contrast to many women today who deny the existence of God—or that God had anything to do with their pregnancy. The Genesis 4:1 Scripture also shows that Adam played a role in God's creative process of reproduction, a fact often ignored by our society in the debate regarding abortion. If we or our partners are pregnant, we should thank God for his confidence in us and his favor in selecting us to care for and raise one or more of his children.

PRAYER FOCUS: God, I pray that you will awaken women who have been deceived into thinking the baby in their womb is not a person but only a parcel of tissue they can choose to remove at their whim. Teach them the truth about children in the womb. Lord, awaken men to stand up, protect, love, cherish, and support their preborn child and their child's mother.

DID YOU KNOW? Studying biblical names and what they mean can be quite revealing about a person's character, purpose, destiny, or creation. Adam, for example, means "man of red earth," describing the very dust God used to create him. Eve means "life" or "life giving," describing her privileged role in carrying the life God had created inside her.[5] See *The Book of Bible Names* for a quick reference on the meaning of many biblical names.

REFLECTIONS

FEBRUARY 6

Deuteronomy 24:16-18 NIV

Fathers shall not be put to death for their children, nor children put to death for their fathers; each is to die for his own sin. Do not deprive the alien or the fatherless of justice, or take the cloak of the widow as a pledge. Remember that you were slaves in Egypt and the LORD your God redeemed you from there. That is why I command you to do this.

Abortion is often obtained to cover up the sins of the fathers, to hide an affair, avoid embarrassment, or allow continual promiscuity without responsibility. Incestuous men often force their daughters to have repeated abortions in order to cover up their crimes. Whatever the reasons, fathers often deprive their innocent children of justice because of their own sin and calloused hearts. God warns such men that they will ultimately be held accountable for their actions. If you are a man who has encouraged, procured, or forced a woman to abort, God wants to forgive you. He is a redeemer who can forgive the most horrible offenses, but he requires repentance followed by an earnest desire to change and help others. God first helped and redeemed us, and therefore, out of gratitude, we should help others discover God and avoid the sins and mistakes we've made.

PRAYER FOCUS: God, forgive me for whatever involvement I have had in aborting a child instead of facing the consequences of my actions. Help me respect life and defend it from this day forward. Father, motivate us to stand up and end abortion in our families and our culture. Holy Spirit, help me live a life of sexual purity and monogamy.

DID YOU KNOW? Male influence is cited by many postabortive women as the single biggest factor in choosing to abort their child. Research shows that male pressure to abort was present in thirty-eight percent and twenty-seven percent of the cases examined.[6] Sadly, many men have tolerated or encouraged abortion because it appears to free them from certain sexual consequences and allow them to escape the responsibility of fatherhood.

REFLECTIONS

FEBRUARY 7

Psalm 30:11-12 NIV

You turned my wailing into dancing; you removed my sackcloth and clothed me with joy, that my heart may sing to you and not be silent. O LORD my God, I will give you thanks forever.

∞

The joy of the Lord comes with freedom for all who repent before God. The Bible says, "If the Son sets you free, you will be free indeed" (John 8:36 NIV). God accepts prayers of contrition, forgives sins completely, and wants all of us to experience his love and liberating joy. We must forgive ourselves for any part we have ever played in abortion, just as God has forgiven us. We must wipe the slate clean. The Enemy will try to steal our joy through condemnation, but don't let him. Satan is defeated when we clothe ourselves in the Word of God and embrace God's promises concerning forgiveness. Read Psalm 32:1-5 and 1 John 1:8-9. These texts tell us that if we confess our sins they will be trodden underfoot and we will be forgiven. Then we must surround ourselves with compassionate brothers and sisters in Christ who can remind us of the truth of God and our immeasurable worth.

PRAYER FOCUS: Thank you, Lord Jesus, for forgiving me. Help me understand that my past sins are covered and that my future sins are paid for as long as I confess them to you and seek healing. God, use my story, failures, and pain to make a difference in the lives of people dealing with similar circumstances.

DID YOU KNOW? John Newton, the famous eighteenth century preacher who wrote the song "Amazing Grace," was a former slave trader and wicked degenerate according to his own testimony before he came to Christ and repented of his sins. Even after conversion Newton struggled with sin and setbacks as he journeyed toward becoming the man Christ enabled him to be. He requested the following epitaph be written on his gravestone:

> JOHN NEWTON, Clerk [preacher]
> Once an infidel and libertine,
> A servant of slaves in Africa,
> Was, by the rich mercy
> Of our Lord and Saviour,
> JESUS CHRIST,
> Preserved, restored, pardoned, and
> Appointed to preach
> The faith he had
> Long laboured to destroy.
> He ministered,
> Near sixteen years at Olney, in Bucks,
> And twenty eight years in this Church.[7]

Praise God that none of us are beyond redemption!

FEBRUARY 8

Colossians 4:2-4 NIV

Devote yourselves to prayer, being watchful and thankful. And pray for us, too, that God may open a door for our message, so that we may proclaim the mystery of Christ, for which I am in chains. Pray that I may proclaim it clearly, as I should.

Prayer is vital in all aspects of our lives, but especially when we take on the Enemy and fight injustice. It is important to pray often for protection, wisdom, and guidance in our efforts to end abortion. We must pray that God will open doors that no one can shut, and give us the courage to proclaim what Scripture says about abortion and the gospel message. We also need to pray for our church leaders and those working within the pro-life movement, asking God to grant them perseverance, wisdom, protection, and the necessary resources in the fight to protect and defend life.

PRAYER FOCUS: Thank you, Lord, for the men and women who serve you in all ways, including in church, missions, and pro-life ministry. Help them follow you diligently and use the resources committed to them to the best of their ability. Watch over them and their families and keep them from temptation and burnout.

DID YOU KNOW? The majority of people who work in pro-life organizations are unpaid volunteers. The passion, sacrifice, and efforts of these individuals cannot be measured or underestimated. For the movement to reach new heights of effectiveness, however, we need more full-time people in the field of pro-life work who are paid competitive salaries. If God has blessed us financially and burdened our hearts to help in this effort, we should consider giving enough money to enable our local pro-life group to hire full-time staffers. These new employees could focus all their time and energy into the various missions for life. In time, the extra man power may increase the organization's revenue to the point where generous help is no longer needed to augment the salaries. We could also offer our professional skills at no charge, helping the local group with Web design, graphic arts, legal representation, copywriting, ad campaigns, marketing, editorial services, and so on. Finally, if we have the means, we could offer ourselves as full-time workers for little or no pay.

REFLECTIONS

FEBRUARY 9

Psalm 82:2-4 ESV

How long will you judge unjustly and show partiality to the wicked? Give justice to the weak and the fatherless; maintain the right of the afflicted and the destitute. Rescue the weak and the needy; deliver them from the hand of the wicked.

The Bible has much to say about our responsibility to the oppressed, afflicted, weak, poor, needy, and fatherless. It is easy to identify those who belong to these groups when we see fatherless children of fallen soldiers, or poor people down at the soup kitchen, or the weak in a hospital bed. What is not so clear is the oppression of people who we can't relate to or don't see, like the child sold into the sexual slave trade, or the preborn baby scheduled for abortion. Legalized abortion has made the child in the womb the most oppressed people group in the world. Global estimates indicate that over forty-two million children are aborted each year. When we legalize or tolerate abortion, we provide sanctuary or partiality to the wicked and allow injustice to run rampant on our most innocent and vulnerable children. Thus, we fail to maintain the rights of the afflicted, weak, fatherless, needy, and destitute neighbors among us by allowing legalized abortion to continue. Who is more destitute than the child scheduled for abortion? Who is weaker than the developing baby in the womb? Who has been abandoned more by his or her father than the child about to be terminated? Who is more fatherless than the child whose father has been stripped of his legal right to decide the fate of his preborn child? When will God's people rise up and defend the afflicted needy children in our land?

PRAYER FOCUS: God, reveal to all Christians how preborn babies scheduled for abortion are part of the weak, needy, fatherless, destitute, poor, and afflicted around us. Help us to bring justice to them and deliver them from the hand of the wicked.

DID YOU KNOW? By the sixth week a developing baby's lungs are beginning to form and their hands and feet have become distinguishable.[8]

REFLECTIONS

FEBRUARY 10

Proverbs 24:10-12 NIV

If you falter in times of trouble, how small is your strength! Rescue those being led away to death; hold back those staggering toward slaughter. If you say, "But we knew nothing about this," does not he who weighs the heart perceive it? Does not he who guards your life know it? Will he not repay each person according to what he has done?

A quick examination of our culture reveals we are living in a time of trouble. Pornography, abortion, violence, and fraud all give clear evidence about the state of our culture and nation. This Scripture from Proverbs chapter twenty-four is to be taken seriously by all believers, especially those who think social issues are not their problem as long as they avoid such behavior. God makes it clear that we are all responsible for the welfare of our neighbor, and we should have as our primary goal their salvation and betterment. This verse is clearly addressing those being led away to death by abortion and all of its victims. We believers need to be directly involved in halting the endless slaughter of babies in the womb. We also need to rescue their deceived parents who are in danger of dying in an unrepentant state without Christ and suffering a spiritual death that is far worse than a physical one.

PRAYER FOCUS: God, help me not to falter in times of trouble. Help me to understand that I am responsible for how I treat my neighbor, and that my neighbor is everyone I share the planet with, including the preborn. Forgive my apathy and indifference to abortion and show me what I can do to bring it to an end.

DID YOU KNOW? 1,188 people have been executed in the United States between 1976 and 2009 for crimes they committed.[9] Of those 1,188 executions, only eleven were females.[10] During this same time period more than forty million innocent babies have been executed—and nearly half of them were female.

REFLECTIONS

FEBRUARY 11

2 Corinthians 7:10-11 NIV

Godly sorrow brings repentance that leads to salvation and leaves no regret, but worldly sorrow brings death. See what this godly sorrow has produced in you: what earnestness, what eagerness to clear yourselves, what indignation, what alarm, what longing, what concern, what readiness to see justice done. At every point you have proved yourselves to be innocent in this matter.

If we are truly sorry for allowing abortion to continue in our land, we must take action against it and do whatever is within our power to abolish it. We must be earnest, eager, outraged, alarmed, concerned, and ready to see justice done! We can vote against abortion, protest the facilities that provide it, encourage our political representatives to stand against it, help men and women in unexpected pregnancies by meeting their physical and financial needs, and support our local pregnancy resource center or pro-life group. Probably the most important thing we can do is educate ourselves about the subject and offer assistance to our family and friends when they face an unexpected pregnancy personally. We must encourage our brothers and sisters in Christ to join with us in this fight and always speak the truth about abortion and the harm it does to men, women, children, and society.

PRAYER FOCUS: God, forgive me and my nation for allowing abortion to continue, and help me make an effort to end it. Lord, use your people, politicians, authors, musicians, doctors, teachers, pastors, and everyday citizens to speak out against the mass killing of innocent preborn children. Give me creative ideas to add fresh thinking and effective strategies to the pro-life movement.

DID YOU KNOW? A study in Finland on pregnancy-related deaths from 1989 to 1994 showed that post-abortive women committed suicide seven times more often than women who carried to term.[11] John C. and Barbara H. Willke's 2003 book *Abortion Questions & Answers* is a great starting resource for educating oneself about abortion.

REFLECTIONS

FEBRUARY 12

Ezekiel 22:29-30 NKJV

The people of the land have used oppressions, committed robbery, and mistreated the poor and needy; and they wrongfully oppress the stranger. So I sought for a man among them who would make a wall, and stand in the gap before Me on behalf of the land, that I should not destroy it; but I found no one.

In addition to being among the poor and the needy, the preborn are clearly treated as strangers among us, being denied the basic human rights the rest of us enjoy. Why? Because they have been stripped by our courts of their personhood. God is looking for people who will stand in the gap on behalf of his little ones, believers who will ask the Lord for mercy so that he will not have to destroy our land! God is looking for strong intercessors and activists who will tirelessly plead for justice. How heartbreaking it is for a nation when God finds no one to answer the call. Our greatest example of someone who stood in the gap for us is Jesus, and we should strive to be like him. It is no coincidence that God asks for men to stand up on behalf of the land because he designed them to be warriors and protectors of his people, especially children.

PRAYER FOCUS: God, teach me to stand in the gap before you and pray effectively using the Word to intercede for your little ones and my nation. Lord, send forth deliverers from among your people, especially men.

DID YOU KNOW? Abraham Lincoln, the great emancipator, and Charles Darwin, the evolutionist, were born on this day in 1809. How a man aligns himself with God can have a tremendous impact for evil or for good.

REFLECTIONS

FEBRUARY 13

Proverbs 14:25-27 ESV

A truthful witness saves lives, but one who breathes out lies is deceitful. In the fear of the LORD one has strong confidence, and his children will have a refuge. The fear of the LORD is a fountain of life, that one may turn away from the snares of death.

The Bible says "The fear of the Lord is the beginning of wisdom, and the knowledge of the Holy One is insight" (Prov. 9:10 ESV). Reverence and respect for God will lead us into agreement with all that he says, allowing us to reflect his character as much as possible in our current state of being redeemed (while still possessing a fallen nature). A truthful witness is one who is in agreement with God and, as a result, will pursue things like justice, charity, and peace. Partnership with God in pursuing these things will often result in saved lives, both physically and spiritually. Contrast this with the one who supports or promotes the lies of abortion, whose deceit leads to the destruction of lives, both physically and spiritually. If we as believers would speak the truth regarding abortion in public, private, and the church, I believe we would turn others from the snares of death and save lives.

PRAYER FOCUS: God, reveal your truth to me through your Word and the Holy Spirit. Give me the courage to speak the truth in love to my family, friends, and neighbors whenever possible. Thank you that your Word is trustworthy and paints an accurate picture of me, and that I can depend on it for answers to all my questions.

DID YOU KNOW? A baby's brain waves can be recorded on an electroencephalogram (EEG) by the fortieth day after conception—or the beginning of the sixth week.[12]

REFLECTIONS

FEBRUARY 14

Song of Solomon 8:6-7 NIV

Place me like a seal over your heart, like a seal on your arm; for love is as strong as death, its jealousy unyielding as the grave. It burns like blazing fire, like a mighty flame. Many waters cannot quench love; rivers cannot wash it away. If one were to give all the wealth of his house for love, it would be utterly scorned.

Love cannot be bought because it is the free gift of God. God's love is certain and constant, and it comes to us through the sacrifice of his Son Jesus. God is jealous for us and desperately wants to fellowship with us as his adopted children for all eternity. Nothing can quench his love—not abortion, not sin, not backsliding, not failure of any kind. Humanity is the pinnacle of God's earthly creation, and we are his treasured possessions. No matter what we've done or where we find ourselves, Jesus is willing to forgive us and can transform our lives. Jesus said, "Come to me, all you who are weary and burdened, and I will give you rest" (Matt. 11:28 NIV).

PRAYER FOCUS: Thank you, Lord Jesus, for loving me no matter what my sins are or have been. Please make me a new person as I give my life and my sins to you. I love you because you first loved me. Help me also to love my neighbor and myself.

DID YOU KNOW? Around six thousand people will celebrate their love by getting married today in the United States.[13] On this Valentine's Day, as we visit one of the nation's many florists or jewelry stores, we can reflect back on what love and commitment is all about, and let Christ be the center of our romance.

REFLECTIONS

FEBRUARY 15

Romans 15:5-6 NASB

Now may the God who gives perseverance and encouragement grant you to be of the same mind with one another according to Christ Jesus, so that with one accord you may with one voice glorify the God and Father of our Lord Jesus Christ.

∞

Unity and peace should be the goal of every organization that seeks to impact the world for Christ and abolish abortion. The Bible says that "if a house is divided against itself, that house will not be able to stand" (Mark 3:25 NASB). When we fight against one another or criticize each other's work openly, airing our differences of opinion in public forums, we hurt our cause and damage our credibility. Abortionists and their supporters are never divided about their goal to keep abortion readily available to all in order to destroy lives, and they will continue to succeed if we are divided and contentious. In order to persevere in this fight, we need to encourage one another in love and good deeds. Though we are many members, let's remember the one body of Christ we belong to!

PRAYER FOCUS: Father, I pray for unity in the body of Christ and unity in the pro-life movement. Give me wisdom in handling disagreements between myself and my brothers and sisters in Christ. Thank you for being in control of every situation. Keep me mindful of your goodness and sovereignty, and help me to rest in you during times of conflict.

DID YOU KNOW? World War II would never have ended when it did if the nations of Great Britain, Russia, the United States, and several other nations had not put aside their differences and worked together to smash fascism. This does not even account for the collaboration and effort of everyday citizens who led resistances, hid Jews, sponsored bond drives, or increased production through hard work and ingenuity. American manufacturing produced more than double the armaments of Germany, Japan, and Italy combined during the war.[14]

REFLECTIONS

FEBRUARY 16

Proverbs 19:9 NKJV

A false witness will not go unpunished, and he who speaks lies shall perish.

The words we speak have tremendous power for life or death, good or evil, blessing or cursing. It is vital that we seek out the truth of God as revealed in his Word, agree with him about all that is written there, and then speak the truth to others for their benefit and ours. When we hear that "a false witness will not go unpunished, and he who speaks lies shall perish," we, as believers, should be encouraged and comforted because it points to the inevitable defeat of our Enemy, the Devil. Satan will be punished, and his future is one of eternal torment and damnation. The Bible says, "When he lies, he speaks his native language, for he is a liar and the father of lies" (John 8:44 NIV). One of his biggest lies is that the preborn baby is not a person. But one day, all his lies will be revealed and the great deceiver will be punished with everlasting destruction!

PRAYER FOCUS: Thank you, God, for Truth and that your Word reveals what is true. Help me to speak the truth and be honest in everything I do. Lord, help my brothers and sisters who have been deceived about the humanity of their baby see the truth and be set free from the trickery of the Devil.

DID YOU KNOW? Margaret Sanger, the founder of Planned Parenthood, was an advocate for eugenics (the belief that the human race is improved by restricting certain people from reproduction), racism, abortion, and infanticide.[15] Her organization holds the horrible distinction of being the nation's leading abortion provider, performing over 250,000 abortions per year.[16]

REFLECTIONS

49

FEBRUARY 17

Matthew 22:17-21 NKJV

"Tell us, therefore, what do You think? Is it lawful to pay taxes to Caesar, or not?" But Jesus perceived their wickedness, and said, "Why do you test Me, you hypocrites? Show Me the tax money." So they brought Him a denarius. And He said to them, "Whose image and inscription is this?" They said to Him, "Caesar's." And He said to them, "Render therefore to Caesar the things that are Caesar's, and to God the things that are God's."

∞

The teachers of the law were hoping to trap Jesus with this question by either making him unpopular with the Jews, who hated Roman rule, or portraying him as a traitor to the Roman Empire. Jesus, however, knew their hearts and gave a response that satisfied both his people and the Roman authority. Just as the Pharisees marveled at his teaching, I am struck by the power of the Lord's words regarding the modern-day abortion controversy. God in his providence has given us a clear picture of how we are to treat preborn children, who are made in God's image. They are to be rendered to their Creator, for they are his and unmistakably bear the divine image. The denarius Jesus referred to in Matthew 22:17-21 displayed the image of Caesar and therefore belonged to Caesar. Human beings are made in the image of God and therefore belong to God:

> Then God said, "Let Us make man in Our image, according to Our likeness; let them have dominion over the fish of the sea, over the birds of the air, and over the cattle, over all the earth and over every creeping thing that creeps on the earth." So God created man in His own image; in the image of God He created him; male and female He created them (Gen. 1:26-27 NKJV).

PRAYER FOCUS: Lord, teach me to revere and respect every human being, for all bear your image and you love and care for each one. Thank you for creating me. Help me bear your image well and become the person you designed me to be for your glory.

DID YOU KNOW? The surgical procedure known as a caesarean section may have been named after Gaius Julius Caesar. Peter Tallack wrote, "Sometimes it is necessary to deliver the baby through a surgical incision in the mother's abdominal wall and uterus—that is, by caesarean section. Legend has it that Julius Caesar was born this way, but the operation may be named from an ancient law, restated by Caesar, that a woman dying in labor must be cut open in the hope of saving the child."[17]

FEBRUARY 18

Deuteronomy 8:17-18 NIV

You may say to yourself, "My power and the strength of my hands have produced this wealth for me." But remember the LORD your God, for it is he who gives you the ability to produce wealth, and so confirms his covenant, which he swore to your forefathers, as it is today.

God is the One who richly gives us all things, including our talents and skills. Everything we possess is a gift from God. All our physical, intellectual, and spiritual abilities came from him. When we discover this truth and begin to embrace it, we become grateful people who are able to live in freedom and generously give to others. Many of God's servants are working hard to put a stop to the travesty of abortion, but they need financial partners to help them accomplish their work. Take time to investigate the local and national groups fighting to restore a culture of life in our nation. And then ask God which ones you should support.

PRAYER FOCUS: Lord, help me be faithful and sow financially into the work to support human life at all levels, even if I don't have much. And as I am faithful in giving, even when it is a small amount, bless me financially so that I can give in abundance to the work of the Kingdom.

DID YOU KNOW? Job was one of the wealthiest people recorded in the Bible. Read the book of Job and find out how a righteous man can and should use great wealth—and ultimately what he puts his trust in.

REFLECTIONS

FEBRUARY 19

James 1:12 ESV

Blessed is the man who remains steadfast under trial, for when he has stood the test he will receive the crown of life, which God has promised to those who love him.

Overcoming the abortion mentality in our nation is an extremely difficult trial requiring that we be steadfast and persevering. Many of the pioneers in the pro-life movement have been fighting the good fight for more than thirty years. It is terribly sad that the culture, while making some small strides, is still widely accepting of abortion for a myriad of reasons, all faulty in their conclusions. It doesn't matter when Christians enter the fray, only that we fight hard and remain vigilant until the mission is accomplished. Fresh troops and reinforcements are vital in any battle, so we must bring our talents and ideas into the fight and labor diligently until the victory is won!

PRAYER FOCUS: God, help me to be accepting of new people and new approaches to protecting the preborn in America and the world. Lord, use my talents, dreams, ideas, and abilities to bring about the end of abortion and the restoration of all those people who have been wounded by it.

DID YOU KNOW? William Wilberforce, who wrote *Real Christianity*, was instrumental in the abolition of slavery throughout the British Empire. His forty-year fight in the British parliament to end the evil of slavery had many ups and downs, with his final success coming just three days before his death.[18] Wilberforce, truly a man of perseverance, can teach all abortion abolitionists by his example to remain steadfast under trial.

REFLECTIONS

FEBRUARY 20

James 5:5-6 NIV

You have lived on earth in luxury and self-indulgence. You have fattened yourselves in the day of slaughter. You have condemned and murdered innocent men, who were not opposing you.

James is warning rich oppressors of the coming judgment of God. These verses should arouse considerable alarm for those of us fortunate enough to live in the United States of America. We are truly blessed among nations, as most of us live in luxury and self-indulgence, compared to the rest of the world. Sadly, during the past forty years our children have been led to the slaughter daily through the widespread abortion that is easily available in our society. Our courts have condemned thousands upon thousands of innocent preborn babies to death, while millions of our citizens have actively participated in the killing, or allowed this grave injustice to continue through inaction and apathy. May God give us the courage to end this atrocity and may he forgive us for our lack of concern and self-interest during this dark time!

PRAYER FOCUS: God, forgive me and my nation for allowing the barbaric act of abortion to continue. Help us have the courage to do whatever we can to restore legal protection for all the citizens of our nation, born or preborn. Thank you, Lord God, for being slow to anger, rich in love, and abounding in mercy.

DID YOU KNOW? By the age of forty-five, forty-three percent of American women will have had at least one abortion, according to the Centers for Disease Control and Prevention.[19] To examine the CDC's latest report on abortion statistics in the United States of America, go to *cdc.gov/reproductivehealth/Data_Stats/Abortion.htm* and click the link below "Abortion Surveillance Reports."

REFLECTIONS

FEBRUARY 21

James 2:24-26 NIV

You see that a person is justified by what he does and not by faith alone. In the same way, was not even Rahab the prostitute considered righteous for what she did when she gave lodging to the spies and sent them off in a different direction? As the body without the spirit is dead, so faith without deeds is dead.

Our faith is conviction leading to action. Faith requires deeds; otherwise, if we do nothing, our faith is dead. Love compels us to act and defend our preborn neighbors who are facing being killed by abortion. God is pleased when we rescue and protect his children. Consider Rahab, a prostitute, who was considered righteous by God because she hid the Jewish spies from her people—who would have killed them if she had not protected them. I believe that as serious and offensive as our sin is to God, he is even more concerned with our lack of love for our fellow human beings. Christ paid for our sins on the cross, and he wants us to be his redeemed messengers of love to a lost and dying world. The two great commandments are to love God and to love each other. Love requires that we reach out and help our preborn neighbors and their parents.

PRAYER FOCUS: Father, thank you for sending your Holy Spirit to guide me and work in me to accomplish your plans. Show me what it is you would have me do about abortion and anything else you have placed on my heart. Give me the courage to act upon what you show me.

DID YOU KNOW? By the seventh week from conception, a baby's tongue has taste buds, their elbows and toes are visible, and all their essential organs have begun to form.[20] In writing about the eyes at this stage, one writer said, "The light-sensitive cells of the retina have formed, and nerve connections from the retina to the brain have been established."[21]

REFLECTIONS

FEBRUARY 22

Revelation 4:11 NASB

Worthy are You, our Lord and our God, to receive glory and honor and power; for You created all things, and because of Your will they existed, and were created.

This window into heaven provides a glorious glimpse of the adoration and praise our Creator deserves. As the twenty-four elders are praising God and casting their crowns before him, they worship the One who lives forever and ever. Their worship confirms what the Bible teaches from Genesis to Revelation—that God alone is the Creator of all things. He created all of us and everything that makes up our universe. Every child is a wanted child because God designed them to live in a particular time and place, and to fulfill a specific, God-ordained purpose. We need to cherish every life, realizing that our ultimate value comes from the Lord God Almighty, and not from anything of our own, such as education, looks, abilities, occupation, or wealth.

PRAYER FOCUS: God, I praise you for making this awesome planet, even though because of our sin it is fallen. Thank you for making my friends and family. I love them dearly! Help me understand that every child scheduled for abortion is someone's son or daughter, who you created to be a father, mother, sister, brother, and friend. And never let me forget that every single person is precious to you.

DID YOU KNOW? The Christian music group Casting Crowns has made reference to abortion in several of their songs. My favorite is "While You Were Sleeping" on the *Lifesong* CD, released in 2005.[22] Pray that more Christian artists of all types would be brave enough to bring the subject of abortion and infanticide out into the light.

REFLECTIONS

FEBRUARY 23

Jeremiah 1:4-5 ESV

Now the word of the LORD came to me, saying, "Before I formed you in the womb I knew you, and before you were born I consecrated you; I appointed you a prophet to the nations."

∞

The Bible affirms in several places that we are full persons from the moment of conception. But from the Lord's statement recorded by the prophet Jeremiah—"Before I formed you in the womb I knew you"—one could argue that personhood begins in the mind of God. Another Scripture that represents this perspective is found in Psalm 139:

For you formed my inward parts; you knitted me together in my mother's womb. I praise you, for I am fearfully and wonderfully made. Wonderful are your works; my soul knows it very well. My frame was not hidden from you, when I was being made in secret, intricately woven in the depths of the earth. Your eyes saw my unformed substance; in your book were written, every one of them, the days that were formed for me, when as yet there was none of them (139: 13-16 ESV).

Just like the plan God had for Jeremiah, he has a plan and a purpose for our lives. Not one person was a random happening or a product of the evolutionary process. We were made by Almighty God, the Maker of heaven and earth, whose ways and thoughts are higher than ours and who is deliberately intentional in all he does. Regardless of our conception circumstance, God wanted us here for his purposes and glory.

PRAYER FOCUS: Thank you, God, that I am not a mistake and that you wanted me from the moment you decided to make me. Reveal to me your plan and the dream you have placed in my heart so that I may accomplish it for your glory.

DID YOU KNOW? Many women who have conceived a child during the horrible crime of rape and have gone on to abort their child report that the abortion is harder to recover from than the rape.[23] What the Enemy intends for evil God works for good. Don't be deceived—all women and their babies are special and valued highly by God. David Reardon writes, "Rebecca Morris became pregnant after being raped by a friend. She had an abortion, at her mother's urging, and she thought this would solve all her problems. But many years later Rebecca still struggles with the emotional effects of the abortion. She says that, 'They say abortion is the easy way out, the best thing for everyone, but they are wrong. It has been over fifteen years, and I still suffer.'"[24]

FEBRUARY 24

1 Timothy 4:4-5 ESV

For everything created by God is good, and nothing is to be rejected if it is received with thanksgiving, for it is made holy by the word of God and prayer.

∞

In chapter four of First Timothy, Paul is contrasting false teachings that forbid marriage and certain foods with proper instruction. But it is here in verse four that we discover the affirmation that everything created by God is good—including any child created as a result of rape or incest. Incest and rape are horrible crimes and are never good, but on the rare occasion when a child is conceived after such an assault there is no doubt that the newly created life is fashioned by God, the giver of all life (John 1:3). These little ones have done nothing wrong (Ezek. 18:20; Rom. 9:11). Nor did they choose the manner of their conception. For reasons known only to God, he chose to bring them forth under adverse circumstances. Looking at these babies through the revelation of Scripture, we can see that God granted conception in part to give a reward and a heritage. Psalm 127:3 says, "Behold, children are a heritage from the Lord, the fruit of the womb a reward." A reward bestowed upon the victimized woman, potential adoptive parents, and society at large. Scripture further teaches that God is sovereign, comforting, and has good future plans for the victim, the baby, and all of us (Prov. 3:5-10; Ps. 30:1-5, 8-12; Jer. 29:11). Initially this seems counterintuitive to us and is hard to see, but it is what the Word teaches. If the woman who finds herself in this painful circumstance will courageously receive the child with thanksgiving, pray often, and remain in the Word of God, God will bless her and reward her faithfulness (Ps. 34). We may never fully understand why God allows such things, but we know he is sovereign, faithful, and good. Perhaps God has a plan for a rape victim's child to become a prosecutor of rapists or someone who helps women in the future who are victims of rape and incest. Maybe the child is the evidence needed to stop an abusive father from continuing to harm his daughters. Or, perhaps this child will be God's greatest gift to its mother, bringing her unspeakable joy! Only God knows, but if the victims of sexual violence who conceive new life remain faithful in this enormously difficult circumstance, God will reveal to them how he makes beauty out of ashes.

PRAYER FOCUS: Lord God, I can trust that you know why I must walk this path, even if I don't right now. Teach me to be like Job and say with confidence, "Though He slay me, yet will I trust Him" (Job 13:15 NKJV).

DID YOU KNOW? Approximately one percent of all abortions committed in the United States are because of rape and incest.[25] If you would like to know more about the impact of abortion on rape and incest victims, read *Victims and Victors*, by David Reardon, Julie Makimaa, and Amy Sobie.

FEBRUARY 25

Isaiah 43:18-19 NASB

Do not call to mind the former things, or ponder things of the past. Behold, I will do something new, now it will spring forth; will you not be aware of it? I will even make a roadway in the wilderness, rivers in the desert.

God wants us to trust him and his ability to change things in our lives. We need to stop focusing on our past sins and hurts and start focusing on the new things God wants to do with us. Perspective plays a huge role in our ability to live in freedom and reach for all that God has for us. To do that we need to stay grounded in the Word and listen to the Holy Spirit so that we adopt God's eternal perspective and perceive the new things that he is doing around us and in us. We are creatures of the familiar who resist change, but we need to let go and let God freely move in us to the point of miracles. I don't know about you, but I long to see God restore the desert areas of my life with streams of living water! God will not fail us. "For I am confident of this very thing, that He who began a good work in you will perfect it until the day of Christ Jesus" (Phil. 1:6 NASB).

PRAYER FOCUS: Lord, I trust my past to you and give you all my heartache and sins. I ask you to set me free from their memory and give me rest. Father, show me the new thing you want to do in my life, and help me accomplish it. Thank you for healing me, loving me, forgiving me, and helping me.

DID YOU KNOW? The Nile River, flowing through Egypt, Ethiopia, Rwanda, North and South Sudan, and several other nations, is the world's longest river, measuring 4,158 miles in length.[26] God has always delighted in making rivers in the desert.

REFLECTIONS

FEBRUARY 26

Psalm 19:7-11 NIV

The law of the LORD is perfect, reviving the soul. The statutes of the LORD are trustworthy, making wise the simple. The precepts of the LORD are right, giving joy to the heart. The commands of the LORD are radiant, giving light to the eyes. The fear of the LORD is pure, enduring forever. The ordinances of the LORD are sure and altogether righteous. They are more precious than gold, than much pure gold; they are sweeter than honey, than honey from the comb. By them is your servant warned; in keeping them there is great reward.

God's Word is restoring, trustworthy, wise, radiant, illuminating, pure, joyous, sure, and righteous. The renewing of our minds comes from reading, studying, memorizing, and applying God's Word. When we spend time reading Scripture aloud and letting the truth of God spill over us, we are warmed and rewarded. The Bible has the answer to all questions and its words of life nourish the soul. We would all profit from the habit of reciting Scripture during our prayer times to claim God's promises, meditating on God's Word by creating Scripture flash cards, or buying the little Scripture cards at Christian bookstores. "Faith comes by hearing, and hearing by the word of God" (Rom. 10:17 NKJV). We must do whatever we can to tune the world out and develop ears to hear what God is saying.

PRAYER FOCUS: Thank you, God, for giving us the Bible. Help me to find time to read it and use creative ways to study and learn it. Lord, help me hide your Word in my heart, believing it before I believe anyone else or even myself.

DID YOU KNOW? The Bible has sold over six billion copies and is the best-selling book of all time. It has been translated into many languages with multiple versions and translations.[27] Clearly the Bible is an inspired book, for no mere fairy tale could have endured so long or been desired by so many over the course of human history.

REFLECTIONS

FEBRUARY 27

James 1:22-25 ESV

But be doers of the word, and not hearers only, deceiving yourselves. For if anyone is a hearer of the word and not a doer, he is like a man who looks intently at his natural face in a mirror. For he looks at himself and goes away and at once forgets what he was like. But the one who looks into the perfect law, the law of liberty, and perseveres, being no hearer who forgets but a doer who acts, he will be blessed in his doing.

The Word of God is living and active and we need to be the same. The Bible is not meant to be a collection of stories for entertainment but rather a guidebook on how to live life, love God, and serve each other. The Bible is practical and applicable to every part of our lives. If we seek we will find, we are told in the gospel of Matthew: "Ask, and it will be given to you; seek, and you will find; knock, and it will be opened to you. For everyone who asks receives, and the one who seeks finds, and to the one who knocks it will be opened" (7:7-8 ESV). But after we find, we must do. We must be doers who act, for James says we are blessed in our doing. The Bible is clear about its opposition to abortion and our collective responsibility to end it. It is up to us to hear God's heart for preborn babies and their parents—and then act upon it. May God grant us the strength and courage to be doers of his Word in this critical area and in all things.

PRAYER FOCUS: Lord, give me the courage and boldness to speak up for the preborn babies who have no voice. Give me a heart for their parents and the grace to offer them assistance. Lord, bathe me in your love and cast out my fear of rejection and ridicule.

DID YOU KNOW? The term *fetus*, used to describe a developing baby from eight weeks until birth, after all of the internal organs and body systems are in place, is a Latin word meaning "young one," or "offspring."[28]

REFLECTIONS

FEBRUARY
28

2 Timothy 1:7-10 NKJV

For God has not given us a spirit of fear, but of power and of love and of a sound mind. Therefore do not be ashamed of the testimony of our Lord, nor of me His prisoner, but share with me in the sufferings for the gospel according to the power of God, who has saved us and called us with a holy calling, not according to our works, but according to His own purpose and grace which was given to us in Christ Jesus before time began, but has now been revealed by the appearing of our Savior Jesus Christ, who has abolished death and brought life and immortality to light through the gospel.

When we get involved in helping someone who is suffering or oppressed, there is often a natural hesitation or fear for our own safety. Beyond this, every believer has to overcome the enemies of the flesh, the world, spiritual forces of wickedness, powers, principalities, and the Devil. Fortunately, the power of God is far greater than all our enemies, including the Enemy himself. It all comes down to who we will believe or trust: God or other people, God or our own flesh, or God or the Enemy? The apostle Peter told us to, "Cast all your anxiety on him because he cares for you" (1 Pet. 5:7 NIV). Take confidence in God and boldly carry out his calling to rescue those who are being led away to slaughter and condemned to death.

If you faint in the day of adversity, your strength is small. Deliver those who are drawn toward death, and hold back those stumbling to the slaughter. If you say, "Surely we did not know this," does not He who weighs the hearts consider it? He who keeps your soul, does He not know it? And will He not render to each man according to his deeds? (Prov. 24:10-12 NKJV).

PRAYER FOCUS: Lord, help me understand the balance between grace and works. I know that I am saved by your grace through faith, but that the fruit of your grace working in my life is obedience to the things you've called me to. Help me be obedient to your call and apply myself to the good works that you prepared in advance for me to do.

DID YOU KNOW? Corrie ten Boom and her family hid Jews during the German occupation of Holland. Facing their fears while trusting God, they accomplished amazing things. Their story is told in the book and movie called *The Hiding Place*. Their faith, conviction, and courage allowed them to live out John 15:13, "Greater love has no one than this, that he lay down his life for his friends" (NIV).

REFLECTIONS

March

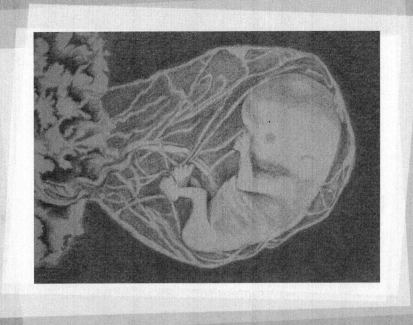

EIGHT WEEKS GESTATION

MARCH 1

Psalm 27:1 NKJV

The L ORD is my light and my salvation; whom shall I fear? The L ORD is the strength of my life; of whom shall I be afraid?

When we embrace the reality that God is on our side, we realize there is nothing to fear because God has promised to protect, defend, and rescue us. We can agree with Scripture when it says, "If God is for us, who can be against us?" (Rom. 8:31 NKJV). The Lord is our light in the darkness, our strength in the battle, and our salvation whether we live or die! When we have entrusted our lives to Jesus, we know our eternity is secure and that death brings us into the presence of the Lord. Paul wrote, "For to me, to live *is* Christ, and to die *is* gain" (Phil. 1:21 NKJV). What can the Enemy do to us when we no longer fear death, when we are confident that the Lord is the strength of our life and that nothing can snatch us from our Savior's hand?

PRAYER FOCUS: Lord Jesus, thank you for freeing me from the fear of death and purchasing my salvation for all eternity. Deliver me from all my fears and release me to trust in your provision, no matter where you send me or what I face.

DID YOU KNOW? The 2007 Heisman Trophy winner, Tim Tebow, from the University of Florida, could have been aborted. When Tim was in the womb, his mother Pam Tebow was told by a doctor that because of an amoebic infection and a possible threat to her health, she should abort Tim. Pam and her husband refused to give in to fear and went ahead with their pregnancy. Little did they know Tim would grow to be 6'3", 235 pounds, and one day win the Heisman Trophy.[1]

REFLECTIONS

MARCH 2

1 John 3:1 NIV

How great is the love the Father has lavished on us, that we should be called children of God! And that is what we are! The reason the world does not know us is that it did not know him.

The issue of abortion centers on children—and not just the ones in the womb. The Bible makes it clear that we are all God's children, the work of his hands. A great truth is that the pregnant mother, expectant father, parents, grandparents, and siblings are all God's children, and, perhaps even more than the preborn baby, they are in need of rescue from the hand of the Enemy. Satan and those who do his bidding seek to destroy not only the physical life of the child but the spiritual life of the parents and their family through abortion. Ending abortion will result in the rescue of children and the protection and salvation of many parents.

PRAYER FOCUS: God, I'm glad you loved me enough to create me and give me the choice to have a relationship with you. Lord, I desire to be your adopted son or daughter, and I want to know you the way you know me. Please come into my life and increase my knowledge of you and my sense of self-worth.

DID YOU KNOW? The word "children" occurs 435 times in the New International Version of the Bible. The opening books in the Old and New Testaments lead in frequency with Genesis using the word forty-two times and Matthew using it nineteen times.[2]

REFLECTIONS

64

MARCH 3

Isaiah 49:15-16 NKJV

Can a woman forget her nursing child, and not have compassion on the son of her womb? Surely they may forget, yet I will not forget you. See, I have inscribed you on the palms of My hands; your walls are continually before Me.

People are capable of great atrocity, even hurting their offspring or the members of their immediate family. Tragically, many parents have neglected, abused, or even killed their children. In Isaiah 49:15-16 God tells us that regardless of our conception, birth, or life circumstance, we are highly valued and wanted by him. In fact, God thinks about us so much that he has written our names on his hands. The God who rules the universe has not forgotten us or abandoned us! He loves us all and desires to provide us with life to the fullest. Our response to his gifts should be to trust him always. We should trust him with our lives and allow him to complete his plans for us. If our parents abandoned or hurt us, we can put our lives in the nail-scarred hands of our Lord and Savior. When we do, God will speak to our hearts a love song and a destiny we can't even imagine.

PRAYER FOCUS: God, communicate your love to me through your Word and Holy Spirit. Show me clearly what you want me to do that is unique to me and that you created me to accomplish. Give me the courage, perseverance, and ability to achieve it, and show me that I can trust you as my parent. Teach me how to trust in you, even if my earthly role models have failed miserably in proving trustworthy.

DID YOU KNOW? Eighty percent of women considering having an abortion reject the idea of abortion after viewing an ultrasound of their developing baby. They decide instead to carry their pregnancy to term.[3] Pictures really do speak a thousand words!

REFLECTIONS

MARCH 4

Exodus 4:11-12 NIV

The LORD said to him, "Who gave man his mouth? Who makes him deaf or mute? Who gives him sight or makes him blind? Is it not I, the LORD? Now go; I will help you speak and will teach you what to say."

∞

This dialogue in the fourth chapter of Exodus occurs as God is speaking to Moses out of the burning bush. Moses is uneasy and uncomfortable with being sent to free the Israelites from the Egyptians. He felt intimidated by what God had asked him to do because he doubted his ability to carry out the assignment. But God knew that Moses would succeed if he trusted in him. It wasn't his ability, but rather God's that would see him through. So often, this is what God is asking all of us to do. We simply need to trust and proceed. How often do we squander our opportunities fretting, worrying, complaining, deciding why it won't work, or wondering how many ways we will fail? Instead, we simply need to trust God and follow wherever he leads. God reassures Moses that he will succeed by pointing out that he is the Maker of all things and, as such, the ultimate power and authority in the universe. He is God! If he is for us, nothing can stand against us. Notice how God, in his comments to Moses, makes no distinction between those he created with disabilities and anyone else. To God all life is precious and valuable regardless of functionality or capability. It is only humankind in its finite and twisted thinking that believes one life is more valuable than another.

PRAYER FOCUS: God, help me see people through your eyes. Give me your eternal perspective rather than my finite perspective. Grant me wisdom and understanding about what is really important in life, and help me trust you when your plans overwhelm me or when my circumstances are very difficult and debilitating.

DID YOU KNOW? Incredibly, roughly sixty percent of people polled believe it is acceptable to abort a child diagnosed with a fetal handicap.[4] This is antithetical to a biblical point of view. Many people born with disabilities, such as Nick Vujicic (motivational speaker, author), Christy Brown (author), Jeff Healey (musician), and Jim Abbott (athlete) have lived extraordinary lives in spite of their disabilities.

REFLECTIONS

MARCH 5

Lamentations 3:22-23 ESV

The steadfast love of the Lord never ceases; his mercies never come to an end; they are new every morning; great is your faithfulness.

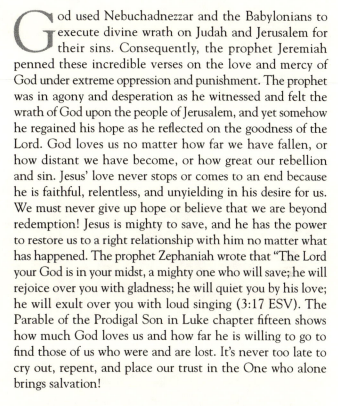

God used Nebuchadnezzar and the Babylonians to execute divine wrath on Judah and Jerusalem for their sins. Consequently, the prophet Jeremiah penned these incredible verses on the love and mercy of God under extreme oppression and punishment. The prophet was in agony and desperation as he witnessed and felt the wrath of God upon the people of Jerusalem, and yet somehow he regained his hope as he reflected on the goodness of the Lord. God loves us no matter how far we have fallen, or how distant we have become, or how great our rebellion and sin. Jesus' love never stops or comes to an end because he is faithful, relentless, and unyielding in his desire for us. We must never give up hope or believe that we are beyond redemption! Jesus is mighty to save, and he has the power to restore us to a right relationship with him no matter what has happened. The prophet Zephaniah wrote that "The Lord your God is in your midst, a mighty one who will save; he will rejoice over you with gladness; he will quiet you by his love; he will exult over you with loud singing (3:17 ESV). The Parable of the Prodigal Son in Luke chapter fifteen shows how much God loves us and how far he is willing to go to find those of us who were and are lost. It's never too late to cry out, repent, and place our trust in the One who alone brings salvation!

PRAYER FOCUS: Lord, your mercy towards me and your unending love for me blow me away. Jesus, I bring before you my sin and ask you to wash me clean and restore a right spirit within me. Help me to overcome temptation, resist the Devil, and trust in your provision. Above all, help me forgive myself. Jesus, give me your peace and show me how far you have removed my sin from me.

DID YOU KNOW? While dying on the cross, Jesus asked the Father to forgive the people who had falsely accused him and demanded his execution (Luke 23:33-34). Jesus is the embodiment of compassion and grace. Spurgeon wrote, "The sinner is the Gospel's reason for existence. If you are un-deserving, ill-deserving, hell-deserving, you are the sort of man for whom the Gospel is ordained and arranged and proclaimed."[5]

MARCH 6

Psalm 94:3-7 ESV

O LORD, how long shall the wicked, how long shall the wicked exult? They pour out their arrogant words; all the evildoers boast. They crush your people, O LORD, and afflict your heritage. They kill the widow and the sojourner, and murder the fatherless; and they say, "The LORD does not see; the God of Jacob does not perceive."

Do not be deceived. God sees oppression and wickedness, and he will not be mocked! God is slow to anger, abounding in love, and rich in forgiveness, not wanting any of his children to perish. God is patient, hoping all of us come to repentance. The gospel of Luke says that "repentance and forgiveness of sins should be proclaimed in [Christ's] name to all nations, beginning from Jerusalem" (24:47 ESV). The psalmist writes, "Why does the wicked man revile God? Why does he say to himself, 'He won't call me to account?' But you, O God, do see trouble and grief; you consider it to take it in hand" (Ps. 10:13-14 NIV). God will not delay his justice forever. Those who support, encourage, and provide abortion arrogantly defy the living God and aid in the destruction and literal crushing of his children. Pro-choice and pro-abortion supporters impose their will upon God's preborn children by condoning their slaughter and denying them their God-given rights of personhood. Destroying God's people, his heritage, is a serious offense. Make no mistake, the preborn baby is oppressed and a member of all the groups God calls us to love, help, and defend, including widows, strangers, the weak, the needy, the poor, and the fatherless. We need to help our brothers and sisters in the womb and those who carry them while there is still time—before God stops being patient and merciful and brings judgment.

PRAYER FOCUS: Lord, I repent of my apathy regarding abortion and commit myself to do whatever I can to promote a culture of life and stop the culture of death abortion creates. Give me a heart and a voice for the weak, needy, poor, fatherless, and oppressed around me.

DID YOU KNOW? Heart disease, typically the leading cause of death in the United States, took the lives of around nineteen million Americans between 1981 and 2007.[6] Abortion, the nation's true leading cause of death, claimed the lives of roughly thirty-four million American children between 1981 and 2007.[7]

REFLECTIONS

MARCH 7

2 Chronicles 14:11 NASB

Then Asa called to the LORD his God and said, "LORD, there is no one besides You to help in the battle between the powerful and those who have no strength; so help us, O LORD our God, for we trust in You, and in Your name have come against this multitude. O LORD, You are our God; let not man prevail against You."

A warrior is best equipped for battle when he knows his role, his strategy, his opponent, his strengths, his weaknesses, and his weapons. Asa knew he was fighting a strong and enormous enemy, and that in his own strength he would not prevail. Humbling himself, Asa chose to rely on his greatest weapon—Almighty God—during the battle. Like Asa, we need to look past the giant of abortion to God's inevitable victory and ask for his help to slay the giant and bring our country back to a respect for all life. If we place our trust in God, fighting in the manner he reveals to us through his Word and prayer, we will achieve victory over all our enemies, whether they are flesh or spirit.

PRAYER FOCUS: Lord God, teach me to hear your voice and to trust in your wisdom and guidance. Thank you for intervening and helping those who have no strength.

DID YOU KNOW? George Müller, a famous Christian orphanage director in the 1800s, ran his ministry entirely by prayer and complete dependence on God's provision. Read about his devout trust in God in the book *George Müller of Bristol: His Life of Prayer and Faith* by A. T. Pierson.

REFLECTIONS

MARCH 8

Jeremiah 29:11 NASB

For I know the plans that I have for you, declares the Lord, plans for welfare and not for calamity to give you a future and a hope.

God loves us and desires to bless us in all we do. His plans are for good and not for evil. He wants to walk in fellowship with us, restoring to us all that humanity's fall from grace in the Garden of Eden and the Enemy have stolen. Will we place our trust in the Lord, lean not on our own feelings and experience, and let him be the guide of our lives? If we do, God promises he will give us a future and a hope. In my experience, nothing brings us a future and a hope more clearly than our children. As God's children, we are a special part of the present and the future. Our devoted lives of service to God bring hope to all who live on earth.

PRAYER FOCUS: God, help me desire good things for others, as you desire good things for me. Lord, let me taste and see that you are good regardless of circumstance. Help me recognize how blessed I am as I take refuge in you. Please protect and sustain my life.

DID YOU KNOW? The human body provides a great example of the intricate and amazing plans of God. All our body systems work together in absolute harmony to create the most complex and amazing beings on earth. Our amazing body contains fifty trillion cells and sixty-two thousand miles of blood vessels. Our heart pumps 3,600 gallons of blood each day. The small intestine is sixteen feet long. The stomach produces half a gallon of hydrochloric acid each day. There are twenty-eight bones in the skull and fifty-eight in the legs and feet.[8] Take a close look at the amazing human body and ask, *How could this come from nothing, be alive only at birth, and be the result of random chance and natural selection?* The answer is, it could not, for there is a God.

REFLECTIONS

MARCH 9

Exodus 23:25-26 NIV

Worship the Lord your God, and his blessing will be on your food and water. I will take away sickness from among you, and none will miscarry or be barren in your land. I will give you a full life span.

God promised his blessing and a full life to the Israelites if they would obey his angel and do all he commanded as they entered the Promised Land. God rewards obedience and the one who faithfully keeps his ways and commands. The body of Christ and our nation will be truly blessed when we turn to God with our whole heart and begin walking in his counsel and his truth. God will bless his people with life and health beyond measure if they collectively obey and walk according to his revealed wisdom. How far would the rate of miscarriage, cancer, and other deadly diseases drop in America if we rendered justice for the preborn and stopped abortion? The Bible teaches that all preborn children, infants, and young children who die reside safely in the arms of God (2 Sam. 12:19-23; Job 3:11-19; Matt. 18:10, 14; Mark. 10:13-16). Additionally, we can expect to be reunited one day in heaven with those in the faith who passed from illness (Matt. 8:11; John 17:20-24; 1 Cor. 15:42-44). Miscarriage, sickness, handicap, and death are all results of the fall of man in the garden, collective disobedience (sin) by God's children on earth, and Satan, who comes to steal, kill, and destroy. Often the outward condition or experience of an individual does not indicate the inward heart of that individual. God knows our story and the reasons for our suffering. Many times when we experience suffering, illness, or death it is not for any overt sin of our own, but rather due to the general state of sin in the world, the Enemy, and the collective climate of the culture—the more wicked the culture the more pain and trouble, the more righteous the culture the more peaceful and blessed (Gen. 3; Job 1:6-22; 2:1-10; Prov. 29:2; Jer. 18:7-10; John 9; Luke 13:1-5, 10-17; Rom. 5). God knows the heart and one's particular situation, and he loves us more than anything on earth (Deut. 7:6-9; Ps. 30:4, 5, 11, 12; John 15:9).

PRAYER FOCUS: God, raise up a unified body of Christians who desire to live according to your commands and principles. Help me to become the kind of person who loves you with my whole heart and walks according to your revealed Truth.

DID YOU KNOW? Several studies indicate there is an increased risk of miscarriage in pregnancies following an abortion. For more information see pages 163-164 in John and Barbara Willke's book, *Abortion Questions & Answers*.

MARCH 10

2 Samuel 14:14 NIV

Like water spilled on the ground, which cannot be recovered, so we must die. But God does not take away life; instead, he devises ways so that a banished person may not remain estranged from him.

It is an unavoidable fact that we will all physically die at some point during this earthly life. What happens after death has been the source of great speculation and debate throughout human history. God, however, has disclosed the end from the beginning and has revealed all truth in his Word (Job 38-42; Isa. 44:7-8; Matt. 10:26-27; 2 Cor. 4:18; Rev. 1:4-8, 17-18). The truth is that every person lives forever after their creation by God, and the choice we make to accept or reject Jesus as our Lord and Savior will determine how and where we spend eternity. Today's Scripture is true that "God does not take away life; instead, he devises ways so that a banished person may not remain estranged from him." The way God has devised is Jesus Christ, who bled and died for our sins on the cross. Jesus said, "I am the way and the truth and the life. No one comes to the Father except through me" (John 14:6 NIV). "The Word became flesh and made his dwelling among us. We have seen his glory, the glory of the One and Only, who came from the Father, full of grace and truth" (John 1:14 NIV).

PRAYER FOCUS: Lord, give me a heart for the lost and the undecided about who Jesus is. Increase my boldness to share my faith. Thank you, God, for sending Jesus to bear my shame and save my life!

DID YOU KNOW? By the tenth week from conception, the baby is developing fingernails, responding to stimulation, and forming buds for their permanent teeth.[9]

REFLECTIONS

MARCH 11

Proverbs 22:2 NKJV

The rich and the poor have this in common, the LORD is the maker of them all.

John 1:3 states, "All things were made through Him, and without Him nothing was made that was made" (NKJV). This confirms the truth that everything is made by Jesus, who is God. Everything includes all preborn children, whether they are in the first seconds of conception or about to be delivered through the birth canal. Abortion clearly takes the life of a person God has created during the early stages of development inside their mother's womb.

PRAYER FOCUS: Lord, forgive us for abortion. We are without excuse to allow such a monstrosity, because the evidence that humans are alive at conception is overwhelming. Science, technology, embryology, common sense, and the Bible all confirm that life begins at conception.

DID YOU KNOW? Ralph Abernathy, a Baptist minister, civil rights movement leader, and close friend of Martin Luther King, Jr. was born on this date in 1926.[10] Every person has a destiny and a calling to fulfill. How much have we missed out on as a nation because of legalized abortion?

REFLECTIONS

MARCH 12

Proverbs 12:6 NIV

The words of the wicked lie in wait for blood, but the speech of the upright rescues them.

∞

The Scriptures affirm that "the tongue has the power of life and death, and those who love it will eat its fruit" (Prov. 18:21 NIV). When it concerns abortion, nothing could be more true! Our words and our willingness to speak the truth about abortion are one of the keys to defeating this idolatrous stronghold of the Enemy. If we surrender our speech to Jesus, we will find that we begin speaking as he would speak, and our words will be full of grace and truth. When our words are pure, loving, compassionate, kind, truthful, and under the control of the Holy Spirit, we will reap a harvest of righteousness and begin seeing our neighbors and their preborn babies rescued from the grip of sin and death.

PRAYER FOCUS: Lord, teach me to gain control over my tongue so I can speak words that bring life. I know this is difficult, but I know that nothing is impossible for you, and I ask in accordance with your will that you would transform my speech to become like yours.

DID YOU KNOW? Before God created heaven, earth, nature, animals, and humans, he spoke. God spoke everything into existence, even us. Read the first chapter of Genesis and note the power of God's tongue. Notice also that everything God created was good, but after the creation of human beings on the sixth day, Scripture says, "it was very good" (Gen. 1:31).

REFLECTIONS

MARCH 13

Ezekiel 18:30-32 NIV

Therefore, O house of Israel, I will judge you, each one according to his ways, declares the Sovereign LORD. Repent! Turn away from all your offenses; then sin will not be your downfall. Rid yourselves of all the offenses you have committed, and get a new heart and a new spirit. Why will you die, O house of Israel? For I take no pleasure in the death of anyone, declares the Sovereign LORD. Repent and live!

The Bible makes it clear that all people will be judged for everything they have ever done, both good and bad. God's law and justice are so perfect that even the slightest offense deserves punishment and separation from a holy God. The book of James says "whoever keeps the whole law and yet stumbles at just one point is guilty of breaking all of it" (2:10 NIV). Yet God did not leave us without hope or a way to be reconciled to him. God's way has always been for us to repent and turn away from our sin; after which he gives us a new heart and spirit. Jesus is the way, and he is available to all who will repent and believe. God has given us the choice to live through Christ or die in our own sin, but he makes it quite clear which path he hopes we will choose. Life! Jesus came to earth to pay the price for our sin and satisfy God's holy justice. The path to abundant life means repenting of our sins and allowing Jesus to bring us new life. God wants us all to live life on earth and in heaven to the fullest. Jesus said, "The thief comes only to steal and kill and destroy; I have come that they may have life, and have it to the full" (John 10:10 NIV). This is why he is so grieved by abortion. The toll it takes in this life and the next is immeasurable.

PRAYER FOCUS: God, I know I have broken your law and sinned against you. I repent of my sins and ask you to forgive me and take control of my life. Help me to get the most out of life by giving me a clean heart through the ministry of the Holy Spirit. Jesus, come live in me and set me free!

DID YOU KNOW? Jesus is in heaven at the right hand of the Father, and he is always praying for us (Heb. 7:25; Isa. 53:12).

REFLECTIONS

MARCH 14

Luke 5:30-32 NASB

The Pharisees and their scribes began grumbling at His disciples, saying, "Why do you eat and drink with the tax collectors and sinners?" And Jesus answered and said to them, "It is not those who are well who need a physician, but those who are sick. I have not come to call the righteous but sinners to repentance."

Jesus paid the price for all mankind with his blood sacrifice on the cross. He has called everyone to repentance because we are all under the curse of sin and death. Romans 3:9-20 makes it clear that no one is righteous and that all people have broken God's law and gone their own way. Jesus died for the Pharisees and scribes, as well as the tax collectors and sinners. The reason the Pharisees didn't recognize Jesus as the Messiah was because they didn't realize who they were as sinners and how much they needed a Savior! I find Jesus' comment pointed and ironic when I think about abortion because the majority of abortions administered in America are to healthy women with healthy babies by a physician who is not treating the sick but those who are well. If healthy men and women facing an unexpected pregnancy would heed the first part of the Lord's advice, they would virtually shut down the abortion industry.

PRAYER FOCUS: Thank you, Jesus, for dying for me. Lord, teach me how your Word can effectively answer the Enemy and combat all of his lies, especially the lies of abortion.

DID YOU KNOW? Abortion is rarely performed to save the life of the mother. Randy Alcorn wrote, "It's an extremely rare case when abortion is required to save the mother's life. While he was U.S. Surgeon General, Dr. C. Everett Koop stated that in thirty-six years as a pediatric surgeon, he was never aware of a single situation in which a preborn child's life had to be taken in order to save the mother's life. He said the use of this argument to justify abortion was a 'smoke screen.'" Alcorn went on to say, "Dr. Landrum Shettles claimed that less than one percent of all abortions are performed to save the mother's life."[11]

REFLECTIONS

MARCH 15

Psalm 32:1-5 NIV

Blessed is he whose transgressions are forgiven, whose sins are covered. Blessed is the man whose sin the LORD does not count against him and in whose spirit is no deceit. When I kept silent, my bones wasted away through my groaning all day long. For day and night your hand was heavy upon me; my strength was sapped as in the heat of summer. Then I acknowledged my sin to you and did not cover up my iniquity. I said, "I will confess my transgressions to the LORD"—and you forgave the guilt of my sin.

It's amazing how different our perspective is from God's perspective. We dread admitting we are wrong and asking for forgiveness because we don't want to seem fallible or bad. God, however, knows that we will be blessed and set free when we humbly admit we have made mistakes and sinned. The real battle is pride. The longer we delay confessing our sin, the heavier our burden will become until it consumes our very life. On the other hand, humility and dependence on God leads to relief and freedom. The Lord said, "Come to me, all you who are weary and burdened, and I will give you rest. Take my yoke upon you and learn from me, for I am gentle and humble in heart, and you will find rest for your souls. For my yoke is easy and my burden is light" (Matt. 11:28-30 NIV). If we will allow God to forgive our sin and transform our lives, we will see that his yoke is easy and his burden is light.

PRAYER FOCUS: God, I confess my sin of _____ to you and ask that you would forgive me and cleanse me from all filth. Give me the power to resist the Devil and keep me away from temptation so that I might not sin against you anymore. Lord, if I should fall again, help me bring my sin before you quickly so that we might be reconciled and resume our intimate fellowship together.

DID YOU KNOW? A growing number of post-abortive men and women who have confessed their sin to the Lord and been set free are speaking out against abortion in the hope that they can keep others from making the same tragic choice they made. One such group can be contacted at *www.silentnomoreawareness.org*. This group offers many resources to help facilitate healing.

REFLECTIONS

MARCH 16

1 John 1:8-9 NKJV

If we say that we have no sin, we deceive ourselves, and the truth is not in us. If we confess our sins, He is faithful and just to forgive us our sins and to cleanse us from all unrighteousness.

We all sin and fall short of God's standard; there is no one who does not sin. And even every believer sins after they have accepted Jesus as their personal Lord and Savior. The question is not whether or not we sin, but how we handle our sin. When we sin, we need to confess it to the Lord and ask Jesus to forgive us, cleanse us, heal us, and give us the ability to resist that sin in the future (1 Kings 8:33-52). If we continue struggling and falling in the same sin, God may want to use members of his body who are especially gifted in the area of deliverance to help us with a particular sin. We should not be afraid to share our struggles with fellow believers we trust. Many people in the body of Christ (the church) have wisdom about how to address specific strongholds of sin (Mark 9:21-29; Acts 5:15-16; 8:6-7; James 5:16).

PRAYER FOCUS: Thank you, Lord, that I can turn to you for help with my sins and that you will always find a way to help me. Lord, I believe you paid for all my sins by dying for me on the cross. I believe the good work you started in me will be completed because of your great love for me (Phil. 1:6). Jesus, I place my trust in you because you alone are faithful.

DID YOU KNOW? Every human being recorded in the Bible struggled with sin except Jesus. Read Romans chapter seven and see how the apostle Paul describes his battle with sin.

REFLECTIONS

78

MARCH 17

1 Peter 2:24 ESV

He himself bore our sins in his body on the tree, that we might die to sin and live to righteousness. By his wounds you have been healed.

Realizing we need a Savior and repenting of our sins is the first step toward healing. Power and healing are available to us because Jesus obediently poured out his life on the cross as the Father's perfect sacrifice of atonement. His life, blood, and death are what allow us to become righteous and live in victory.

PRAYER FOCUS: Thank you, Jesus, for dying on the cross for me and allowing me to have fellowship with the Father through your sacrifice of love. I love you, Lord, and I am grateful for everything you have given me and done for me. I am especially grateful for your sacrifice upon the cross that secured my redemption.

DID YOU KNOW? Jesus suffered spiritually, emotionally, and physically during his crucifixion on the cross for our atonement (reconciliation with God). He suffered spiritually when he was forsaken by his Father and the weight of all sin was poured upon him. Emotionally, Jesus suffered when he was falsely accused, abandoned by his disciples, mocked, cursed, and spat upon. Finally, he suffered physically when he was beaten, scourged, marched to the execution site, nailed to the cross, and pierced with a Roman spear (Matt. 26; 27; John 18; 19). For a detailed medical description of the bloody price our Lord paid for our sin on the cross, see Josh McDowell's *The New Evidence that Demands a Verdict*.

REFLECTIONS

MARCH 18

Psalm 19:1-4 NIV

The heavens declare the glory of God; the skies proclaim the work of his hands. Day after day they pour forth speech; night after night they display knowledge. There is no speech or language where their voice is not heard. Their voice goes out into all the earth, their words to the ends of the world.

The sun, moon, stars and planets constantly speak of the glorious God and his marvelous creation. God's spectacular canopy is seen by all people in every generation throughout the whole earth, so that no one is without the testimony of his supremacy, splendor, and majesty. God's creation continually speaks about its Designer. How shameful it is that the very pinnacle of God's creation has rejected creation's testimony and murdered the very work of God's own hands through abortion!

PRAYER FOCUS: Lord, "Your works are wonderful, I know that full well" (Ps. 139:14 NIV). God, give me ears to hear you speak through your creation, and eyes to see you in everything you have made.

DID YOU KNOW? According to *Firefly's World of Facts*, "Our Solar System is only one of 100—200 billion stars in the Milky Way, which is 100,000 light years in diameter."[12] It is important to note that if our earth were even slightly out of orbit, it would fail to support life as we know it.[13] God's design is so marvelous and overwhelming it deserves to be studied. Two thought-provoking books on the subject are *The Witness of the Stars* by E. W. Bullinger and *The Evidential Power of Beauty* by Thomas Dubay, S. M.

REFLECTIONS

MARCH 19

Hebrews 4:12-13 NKJV

For the word of God is living and powerful, and sharper than any two-edged sword, piercing even to the division of soul and spirit, and of joints and marrow, and is a discerner of the thoughts and intents of the heart. And there is no creature hidden from His sight, but all things are naked and open to the eyes of Him to whom we must give account.

God's Word is penetrating and powerful to expose our hearts and render us completely defenseless to the wisdom of the Lord. When we hold our hearts up to the revealed light of Scripture, we see clearly that we have nothing to boast about. We are desperately wicked and in need of a Savior. This same revealed light, however, bathes us in such a glorious, pure, and unrestrained love that we can barely contain the ecstasy we feel as we melt in our Father's care, compassion, and desire for us! Nothing is hidden from God, but all things are naked and open to the eyes of him to whom we must give account for every secret done in the dark or every act done in the light.

PRAYER FOCUS: Lord Jesus, as I examine your Word, let it examine me. Reveal to me the sins and stumbling blocks in my life that I need to bring to the cross. Make me new, Lord, and wash me clean. Thank you for your overwhelming love and comfort. Even when I'm wounded, I know you walk beside me.

DID YOU KNOW? The Bible was written on three continents—Africa, Asia, and Europe—and in three languages—Hebrew, Aramaic, and Greek.[14]

REFLECTIONS

MARCH 20

Nahum 3:1 NIV

Woe to the city of blood, full of lies, full of plunder, never without victims!

This warning was originally issued to the city of Nineveh, most likely before its fall around 612 BC. It is interesting to note that God had already spared Nineveh from judgment due to her repentance during the time of Jonah. The prophet Nahum is prophesying new destruction upon Nineveh because of her bloodshed and lies. "Woe to the city of blood." I believe the prophetic words spoken to Nineveh 2,600 years ago could be just as easily applied to New York City, Chicago, Los Angeles, or your hometown. The bloodshed of abortion flows from our cities as our courts, government, and people continue upholding the abortion industry's lies. Around 3,300 children are killed each day in our country due to legalized abortion! This atrocity springs from a foundation of lies cleverly hidden in nebulous and subjective terms like *choice, safety, privacy, health, "quality of life,"* and *women's rights.* Psalm 5:6 says, "You destroy those who tell lies; bloodthirsty and deceitful men the Lord abhors" (NIV). It's time to stop listening to lies and start listening to God, or we will surely end up like Nineveh!

PRAYER FOCUS: Thank you, God, for your slowness to anger and your abundant mercy. I plead forgiveness for my nation and our sin of shedding innocent blood. Lord, only Christ's blood is sufficient to atone for our national guilt. Please hasten our repentance and give us time to abolish abortion, avoiding your corrective judgment upon us.

DID YOU KNOW? The circulation of the mother's blood and her baby's blood are side by side in the womb, but they never mix.[15] This is one of the many scientific facts that refute the lie that the baby is part of the woman's body.

REFLECTIONS

MARCH 21

Exodus 23:6-7 NASB

You shall not pervert the justice due to your needy brother in his dispute. Keep far from a false charge, and do not kill the innocent or the righteous, for I will not acquit the guilty.

Legalized abortion perverts all justice. It does everything these verses in Exodus command us not to do. Abortion denies justice to our needy preborn neighbors, requires that a false charge of non-personhood be established and maintained, and kills thousands of innocent men and women every day. Unlike the atrocities of slavery or the Holocaust during World War II, abortion is an attack on the whole human race, reaching every ethnic group and gender. I believe abortion is the greatest attempt so far on the part of Satan to destroy the work of God's hand and those who are made in the divine image.

PRAYER FOCUS: God, help me to stand against abortion in my words and actions. I want to become a tangible solution to this problem in our nation and the world. Lord, only you can end this atrocity, so please teach me to pray effectively against abortion and release the power of the Holy Spirit living in me.

DID YOU KNOW? Many nations of the world allow legalized abortion with varying degrees of restriction. Conservative estimates place the worldwide abortion total at around forty-two million babies per year.[16] For more information on worldwide abortion laws, go to *www.pregnantpause.org* and click "legislation" under the category Law & Action.

REFLECTIONS

MARCH 22

Matthew 26:28 ESV

"This is my blood of the covenant, which is poured out for many for the forgiveness of sins."

Jesus' blood shed on the cross is the ultimate and final payment for our offense of sin. His atonement was poured out for all humankind, and all those who believe he died for their sins and place their trust in him as God's perfect sacrifice will be adopted and redeemed. Jesus' blood covers a multitude of sins and delivers Christians from death. Nothing in all creation will separate us from Jesus and his love if we confess him and ask him to bear our burden of sin. Jesus would not have endured such a painful and horrific death if we were not worth saving! We must never underestimate God's love for us and our intrinsic value to him. Jesus will forgive any sin if we ask him to forgive us and sincerely repent.

PRAYER FOCUS: Jesus, I believe in you! Please forgive my sins and create in me a transformed heart and a new spirit. Open my eyes to see and my ears to hear your voice and your Word. Show me the way to go and then help me walk it out. Thank you for loving me even when I am not very lovely.

DID YOU KNOW? Blood is vital to life. "The cardiovascular system is one of the first major systems to start working in the embryo. Without a heart and blood vessels, there is no way to deliver the food and oxygen the embryo needs to flourish."[17] God said that "the life of a creature is in the blood, and I have given it to you to make atonement for yourselves on the altar; it is the blood that makes atonement for one's life" (Lev. 17:11 NIV). This is as true in the biological realm as it is in the spiritual realm—through faith in Jesus Christ.

REFLECTIONS

MARCH 23

Psalm 107:1-3 NKJV

Oh, give thanks to the Lord, for He is good! For His mercy endures forever. Let the redeemed of the Lord say so, whom He has redeemed from the hand of the enemy, and gathered out of the lands, from the east and from the west, from the north and from the south.

Let the sons and the daughters arise and let the redeemed of the Lord proclaim the goodness of our God in the land of the living! The exhortation at the beginning of this great psalm of deliverance is foundational to the call to liberate the preborn and minister to their parents. It is precisely because our God has delivered and redeemed us from the great Enemy of life that we should go and rescue the preborn and their parents. We must strive to be like our heavenly Father in every way. If God rescues, so should we. If God loves, so should we. If God heals, so should we. If God forgives, so should we. Church, let's love the least of these and in so doing let's affirm that our God is good!

PRAYER FOCUS: Lord God, thank you for rescuing me from darkness and giving me the joy of your salvation. Great is your love! Your mercies endure forever. Help me love the least of these, my brethren, whenever they are in need.

DID YOU KNOW? Goodness is a fruit of the Spirit (Gal.5:22). The New King James Version translation of the Bible refers to goodness or good over 740 times.[18] If you have not experienced the goodness of God, read Psalm 34:8 and ask him to let you taste it.

REFLECTIONS

MARCH
24

Psalm 94:16 NASB

Who will stand up for me against evildoers? Who will take his stand for me against those who do wickedness?

As God's people, we need to stand for truth. We need to take a stand against those ideas and actions that are wicked. As Edmund Burke allegedly said, "All that is necessary for the triumph of evil is for good men to do nothing." God has appointed us as watchmen over his people, and we need to sound the alarm and awaken all to the atrocity of abortion.

PRAYER FOCUS: God, give me the courage to engage the culture and promote the sanctity of human life. Holy Spirit, guard my heart against discouragement, burnout, and apathy, and help me persevere for as long as it takes to see justice done.

DID YOU KNOW? God has always sent his watchmen during difficult times to challenge the status quo and bring help to the people. How different would the world be if watchmen like Moses, Esther, William Wilberforce, Martin Luther King, Jr., or Corrie ten Boom had refused to take a stand and voice the truth?

REFLECTIONS

MARCH 25

Isaiah 64:6-8 NASB

For all of us have become like one who is unclean, and all our righteous deeds are like a filthy garment; and all of us wither like a leaf, and our iniquities, like the wind, take us away. There is no one who calls on Your name, who arouses himself to take hold of You; for You have hidden Your face from us and have delivered us into the power of our iniquities. But now, O LORD, You are our Father, we are the clay, and You our potter; and all of us are the work of Your hand.

We are all fallen and wayward, and that is true even of people who believe in Christ. Without the grace and love of our Father, we would all languish in our sins and ultimately perish. The question we need to ask ourselves is, whose hands are we in? Are we in the hands of our Creator God, being molded in his image? Or are we in the hands of the world, being molded in its image? The One who made us knows best how to form and develop us into a holy people, a blessed nation. If we give our fears, our hopes, our dreams, our sins, our troubles, and our very lives to God, we can watch him make beauty out of ashes.

PRAYER FOCUS: God, I thank you that every person you have made from the foundation of the world is important to you because they are the work of your hand. Knowing that I came from you makes me feel appreciated, loved, and special. Jesus, please continue what you started in me, teach me what is best, and teach me the way I should go (Isa. 48:17-19).

DID YOU KNOW? By the twelfth week of gestation, a baby's sex is clearly distinguishable, tiny hairs have begun to grow, and she can make a fist with her fingers.[19]

REFLECTIONS

MARCH 26

Acts 10:34-35 ESV

So Peter opened his mouth and said: "Truly I understand that God shows no partiality, but in every nation anyone who fears him and does what is right is acceptable to him."

∞

Peter is realizing through revelation and the outpouring of God's Spirit on both the Jews and the Gentiles that God is Lord of all and richly blesses all who call on him. If we respect God and do what is right, we will be accepted and blessed regardless of who we are or where we live. What greater respect could we show to God than to respect every life he has created, while laboring diligently to support and care for all human beings? The Lord has revealed to us what is good and what we must do, "to do justice, and to love kindness, and to walk humbly with your God" (Mic. 6:8 ESV). Abortion is incompatible with any of these things.

PRAYER FOCUS: God, teach me to do what is right and to love what you love. Give me your eyes to see and your ears to hear. Lord, you love the least of these, my brothers and sisters, and your ear is attentive to their prayers. Help me to be like you and love your people from every tribe, tongue, and nation, born or preborn.

DID YOU KNOW? There are an estimated two billion Christians in the world, making Christianity the largest faith on earth.[20] Jesus said, "By their fruits you will know them" (Matt. 7:20 NKJV). I can think of no better fruit to evidence the authenticity of Christ and the gospel than the billions of lives, past and present, which have been improved by their relationship with the Savior.

REFLECTIONS

MARCH 27

Isaiah 58:2-4 NIV

For day after day they seek me out; they seem eager to know my ways, as if they were a nation that does what is right and has not forsaken the commands of its God. They ask me for just decisions and seem eager for God to come near them. "Why have we fasted," they say, "and you have not seen it? Why have we humbled ourselves, and you have not noticed?" Yet on the day of your fasting, you do as you please and exploit all your workers. Your fasting ends in quarreling and strife, and in striking each other with wicked fists. You cannot fast as you do today and expect your voice to be heard on high.

Why is the church in America often stymied or ineffective? Perhaps it is because we have followed too closely the world's system and failed to follow the teachings of Scripture and the Lord's commands. We often seek out human solutions or institutions to solve our problems, rather than following God's prescribed plan for healing and victory. We fast and we pray, but then we fail to take action and cease to become lights shining before humanity. Or worse, we fast and pray and then let our lives and our testimony degenerate into wickedness. We would do well to heed the words of James, "Faith by itself, if it is not accompanied by action, is dead" (James 2:17 NIV). Read tomorrow's entry and find out how we can be assured that God will hear our voice and honor our fast.

PRAYER FOCUS: Lord, help me understand that your ways are not our ways. Give me the discernment to separate the two, and help me hear your voice and obey your path. Increase my knowledge of your Word so I can reconcile your voice with your revealed Word.

DID YOU KNOW? Fasting (abstaining from food to concentrate on God) has a rich biblical heritage and is presented in the Bible as a vital tool in the believer's life to effect change. Three worthwhile books on the subject are *Fasting* and *Shaping History through Prayer and Fasting* by Derek Prince, and *A Hunger for God* by John Piper.

REFLECTIONS

MARCH 28

Isaiah 58:6-9 NIV

Is not this the kind of fasting I have chosen: to loose the chains of injustice and untie the cords of the yoke, to set the oppressed free and break every yoke? Is it not to share your food with the hungry and to provide the poor wanderer with shelter—when you see the naked, to clothe him, and not to turn away from your own flesh and blood? Then your light will break forth like the dawn, and your healing will quickly appear; then your righteousness will go before you, and the glory of the LORD will be your rear guard. Then you will call, and the LORD will answer; you will cry for help, and he will say: Here am I.

Perhaps the answer to global warming is not lower emissions and greater conservation. Perhaps the answer to our economic woes is not more government regulation or tax cuts. Maybe the best plan for healing and change is to honor God and revere what he has made! We are all called to love our neighbor and be good stewards of the planet. But how can we expect good things from a just God when we kill his children at a rate of over three thousand per day? How can we expect a change in our climate while we greedily exploit the poor and the needy? How can we request financial blessing from God when our children perish daily in the womb and faint from hunger at the head of every street (Lam. 2:19)? The answer is that we cannot. But if we set the oppressed children in the womb free, and break the yoke of abortion; if we share our monetary resources with the poor, and feed the hungry; if we clothe the naked, reach out to the orphan and visit the sick; then our healing will quickly appear and our light will shine before the world. God alone can change the climate, and all the wealth of the world is his: "Yours, O Lord, is the greatness and the power and the glory and the majesty and the splendor, for everything in heaven and earth is yours. Yours, O Lord, is the kingdom; you are exalted as head over all. Wealth and honor come from you; you are the ruler of all things. In your hands are strength and power to exalt and give strength to all" (1 Chron. 29:11-12 NIV). The sooner we follow God's plan, the better off we will be, for his ways bless not only us and our children, but our children's children.

PRAYER FOCUS: God, I'm sorry I have failed to recognize the needs of the oppressed and hurting people around me. Lord, would you give me eyes to see and ears to hear the needs of your people? And give me the resources necessary to meet the needs I see.

DID YOU KNOW? Esther fasted in accordance with the principles described in Isaiah chapter fifty-eight. The book of Esther, chapters four through eight (especially 4:7-16), shows how her actions brought about great change for her people and nation.

MARCH 29

Jeremiah 18:7-10 NKJV

The instant I speak concerning a nation and concerning a kingdom, to pluck up, to pull down, and to destroy it, if that nation against whom I have spoken turns from its evil, I will relent of the disaster that I thought to bring upon it. And the instant I speak concerning a nation and concerning a kingdom, to build and to plant it, if it does evil in My sight so that it does not obey My voice, then I will relent concerning the good with which I said I would benefit it.

God is sovereign. He raises up leaders, topples kings, and presides over the affairs of nations. God's timing is not ours, and while it may appear as though God is slow to render justice when a nation abandons his ways and oppresses his people, God will ultimately tear down such a nation. He is rich in love, slow to anger, and abundantly merciful. He is good to both the righteous and the wicked. But God will not remain neutral forever, and when he acts, he is decisive and quick. If our nation does not correct the abuse of abortion and follow God's ways, it is only a matter of time before we will falter and be delivered into the hands of our enemies. The blessing or cursing of a nation lies in the conduct of its people. Will we repent and do what is right, or will we continue in rebellion and receive God's just punishment?

PRAYER FOCUS: Lord God, forgive me and my nation for our rebellion and sin. Help us to know your truth and to put it into practice. Thank you, heavenly Father, for your patience in the midst of our sin. Give us time to repent and do what is right as a nation.

DID YOU KNOW? The number of abortions committed in the United States every four years is almost as great as the number of Jews murdered during the Holocaust. Shamefully, our national holocaust is already six to seven times longer than the one in Europe during WWII.

REFLECTIONS

MARCH 30

Psalm 76:7-9 NKJV

You, Yourself, are to be feared; and who may stand in Your presence when once You are angry? You caused judgment to be heard from heaven; the earth feared and was still, when God arose to judgment, to deliver all the oppressed of the earth.

God alone is the One we should fear and to whom we must give an account! Sooner or later, he is coming in judgment to set the record straight and render justice for the oppressed. Even as the land is still before Almighty God, we must also be still and know that he is God (Ps. 46:10). It should send great shivers down our spines to think of facing our Creator with the blood of his preborn children on our hands. Make no mistake, if we do not repent and end abortion in our land, God will!

PRAYER FOCUS: Lord, forgive me for my part in this present wickedness and restore me to a healthy relationship with you. Lord, I understand I must take action against abortion, regardless of my own level of complicity. Help me find ways to help your oppressed people in the womb.

DID YOU KNOW? Abortion has made human embryos and fetuses the most oppressed people group in the world. Scott Klusendorf, defending the humanity of human embryos, cited the following conclusions made by the National Bioethics Advisory Commission and the Ramsey Colloquium: "The report from the Advisory Commission describes the human embryo from its earliest stages as a living organism and a 'developing form of human life.' The highly respected 1995 Ramsey Colloquium statement on embryo research acknowledges: The [embryo] is human; it will not articulate itself into some other kind of animal. Any being that is human is a human being. If it is objected that, at five days or fifteen days, the embryo does not look like a human being, it must be pointed out that this is precisely what a human being looks like—and what each of us looked like—at five or fifteen days of development."[21]

REFLECTIONS

MARCH 31

Matthew 12:35-37 NASB

The good man brings out of his good treasure what is good; and the evil man brings out of his evil treasure what is evil. But I tell you that every careless word that people speak, they shall give an accounting for it in the day of judgment. For by your words you will be justified, and by your words you will be condemned.

Our words matter. They can be a great force for good or evil. Paul said, "Speaking the truth in love, we will in all things grow up into him who is the Head, that is, Christ" (Eph. 4:15 NIV). The way we speak the truth in love about other men and women can shape the minds of our families and culture. We must always ask God to guard our speech and keep us from speaking things that bring death. For far too long we have spoken terms like "choice," "my body," "health of the mother," and "women's rights," to the exclusion of one group in preference to another. We cannot be for women's rights and then kill fifty million preborn children, half of whom are female. We cannot protect an individual's rights to their body by ensuring their right to destroy another individual's body. We cannot give one person the choice to kill and refuse another person the choice to live. We cannot protect women's health by allowing them to undergo an unnecessary procedure that can result in all sorts of health problems and even death. Words have meaning, and if we do not fight to reclaim the meaning of them, they will be used to justify the unjustifiable.

PRAYER FOCUS: Lord, teach me to speak what is true, tempered by grace. Give me a thirst for your Word so that I know what is true and what is false.

DID YOU KNOW? *The Oxford English Dictionary* defines the word *conception* as "the creation of a child in the womb."[22] Comparatively, *The American Heritage Dictionary* defines the word as "the formation of a zygote capable of survival and maturation in normal conditions."[23] While taking a different approach, both definitions affirm the truth that life begins at conception.

REFLECTIONS

April

TWELVE WEEKS GESTATION

APRIL 1

1 Timothy 4:7-8 ESV

Have nothing to do with irreverent, silly myths. Rather train yourself for godliness; for while bodily training is of some value, godliness is of value in every way, as it holds promise for the present life and also for the life to come.

On this day of playful deceitfulness, it is important to remember those things that are dependable and that truly have value. People are the most valuable entity in all creation, and God has given us a treasure book of information on how to treat them. This treasure book of wisdom, however, will do us no good unless we read it. Reading and studying the Bible needs to be a regular part of our lives as Christians. We need to "work out" in the things of God so that we know the truth and are ready to act upon it! The Bible is the greatest resource on earth, and the better we understand it, the better we will live out our faith and impact the world for Christ. It is a myth that the preborn are not persons, and the Bible has told us so.

PRAYER FOCUS: God, help me understand that I need to make you a daily priority just like exercise. Show me that physical health is good, but that spiritual health is better and ultimately leads to greater physical health as well.

DID YOU KNOW? On this day in 1996, Taco Bell took out a full-page ad in *The New York Times* announcing they had purchased the Liberty Bell to "reduce the country's debts." They said they were renaming it the "Taco Liberty Bell."[1] The Bible says that "a joyful heart is good medicine" (Prov. 17:22 ESV). So have some fun today.

REFLECTIONS

APRIL 2

Psalm 34:8 HCSB

Taste and see that the Lord is good. How happy is the man who takes refuge in Him!

∞

Is the Lord your refuge, the One in whom you place your trust? My wife and I are always trying to get our kids to eat something new. We know our kids will like the unfamiliar food if they will taste it and learn what we have already discovered: that this food is yummy! At first there is resistance and distrust, but if they work up the courage and try it, they discover more often than not that this stuff is good! God is offering us the same proposition. He knows what we need and how to meet our needs, but can we trust him? God says, "Go ahead, taste me, try me in this, and see that I am good!" If we give God our worries, our fears, our finances, and our lives, we will see through experience that God is truly good. And we will be happy for taking refuge in him.

PRAYER FOCUS: God, show me that you are good! I want to taste your goodness and feel the joy of your salvation. Lord, increase my faith in you by manifesting your presence in my life in tangible, measurable ways.

DID YOU KNOW? God is good to everyone he has made (Ps. 145:8-10; Matt. 5:45). He gives us life and breath, sunshine and rain. God gives us the capacity to think and dream, love and laugh. He gives us beauty and passion, strength and tenderness. The goodness of God is all around us, and all we have to do is look for it.

REFLECTIONS

APRIL 3

Psalm 10:1-3 NIV

Why, O LORD, do you stand far off? Why do you hide yourself in times of trouble? In his arrogance the wicked man hunts down the weak, who are caught in the schemes he devises. He boasts of the cravings of his heart; he blesses the greedy and reviles the LORD.

Why does God allow the wicked time on earth? Why doesn't he render immediate justice? God allows the wicked time on earth because of his fairness, love, and compassion. If God rendered immediate justice to the wicked, the planet would be uninhabited, and the human race would be extinct. For we are all fallen and prone to wickedness. God in his great mercy allows us time to repent and realize our need for his governance. Apart from the Lord, we are wayward and can do nothing truly pure or good. Of all the wicked things humans have devised, abortion is truly one of the most horrible. Psalm 10 accurately describes the wickedness of abortion and how it is arrived at and practiced in our land.

PRAYER FOCUS: Lord, thank you that my wickedness doesn't have to be the end of the story if I repent. I know you can make beauty out of ashes. Jesus, help me abstain from personal wickedness and fight against any form of wickedness in my culture.

DID YOU KNOW? Basil of Caesarea (329-379 AD), a leader in the Greek Orthodox Church, fought the evils of heresy and abortion during his ministry. To read more about his contribution see John Ensor's *Answering the Call*.[2]

REFLECTIONS

APRIL 4

Psalm 10:4-8 NIV

In his pride the wicked does not seek him; in all his thoughts there is no room for God. His ways are always prosperous; he is haughty and your laws are far from him; he sneers at all his enemies. He says to himself, "Nothing will shake me; I'll always be happy and never have trouble." His mouth is full of curses and lies and threats; trouble and evil are under his tongue. He lies in wait near the villages; from ambush he murders the innocent, watching in secret for his victims.

Arrogance and pride are at the heart of wickedness. The wicked presume they know more than God or anyone else. They justify their actions by flaunting their wealth and possessions, believing their affluence lends credibility to their methods. The wicked mock their opposition and spew out from their lips all sorts of vile hatred and deception. If they follow this destructive path long enough, they will eventually prey upon the weak and murder the innocent. The wicked are slow to perceive God's heart and fail to account for his judgment, but God will judge everyone according to his or her works. If we are involved with abortion, we must repent and taste the restoration of the Lord. Whatever restitution he requires will be well worth the effort!

PRAYER FOCUS: Lord, I'm sorry I have participated in abortion or any other form of wickedness. Teach me the right path to follow and the right way to treat people. Jesus, I long to be good like you. Come into my heart and make me new. Thank you that no matter how far I have fallen, you can redeem me, for nothing is impossible with you.

DID YOU KNOW? Martin Luther King, Jr. was assassinated on this day in 1968. Whether we live or die, God is extremely pleased with those who stand up against wickedness (John 12:24-25).

REFLECTIONS

APRIL 5

Psalm 10:9-14 NIV

He lies in wait like a lion in cover; he lies in wait to catch the helpless; he catches the helpless and drags them off in his net. His victims are crushed, they collapse; they fall under his strength. He says to himself, "God has forgotten; he covers his face and never sees." Arise, Lord! Lift up your hand, O God. Do not forget the helpless. Why does the wicked man revile God? Why does he say to himself, "He won't call me to account?" But you, O God, do see trouble and grief; you consider it to take it in hand. The victim commits himself to you; you are the helper of the fatherless.

∞

Planned Parenthood (the nation's largest provider of abortions) lies in wait in our poorest neighborhoods for the confused and needy to encourage and guide them in the destruction of their children. In their arrogance, they believe they are helping people and only removing an unfortunate burden, a blob of tissue. They fail to consult God about the beginning of life and the value of every member of the human race. They deny or ignore that we are full human beings from the moment of conception. Many embryos and fetuses are crushed by the abortionist and fall under their strength. Arise, Lord! End abortion in America. Do not forget the helpless. Be their helper and be our helper both now and forever!

PRAYER FOCUS: Lord God, only you can change our hearts and overcome abortion. Please bring repentance to those involved in Planned Parenthood and bring healing in our land. Wake up your entire church to the needs of the least of these our brothers and sisters in the womb.

DID YOU KNOW? Verse 10 in Psalm 10 accurately describes a Dilatation and Evacuation abortion: "His victims are crushed, they collapse; they fall under his strength." See *Abortion Questions & Answers* by John and Barbara Willke (page 141) for a brief description of the horribleness of a D&E abortion.

REFLECTIONS

APRIL 6

Luke 6:36-38 HCSB

Be merciful, just as your Father also is merciful. Do not judge, and you will not be judged. Do not condemn, and you will not be condemned. Forgive, and you will be forgiven. Give, and it will be given to you; a good measure—pressed down, shaken together, and running over—will be poured into your lap. For with the measure you use, it will be measured back to you.

Nothing illustrates mercy and forgiveness better than a story from Corrie ten Boom's ministry shortly after WWII at a church in Munich. The following is an excerpt from Rusty Wright's article for *womentodaymagazine.com* entitled "Forgiveness, Reconciliation, and You." Wright gives the primary source as "Death Camp Revisited," *Worldwide Challenge*, July/August 1994, 35-36.

"When we confess our sins," Corrie explained, "God casts them into the deepest ocean, gone forever." After her presentation, she recognized a man approaching her, a guard from Ravensbruck, before whom she had had to walk naked. Chilling memories flooded back. "A fine message, *Fraulein!*" said the man. "How good it is to know that, as you say, all our sins are at the bottom of the sea!" He extended his hand in greeting. Corrie recalled, "I, who had spoken so glibly of forgiveness, fumbled in my pocketbook rather than take that hand. He would not remember me. . . . But I remembered him and the leather crop swinging from his belt. I was face to face with one of my captors, and my blood seemed to freeze." The man continued: "You mentioned Ravensbruck in your talk. . . . I was a guard there. . . . But since that time . . . I have become a Christian. I know that God has forgiven me for the cruel things I did there, but I would like to hear it from your lips as well, *Fraulein*." He extended his hand again. "Will you forgive me?" **Corrie stood there, unable to forgive.** As anger and vengeance raged inside her, she remembered Jesus' death for this man. How could she refuse? But she lacked the strength. She silently asked God to forgive her and help her forgive him. As she took his hand, she felt a healing warmth flooding her body. "I forgive you, brother!" she cried, "With all my heart." "And so," Corrie later recalled, "I discovered that it is not on our forgiveness any more than on our goodness that the world's healing hinges, but on [God's]. When He tells us to love our enemies, He gives, along with the command, the love itself."

PRAYER FOCUS: Jesus, I need your help to forgive _____. Please give me the ability to surrender myself to you, let go of my hurt, and release those who have sinned against me so that I can be free!

DID YOU KNOW? Corrie ten Boom was released from Ravensbruck, the notorious women's concentration camp, because of a clerical error that occurred just one week before all the women in her age group were taken to the gas chamber.[3]

APRIL 7

Psalm 119:11 NKJV

Your word I have hidden in my heart, that I might not sin against You!

How do we stay grounded and steadfast in today's frantic culture? We must spend time with our Father and learn his counsel. The psalmist knew that for him to please God, he must know God's truth and live by it. He spent hours of time in God's Word—enough time to effectively hide God's Word in his heart. The closer we are to God, the farther away from sin we will be. Memorize Scripture and let it become an integral part of your day.

PRAYER FOCUS: God, help me find creative ways to read and listen to your Word. Lead me to creative resources to nourish my soul with your teaching and your wisdom. Help me find a church that cherishes the Bible and teaches it in a serious way. Allow me to store up your Word in my heart so that I can recall it when the Enemy attacks me or when a witness opportunity presents itself.

DID YOU KNOW? Psalm 119 is the longest psalm in the Bible. It mentions God's Word in almost every verse. The psalm itself is an acrostic poem with twenty-two stanzas using each word of the Hebrew alphabet in sequence. Each stanza has eight verses that begin with the appropriate numerical letter as it relates to the order of the Hebrew alphabet.[4]

REFLECTIONS

APRIL 8

Luke 1:34-37 HCSB

Mary asked the angel, "How can this be, since I have not been intimate with a man?" The angel replied to her: "The Holy Spirit will come upon you, and the power of the Most High will overshadow you. Therefore the holy One to be born will be called the Son of God. And consider your relative Elizabeth—even she has conceived a son in her old age, and this is the sixth month for her who was called barren. For nothing will be impossible with God."

If God did not value the process of embryonic and fetal development, then why did he send his only begotten Son through the womb? Jesus was a zygote, an embryo, and a fetus before he was a tiny baby wrapped in swaddling clothes and placed in a manger! God directly oversees the creation of his people from the moment of conception. Consider Elizabeth's story in the first chapter of the gospel of Luke—God made her womb fertile in her old age after years of barrenness. He knew she was in the sixth month of gestation, and he had intimate knowledge of the baby's gender and purpose. Have no doubt that God is the Author and Creator of all life!

PRAYER FOCUS: Lord, I am inspired by your miraculous power and the knowledge that nothing is impossible with you. I praise you that Jesus, my Judge, shared in my humanity from conception until his earthly death. How qualified you are, Lord Jesus, to render a just verdict concerning me. Help me believe that you can accomplish great things with my life, and give me the grace and courage to act on what I believe.

DID YOU KNOW? In the third month of pregnancy, a baby's nervous system is generating an average of 2.5 million neurons every minute.[5]

REFLECTIONS

APRIL 9

Psalm 50:10-12 NASB

For every beast of the forest is Mine, the cattle on a thousand hills. I know every bird of the mountains, and everything that moves in the field is Mine. If I were hungry I would not tell you, for the world is Mine, and all it contains.

God is the sovereign Creator, and everything he has made is his, including the preborn of every species. The riches of God's wisdom and knowledge are too great for us to fathom. Notice how intimately involved and observant God is concerning his creation. He knows every beast and every bird. Indeed, as Jesus affirmed in Luke 12:7, "the very hairs of your head are all numbered. Do not fear; you are more valuable than many sparrows" (NASB). God keeps his eye on the sparrow, but we are of far greater value than they. How shameful it is when we presume to know who should live and who should die in the womb!

PRAYER FOCUS: Lord, when I think of the wonders of your creation, I am in awe. I am the clay and you are the potter, so mold me in the way you would have me go. Lord, you are worthy of all praise and adoration. You are the Mighty God, Everlasting Father, and my Prince of Peace!

DID YOU KNOW? Scientists still don't know how many species live on earth. The World Resources Institute (*wri.org*) said this: "Surprisingly, scientists have a better understanding of how many stars there are in the galaxy than how many species there are on Earth. Estimates of global species diversity have varied from 2 million to 100 million species, with a best estimate of somewhere near 10 million, and only 1.4 million have actually been named."[6]

REFLECTIONS

APRIL 10

Psalm 94:20-21 ESV

Can wicked rulers be allied with you, those who frame injustice by statute? They band together against the life of the righteous and condemn the innocent to death.

∞

The apostle Paul said there is no authority except from God, who clearly establishes all authority (Romans 13:1-7). The Bible makes it clear, however, that God does not always approve of how those in authority exercise their authority. We all have been given free will, and governments are no exception. The ninety-fourth psalm asks if a corrupt government or ruler can be allied with God. The psalmist goes on to conclude that God will repay evil rulers for their wickedness and destroy them: "He will bring back on them their iniquity and wipe them out for their wickedness; the Lord our God will wipe them out" (94:23 ESV). While God has used wicked nations at times to achieve his purposes, he never exonerates them from judgment. The psalmist also tells us how to spot an unjust government. It is one that is opposed to God's righteous people and one that condemns the innocent to death. Our government and nation will not survive for very long if we continue supporting abortion on demand and denying the preborn justice.

PRAYER FOCUS: Jesus, I pray for my government and those in positions of authority. Help them champion justice and have the general well-being of all our citizens in mind when they make decisions. Give us God-fearing presidents like George Washington, John Adams, and Abraham Lincoln. Motivate our congresspeople and senators to pray diligently before they introduce legislation or vote.

DID YOU KNOW? Abraham Lincoln and the U.S. Senate established a national day of prayer and fasting to be carried out on April 30, 1863. The proclamation opens with these words: "Whereas, the Senate of the United States, devoutly recognizing the Supreme Authority and Just Government of Almighty God, in all the affairs of men and of nations, has, by a resolution, requested the President to designate and set apart a day for National prayer and humiliation: And whereas, it is the duty of nations, as well as of men, to own their dependence upon the overruling power of God, to confess their sins and transgressions, in humble sorrow, yet with assured hope that genuine repentance will lead to mercy and pardon; and to recognize the sublime truth, announced in the Holy Scriptures and proven by all history, that those nations only are blessed whose God is the Lord."[7]

APRIL 11

Exodus 1:15-21 HCSB

Then the king of Egypt said to the Hebrew midwives, one of whom was named Shiphrah and the other Puah, "When you help the Hebrew women give birth, observe them as they deliver. If the child is a son, kill him, but if it's a daughter, she may live." The Hebrew midwives, however, feared God and did not do as the king of Egypt had told them; they let the boys live. So the king of Egypt summoned the midwives and asked them, "Why have you done this and let the boys live?" The midwives said to Pharaoh, "The Hebrew women are not like the Egyptian women, for they are vigorous and give birth before a midwife can get to them." So God was good to the midwives, and the people multiplied and became very numerous. Since the midwives feared God, He gave them families.

Why did God bless the Hebrew midwives after they disobeyed a direct order from the king and lied? God blessed them because his laws are above the laws of man, and God rewards those who honor him. The midwives feared God and understood that the king's order was an immoral one, for to obey the king would be to disobey their Creator. We are all encouraged to obey our governing authorities—until they willfully violate God's higher law. Then it is our duty to obey God. As Peter and the other apostles said, "We must obey God rather than men" (Acts 5:29 HCSB). Abortion is wrong, and it should not be tolerated simply because it is sanctioned by the government.

PRAYER FOCUS: God, please wake my government up and help them see that their primary role is to protect our citizens, not harm them. Jesus, put men and women in office of the highest moral character who will defend our most cherished principals of the right to life, liberty, and the pursuit of happiness.

DID YOU KNOW? A young German student named Sophie Scholl stood up against the Nazis during WWII and paid for it with her life. Watch her story in the 2005 German movie, *Sophie Scholl, the Final Days*.

REFLECTIONS

APRIL 12

1 John 4:7 NKJV

Beloved, let us love one another, for love is of God; and everyone who loves is born of God and knows God.

God is love, and Jesus demonstrated it powerfully when he walked among us in Palestine. Love is the supreme goal of a redeemed life. We must receive love from God, share love with others, and lavish love on our children. The Bible says, "Above all things have fervent love for one another, for 'love will cover a multitude of sins'" (1 Pet. 4:8 NKJV). And, "We know that we have passed from death to life, because we love our brothers. Anyone who does not love remains in death" (1 John 3:14 NIV). Only God's love is sufficient to save our souls, satisfy our longing, and heal our brokenness. God's love will train us in righteousness and spill over on our neighbors!

PRAYER FOCUS: God, thank you for loving me regardless of the mess I've made or the state I'm in. Lord, help me perceive the never-ending supply of love you shower upon me. Show me how to give what I have been given and provide me with abundant opportunities to love as I have been loved.

DID YOU KNOW? *Webster's Compact Dictionary* defines *love* as "a passionate affection for another person."[8] No wonder we call the sacrifice of Christ the "Passion." He is so passionate about us he was willing to be humiliated and murdered for our affection. Pause a moment and realize that you and I are God's passion!

REFLECTIONS

APRIL 13

Isaiah 5:20-23 ESV

Woe to those who call evil good and good evil, who put darkness for light and light for darkness, who put bitter for sweet and sweet for bitter! Woe to those who are wise in their own eyes, and shrewd in their own sight! Woe to those who are heroes at drinking wine, and valiant men in mixing strong drink, who acquit the guilty for a bribe, and deprive the innocent of his right!

These verses offer a sober warning to anyone steeped in pride, aloof, or pursuing pleasure during seasons of injustice. How often throughout history has the oppressor justified their oppression by arguing its "goodness"? Slavery was said to be good for the poor ignorant slave and offered him a better life than the one he was abducted from. The extermination of the Jews was said to be good for the German people and their economy. Abortion is said to be good for women, so much so that their right to have one must be protected for the sake of their health. How far have we fallen when we call abortion good and those who oppose it evil? We are truly lost and in darkness when we give our mothers the right to kill and withhold our children's right to live!

PRAYER FOCUS: Jesus, forgive me for my tolerance of abortion. Forgive my failure to recognize what abortion is and who it harms. Lord, the Enemy of our soul means abortion for evil, but you can work it together for good if we repent and take action. Lord, give me the courage to live what I believe and speak what I know is true.

DID YOU KNOW? At the beginning of the second trimester, a baby's toenails begin to develop, their ears stand out from their head, and they will grow more in the next four weeks than at any other time during the pregnancy.[9]

REFLECTIONS

APRIL 14

John 14:5-6 HCSB

"Lord," Thomas said, "we don't know where You're going. How can we know the way?" Jesus told them, "I am the way, the truth, and the life. No one comes to the Father except through Me."

In this passage Jesus is talking to his disciples about his return to the Father in heaven. Thomas, along with the other disciples, is bewildered and confused, so he asks Jesus for greater clarification. Just like Thomas, many of us are confused about the truth or the right path to follow. Jesus' response is for all of us who are lost or confused. He said, "I am the way, the truth, and the life." Jesus is sufficient to supply all our needs and answer all our questions. He is the way to heaven, the revealer of all truth, and the Creator of all life. When we place our trust in Jesus and meditate on his Word, we will not be disappointed! The rock-bottom teaching of Christianity is that there is only one way to the Father, and that is through belief in the Son.

PRAYER FOCUS: Jesus, I believe in you. Help me to know you in spirit and in truth. Reveal yourself to me in the Bible and through the Holy Spirit. Thank you for loving me even when I lack discernment and illumination.

DID YOU KNOW? The ancient Jewish historian Josephus (circa 37-100 AD) confirmed in his writings that Jesus was a real person of history. There is much additional non-Christian support for the historicity and authenticity of the New Testament narrative, as can be seen in Josh McDowell's *The New Evidence that Demands a Verdict*.

REFLECTIONS

APRIL 15

Romans 13:1, 6-7 NIV

Everyone must submit himself to the governing authorities, for there is no authority except that which God has established. The authorities that exist have been established by God. . . . This is also why you pay taxes, for the authorities are God's servants, who give their full time to governing. Give everyone what you owe him: If you owe taxes, pay taxes; if revenue, then revenue; if respect, then respect; if honor, then honor.

It's important to remember why we pay taxes. We pay taxes because the government is an institution established by God for the dissemination of justice and the good of the people. In addition to our taxes, we must assist our government representatives by praying for them and helping them understand how to govern correctly. It would be a different world if all government authorities understood that they are God's servants and acted accordingly. God has given all of us, including those who govern, free will. One does not have to look far to see that many servants of God have failed to govern correctly. Servants like Pharaoh, Nero, and Hitler governed horribly, while servants like David, Washington, and Lincoln governed well. In chapters twenty-one through twenty-four of Second Kings we learn about God's two servant rulers, Manasseh and Josiah. God praised and approved of Josiah, but Manasseh decided not to serve the Lord and instead to pursue wickedness. God is sovereign, but man decides whom he shall serve. "But if serving the Lord seems undesirable to you, then choose for yourselves this day whom you will serve, whether the gods your forefathers served beyond the River, or the gods of the Amorites, in whose land you are living. But as for me and my household, we will serve the Lord" (Josh. 24:15 NIV).

PRAYER FOCUS: Lord, help all our leaders choose to serve you and do what's best for the people. Give them courage, strength, protection, and provision. Help them to know your truth and do what is right, regardless of the consequences.

DID YOU KNOW? Many of the ideas that form our Bill of Rights came from the Puritans of the Massachusetts Bay Colony. Their "Body of Liberties" passed in 1641 stated that "it was a violation of common law to impose taxation without representation" and "that no one shall be deprived of life, liberty, or property without due process of law."[10] Read more about our national Christian heritage in the book *Faith and Freedom* by Benjamin Hart.

REFLECTIONS

APRIL 16

2 Samuel 23:2-4 ESV

The Spirit of the LORD speaks by me; his word is on my tongue. The God of Israel has spoken; the Rock of Israel has said to me: When one rules justly over men, ruling in the fear of God, he dawns on them like the morning light, like the sun shining forth on a cloudless morning, like rain that makes the grass to sprout from the earth.

~

David, the great king of Israel, is speaking about the proper way to rule. A great ruler or government official is a just person who rules in the fear of God. In other words, they revere God and God's perspective as shown in his revealed Word. Great rulers make sure they align with what God says, that they are in agreement with it, and that they see to it that the people receive justice. God-fearing leaders bring light, truth, and justice to the people. Far from taking away their people's freedom and killing the smallest and most defenseless, godly governments protect the life and freedom of all citizens. We need more servants in government who will shine the light of truth into the darkness of abortion.

PRAYER FOCUS: God, please give us godly leaders who will fight for all our citizens, born or preborn. Help them understand your truth, pursue righteousness, and seek justice at all times. God, if you want me to serve in government, speak to my heart and present me with opportunities to lead.

DID YOU KNOW? George Washington, our first president and beloved patriot, made the following remark to the United States legislature: "I now make it my earnest prayer that God would . . . most graciously be pleased to dispose us all to do justice, to love mercy, and to demean ourselves with that charity, humility, and pacific temper of the mind which were the characteristics of the Divine Author of our blessed religion."[11] Indeed, our government would shine forth like the sun if our leaders sought to walk out Micah 6:8 in their governance: "He has told you, O man, what is good; and what does the Lord require of you but to do justice, and to love kindness, and to walk humbly with your God?" (ESV).

REFLECTIONS

APRIL 17

Psalm 119:57-60 HCSB

The LORD is my portion; I have promised to keep Your words. I have sought Your favor with all my heart; be gracious to me according to Your promise. I thought about my ways and turned my steps back to Your decrees. I hurried, not hesitating to keep Your commands.

God wants to improve personal morality as he changes social or legislative morality. Often he is not seeking to change people through politics or the law, but rather to change politics and the law through people (2 Kings 22:3-13, 18-20; 23:1-25; Luke 19:1-9). People are the key and ultimately what matters! For the good of the people, abortion must end. We will succeed in any endeavor or leadership position if we align ourselves with God. If we have gone astray, we can think about our ways and turn our steps back to God's ways. The man or woman who does this will prosper. As we read in the book of Joshua, "This book of instruction must not depart from your mouth; you are to recite it day and night so that you may carefully observe everything written in it. For then you will prosper and succeed in whatever you do" (1:8 HCSB).

PRAYER FOCUS: Lord, I'm glad you are my portion. Help me to keep your words and your commands. Jesus, I'm seeking your favor. Please be gracious to me and fulfill your promises to me.

DID YOU KNOW? Toward the close of his book *Real Christianity*, William Wilberforce wrote these insightful words about his hope for his nation and the power of God working through faithful servants to heal their land: "I find it necessary to affirm that the problems we face nationally and internationally are a direct result of the decline of faith and morality in our nation. My only hope of a prosperous future for this country rests not on the size and firepower of our military, nor on the wisdom of its leaders, nor on the spirit of her people, but only on the love and obedience of the people who name themselves after Christ, that their prayers might be heard and for the sake of these, God might look upon us with favor."[12]

REFLECTIONS

_____

_____

_____

_____

APRIL
18

Acts 17:24-28 NASB

The God who made the world and all things in it, since He is Lord of heaven and earth, does not dwell in temples made with hands; nor is He served by human hands, as though He needed anything, since He Himself gives to all people life and breath and all things; and He made from one man every nation of mankind to live on all the face of the earth, having determined their appointed times and the boundaries of their habitation, that they would seek God, if perhaps they might grope for Him and find Him, though He is not far from each one of us; for in Him we live and move and exist, as even some of your own poets have said, "For we also are His children."

When the apostle Paul preached in Athens on Mars Hill, he affirmed the truth that God is the Creator of all life. God personally determines our time to live and our place of birth. Paul goes on to say why God made us: ". . . that they would seek God, if perhaps they might grope for Him and find Him, though He is not far from each one of us" (Acts 17:27 NASB). We are made to seek and find our Creator so we can go from being his created offspring to his spiritual offspring through faith in Jesus Christ. We are all God's children, but only those who trust in Christ will become sons and daughters of God. Let us praise God today, for we live and move and exist only because of his great goodness. God is not far from us, and we can all reach out to him and discover his loving plans for our lives.

PRAYER FOCUS: God, I'm so glad you chose to give me life. Help me perceive your presence and find you in everything that has been made. Lord, thank you for providing everything I need, and teach me to seek you first in all things.

DID YOU KNOW? A preborn baby's fingerprints begin to form in the tenth week of gestation and are complete by the seventeenth week. No two sets of fingerprints are alike.[13] Fingerprints are one of many ways God reveals our uniqueness.

REFLECTIONS

APRIL 19

Deuteronomy 30:15-16 NKJV

See, I have set before you today life and good, death and evil, in that I command you today to love the LORD your God, to walk in His ways, and to keep His commandments, His statutes, and His judgments, that you may live and multiply; and the LORD your God will bless you in the land which you go to possess.

Moses is speaking to the people of Israel before Joshua takes them into the Promised Land. Moses' words still ring true today as God continually sets before each one of us the choice of good and evil, life and death. How we choose determines our own fate and the fate of others. If we follow God's ways and teachings, we will experience abundance and life. If we follow our own ways or teachings that are contrary to God's, we will experience waywardness, evil, and death. We must choose this day whom we will trust with our lives. If we choose God, we will live a life full of God's love and grace.

PRAYER FOCUS: God, I'm glad I'm not a robot and that I'm free to choose. Please teach me right from wrong and help me choose to do what is right. Lord, help me be an instrument for good and not evil so that I will bless my family, friends, and nation.

DID YOU KNOW? On this date in 1995, Timothy McVeigh decided to choose evil and death when he bombed the Alfred P. Murrah Federal Building in Oklahoma City, Oklahoma. The attack killed 168 people, including nineteen children. McVeigh was executed on June 11, 2001.[14] If McVeigh had chosen life on April 19, 1995, the world would be a far better place for the 168 victims, their families, McVeigh, and our nation.

REFLECTIONS

APRIL 20

Deuteronomy 33:26-27 NIV

There is none like the God of Jeshurun, who rides on the heavens to help you and on the clouds in his majesty. The eternal God is your refuge, and underneath are the everlasting arms. He will drive out your enemy before you, saying, "Destroy him!"

Deuteronomy 33:26-27 was part of Moses' blessing upon the tribe of Asher. How comforting it is to know that the eternal God is our refuge who rides on the heavens to help us. He is good to all. Whether we live or die, we can trust in his mercy and justice. We can place our painful pasts, perplexing presents, or uncertain futures in God's everlasting arms and feel the security of the Father's embrace. God knows our circumstances, heartaches, and fears. We can trust him, knowing he will ultimately destroy our enemies and give us rest.

PRAYER FOCUS: God, I'm so hurt by _____. Please provide me with your refuge and give me peace. Lord, I know the secret things belong to you (Deut. 29:29) and that all my questions will one day be satisfied. But for now help me see beyond my pain and circumstance. Teach me to walk by faith, because today it's not easy!

DID YOU KNOW? The word *Jeshurun* means "upright one," and was sometimes used in the Bible to refer to Israel.[15]

REFLECTIONS

APRIL 21

Romans 1:16-17 HCSB

For I am not ashamed of the gospel, because it is God's power for salvation to everyone who believes, first to the Jew, and also to the Greek. For in it God's righteousness is revealed from faith to faith, just as it is written: The righteous will live by faith.

We should never be ashamed of the God who gave us life and the way of redemption. Rather, we must share the gospel with others because it holds the power of God to transform their lives and lead them to salvation. God's offer of salvation extends to all the people he has made or will make in the future. God does rescue and save the aborted child, but just like you and me, he would rather see them live and make the choice to live by faith. God created us to live! The righteous cannot live by faith if they are deprived of the fundamental right to life.

PRAYER FOCUS: Jesus, help me see past the world and all the confusion to the reality that you came to bring life! You are the living God who gives each of us life. You give life to both flesh and spirit. Please ignite my spirit and show me how to love life regardless of stage, function, or form. Give me a deep respect and reverence for you and everything made in your image.

DID YOU KNOW? Paul, the writer of Romans, was beheaded in Rome around AD 67.[16] Not even prison or a violent death could make Paul ashamed of the gospel!

REFLECTIONS

APRIL 22

Romans 15:1-4 NASB

Now we who are strong ought to bear the weaknesses of those without strength and not just please ourselves. Each of us is to please his neighbor for his good, to his edification. For even Christ did not please Himself; but as it is written, "The reproaches of those who reproached You fell on Me." For whatever was written in earlier times was written for our instruction, so that through perseverance and the encouragement of the Scriptures we might have hope.

It is important to understand that our second greatest mandate as believers is to love and care for our neighbors. From the least to the greatest, all people are important to God and qualify as our neighbor. Certainly, the preborn are the least of these among us and are without strength to defend themselves against the evil of abortion. Our mandate as people who have the strength mentally, physically, financially and politically is to cry out for their lives and help them. In other words, to give of ourselves just as Jesus gave of himself for us. The apostle Paul knew that whatever the Holy Spirit communicated through the Hebrew Scriptures was applicable and vital for his time period. And we know the Old Testament and the New Testament are both applicable and vital to our time now. The Word of God is not silent about abortion and, therefore, we cannot remain silent. We must take action and bring abortion to an end.

PRAYER FOCUS: God, give me the courage, opportunity, and ability to defend the weak. Lord, I can't address everything that is wrong around me, but I can do something. Show me what I can do. I'm overwhelmed by your love and patience in the midst of this tragedy. You are truly good.

DID YOU KNOW? There are thousands of pro-life organizations and pregnancy resource centers in our nation. Contact one and get involved with helping the weak. A good place to start is *www.care-net.org*.

REFLECTIONS

APRIL 23

Philemon 4-7 NIV

I always thank my God as I remember you in my prayers, because I hear about your faith in the Lord Jesus and your love for all the saints. I pray that you may be active in sharing your faith, so that you will have a full understanding of every good thing we have in Christ. Your love has given me great joy and encouragement, because you, brother, have refreshed the hearts of the saints.

In our efforts to help the preborn and our neighbors, we can often feel alone and isolated. It is important to remember that we are never alone, for God and our fellow saints are always with us in spirit and in prayer. Prayer is a great uniting force. As long as we are praying for one another, we are spiritually united, waiting for God to respond to our corporate prayers. Just knowing there are believers all over the world working to abolish the killing of preborn children is a great encouragement. We need to pray for all our brothers and sisters not only here but all around the world. We need to pray they will have favor, grace, humility, perseverance, and provision for ministry. Other believers who work the fields today, as well as those who have gone before us, can give us the encouragement we need for the weighty work we do. Above all, we can take great comfort in the knowledge that as we serve the Lord, our work will encourage others.

PRAYER FOCUS: God, bless your ministers and priests, and all who serve you around the globe. Protect them and their families from the Enemy. Give them strength, courage, and stability. Provide for their ministries and fill them with your love as they love your people.

DID YOU KNOW? By sixteen weeks a baby roughly five and one-half inches long can grasp, bend, flex, and twist their fingers, wrists, legs, and toes. They are also beginning to develop spatial awareness.[17]

REFLECTIONS

APRIL 24

Malachi 4:5-6 ESV

Behold, I will send you Elijah the prophet before the great and awesome day of the Lord comes. And he will turn the hearts of fathers to their children and the hearts of children to their fathers, lest I come and strike the land with a decree of utter destruction.

In this culture of high divorce rates, overcrowded prisons, and countless children being raised in fatherless homes, we need to pray that God will send forth men in the spirit and power of Elijah, men who can turn the tide in our culture. Elijah was one of Israel's great prophets, and John the Baptist, who came in the spirit and power of Elijah, was hailed by Jesus as the greatest man born of women. Both of these servants of God pointed to the Father and loved his children. Elijah and John were courageous men who told the truth and honored God. We need men who will stand in the gap for their children, their families, and the land. We need fathers who will love their children and children who will honor their fathers.

PRAYER FOCUS: God, send us men who will love their children and mentor them. Help our young people respect their elders, honor authority, and obey their parents. Lord, give those fathers who have made mistakes with their families the courage to ask for forgiveness and make a fresh start. Honor their efforts and bless them as they attempt to reconcile with those they love. Give men a heart for their children and their children a heart for them.

DID YOU KNOW? Men currently have no legal rights regarding the life of their preborn child. If the mother decides to abort against the father's wishes, the father has no legal recourse.

REFLECTIONS

APRIL 25

Luke 18:15-17 NASB

And they were bringing even their babies to Him so that He would touch them, but when the disciples saw it, they began rebuking them. But Jesus called for them, saying, "Permit the children to come to Me, and do not hinder them, for the kingdom of God belongs to such as these. Truly I say to you, whoever does not receive the kingdom of God like a child will not enter it at all."

Children have often been overlooked or undervalued in society. Jesus' disciples felt that he should not be troubled by the wishes of parents concerning their immature little ones, but Jesus valued the babies regardless of development or position. Not only did the Lord permit the children to come, he used the opportunity to teach his followers about faith and what they could learn from children. One of the best qualities children possess is that they are trusting, especially of their parents and those in authority. Jesus was teaching his disciples that only those who approach their faith like a little child and trust God completely will follow him into the Kingdom he has prepared for them. Jesus does not want us to hinder the little children from being born but rather to let them come and see for themselves who this Jesus is.

PRAYER FOCUS: Jesus, forgive us for thinking there are children who are unwanted or who are a nuisance. Direct our steps to remove abortion from our lives, our churches, and our society. Lord, lead me to trust you like a child with unclouded belief and total abandon.

DID YOU KNOW? Colorado was the first state in our nation to legalize abortion on this day in 1967.[18]

REFLECTIONS

APRIL 26

Lamentations 3:48-50 HCSB

My eyes flow with streams of tears because of the destruction of my dear people. My eyes overflow unceasingly, without end, until the LORD looks down from heaven and sees.

The prophet Jeremiah was brokenhearted over the destruction and oppression of the women and children of Jerusalem under the brutal attack of the Babylonians. He intercedes for them in tears until the Lord looks down from heaven and provides relief to the people. Just like Jeremiah, we need to intercede for our nation and our people. Our women and men are being lied to and destroyed by deceptive pro-choice policies and rhetoric, while our children are being daily led to the slaughter of abortion. It's time to cry out to the Lord with tears of repentance and intercession for the liberation of our people and the end of the madness of abortion.

PRAYER FOCUS: Lord, please do not forget the work of your own hands. Deliver us from our sins and restore to us a renewed sense of truth and worth. Forgive us for the blood we have shed and save us from the misery of death. You have set before us life and death. Help us choose life!

DID YOU KNOW? The shortest verse in the Bible is John 11:35, "*Jesus wept.*" Our Lord knew how to grieve and make intercession with tears. To see just how effective the ministry of tears can be, apply the wisdom of Psalm 126:5-6: "Those who sow in tears will reap with shouts of joy. Though one goes along weeping, carrying the bag of seed, he will surely come back with shouts of joy, carrying his sheaves" (HCSB).

REFLECTIONS

APRIL 27

Psalm 128 NKJV

Blessed is every one who fears the LORD, who walks in His ways. When you eat the labor of your hands, you shall be happy, and it shall be well with you. Your wife shall be like a fruitful vine in the very heart of your house, your children like olive plants all around your table. Behold, thus shall the man be blessed who fears the LORD. The LORD bless you out of Zion, and may you see the good of Jerusalem all the days of your life. Yes, may you see your children's children. Peace be upon Israel!

When we revere the Lord and practice the things he has taught us through his Word, we will be blessed. Following God's plan keeps us from making bad choices that could result in our harm or death. It also allows us to benefit from our Father's wisdom and make wise choices concerning our families, our finances, friendships, marriages, jobs, and many other things. The specific blessings listed for honoring God are happiness, contentment, a faithful wife, abundant children who are healthy and strong, a long life, a prosperous nation, and a blessed posterity. God highly values families and children. When our culture looks down on large families or undervalues children in the womb, it is easy to see that social values are out of step with God's values. It is obvious that God values every life, every child, and so must we.

PRAYER FOCUS: Creator of life, give me a grateful heart for children, especially the ones you have already blessed me with.

DID YOU KNOW? Children are more than a blessing. They are quite literally the future! Peggy Noonan communicated this great truth beautifully in the epilogue of her book about Ronald Reagan entitled *When Character was King*. She wrote: "The little bodies of children are the repositories of the greatness of a future age. And they must be encouraged, must eat from the tales of those who've gone before, and brandished their swords, and slayed dragons."[19] One of the dragons yet to be slain is abortion.

REFLECTIONS

121

APRIL 28

Luke 11:46 NIV

Jesus replied, "And you experts in the law, woe to you, because you load people down with burdens they can hardly carry, and you yourselves will not lift one finger to help them."

It is an awesome responsibility to lead and teach God's people. We should all continually pray for protection, provision, wisdom, favor, grace, and knowledge for our pastors and teachers. No pastor or leader is perfect. We all commit sin and make errors from time to time. Jesus isn't speaking in Luke 11:46 about what we teach as much as how we teach. Those who teach must lead by action and involvement, not by words alone. It's bad enough to overburden people, but it is a grievous sin when a leader will not share the burden with the people. If we ask people to fast, we need to fast. If we ask people to give financially, we need to give financially. If we ask people to engage in nonviolent civil disobedience, we need to lead the civil disobedience. Those of us who lead must lead in humility, action, and truth.

PRAYER FOCUS: Jesus, watch over and bless those men and women in leadership and teaching roles. Help them to have discernment, wisdom, compassion, and love when dealing with people and ministry. Lord, help us all to be doers of the Word and not just hearers only.

DID YOU KNOW? Martin Luther King was arrested in April, 1963, for anti-segregation protests in Alabama. During his jail time King wrote his famous *Letter from a Birmingham Jail* in which he wrote, "Injustice anywhere is a threat to justice everywhere."[20] Jim Elliot, in response to a letter written by his parents expressing their hopes that he might remain in America and minister here, wrote, "Surely those who know the great passionate heart of Jehovah must deny their own loves to share in the expression of His. Consider the call from the Throne above, 'Go ye,' and from round about, 'Come over and help us,' and even the call from the damned souls below, 'Send Lazarus to my brothers, that they come not to this place.' Impelled, then, by these voices, I dare not stay home while Quichuas perish." Both men are examples of leaders who led with actions as well as words.[21]

REFLECTIONS

APRIL 29

Hebrews 6:10 NIV

God is not unjust; he will not forget your work and the love you have shown him as you have helped his people and continue to help them.

God rewards those who love their neighbor, help their brother, and care for the least of these among us. Take heart today and realize that God sees all your good deeds and loving acts. He takes them into consideration when preparing your heavenly reward, whether your work is as well-recognized and acknowledged as Billy Graham's or Mother Teresa's, or whether it is as unheralded as a small town youth pastor's. God knows your deeds and will render to each person according to what they did with their time and talents. The world and fellow believers may fail to recognize your efforts to love God's people, but God will not.

PRAYER FOCUS: God, help me understand that I live for an audience of One. Use me to help people and love them like Jesus whenever and wherever I have the opportunity. Give me a humble spirit and a clean mind so I can represent you favorably to others.

DID YOU KNOW? The word "reward" is used over eighty times in the English Bible, according to *The New Strong's Exhaustive Concordance of the Bible*. The first time the word appears is in Genesis 15:1, and the last time is in Revelation 22:12.[22] Take a look at the eleventh chapter of Hebrews to observe how many times the heroes of the faith were honoring God, helping others, or looking ahead to their reward.

REFLECTIONS

APRIL 30

Exodus 21:22-24 NKJV

If men fight, and hurt a woman with child, so that she gives birth prematurely, yet no harm follows, he shall surely be punished accordingly as the woman's husband imposes on him; and he shall pay as the judges determine. But if any harm follows, then you shall give life for life, eye for eye, tooth for tooth, hand for hand, foot for foot.

These verses from the book of Exodus are part of a list of laws given to the Israelites following Moses' encounter with God on Mount Sinai. This law is instructing the people of Israel about how to deal with accidental prenatal and maternal injury or death. These verses clearly establish the personhood of a developing baby. Notice the woman is with child, not with a blob of tissue. God clearly acknowledges in these verses that there are stages of development in a child's journey in the womb. He knows some premature births occur in the later stages of gestation and will result in survival, while others take place in the first trimester and likely will not survive. This is why God mandates a sliding scale of punishment options. Further still, in the case where both the mother and her child survive the incident, the guilty man is still fined by the husband as a way to reinforce the value of human life and teach him to be more careful when he gets physical. Finally, God allows all three members of the family an equal part in the process as he is concerned for the mother, her child, and the husband.

PRAYER FOCUS: Father, your Word is so clear that life begins at conception. Forgive us for our arrogance and our practice of abortion.

DID YOU KNOW? Adam Clarke's Bible commentary, published in the early 1800s, took him over forty years to complete.[23] In it Clarke interprets today's verses in Exodus to apply to both mother and child. Biblical scholars and theologians have a rich history of defending life in the womb. A great resource for discovering the pro-life history of the church is George Grant's book, *Third Time Around: A History of the Pro-Life Movement from the First Century to the Present*.

REFLECTIONS

May

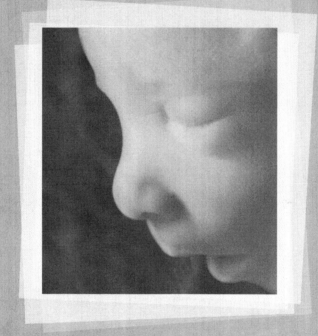

SIXTEEN WEEKS GESTATION

MAY 1

Psalm 78:5-7 HCSB

He established a testimony in Jacob and set up a law in Israel, which He commanded our fathers to teach to their children so that a future generation—children yet to be born—might know. They were to rise and tell their children so that they might put their confidence in God and not forget God's works, but keep His commands.

We are all called by God to teach our children his ways. God wants every generation to know of his love and passion for them. The Bible says, "Train a child in the way he should go, and when he is old he will not turn from it" (Prov. 22:6 NIV). God's plan of redemption is for all of us, including even children yet to be born. Tragically, we have collectively chosen to abandon millions of God's children each year by allowing them to be aborted while they develop in the womb. Our nation's future is literally and spiritually at stake if we continue tolerating this slaughter of the innocents.

PRAYER FOCUS: God, you are holy and awesome! Thank you for life and for my children. Lord, grant me wisdom and show me your truth so that I can share it with my children. God, in your great goodness, give my children ears to hear and eyes to see what I teach them.

DID YOU KNOW? At around seventeen to eighteen weeks, women begin feeling their baby move for the first time. While this is a new experience for mom, the baby has already been moving since week eight without the mother's knowledge.[1]

REFLECTIONS

MAY 2

Jeremiah 8:5-6 ESV

Why then has this people turned away in perpetual backsliding? They hold fast to deceit; they refuse to return. I have paid attention and listened, but they have not spoken rightly; no man relents of his evil, saying, "What have I done?" Everyone turns to his own course, like a horse plunging headlong into battle.

Why do we turn away from God and resist the truth? Why do we run to familiar sins in times of stress and fatigue? Why do we give ourselves over to things we know are not good for us? Perhaps it is because we fall for the lies of the Enemy and fail to trust that God is good. No matter what the offense or how long we have struggled with it, God is waiting patiently for us to repent. He is listening and ready to bring healing and restoration to our wounded lives and damaged souls. The first step toward restoration is to abandon deceit and discover the truth. The gospel of John says, "Sanctify them in the truth; your word is truth" (17:17 ESV). Since God's Word is truth we need to spend time in it to sharpen our internal lie detector. Second, we need to return to our loving Father and trust him to be good to us. Finally, we must be honest with God and confess our part in the problems we have created or the sins we have committed. Either we follow the wisdom of God, or like everyone who has rejected God before us, we will follow our own course and plunge headlong into trouble and misery.

PRAYER FOCUS: God, today I'm returning to you. Teach me your truth and show me that I can trust you to care for me. Forgive me, Lord, for what I have done and help me resist the temptation to do it again in the future.

DID YOU KNOW? Kyle Busch (NASCAR, 2004 Busch Series Rookie of the Year), Sarah Hughes (figure skater, 2002 Olympic gold medalist), and Kay Panabaker (television and film actress, graduated high school valedictorian at the age of thirteen) all were born on this day and could have been aborted under *Roe v Wade/Doe v. Bolton*.[2]

REFLECTIONS

MAY 3

Isaiah 55:6-7 NASB

Seek the L ORD while He may be found; call upon Him while He is near. Let the wicked forsake his way and the unrighteous man his thoughts; and let him return to the L ORD, and He will have compassion on him, and to our God, for He will abundantly pardon.

The Lord is near the brokenhearted, and he will not reject a contrite spirit. Jesus said, "Behold, I stand at the door and knock; if anyone hears My voice and opens the door, I will come in to him and will dine with him, and he with Me" (Rev. 3:20 NASB). We can return to the Lord for he is compassionate and forgiving. How long will we keep our sins a secret and rebel against God? How long will America continue killing children and pretend we care about justice and "the least of these"? We desperately need the Lord's pardon for all the injustice our society has perpetrated on the preborn. But will we ask for it? Jesus will not impact our lives or the life of our nation if we leave him outside the door knocking and refuse to open the door and let him in. We must repent and allow all God's children to live!

PRAYER FOCUS: Jesus, give me the courage to speak out against the injustice of abortion. Lord, I want to be a voice for the voiceless and a person who makes a difference for the least of these, my brothers and sisters, in the womb.

DID YOU KNOW? In 1852 Frederick Douglass gave a searing speech and powerful rebuke of our nation concerning slavery during a Fourth of July celebration in Rochester, New York. His words carried weight both then and now: "My subject, then, fellow citizens, is American slavery. I shall see this day and its popular characteristics from the slave's point of view. Standing there identified with the American bondman, making his wrongs mine, I do not hesitate to declare, with all my soul, that the character and conduct of this nation never looked blacker to me than on this Fourth of July. Whether we turn to the declarations of the past or to the professions of the present, the conduct of the nation seems equally hideous and revolting. America is false to the past, false to the present, and solemnly binds herself to be false to the future. Standing with God and the crushed and bleeding slave on this occasion, I will, in the name of humanity which is outraged, in the name of liberty which is fettered, in the name of the Constitution and the Bible which are disregarded and trampled upon, dare to call in question and to denounce, with all the emphasis I can command, everything that serves to perpetuate slavery—the great sin and shame of America!" Regarding the church he said, "The American church is guilty, when viewed in connection with what it is doing to uphold slavery; but it is superlatively guilty when viewed in connection with its ability to abolish slavery."[3] One wonders what the abolitionist would say about abortion.

MAY 4

1 Thessalonians 5:14-15 HCSB

And we exhort you, brothers: warn those who are irresponsible, comfort the discouraged, help the weak, be patient with everyone. See to it that no one repays evil for evil to anyone, but always pursue what is good for one another and for all.

Here Paul is advising the Thessalonians at the close of his letter about how to treat one another. How can we apply Paul's exhortation to the critical subject of abortion? First, we must be good to our brothers in Christ and to everyone else with whom we share the planet. This includes helping our weak, preborn neighbors. The law of love compels us to do what is good by fighting to abolish abortion. Second, we need to be kind to the deceived people who are pro-choice and the parents who consent to abortion. Third, we must be patient with other believers in the church when they are slow to action or ignorant. In our patience, however, we must warn those who are lazy or idle that the Lord has called them to love everyone, including the child in the womb. Finally, we can encourage those who have become disheartened in the mission for life with the comfort we ourselves have received from God.

PRAYER FOCUS: Lord Jesus, I want to be like you and do what is right and good. Help me be active in my church and my community by loving people and meeting their needs. Give me a heart for the preborn and those who are suffering. Let me be a part of the solution to the problem of legalized abortion.

DID YOU KNOW? William Lloyd Garrison (1805-1879), the American abolitionist and journalist, wrote a letter of exhortation and affection to his son on New Year's Eve, which said: "May you ever keep in the right path, shun the very appearance of evil, be superior to every evil temptation, and reverently seek to know and do the will of God. May your moral vision ever be clear to discern the right from the wrong, your conscience ever clean and vital, your heart ever tender and affectionate, your spirit ever pure and elevated. May you be prudent and economical without being parsimonious, and generous and philanthropic without being credulous and inconsiderate. May your interest in all the reforms of the day—especially in the cause of the imbruted slave—grow more and more vital, impelling you to the performance of high moral achievements in behalf of suffering humanity, and making your life a blessing to the world. May you be delivered from 'that fear of man which bringeth a snare,' in sustaining what is just, following what is good, and adhering to what is right. May you never go with the multitude to do evil, but be willing to stand alone, if need be, with God and the truth, even if it bring you to the cross or the stake."[4]

MAY 5

Daniel 9:4-6 ESV

I prayed to the Lord my God and made confession, saying, "O Lord, the great and awesome God, who keeps covenant and steadfast love with those who love him and keep his commandments, we have sinned and done wrong and acted wickedly and rebelled, turning aside from your commandments and rules. We have not listened to your servants the prophets, who spoke in your name to our kings, our princes, and our fathers, and to all the people of the land."

Prayer is vital in our fight to stop the insanity of abortion, but how should we pray? The prophet Daniel has provided us with a great example of how to pray for a wayward people in danger of imminent judgment. He begins his intercession by glorifying God and humbling himself, after which he makes confession to the Lord of the people's corporate sins. Scripture tells us that Daniel was a very righteous man who was pleasing to the Lord, and yet he willingly identifies himself with Israel in their sin. Daniel does not waste time with excuses or explanations; he unequivocally repents for his sins and the sins of his nation. Like the prophet, we need to glorify our loving God for his patience and mercy, and then completely and honestly repent for the sin of abortion.

PRAYER FOCUS: O Lord, there is none like you! You alone are righteous and holy. Your great goodness and grace are far beyond my capacity to fathom. We have sinned and acted wickedly by breaking your commands and putting your children to death even before they are born. We have turned away from your truth and have not listened to your Word, medical science, ultrasound technology, pro-life leaders, and your servants in the church who have told us the truth about killing little babies. Please forgive us, Almighty God!

DID YOU KNOW? God sent the angel Gabriel to personally answer Daniel's prayer. "While I was speaking and praying, confessing my sin and the sin of my people Israel, and presenting my plea before the Lord my God for the holy hill of my God, while I was speaking in prayer, the man Gabriel, whom I had seen in the vision at the first, came to me in swift flight at the time of the evening sacrifice. He made me understand, speaking with me and saying, 'O Daniel, I have now come out to give you insight and understanding. At the beginning of your pleas for mercy a word went out, and I have come to tell it to you, for you are greatly loved. Therefore consider the word and understand the vision'" (Dan. 9:20-23 ESV).

MAY 6

Daniel 9:8-11 ESV

To us, O LORD, belongs open shame, to our kings, to our princes, and to our fathers, because we have sinned against you. To the Lord our God belong mercy and forgiveness, for we have rebelled against him and have not obeyed the voice of the LORD our God by walking in his laws, which he set before us by his servants the prophets. All Israel has transgressed your law and turned aside, refusing to obey your voice. And the curse and oath that are written in the Law of Moses the servant of God have been poured out upon us, because we have sinned against him.

To America belongs open shame. Shame to our courts, to our congresspeople, to our presidents, and to all our citizens, because we have sinned against our Creator by allowing abortion to be legal in our land. We have not obeyed the voice of God concerning the sanctity of human life or walked in his ways of purity, responsibility, and self-control. We are deserving of God's wrath because we have sinned against him by destroying what is made in the divine image, our children in the womb. Thankfully, mercy and forgiveness belong to our God, who is slow to anger, rich in love, and abounding in mercy. Let us hope he hears our prayers and honors our repentance.

PRAYER FOCUS: God, we are all guilty of allowing abortion to continue in our land. Please forgive us our trespass and allow us time to make the future a better place for all your children.

DID YOU KNOW? In 2005 the United States aborted roughly 1.2 million children in legalized abortion facilities.[5] While this figure is staggering enough, it does not include unreported abortions, chemical abortions (RU-486, morning after pill), or birth control abortions (IUD, Norplant).

REFLECTIONS

MAY 7

Daniel 9:17-19 ESV

Now therefore, O our God, listen to the prayer of your servant and to his pleas for mercy, and for your own sake, O Lord, make your face to shine upon your sanctuary, which is desolate. O my God, incline your ear and hear. Open your eyes and see our desolations, and the city that is called by your name. For we do not present our pleas before you because of our righteousness, but because of your great mercy. O Lord, hear; O Lord, forgive. O Lord, pay attention and act. Delay not, for your own sake, O my God, because your city and your people are called by your name.

Daniel finishes this great prayer of repentance by pleading with God to listen and be merciful. Daniel does not make this request of God because he is righteous, or because he has earned God's favor. He makes it because he knows God will not let himself be defamed or share his glory with another. In Isaiah 48:11, we read, "For my own sake, for my own sake, I do it, for how should my name be profaned? My glory I will not give to another" (ESV). Daniel knows God is abundantly merciful, and only he can act to save his people from destruction. We cannot end abortion without God. Only He has the power and the mercy to intervene and stop this holocaust. We must plead with God to forgive us acting for his name's sake on behalf of all the people whom he loves.

PRAYER FOCUS: O our God, listen to our prayer to end abortion not because we are righteous, but because you are righteous and your people are the work of your hands. O Lord, hear the preborn's cry for mercy and send them deliverers, men and women of integrity who will fight for justice.

DID YOU KNOW? E. M. Bounds wrote in his book *Power through Prayer*, "No learning can make up for the failure to pray. No earnestness, no diligence, no study, no gifts will supply its lack."[6] We must pray before, during, and after our endeavors if they are to be successful.

REFLECTIONS

MAY 8

Psalm 22:30-31 HCSB

Descendants will serve Him; the next generation will be told about the Lord. They will come and tell a people yet to be born about His righteousness—what He has done.

Psalm 22, written by David, has many prophetic utterances about Christ's final moments on the cross. Jesus even quoted the first verse of this psalm during his crucifixion. Psalm 22 accurately describes the mocking crowds, his pierced hands and feet, disjointed bones, and the casting of lots for his clothing. Still, the most amazing prophecy that was fulfilled might be this last one at the end of the psalm. "Descendants will serve Him." How could a man who had no wife or children have descendants to serve him? How could he be sure that his story of life and death would be told to endless generations when he was relatively unknown and died a criminal's death? Because Jesus was no ordinary criminal! He is the righteous Son of God who took away the sins of the world. Those of us who know Christ, seeing him even through darkened glass, can tell of his righteousness. Millions testify about how he has rescued them from darkness and brought them into his marvelous light. The apostles, martyrs, priests, pastors, teachers, and ordinary believers over the past two thousand years have done exactly what verses thirty and thirty-one predict. Why have they done it? "They will come and tell a people yet to be born about His righteousness." This includes people like you and me and our children—born and preborn.

PRAYER FOCUS: Jesus, I thank you that your plan of redemption extends to all people and every generation. Lord, I want to tell of your glory and the wonders of your love, so please put a song in my heart and courage on my lips.

DID YOU KNOW? Psalm 22 was written approximately nine hundred years before Jesus was conceived.[7]

REFLECTIONS

MAY 9

Matthew 5:17-18 NASB

Do not think that I came to abolish the Law or the Prophets; I did not come to abolish but to fulfill. For truly I say to you, until heaven and earth pass away, not the smallest letter or stroke shall pass from the Law until all is accomplished.

God's Word is true and will stand the test of time until all that he intended is accomplished. Jesus is the Promised One who fulfilled the Hebrew prophecies and brokered a New Covenant with his blood. All who are heavy laden can come to Jesus, and he will offer rest as he daily bears our burdens. Let the Lord of Glory wash us clean and change our clothes (Zechariah 3). We can wholeheartedly trust the Bible and know that all the revealed wisdom of God is found within its pages.

PRAYER FOCUS: Jesus, I believe that the whole Bible is true and profitable for teaching, correcting, and training me in righteousness. Thank you for the rich treasure of your revealed Word. Give me a passion to read it, know it, and memorize it.

DID YOU KNOW? The Hebrew Old Testament has twenty-four books. The twenty-four books are further divided into three sections. The sections are the Law (*Torah*, first five books), the Prophets (*Nebhim*, twenty-one books), and the Writings (*Kethubhim*, thirteen books). The Hebrew manuscripts do not divide Kings, Chronicles, Samuel, Ezra-Nehemiah, and the twelve Later Prophets, totaling five books instead of the twenty books in our modern rendering.[8] All modern English Bibles divide the Old Testament into thirty-nine separate books. For more information, see Chapter 2, in *The New Evidence that Demands a Verdict*, by Josh McDowell.

REFLECTIONS

MAY 10

Luke 21:23-24 NKJV

But woe to those who are pregnant and to those who are nursing babies in those days! For there will be great distress in the land and wrath upon this people. And they will fall by the edge of the sword, and be led away captive into all nations. And Jerusalem will be trampled by Gentiles until the times of the Gentiles are fulfilled.

Jesus is answering questions and teaching in the temple complex when he begins to tell people about the last days before his return. As he talks about persecution, wars, earthquakes, famine, and hatred, Jesus pauses to ponder the fate of young mothers with infants and pregnant mothers during this awful time. How remarkable that even in the throes of wrath and judgment, the Savior's heart goes out to the little ones and the least of these. His heart breaks for the innocent children who will be caught in the middle of this misery. He knows it will be equally hard for both types of women because their children, divided by development and time, are living persons. The maternal agony and worry will be the same if the child is eighteen months old or fourteen weeks gestation. Our Lord is well aware that life begins at conception, and from that point forward it is sacred.

PRAYER FOCUS: Lord, help me diligently love your people until you return. Jesus, please be merciful to our mothers and children when you return, and strengthen the mother/child bond so that the idea of abortion becomes unthinkable to young women. Help women to be nurturing and men to be loving and protective.

DID YOU KNOW? Doctors have discovered that viewing an ultrasound during pregnancy increases the bond between parent and child.[9] Peter Tallack wrote this about ultrasound scans: "Using ultrasound to peer into the womb has revolutionized our understanding of fetal development and care for the mother."[10]

REFLECTIONS

135

MAY 11

Isaiah 54:10 HCSB

"Though the mountains move and the hills shake, My love will not be removed from you and My covenant of peace will not be shaken," says your compassionate LORD.

God reassures Israel his love for them will never be removed, even after rebuke and punishment. Our God does not stay angry with us for long. He loves to forgive a repentant people. When trials and judgments come or our lives are shaken by a death or illness, God is by our side. He will not relent in his efforts to bring us peace now and in the age to come. He will never remove his love from us even in times of rebellion and sin, for he is always knocking at the door, wooing our hearts to rest in his salvation. We can trust the Lord with our doubts and difficulties because our God is a God of great and unending compassion. We can put our lives in Jesus' nail-scarred hands and feel the strength of the Father as he cares for us!

PRAYER FOCUS: God, sometimes I can't believe you still love me when I think of how much I've blown it. How can you rescue me time after time? Lord, give me a revelation of how deep and wide your love for me is, and teach me to rest in your love and perfect peace.

DID YOU KNOW? The Romans and the Jews did not take the life of Jesus on Calvary. He laid His life down of his own accord. He said, "I am the good shepherd. I know My own sheep, and they know Me, as the Father knows Me, and I know the Father. I lay down My life for the sheep. But I have other sheep that are not of this fold; I must bring them also, and they will listen to My voice. Then there will be one flock, one shepherd. This is why the Father loves Me, because I am laying down My life so I may take it up again. No one takes it from Me, but I lay it down on My own. I have the right to lay it down, and I have the right to take it up again. I have received this command from My Father" (John 10:14-18 HCSB). Christ laid his life down for you and me, while we were still sinners, because he loves us. After all, the Son of Man has come to save the lost (Matt. 18:11-13).

REFLECTIONS

_____

_____

_____

MAY 12

Luke 19:4-10 NIV

So he ran ahead and climbed a sycamore-fig tree to see him, since Jesus was coming that way. When Jesus reached the spot, he looked up and said to him, "Zacchaeus, come down immediately. I must stay at your house today." So he came down at once and welcomed him gladly. All the people saw this and began to mutter, "He has gone to be the guest of a 'sinner.'" But Zacchaeus stood up and said to the Lord, "Look, Lord! Here and now I give half of my possessions to the poor, and if I have cheated anybody out of anything, I will pay back four times the amount." Jesus said to him, "Today salvation has come to this house, because this man, too, is a son of Abraham. For the Son of Man came to seek and to save what was lost."

Zacchaeus wanted to know Jesus so much that he climbed a tree in a hostile environment just to see him. Are we running to meet the Savior? Do we want to know him better? Will we pursue the Lord like Zacchaeus, with effort and vigor? To do so we need to stop worrying about what others around us are saying or thinking about us. We just have to go for it; this is about us and the Savior, the Creator God. Zacchaeus demonstrated his heart for God through public repentance, followed by the accompanying actions to prove the genuineness of his heart change. Jesus accepted Zacchaeus's repentance because his belief was followed by action. Abraham's bloodline is not enough, for we must also be born of God's Spirit. When we are born of the Spirit, we will become like our Father—truly committed sons and daughters of God, loving what he loves, hating what he hates, caring for our neighbors, and helping the least of these.

PRAYER FOCUS: God, mold me and make me into a believer who echoes your heart. Teach me to be the same in word and action, and give me the courage to do what is right even when other people reject me or think I'm unworthy. Jesus, I'm so glad you sought me and saved me from my sins.

DID YOU KNOW? John Newton, an Anglican pastor, songwriter, and former slave ship captain, once wrote, "This is faith; a renouncing of everything we are apt to call our own, and relying wholly upon the blood, righteousness, and intercession of Jesus."[11] Zacchaeus changed in a moment from a taker to a giver because he met the Savior and was overwhelmed and freed by what he had been given.

REFLECTIONS

MAY 13

Matthew 23:23-24 NASB

Woe to you, scribes and Pharisees, hypocrites! For you tithe mint and dill and cummin, and have neglected the weightier provisions of the law: justice and mercy and faithfulness; but these are the things you should have done without neglecting the others. You blind guides, who strain out a gnat and swallow a camel!

In the Matthew 23:23-24 text Jesus is rebuking the Pharisees for majoring in the minors. They had it backwards. They thought the observance of external customs and practices was more important than loving God and their neighbors. Yes, we should tithe and bring our Bibles to church, but how we pursue justice, show mercy, and remain faithful is far more important to God. God wants us to strive to be like him, forever faithful, lovers of justice, and overwhelmingly merciful. It is our responsibility to intervene when people are hurting. God calls us to help the innocent, weak, and fatherless. We must pursue justice and equal protection for the preborn. At the same time, we need to forgive and extend mercy to post-abortive parents, helping them in any way possible. If we remain faithful to our Lord and his principles, we can save our children, love God's people, and heal our nation.

PRAYER FOCUS: God, help me become concerned about justice and the rights of every citizen. Give me the discernment to separate truth from falsehood. Give me the capacity to forgive and be merciful. God, be faithful to me in good times and bad so I can learn what it means to be faithful.

DID YOU KNOW? William Wilberforce, the British abolitionist of the eighteenth century who spent most of his life doing the Father's business, wrote a great book about living the Christian life entitled *Real Christianity*. In it he summarized the principle of striving to be like God when he wrote, "Attempt to be an imitator of Christ in your behavior. His goal was always to do the will of the Father. Yours should be the same. Do justice. Show mercy. Be about the Father's business."[12]

REFLECTIONS

MAY 14

Psalm 7:1-2 NKJV

O LORD my God, in You I put my trust; save me from all those who persecute me; and deliver me, lest they tear me like a lion, rending me in pieces, while there is none to deliver.

Very often in the Psalms David cries out to God to save him from his persecution. He laments his desperate condition of being hunted by men who are trying to kill him. I believe David's cry is echoed throughout all generations by those who are being persecuted, but especially by the preborn. The most innocent among us are crying out to God saying, "Save us, God. Only you can save us from those who pursue us. We are weak and defenseless. Send deliverers to help us, or we will surely be ripped to pieces and aborted. Please help us!" God works in mysterious ways, and he can deliver by supernatural means, but more often than not it seems he uses his people to accomplish his plans. He used Moses to bring the Israelites out of Egypt. He used Rahab to hide the spies. He used William Wilberforce to convince the British parliament to abolish the slave trade. He used Martin Luther King, Jr. to champion civil rights and racial equality. Perhaps God wants to use us to end the destruction of his children in the womb. If he is calling us, we must not delay, or there will be none to deliver.

PRAYER FOCUS: God, speak to me and tell me how I can join the fight to end abortion. Lord, you are awesome and beyond compare. Please save your children and use me in whatever capacity I would serve you best. I can hear the cry of the preborn, and I know you have been overwhelmingly merciful to our nation. Please forgive us!

DID YOU KNOW? The most common abortion methods (suction-aspiration, dilation and curettage, and dilation and evacuation) all tear the baby to pieces inside the womb.[13] For a description of these methods, see chapter nineteen in John C. and Barbara H. Willke's *Abortion Questions & Answers*, or go to nrlc.org.

REFLECTIONS

MAY 15

Job 31:13-15 HCSB

If I have dismissed the case of my male or female servants when they made a complaint against me, what could I do when God stands up to judge? How should I answer Him when He calls me to account? Did not the One who made me in the womb also make them? Did not the same God form us both in the womb?

∞

The Bible says Job was a man of perfect integrity and the greatest of all the people of the east (Job 1:1-3). His story is one of personal tragedy, spiritual testing, and triumph. In Job's final claim of innocence, we find one of the Bible's most powerful verses about the personhood of every human life created in the womb. Job, through a series of questions, affirms that his life and the life of his male and female servants were initiated, directed, and valued from the womb by Almighty God. "Did not the One who made me in the womb also make them? Did not the same God form us both in the womb?" God knew all of them from the moment of conception and considered them equal. Job makes this point clear when he argues that if he failed to treat his servants with the respect they were due, God would judge him harshly, because they were just as valuable and precious to the Father as he was. Every person is precious, valuable, loved, and formed by God from the moment of conception.

PRAYER FOCUS: Almighty God, your Word is full of hidden treasure and life. Great and awesome are you, Lord. Thank you for creating me and my family and my friends. Awaken your church to the value of all life and motivate them to stand in the gap for your preborn children.

DID YOU KNOW? Horton, the good elephant in Dr. Seuss's classic story *Horton Hears a Who*, first heard the Who's cry for help on this date. The opening words in Horton's epic adventure are, "On the fifteenth of May, in the jungle of Nool…"[14] This beautiful story, written well before abortion was available on demand, provides one of the greatest allegories for the pro-life struggle. Pick up a copy and read it to your children. After all, "a person is a person, no matter how small!"

REFLECTIONS

MAY 16

Habakkuk 1:2-4 NIV

How long, O LORD, must I call for help, but you do not listen? Or cry out to you, "Violence!" but you do not save? Why do you make me look at injustice? Why do you tolerate wrong? Destruction and violence are before me; there is strife, and conflict abounds. Therefore the law is paralyzed, and justice never prevails. The wicked hem in the righteous, so that justice is perverted.

∞

I am sure we have all at times run out of patience and had a few questions for God. We're not alone—just ask Job or Habakkuk. Habakkuk was grieved by the people's rebellion and sin and God's apparent slow response. Why is God slow to respond or seemingly absent in times of trouble? I believe it is because he allows people free choice and is patiently waiting for their repentance before bringing judgment. God operates with complete knowledge and looks at life from an eternal perspective. He knows how long our lives on earth will be, where we will spend eternity, and what is at stake for both the victim and the victimizer. God doesn't want anyone to perish. In his abundant wisdom, great mercy, and perfect timing, God will answer our prayers. And in eternity we will understand the reasons why difficult things happened or why God responded the way he did. For now, we must be content to cry out for justice, trust in the Lord, and plead with him to use his people and his power to help us overcome abortion. On the question of abortion, the wicked have hemmed in the righteous by making us think that abortion is an individual choice or a private matter. Yet just the opposite is true, for the good of our neighbor is our primary concern, and abortion harms people of every race, gender, and creed.

PRAYER FOCUS: Lord Jesus, help me understand that I can trust you even when I can't make sense of things or understand why they happen. God, give me a heart that cries out for justice and the desire to make things in my family, community, and world better. Help me see things from your perspective instead of mine.

DID YOU KNOW? Ginny Owens, the contemporary Christian musician, is blind.[15] She has written a powerful song titled "This Road," which is about trusting God when we don't see his plan or purpose. Listen to this powerful song and artist on the album *Something More*, released by Rocketown Records.

REFLECTIONS

MAY 17

Zephaniah 3:17 HCSB

Yahweh your God is among you, a warrior who saves. He will rejoice over you with gladness. He will bring you quietness with His love. He will delight in you with shouts of joy.

We are never alone because God is always present. God is a warrior who fights to the death for our salvation. He rejoices over one who was lost more than ninety-nine who are safe in his arms (Matt. 18:12-14). It is not the will of God that anyone perishes. In fact, it makes God glad to think about us and our friends. In the midst of great tragedy and despair, he quiets our souls with his unfailing and surpassing love. He delights in everything and everyone he has made. Praise and honor are due him for he was and is and is to come. Nothing in all creation compares with Yahweh, and he thinks nothing he has created compares to us!

PRAYER FOCUS: Jesus, there is none like you! You are the Mighty God who laid down his life for me and everyone you have ever created. Holy is the Lamb and worthy of honor and praise. Lord, I want to be like you and love your people!

DID YOU KNOW? Horatio Spafford wrote the hymn "It Is Well with My Soul" after the tragic death of his four daughters. The girls' ship sank when it collided with another vessel while crossing the Atlantic Ocean. Prior to this tragedy, Horatio had already lost his son to scarlet fever and a great deal of his finances in the Chicago Fire of 1871. Horatio and his wife later moved to Jerusalem and founded a ministry to serve the poor.[16] Only the Prince of Peace can overcome the darkness and quiet our souls with his love!

REFLECTIONS

MAY 18

1 Samuel 26:23-25 ESV

"The LORD rewards every man for his righteousness and his faithfulness, for the LORD gave you into my hand today, and I would not put out my hand against the LORD's anointed. Behold, as your life was precious this day in my sight, so may my life be precious in the sight of the LORD, and may he deliver me out of all tribulation." Then Saul said to David, "Blessed be you, my son David! You will do many things and will succeed in them."

This conversation takes place between David and Saul after David has captured Saul's spear and jar of water from the middle of three thousand sleeping soldiers. Saul and the soldiers had been tracking David in order to take his life. David, despite being encouraged by Abishai to kill Saul, showed great reverence for God's anointed leader and the proper respect for the sacredness of human life. David also understood that the way he valued life would be the measure with which his own life would be valued. Saul acknowledged David's righteousness and predicted that his future would be blessed with success and favor. David was a man after God's heart for many reasons, but I have no doubt one of them was his respect for the life of his fellow citizens.

PRAYER FOCUS: God, help me respect those who are in authority over me and help me settle any disagreements with them in a humble manner. Lord, help me value every human life.

DID YOU KNOW? Babies in the womb can dream. Peter Tallack wrote the following about twenty-one-week-old babies: "At twenty-one weeks rapid eye movements begin—an activity associated with dreaming in which the eyes flicker back and forth behind closed eyelids. When a loud vibrating noise source is applied to the mother's abdomen, the fetus responds by blinking and starting—a reaction that usually develops earlier in girls than boys. The fetus's vocal cords are functioning—she can get hiccups—and movements such as grasping and pedaling are coordinated."[17]

REFLECTIONS

MAY 19

John 5:24 NKJV

Most assuredly, I say to you, he who hears My word and believes in Him who sent Me has everlasting life, and shall not come into judgment, but has passed from death into life.

Jesus is truly life-giving. He created all life, sustains life, and died so that we could have fellowship with him for all eternity. His words are the words of life and truth. If we accept his words that point to our loving Father, we will discover truth and be transformed by the power of the Spirit into new creatures. Judgment will no longer dominate our thoughts or cloud our future because we have tasted the Living Water and been set free! Paul proclaims in 2 Corinthians 3:17, "Now the Lord is the Spirit; and where the Spirit of the Lord is, there is freedom" (ESV). It is good and pleasant to dwell in the house of the Lord, under the shadow of his wings.

PRAYER FOCUS: Jesus, I believe you are the Son of the living God, who honored the Father and died for my transgressions. I place my faith and trust in you, knowing that you will bridge the gap for me and bring me safely into eternity. I am overwhelmed by your compassion and love for me. Please allow me to return the favor by loving you and all the people you have made to the best of my ability.

DID YOU KNOW? The standard calendar abbreviations for time meet at the birth of Jesus of Nazareth. B.C. stands for "Before Christ" and A.D. stands for *anno domini*, a Latin phrase meaning "In the year of our Lord."[18] Sadly, new terms are being implemented today in an attempt to remove the centrality of the Advent of Christ.

REFLECTIONS

_____

_____

_____

_____

_____

_____

_____

_____

MAY 20

Proverbs 10:2 ESV

Treasures gained by wickedness do not profit, but righteousness delivers from death.

If we make our living by abortion, embezzlement, extortion, drug trafficking, or any other wicked pursuit, we must repent and follow the example of Zacchaeus in Luke chapter nineteen. Proverbs 10:2 does not say money cannot be gained from wicked endeavors, only that it does not profit. "For what does it profit a man to gain the whole world and forfeit his soul?" (Mark 8:36 ESV). What we do matters both now and in eternity because we will stand before Almighty God and give an account for the things we have done. With God's help, we must overcome our nature and strive to do what is right. Jesus, in his righteousness, delivers from death those who trust in him for salvation. All who trust Christ have his righteousness imputed to them. It behooves us then to use his indwelling righteousness to deliver the preborn from death and fight against the evil of abortion.

PRAYER FOCUS: God, bless the work of my hands and provide for me through honest labor. Lord, teach me to consider others to be better than myself, and help me to become a person who tithes and gives generously to worthy endeavors. I want to be useful in the kingdom of God and store up my treasure in heaven.

DID YOU KNOW? Abortion negatively impacts our economy in different ways. First, we have fifty million fewer workers, plus their potential offspring, contributing to social security. Second, there are fewer people buying goods, producing goods, and paying taxes in our nation. Third, the loss of man power and innovation will have a huge economic impact on our aging population in the decades to come.[19]

REFLECTIONS

MAY 21

1 Peter 4:17-19 NIV

For it is time for judgment to begin with the family of God; and if it begins with us, what will the outcome be for those who do not obey the gospel of God? And, "If it is hard for the righteous to be saved, what will become of the ungodly and the sinner?" So then, those who suffer according to God's will should commit themselves to their faithful Creator and continue to do good.

Peter is talking about suffering for the gospel and Christ. What better way is there to suffer for Christ than to love God's people? It was Jesus who said to Simon Peter, "Simon son of John, do you truly love me?" He answered, "Yes, Lord, you know that I love you." Jesus said, "Take care of my sheep" (John 21:16 NIV). It is time for judgment to come to the family of God. We cannot sit idly by and allow our fellow citizens to die without hearing the gospel or to be destroyed in the womb. Fighting abortion is in accordance with God's will, so let's commit ourselves to fight for the good of all people, even if we suffer for it. Our loving Creator is faithful to reward us and help us bring about a good result. Those in the church who have remained on the sideline need to get in the game and help us turn the tide, while those in the church who have committed abortion need to call an injury time-out, seek forgiveness, and report back for duty when they've healed. God is looking for the entire family to get involved and take care of his sheep.

PRAYER FOCUS: Lord, I want to do my part. Show me what I can do, be it spiritual, financial, or physical. Use my talents and abilities to make a difference in my church, community, and nation. Lord, end abortion and use me to be a part of the solution.

DID YOU KNOW? The creation of female germ cells (eggs) begins before birth when the female fetus is only three months old.[20]

REFLECTIONS

MAY 22

Galatians 6:9-10 NASB

Let us not lose heart in doing good, for in due time we will reap if we do not grow weary. So then, while we have opportunity, let us do good to all people, and especially to those who are of the household of the faith.

It is hard to swim upstream in a culture of relativism, especially when trying to help others see the urgent need to abolish abortion. One can feel abandoned, alone, or attacked. But Paul exhorts us not to lose heart when we are trying to accomplish what is good and right. Each of us has the God-given responsibility to save innocent lives by speaking out against the horrors of abortion to our family, neighbors, and friends. We can put our time, talent, and money into making a difference in the life of a child. We can help heal our brothers and sisters in Christ who have fallen victim to the lie that abortion is not a great evil. We can adopt children who would otherwise be terminated in pregnancy. We can help women experiencing an unexpected pregnancy with their lodging, finances, and medical bills. We can pursue change in the halls of government. There is so much we can and must do. Will we do it?

PRAYER FOCUS: God, give me the strength to be good to your people and love them sacrificially. Help me take hold of the opportunities I have within my community to turn the tide in the abortion battle. Use me to encourage my brothers and sisters in Christ to join me in these efforts.

DID YOU KNOW? Oscar Schindler was a German industrialist who employed many Jewish people in his enamelware and ammunitions factories during WWII. Schindler saved over one thousand Jews who worked for him during the Holocaust. Schindler made tremendous financial sacrifices to ensure their safety.[21] If you have not done so already, I encourage you to watch the movie *Schindler's List*, based on his moving story, directed by Steven Spielberg.

REFLECTIONS

MAY 23

James 5:19-20 HCSB

My brothers, if any among you strays from the truth, and someone turns him back, let him know that whoever turns a sinner from the error of his way will save his life from death and cover a multitude of sins.

∞

Before James wrote these words, he was talking about effective prayer and the earnest prayers of Elijah. When our friends, neighbors, and loved ones have strayed from the truth, the most important thing we can do is to pray for them earnestly. We need to love them with grace and truth, praying often to the One who can change their heart. And that goes for us, too, when we have strayed from the truth. Jesus can change our hearts, and it is never too late to return to Christ and his people who love us. We are God's passion and he is longing to save our lives from destruction. We can repent of the error of our ways and return to our loving Father, who looks expectantly for us, ready to forgive. No one will ever love us as much as Jesus. His love covers a multitude of sins, including yours and mine.

PRAYER FOCUS: Lord Jesus, show me that I am your child and that you love me regardless of what I have done. Wash me clean and help me to choose a better course than the one I am on. Jesus, I pray for the salvation and restoration of all the abortionists and their staff of employees. Do not forsake them, for they are the work of your hands. Redeem their lives just as you have redeemed mine.

DID YOU KNOW? The apostle Paul, who wrote the majority of the epistles, wrote "Christ Jesus came into the world to save sinners—and I am the worst of them" (1 Tim. 1:15 HCSB). Before his conversion experience on the road to Damascus, Paul severely persecuted the early church. He wrote, "For you have heard about my former way of life in Judaism: I persecuted God's church to an extreme degree and tried to destroy it" (Gal. 1:13 HCSB). It's not about our sin—it's about our Savior. Jesus will make us new!

REFLECTIONS

MAY 24

Job 31:21-23 NIV

If I have raised my hand against the fatherless, knowing that I had influence in court, then let my arm fall from the shoulder, let it be broken off at the joint. For I dreaded destruction from God, and for fear of his splendor I could not do such things.

Why have we committed abortion? Why have we tolerated the mass killing of developing human beings? Why have we failed to take the destruction of children seriously? We have done these things because we have lost the fear of God. For many, it has been too easy to excuse this sin in light of his grace. In our ignorance, we think that God is just like us, but Job knew better. He knew that God loved the least of these and expected us to do the same, regardless of what the law said or the courts allowed. Woe to us and to our courts for we have raised our hand against the fatherless and failed to take care of the least of these in the womb.

PRAYER FOCUS: Forgive us, O God, for we have failed to marvel at your splendor, your creation, and your children. Forgive our leaders, judges, politicians, pastors, and people in authority who have supported or championed abortion. Lord, help us to understand that you are just and holy. Let us love what you love and end the slaughter of your preborn children.

DID YOU KNOW? The Dred Scott v. Sanford Supreme Court decision in 1857 said that black slaves were not "legal persons" and therefore they were the property of the slave owner. Similarly, the Roe v. Wade Supreme Court decision in 1973 said that the preborn are not persons and are the property of the mother. Regrettably, both cases were decided by a 7-2 majority.[22] The Emancipation Proclamation of President Lincoln invalidated the Dred Scott decision. What will invalidate the Supreme Court's grotesque decision of 1973?

REFLECTIONS

MAY 25

Nehemiah 9:26-28 NASB

But they became disobedient and rebelled against You, and cast Your law behind their backs and killed Your prophets who had admonished them so that they might return to You, and they committed great blasphemies. Therefore You delivered them into the hand of their oppressors who oppressed them, but when they cried to You in the time of their distress, You heard from heaven, and according to Your great compassion You gave them deliverers who delivered them from the hand of their oppressors. But as soon as they had rest, they did evil again before You; therefore You abandoned them to the hand of their enemies, so that they ruled over them. When they cried again to You, You heard from heaven, and many times You rescued them according to Your compassion.

The prophet Nehemiah's recounting of Israel's past sins and deliverance is an amazing passage of Scripture. Is there a better description of human depravity and the glorious goodness of God? Regardless of our past, when we turn to God he is compassionate and forgiving because of his great love for us. God will deliver us, but we should not be so naive as to believe there won't be consequences for our sin. Sin brings consequences and even death. If we engage in fornication or adultery, we may get herpes, syphilis, or AIDS. If we steal at work, we may get fired or go to prison. If we do drugs, we may ruin our health and our relationships. God can transform our futures, but he may not undo the consequences of our past. He will, however, give us the grace to live with the consequences of what we have done.

PRAYER FOCUS: Father God, bring me revelation today that it is never too late to confess my sins to you and be restored to a right relationship with you. Help me overcome the pain of the past and pursue a better future. Lord, I love that you never give up on me or fail to be compassionate towards me.

DID YOU KNOW? Post-abortion syndrome is a form of post-traumatic stress disorder.[23] Post-abortion syndrome affects many people who have had an abortion. Three books that can assist people who are dealing with the after-effects of abortion are *Forgiven and Set Free* by Linda Cochrane, *David's Harp* by Richard Beattie, and *Real Abortion Stories: the Hurting and the Healing*, edited by Barbara Horak.

REFLECTIONS

MAY 26

Psalm 36:5-9 ESV

Your steadfast love, O Lord, extends to the heavens, your faithfulness to the clouds. Your righteousness is like the mountains of God; your judgments are like the great deep; man and beast you save, O Lord. How precious is your steadfast love, O God! The children of mankind take refuge in the shadow of your wings. They feast on the abundance of your house, and you give them drink from the river of your delights. For with you is the fountain of life; in your light do we see light.

God loves us intently! His love is beyond compare or measure. He is faithful, righteous, and just. We can all take refuge in the shadow of his wings. Every day we taste the goodness of God in the food we eat, the intellect we enjoy, the air we breathe, and the water we drink. This marvelous planet was designed by God specifically for us. The Earth's vast resources and species were created for our enjoyment and sustenance. God is good to everyone he has made, especially his children. Jesus is the fountain of life, and in his light we can see all things. God never intended for nature to be equal with people, or for people to harm their children. God intended for us to care for the things he has made so that those things could continue to support us and our offspring.

PRAYER FOCUS: God, thank you for your steadfast love! I marvel at your creation and the beauty it contains. Help me respect the planet and the people upon it. Teach me to be a good steward of the things you made.

DID YOU KNOW? Cumulus, altostratus, and cirrus are types of clouds. In all, there are ten types of clouds, each with a distinct shape. Everest and K2 are the world's tallest mountains, with heights over 29,000 and 28,000 feet, respectively. The Pacific Ocean is the world's deepest, averaging 13,000 feet. In fact, the Pacific Ocean is more than twenty-five percent larger than the land area that makes up our entire planet.[24] May we never fail to catch a glimpse of God in his awesome creation!

REFLECTIONS

___

___

___

___

___

___

MAY
27

Acts 2:38-39 NKJV

Then Peter said to them,
"Repent, and let every one
of you be baptized in the
name of Jesus Christ for the
remission of sins; and you
shall receive the gift of the
Holy Spirit. For the promise
is to you and to your children,
and to all who are afar off,
as many as the Lord our
God will call."

Peter, speaking to an international crowd on the Day of Pentecost, affirms that Christ's offer of redemption extends to all people, even those who will be created in the future. Jesus died for all people—old, young, preborn, and future unborn. He died for our redemption from sin just as surely as he died for Peter and the men listening to him on the Day of Pentecost. People living today could not have been imagined two thousand years ago, except by God. God alone knew us. Life and death belong in the hands of God and should only be determined by him as Creator. He alone brings people to life and he alone should determine when they die. Abortion, euthanasia, and murder highly offend God because people dare to fulfill a right of God, the right to decide when earthly life begins and ends.

PRAYER FOCUS: Lord, thank you for considering all those who are far off in your plans of redemption. Fill me each day with your Holy Spirit and direct my steps. Show me how to make the world a better place for my children and my children's children.

DID YOU KNOW? In 2005 the death toll from abortion in the United States was double the number of deaths from cancer. According to the U.S. Department of Health and Human Services at *cdc.gov*, the number of cancer deaths for all of 2005 was 559,312(No. 2). Some other leading causes of death recorded in the top ten were heart disease—652,091(No. 1); stroke—143,579(No. 3); accidents—117,809(No. 5); and diabetes—75,119(No. 6).[25] The abortion total for 2005 was roughly 1.2 million.[26]

REFLECTIONS

MAY 28

Matthew 10:16-20 NASB

Behold, I send you out as sheep in the midst of wolves; so be shrewd as serpents and innocent as doves. But beware of men, for they will hand you over to the courts and scourge you in their synagogues; and you will even be brought before governors and kings for My sake, as a testimony to them and to the Gentiles. But when they hand you over, do not worry about how or what you are to say; for it will be given you in that hour what you are to say. For it is not you who speak, but it is the Spirit of your Father who speaks in you.

Jesus knew his followers would face trials and tribulations as they spread the gospel message. He knew they would be persecuted facing religious and civil resistance. Many believers throughout church history have suffered through similar trials as they have preached the gospel or championed the cause of justice. We should not be surprised if we get arrested or ridiculed for our attempts to defend the rights of the preborn. Civil disobedience can be costly, but Jesus promised us we would never go alone. The Lord will go with us and help us. The difficult circumstances we face can be a great witness to those in government or positions of authority. If we are bold and courageous, God will give us the words to speak at just the right time to advance the cause of justice, especially when we conduct our own affairs with innocence and wisdom.

PRAYER FOCUS: Lord, give me the courage to speak out against injustice and the words to be effective in the cause of justice. Jesus, raise up people who are not afraid to voice your truth and do what is right.

DID YOU KNOW? In May of 1961, a small group of citizens known as the "freedom riders" began riding buses into the South to challenge existing Jim Crow laws that mandated racial segregation. Emboldened by the 1960 Supreme Court ruling Boynton v. Virginia, which desegregated bus terminals throughout the southern states, the group took to the road with courage and solidarity.[27] When the nation witnessed the violence and ill treatment endured by the brave freedom riders, it pricked the conscience of the people and bolstered the emerging civil rights movement in America.

REFLECTIONS

MAY 29

Esther 4:11-16 NKJV

"All the king's servants and the people of the king's provinces know that any man or woman who goes into the inner court to the king, who has not been called, he has but one law: put all to death, except the one to whom the king holds out the golden scepter, that he may live. Yet I myself have not been called to go in to the king these thirty days." So they told Mordecai Esther's words. And Mordecai told them to answer Esther: "Do not think in your heart that you will escape in the king's palace any more than all the other Jews. For if you remain completely silent at this time, relief and deliverance will arise for the Jews from another place, but you and your father's house will perish. Yet who knows whether you have come to the kingdom for such a time as this?" Then Esther told them to reply to Mordecai: "Go, gather all the Jews who are present in Shushan, and fast for me; neither eat nor drink for three days, night or day. My maids and I will fast likewise. And so I will go to the king, which is against the law; and if I perish, I perish!

Evil Haman was plotting to kill all the Jewish people in the kingdom of Persia. However, God had raised Esther to the position of queen in order to use her as an instrument of deliverance for the Jewish people. God granted Esther the beauty, favor, and opportunity to become queen, but he left her the choice to deliver the people or let them perish. Would she dare violate the king's law at the risk of her own life to save her people, or would she keep silent and perhaps spare her own life? King Ahasuerus had no knowledge at the time that his queen was of Jewish descent, which gave Esther an opportunity to remain out of danger from Haman's plan. Esther, to her credit, remembered that her God was mighty to save and took Mordecai's words to heart. She realized that God had placed her there at that time to reflect his love through being strong and courageous. Esther also realized she could not bring down Haman or violate the king's law without divine intervention. So she enlisted the corporate prayer and fasting of all the Jews living in Persia. After three days of intense prayer and fasting, Esther took the final step in deliverance: she acted. She lived what James taught, "faith by itself, if it does not have works, is dead" (2:17 NKJV), and because of her faithful civil disobedience, all the Jews were saved from Haman's plot.

PRAYER FOCUS: Lord Jesus, send us deliverers who will take action against abortion. Heavenly Father, teach me how to pray and fast effectively for your children.

DID YOU KNOW? Esther was an orphan. Esther's cousin, Mordecai, was a great influence in her life because he too lived out the teaching of James 1:27. James wrote, "Pure and undefiled religion before God and the Father is this: to visit orphans and widows in their trouble, and to keep oneself unspotted from the world" (NKJV). "And Mordecai had brought up Hadassah, that is, Esther, his uncle's daughter, for she had neither father nor mother. The young woman was lovely and beautiful. When her father and mother died, Mordecai took her as his own daughter" (Esther 2:7 NKJV).

REFLECTIONS

MAY 30

Joshua 1:8-9 HCSB

This book of instruction must not depart from your mouth; you are to recite it day and night, so that you may carefully observe everything written in it. For then you will prosper and succeed in whatever you do. Haven't I commanded you: be strong and courageous? Do not be afraid or discouraged, for the LORD your God is with you wherever you go.

God knew there were giants waiting in the land for Joshua and the people when he told the Israelites not to be afraid because he would always be with them. God was directing Joshua to the one source that would provide both encouragement and equipping. Are you facing a difficult pregnancy? Have you recently lost your job? Is your marriage breaking apart? Are you struggling with sin? Be strong and courageous as you face your giants, resist fear and discouragement, and cry out to the Lord, for he is with you. Hope is waiting in the words of Scripture. We can all increase our faith to believe we can overcome any obstacle or face any challenge because God delights in us. He is mighty to save and sufficient to bring about change. Like Joshua, we will succeed when we turn to the Word of God and meditate upon it day and night. We need to pick up the Bible each day and ask the Holy Spirit to help us face our giants. To be strong and courageous we need faith, and "faith comes from what is heard, and what is heard comes through the message about Christ" (Rom. 10:17 HCSB).

PRAYER FOCUS: Lamb of God, Holy and Anointed One, fall afresh on me. Restore the dry bones of my soul and lead me beside still waters. Show me the hidden things and reveal your truth to me. Increase my faith as I read your Word, and calm my fears.

DID YOU KNOW? Planned Parenthood's Annual Report for 2007-2008 shows that the organization received $349 million in government grants and contracts and an additional $186 million from contributions and bequests for the year ending June 30, 2008. They estimate these two sources made up fifty-eight percent of their revenue for the year. Additionally, this same report claims they performed 289,750 abortions in 2006 and 305,310 abortions in 2007.[28] This abortion giant will fall like Goliath when we place our trust in God and pick up our five smooth stones.

REFLECTIONS

MAY 31

Amos 5:14-15 NIV

Seek good, not evil, that you may live. Then the LORD God Almighty will be with you, just as you say he is. Hate evil, love good; maintain justice in the courts. Perhaps the LORD God Almighty will have mercy on the remnant of Joseph.

Do we seek to do what is good? Are we actively helping others? Giving our time and money helping others will enhance our life and give us purpose. Serving others will diminish our own problems or, at the very least, the amount of time spent worrying about them. One of the best ways to diminish sin is to spend time pursuing God and ministering to his church. Sin often overtakes us when we are self-focused, alone, tired, or bored. But if we get busy living, serving, and loving our neighbors, we will find there is less time to sin or wallow in our own misery. Doing good brings life! America, it is time to hate abortion and the way it harms our women, men, children, and all of society. It is time we love saving babies, helping destitute women and men, restoring sexual purity and marriages, and returning justice to our courts. If we do these things as a nation, perhaps God will be merciful to us.

PRAYER FOCUS: Jesus, teach me through the Holy Spirit and your Word what is evil and what is good. Give me eyes to see and ears to hear what the Spirit says, and develop in me a hatred of sin and a longing for love, joy, peace, patience, kindness, goodness, and faithfulness (Gal. 5:22).

DID YOU KNOW? Joni Eareckson Tada suffered a spinal cord injury in her teens that left her a quadriplegic. She has since become a painter, author, singer, actress, radio personality, and public servant. One of her greatest achievements has been founding Wheels for the World, an organization that refurbishes wheelchairs and provides them to disabled people in third world countries. As of 2005, the organization had sent more than thirty-five thousand wheelchairs to over seventy nations.[29] Through her faith in Christ, Joni has influenced and helped thousands of people during her life.

REFLECTIONS

June

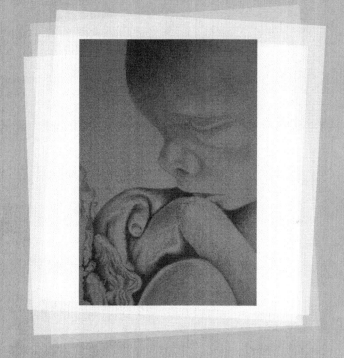

TWENTY WEEKS GESTATION

JUNE 1

Titus 2:11-14 HCSB

For the grace of God has appeared with salvation for all people, instructing us to deny godlessness and worldly lusts and to live in a sensible, righteous, and godly way in the present age, while we wait for the blessed hope and appearing of the glory of our great God and Savior, Jesus Christ. He gave Himself for us to redeem us from all lawlessness and to cleanse for Himself a people for His own possession, eager to do good works.

It is a wonderful thing to know God's grace and salvation are available to all. Through his inner presence and grace, we can overcome our worldly passions and sins. As the Holy Spirit takes hold of us, we begin living more sensible, righteous, self-controlled, and peaceful lives. Jesus has redeemed us, and someday he is returning for us. But until he returns, we have a job to do, and that job is to be God's special people on earth, who love him and his children. We are to be a people eager to do good works, like feeding the hungry, clothing the naked, visiting those in prison, caring for the sick, and pursuing justice for the preborn. Quite simply, our job is to assist others and help them find the Savior.

PRAYER FOCUS: Almighty God, maker of heaven and earth, help me live a godly life. I want to be your ambassador of goodwill and love. Show me how I can best serve your Kingdom. Give me a passion for the lost and the courage to share my faith with others. Lord Jesus, I am so grateful you paid the price for my sin and the sin of the world.

DID YOU KNOW? By twenty-five weeks gestation, a baby's skeleton is completely assembled. The baby's forming spine consists of thirty-three rings, 150 joints, and one thousand ligaments. At birth, babies have three hundred separate bones, but by adulthood some of those bones have fused, leaving 206.[1]

REFLECTIONS

JUNE 2

Obadiah 15 NASB

For the day of the Lord draws near on all the nations. As you have done, it will be done to you. Your dealings will return on your own head.

God is just. His judgment will be in equal proportion to what we deserve without the appeasing or atoning of our sin through faith in Christ. When Jesus returns, he will judge all the nations of the world. Those nations that have kept their way pure and have stood for justice, equality, goodness, and the sacredness of human life will fare best. Meanwhile, those nations that stood for tyranny, oppression, greed, and murder will be repaid in kind. Our national conduct matters. It is time for our government of the people, by the people, and for the people to stand for all the people, both born and preborn!

PRAYER FOCUS: Righteous God, I thank you for your many blessings to our nation in the past and presently. Lord, many times my nation has failed to do the right thing, but often we have adopted a better course later on. Forgive this current iniquity and lead us on a path to place abortion in the history books along with slavery, Native American abuses, restricted voting rights, internment, and segregation. Return us, Lord, to one nation under God, with liberty and justice for all.

DID YOU KNOW? Abraham Lincoln spoke the following words during his second inaugural address, less than two months before his assassination: "Fondly do we hope—fervently do we pray—that this mighty scourge of war may speedily pass away. Yet, if God wills that it continue, until all the wealth piled by the bond-man's two hundred and fifty years of unrequited toil shall be sunk, and until every drop of blood drawn with the lash, shall be paid by another drawn with the sword, as was said three thousand years ago, so still it must be said 'the judgments of the Lord, are true and righteous altogether.' With malice toward none; with charity for all; with firmness in the right, as God gives us to see the right, let us strive on to finish the work we are in; to bind up the nation's wounds."[2] Our nation would do well to remember the cost of the Civil War and abolish abortion now. If, as Lincoln perceived, the severity of the Civil War was due in part to God's judgment for slavery, what might be experienced by our nation today if abortion continues and God releases his judgment upon the land?

JUNE 3

Numbers 35:33 ESV

You shall not pollute the land in which you live, for blood pollutes the land, and no atonement can be made for the land for the blood that is shed in it, except by the blood of the one who shed it.

God spoke these words to Moses after giving him instructions on how to handle the crime of murder. The Old Testament law was clear that justice was to be administered in kind—bruise for bruise, wound for wound, and life for life. No atonement was to be made for murder except by taking the life of the one who shed blood. Life is sacred to God, and, therefore, murder is unacceptable. Those who had willfully taken a life could only atone for their sin through the shedding of their own lifeblood. Thankfully, Jesus' blood is perfectly atoning and sufficient to cover all sin, including murder. Jesus, however, did not come to abolish Old Testament truth but to fulfill it. Therefore, the best way for us to live is to accept Christ's gift of atonement and ask the Holy Spirit to help us keep God's commands for right living. Only then will we be blessed with abundant life through the provision of Christ and the wisdom of God's counsel. Abortion has thoroughly polluted our land, making it necessary to appeal to the blood-atoning mercy of Christ. But we also need to stop shedding innocent blood. Even in the midst of mercy there will be consequences for the murder of God's children. Let us do our part to stop the bloodshed while we are still experiencing the overwhelming grace of God.

PRAYER FOCUS: Lord, I am overwhelmed by your grace and mercy. I see your goodness in the midst of our depravity. You continue to uphold the universe by the word of your power, giving us life and breath, sunshine and rain. I'm amazed by you! God, you truly are good to the sinner and the saint!

DID YOU KNOW? First Chronicles 22:5-10 tells us that King David was not allowed to build the Lord's temple because of all the blood he had spilled in his lifetime. That task was left to David's son Solomon. God takes all spilt blood seriously, even the blood of our enemies spilt during war.

REFLECTIONS

JUNE 4

3 John 11 NKJV

Beloved, do not imitate what is evil, but what is good. He who does good is of God, but he who does evil has not seen God.

As Christians we are called to be imitators of Christ. Jesus is entirely good. He healed the sick, fed the hungry, raised the dead, taught the truth, and forgave his enemies. How did the man from Nazareth live so flawlessly, love so deeply, and endure so much grief for sinners? Because he had seen the Father. Jesus said, "Most assuredly, I say to you, the Son can do nothing of Himself, but what He sees the Father do; for whatever He does, the Son also does in like manner" (John 5:19 NKJV). Oh, to have seen the beauty, majesty, grace, and goodness of the Father! To see God is to love him and to marvel at his grandeur. Even though we see through a glass darkly, to see at all makes us long to be like our Savior. When we find ourselves pursuing or practicing evil, we need to take a fresh look at God, for clearly in that case we have not seen our Creator, the great I Am!

PRAYER FOCUS: Holy and indescribable God, show me your radiant goodness, endless love, and unsearchable wisdom. Open my eyes to see who you are and who I am in you. Teach me to imitate your Son Jesus in my thoughts, words, and actions.

DID YOU KNOW? Martin Luther King, Jr.'s last speech before a Memphis crowd of striking sanitation workers was extemporaneous. On April 3, 1968, King closed with these immortal words the night before his assassination: "Like anybody, I would like to live a long life. Longevity has its place. But I'm not concerned about that now. I just want to do God's will. And he's allowed me to go up to the mountain. And I've looked over. And I've seen the Promised Land. I may not get there with you. But I want you to know tonight, that we, as a people, will get to the Promised Land! And so I'm happy, tonight. I'm not worried about anything. I'm not fearing any man! Mine eyes have seen the glory of the coming of the Lord!"[3]

REFLECTIONS

JUNE 5

Mark 5:35-36 HCSB

While He was still speaking, people came from the synagogue leader's house and said, "Your daughter is dead. Why bother the Teacher anymore?" But when Jesus overheard what was said, He told the synagogue leader, "Don't be afraid. Only believe."

∞

"It's impossible to abolish slavery from the British Empire." "Segregation will never end." "Our country will not give former slaves or women the right to vote." "Abortion is here to stay, so you might as well get used to it." But Jesus said, "Everything is possible to the one who believes" (Mark 9:23 HCSB) and "What is impossible with men is possible with God" (Luke 18:27 HCSB). We must never give in to lies and rhetoric, but we must put aside our fears and believe in the power of God working through his people to accomplish mighty things. "It's impossible to raise people from the dead." Tell that to Jairus, the synagogue leader, and his daughter (Matt. 9:18-26). Abortion will find its way to the ash heap of history where it belongs. All that remains is for us to conquer our fear and believe. Jesus said, "I assure you: The one who believes in Me will also do the works that I do. And he will do even greater works than these, because I am going to the Father" (John 14:12 HCSB).

PRAYER FOCUS: Jesus, take away my spirit of fear and give me a spirit of power, of love, and of a sound mind. Take away my doubts and give me a heart to believe like David. Stir your church, Lord, to rise up and end abortion in our nation.

DID YOU KNOW? Franklin Delano Roosevelt, the thirty-second president of the United States, was elected to office four times. Roosevelt led our nation out of the Great Depression and through the majority of World War II. He served from 1933 to 1945. During his first inauguration, Roosevelt spoke the now famous words, "The only thing we have to fear is fear itself."[4] Roosevelt rightly understood that for him to lead our nation through difficult times he would first have to destroy the enemy of fear.

REFLECTIONS

JUNE 6

1 Chronicles 5:18-20 NASB

The sons of Reuben and the Gadites and the half-tribe of Manasseh, consisting of valiant men, men who bore shield and sword and shot with bow and were skillful in battle, were 44,760, who went to war. They made war against the Hagrites, Jetur, Naphish and Nodab. They were helped against them, and the Hagrites and all who were with them were given into their hand; for they cried out to God in the battle, and He answered their prayers because they trusted in Him.

∞

On June 6, 1944, 2,500 brave men gave their lives destroying Hitler's Atlantic Wall. As a boy, I grew up fascinated by WWII and what Tom Brokaw called "the greatest generation." Their acts of heroism and their monumental achievements of victory and bravery always inspired me. I think what I liked best about their exploits was that they were the good guys, who smashed fascism and ended the Holocaust. They truly fought for freedom and justice, making the world a better place. They achieved this through their "blood, toil, tears, and sweat" as Churchill so eloquently stated. As I reflect over the freedoms they fought so hard to protect, I wonder how most of them would feel about the tragedy of abortion and all the people whose freedom it strips. Certainly they gave their blood for their brothers in arms and their families back home, but they also knew their great sacrifice was for all of us and our children's children. How sad it is that this great nation and its people who spilled blood to stop oppression and tyranny have now allowed an even greater tyranny, the tyranny of abortion. With more than three thousand of our citizens being aborted each day over the past thirty-seven years, every day has become as costly as D-Day.

PRAYER FOCUS: Lord Jesus, protect our troops and all those who serve in our national defense. God, help us to fight only as a last resort or when the cause is just. You answer the prayers of those who trust in you, and so may "In God we trust" be the attitude of our hearts and not just a slogan on our money.

DID YOU KNOW? Lt. Richard Winters of the 101st Airborne won the Distinguished Service Cross on D-Day. Winters's group was outnumbered five to one when they attacked a battery of 105mm guns guarded by fifty enemy soldiers. Winters later wrote in his journal that he "did not forget to get on my knees and thank God for helping me to live through this day and ask for his help on D plus one."[5] You can follow the story of the 101st and Lt. Winters in the HBO mini-series *Band of Brothers*.

REFLECTIONS

163

JUNE 7

Ephesians 6:10-13 NIV

Finally, be strong in the Lord and in his mighty power. Put on the full armor of God so that you can take your stand against the devil's schemes. For our struggle is not against flesh and blood, but against the rulers, against the authorities, against the powers of this dark world and against the spiritual forces of evil in the heavenly realms. Therefore put on the full armor of God, so that when the day of evil comes, you may be able to stand your ground, and after you have done everything, to stand.

Our struggle is not against deceived men and women who abort their babies, or pro-abortion and pro-choice supporters, or even against abortion doctors who grow wealthy on the killing of the preborn. Rather, our struggle is against the hateful Enemy of God and his spiritual forces of wickedness, forces that help the Devil steal, kill, and destroy. Abortion is too heinous and wicked, and too illogical, to be devised by the human mind alone. Abortion is straight from the pit of hell, designed to murder millions of human beings who are made in the image of God. Satan hates the Lord and will do everything in his power to destroy the object of God's affection! Christ is the head, but we are the body here on earth. The church must rise and be God's hands and feet during this dark time. We must put on the full armor of God and take our stand in preparation for the day of evil.

PRAYER FOCUS: Lord of life, do not let yourself be defamed nor share your glory with another. Jesus, help the powerless against the mighty. Lord, supernaturally intervene in the heavens and give us the victory over those who oppose us. Protect us, Lord, and keep us hidden in you.

DID YOU KNOW? Humility is one of our greatest weapons against the enemy. "He mocks proud mockers but gives grace to the humble" (Prov. 3:34 NIV). And James repeats, "He gives us more grace. That is why Scripture says: 'God opposes the proud but gives grace to the humble'" (James 4:6 NIV). Even the archangel Michael used humility when dealing with the Devil: "The archangel Michael, when he was disputing with the devil about the body of Moses, did not dare to bring a slanderous accusation against him, but said, 'The Lord rebuke you!'" (Jude 9 NIV).

REFLECTIONS

JUNE 8

Ephesians 6:14-18 NIV

Stand firm then, with the belt of truth buckled around your waist, with the breastplate of righteousness in place, and with your feet fitted with the readiness that comes from the gospel of peace. In addition to all this, take up the shield of faith, with which you can extinguish all the flaming arrows of the evil one. Take the helmet of salvation and the sword of the Spirit, which is the word of God. And pray in the Spirit on all occasions with all kinds of prayers and requests. With this in mind, be alert and always keep on praying for all the saints.

How do we fight the Enemy? We fight the Evil One by standing firm in our full armor while trusting Almighty God. We secure tightly the truth of God around the core of our being so that we know who God is and who we are in Christ. We adopt the righteousness of Christ and place it over our heart. We make ourselves ready to advance the gospel of peace at every opportunity and during any season. We hold on to our faith believing that God loves us and will never let us go or allow us to fail. Even when the Evil One condemns us, we will trust in our Father's provision. We will know that the helmet protects the head and that the Head of the body of Christ protects us. Christ's salvation is impenetrable, incorruptible, and completely sufficient. We will speak the words of life and listen to how those words apply to us. We will not listen to the Enemy, and we will answer him with Scripture when he accuses us or tempts us. More than anything else, we will pray to the One who can save our souls from death. We will pray in the Spirit earnestly, often, and as he taught us to pray. Finally, we will stay alert and do what is good. Paul said, "Do not be overcome by evil, but overcome evil with good" (Rom. 12:21 NIV).

PRAYER FOCUS: Father, use your Word to be "a lamp unto my feet and a light unto my path" (Ps. 119:105 KJV). Keep me safe in the palm of your hand, and show me how to pray effectively. God, grant me discernment when I battle spiritual forces of wickedness, and help me remember the battle belongs to you. My job is simply to love your people and be good to them.

DID YOU KNOW? Prayer is one of our best weapons against the enemy because it motivates God to fight for us. James 5:16 states, "Confess your sins to each other and pray for each other so that you may be healed. The prayer of a righteous man is powerful and effective" (NIV). There is no more righteous man than Jesus, and he is seated at the right hand of God praying for you and me.

REFLECTIONS

JUNE 9

John 8:44 ESV

You are of your father the devil, and your will is to do your father's desires. He was a murderer from the beginning, and has nothing to do with the truth, because there is no truth in him. When he lies, he speaks out of his own character, for he is a liar and the father of lies.

The Devil is a master of deception and falsehood and he takes particular delight in destroying self-worth. He wants us to believe we are worthless, unworthy of love, unwanted, beyond hope, and unredeemable. He wants us to believe that a child in the womb is just a blob of tissue without viability, part of the mother's body that places undue and unwelcome strain on her. One of the Evil One's greatest lies is that the preborn child is not a person—a lie that is contrary not only to God's revealed truth, but also to science, embryology, ultrasound evidence, biology, logic, and common sense. Satan was a murderer from the beginning, and his murderous lie of abortion has led to the premature death of more than fifty million people in the United States alone.

PRAYER FOCUS: Lord, help me perceive the lies of the Enemy and combat them with the truth. Lord Jesus, I know Satan wants to destroy everyone touched by abortion. I am praying for them today and asking you to heal and restore them. God, I'm sorry my nation has allowed all these children to die, and I am going to do my part to oppose abortion and expose these lies.

DID YOU KNOW? Spiritual warfare is a reality in the believer's life and something we all need to be prepared for. Peter wrote this: "Be sober-minded; be watchful. Your adversary the devil prowls around like a roaring lion, seeking someone to devour. Resist him, firm in your faith, knowing that the same kinds of suffering are being experienced by your brotherhood throughout the world. And after you have suffered a little while, the God of all grace, who has called you to his eternal glory in Christ, will himself restore, confirm, strengthen, and establish you" (1 Pet. 5:8-10 ESV). Two good books to read on spiritual warfare are *Spiritual Warfare* by Dean Sherman, and *Needless Casualties of War* by John Paul Jackson.

REFLECTIONS

JUNE 10

Haggai 1:14-15 NKJV

So the LORD stirred up the spirit of Zerubbabel the son of Shealtiel, governor of Judah, and the spirit of Joshua the son of Jehozadak, the high priest, and the spirit of all the remnant of the people; and they came and worked on the house of the LORD of hosts, their God, on the twenty-fourth day of the sixth month, in the second year of King Darius.

In the Old Testament book of Haggai, the children of Israel had recently returned to Jerusalem, after being in exile, with the goal of rebuilding the Lord's temple. After facing opposition, however, the people had stopped working on God's house and turned their attention to their own affairs and homes (Hag. 1:1-11). God sent the prophet Haggai to help the people get back on track. Haggai helped them see that their neglect of the affairs and concerns of God was the reason their divine favor and blessing had dried up. The people had become discouraged, distracted, and apathetic. God sent his Word through the prophet and personally stirred up the spirits of politicians, spiritual leaders, and everyday citizens to take action, reversing the present course of the people. How can we build bigger homes, increase our retirement portfolios, and buy the latest gadgets when God's children are dying at a rate of over three thousand per day? Perhaps we have forgotten the concerns and affairs of the Savior. God stirs up our spirits to act, but it is up to us to keep them stirred up and attend to the work of the Father. Paul wrote to Timothy, "Therefore I remind you to stir up the gift of God which is in you through the laying on of my hands" (2 Tim. 1:6 NKJV). If God has stirred you to take action against abortion, take courage today and continue working until the task is done!

PRAYER FOCUS: Lord of Hosts, stir up my spirit to love the least of these in the womb. Give me a passion for life and truth. Help me to work even when I am tired or discouraged. Jesus, you have given me all things to enjoy, but don't allow me to place my things above you or your people.

DID YOU KNOW? Zerubbabel's name appears in both genealogical lists of Jesus. Look for it in Matthew chapter one and Luke chapter three. To read an interesting discussion on how the genealogies of Jesus show how he was both human and divine, read *Number in Scripture* by E. W. Bullinger.

REFLECTIONS

JUNE 11

1 Corinthians 1:26-31 HCSB

Brothers, consider your calling: Not many are wise from a human perspective, not many powerful, not many of noble birth. Instead, God has chosen what is foolish in the world to shame the wise, and God has chosen what is weak in the world to shame the strong. God has chosen what is insignificant and despised in the world—what is viewed as nothing—to bring to nothing what is viewed as something, so that no one can boast in His presence. But it is from Him that you are in Christ Jesus, who became God-given wisdom for us—our righteousness, sanctification, and redemption, in order that, as it is written: The one who boasts must boast in the Lord.

∞

We have nothing to boast about, especially when we measure ourselves against the standards of God. Still, God has chosen and appointed imperfect people to do his work throughout human history. We are all called to share the gospel and love our neighbor. We have something to offer our fellow believers and the world, and we cannot allow the Enemy to rob us of our calling by accusing us of being insignificant, inept, sinful, weak, or foolish. We are made in the image of God, bought with a price, covered by his righteousness, sanctified by his holiness, and redeemed by his love. The Word of God says we are in Christ Jesus, who became God-given wisdom for us, as well as our righteousness, sanctification, and redemption. We are qualified and ready to shame the wise, the strong, and the things that are viewed as something.

PRAYER FOCUS: God, I thank you that I don't have to be a somebody in the world's eyes to be a somebody in yours. Lord Jesus, reveal to me my calling and help me to walk it out. I am the clay and you are the potter, so make me into what you desire for me to be.

DID YOU KNOW? According to Judges chapters six through eight, Gideon defeated the Midianites, Amalekites, and the peoples of the East with a force of a mere three hundred men. Yet notice how Gideon viewed himself before he was called: "The Lord turned to him and said, 'Go in the strength you have and deliver Israel from the power of Midian. Am I not sending you?' He said to Him, 'Please, Lord, how can I deliver Israel? Look, my family is the weakest in Manasseh, and I am the youngest in my father's house.' 'But I will be with you,' the Lord said to him. 'You will strike Midian down as if it were one man'" (Judg. 6:14-16 HCSB).

REFLECTIONS

JUNE 12

Philippians 4:4-9 NKJV

Rejoice in the Lord always. Again I will say, rejoice! Let your gentleness be known to all men. The Lord is at hand. Be anxious for nothing, but in everything by prayer and supplication, with thanksgiving, let your requests be made known to God; and the peace of God, which surpasses all understanding, will guard your hearts and minds through Christ Jesus. Finally, brethren, whatever things are true, whatever things are noble, whatever things are just, whatever things are pure, whatever things are lovely, whatever things are of good report, if there is any virtue and if there is anything praiseworthy—meditate on these things. The things which you learned and received and heard and saw in me, these do, and the God of peace will be with you.

No matter how difficult or negative our circumstances, we can always rejoice in the Lord. We have it on the authority of his Word that he will never leave us nor forsake us. God has good things in store for us. The psalmist put it this way: "The LORD is good to all, and His tender mercies are over all His works. Your kingdom is an everlasting kingdom, and Your dominion endures throughout all generations. The LORD upholds all who fall, and raises up all who are bowed down" (Ps. 145:9, 13-14 NKJV). We may face hardship, abuse, imprisonment, loss, ostracism, and death, but the Lord will gather us in his loving embrace both now and forever. Paul instructs us to be gentle to all people—let your gentleness be known to all, he says. Abortion is the opposite of gentleness. If our anxiety is stirred while we are pursuing justice for the preborn, we need to give it to the Lord in prayer. We can thank God for his marvelous deeds and request his protection and favor. He will grant us the courage and the peace to achieve and endure the unthinkable. We need to speak the truth about abortion because doing so is noble, just, pure, and admirable. Brothers and sisters, it is praiseworthy, lovely, and virtuous to intervene on behalf of the oppressed, the needy, the fatherless, the stranger, and the poor.

PRAYER FOCUS: Lord, "I will praise You, for I am fearfully and wonderfully made; marvelous are Your works, and that my soul knows very well" (Ps. 139:14 NKJV). I rejoice in you. It is my joy to serve the Creator of the universe. Sustain me in my efforts to love your people and do what is right. Lord, I love you more than words can express.

DID YOU KNOW? Medgar Evers was assassinated on this day in 1963. The former WWII veteran and civil rights activist was murdered in front of his home. Byron De La Beckwith was convicted of the crime thirty-one years later.[6] Evers did what was right and good, influencing thousands during his lifetime and many more after his death. God works all things for good in his timing.

REFLECTIONS

JUNE 13

2 Thessalonians 1:6-9 NIV

God is just: He will pay back trouble to those who trouble you and give relief to you who are troubled, and to us as well. This will happen when the Lord Jesus is revealed from heaven in blazing fire with his powerful angels. He will punish those who do not know God and do not obey the gospel of our Lord Jesus. They will be punished with everlasting destruction and shut out from the presence of the Lord and from the majesty of his power.

We serve a just God. Ultimate justice will be accomplished when Jesus returns and all people are judged according to what they have done, both good and bad. Adolf Hitler will pay for his crimes against humanity, as will Joseph Stalin, Pol Pot, and Joseph Kony, along with all who are responsible for mass murder. Margaret Sanger and Planned Parenthood will also receive justice for the millions of aborted babies who died in their facilities. The child predator who was never caught and the people who work in the sex slave trades will answer to Almighty God. Justice will be served because God is good and righteous. We all want justice, but none of us is without transgression. How then do we survive God's justice? By pursuing what is right and placing our faith in Jesus, trusting him to bridge the gap when we sin and fall short. Hell is real, and the worst thing about it is being shut out for all eternity from the presence of Jesus and the majesty of his power.

PRAYER FOCUS: Lord God, I am glad you are just and that you will be just concerning me. Forgive my sins and help me live according to your commands and principles, because I know you only want what is best for me. Father God, forgive those involved in Planned Parenthood, for they know not what they do. Change their hearts and minds to love your children and care for them.

DID YOU KNOW? Thomas Jefferson wrote the following comments about slavery and justice in his book *Notes on the State of Virginia:* "And can the liberties of a nation be thought secure when we have removed their only firm basis, a conviction in the minds of the people that these liberties are of the gift of God? That they are not to be violated but with his wrath? Indeed, I tremble for my country when I reflect that God is just; that His justice cannot sleep forever."[7] Have we in this country lost the fear of God?

REFLECTIONS

JUNE 14

Judges 13:2-5 NASB

There was a certain man of Zorah, of the family of the Danites, whose name was Manoah; and his wife was barren and had borne no children. Then the angel of the LORD appeared to the woman and said to her, 'Behold now, you are barren and have borne no children, but you shall conceive and give birth to a son. Now therefore, be careful not to drink wine or strong drink, nor eat any unclean thing. For behold, you shall conceive and give birth to a son, and no razor shall come upon his head, for the boy shall be a Nazirite to God from the womb; and he shall begin to deliver Israel from the hands of the Philistines.

This account of Samson's conception and birth clearly demonstrates that God is the creator and giver of life in the womb. God knew Samson's calling, gender, and the exact time of his conception, development in the womb, and birth. The Lord also clearly healed and reversed whatever was causing Samson's mother to be infertile. God sent Samson to deliver the Israelites from Philistine captivity. According to Judges 10:6-8, the Israelites were in captivity because they refused to serve the Lord and instead had served the pagan gods of Baal, Ashtaroth, and several other false gods. It's worth noting that the worship of Baal and Molech, the god of the people of Ammon, often involved child sacrifice (Lev. 18:21; Jer. 19:4-5). Sadly, Samson did not achieve his full potential because he failed to keep his way pure and fulfill the Nazirite vow. God still used Samson in spite of his sins, but Samson could have achieved greatness if he had followed the commands of God more completely.

PRAYER FOCUS: Lord, forgive us for being unconcerned about the plight of our brothers and sisters in the womb. Help me to discern who my enemies are and don't let me be lulled to sleep by their rhetoric and lies. Holy Spirit, keep me from giving my strength to worldly passions and sin.

DID YOU KNOW? By the twenty-fourth week of gestation, a baby's eyebrows appear and all the components of the eye are developed.[8] Only God could make our complex eyes.

REFLECTIONS

JUNE
15

Jonah 2:8 NIV

Those who cling to worthless idols forfeit the grace that could be theirs.

∞

Jesus is the only road to salvation. Though we can look for love and fulfillment in many directions, only Jesus Christ can meet our deepest needs and deliver us from the power of sin. Have we walked down many roads, only to discover a dead end? Drugs, sexual pleasures, materialism, fame, and escapism will never satisfy the soul. In the end they will be found temporary and eternally worthless. Why should we spend our lives pursuing one sexual encounter after another, never tasting true intimacy and the commitment of authentic love in marriage? Why spend our days clouded by chemicals, failing to experience, with clarity of mind, the beauty of the world or the depth of the soul? Why spend all of our available time and energy accumulating wealth and possessions, only to discover we can't buy the things that really matter? Why give in to fear and abortion, cheating ourselves out of a loving relationship filled with joy and wonder? God can miraculously provide for us and our children. Life on earth is short, and what a tragedy it would be for us to realize too late that our pursuit of worthless idols has caused us to forfeit the grace of God. Jesus will give us more than we can imagine when we place our trust in him. And when we do place our trust in him we discover that "God will meet all your needs according to his glorious riches in Christ Jesus" (Phil. 4:19 NIV).

PRAYER FOCUS: God, I choose life today! Help me throw off any hindrances and the sins that so easily entangle me as I run towards you; let me fix my eyes on you as the author and perfecter of my faith (Heb. 12:1-2). Increase my hope and peace each day as I look to you.

DID YOU KNOW? Jonah spent three days and nights in the belly of a whale before he prayed to the Lord for deliverance (Jonah 1:17; 2:1-2). We all sin and make poor decisions. But our sins and poor decisions do not have to be the end of the story. We can repent and ask God to give us another chance.

REFLECTIONS

JUNE 16

Psalm 150 ESV

Praise the LORD! Praise God in his sanctuary; praise him in his mighty heavens! Praise him for his mighty deeds; praise him according to his excellent greatness! Praise him with trumpet sound; praise him with lute and harp! Praise him with tambourine and dance; praise him with strings and pipe! Praise him with sounding cymbals; praise him with loud clashing cymbals! Let everything that has breath praise the LORD! Praise the LORD!

Any one of us can experience greater intimacy with the Lord. We can all draw closer to the Lord through praise, deepening our fellowship with him. God inhabits the praises of his people (Ps. 22:3; 148:13-14; Matt. 18:20), so we may always worship him with song and thanksgiving, with our whole body and soul. And as we do, the Lord will minister to our hearts and minds, flooding our souls with his presence. Let all creation praise the Maker of the universe! There is none like the Lord God; he is the Bright Morning Star, the Beginning and the End. The great God of our fathers who was, and is, and is to come! Let us praise him because his works are wonderful. Let us praise him because he made us, gives us children, blesses our marriages, and because he loves us so much. Worthy is the Lamb.

PRAYER FOCUS: Almighty God, loving Father, Prince of Peace, you alone are worthy of praise! You are the source of life, and "every good gift and every perfect gift is from above, coming down from the Father of lights with whom there is no variation or shadow due to change" (James 1:17 ESV). Mighty God, nothing compares with you. Thank you for my life, breath, shelter, clothes, food, family, friends, and faith. Draw near to me, God, as I draw near to you (James 4:8).

DID YOU KNOW? The Hebrew title for the book of Psalms is *Sepher Tehillim*, which means "Book of Praises."[9]

REFLECTIONS

JUNE 17

Joel 1:2-3 ESV

Hear this, you elders; give ear, all inhabitants of the land! Has such a thing happened in your days, or in the days of your fathers? Tell your children of it, and let your children tell their children, and their children to another generation.

The prophet Joel is astounded by God's judgment upon the land. A swarm of locusts had destroyed all the vegetation of Judah. He calls on all people to never forget both the plague and the behavior that brought it forth. Joel the seer goes on to make a passionate plea for repentance by the whole nation, from its priests to its nursing babes. Joel understood it wasn't just his current generation that needed to remember the horror, but future generations as well. I wonder how Joel would react to the modern-day horror of abortion. He might well say, "Has such a thing happened in your days, or the days of your fathers? Tell your children who survive about it, and let them tell their children who survive, and their children who survive to another generation." What sort of devastation will we incur for the slaughter of nearly a quarter of the babies conceived each year in the United States of America?

PRAYER FOCUS: Lord Jesus, bring us to our senses and help us see the devastation on the horizon. Lord, forgive your church and the world for aborting babies. Jesus, give us the courage and the desire to repent. Allow us to take back the territory we have abdicated through our involvement with abortion.

DID YOU KNOW? The word *elders* in today's Scripture probably refers to the oldest and potentially wisest among the people.[10] We would do well to listen to the counsel of those who have seen our culture both before and after legalized abortion. "Remember the days of old; consider the years of many generations; ask your father, and he will show you, your elders, and they will tell you" (Deut. 32:7 ESV). Sadly, with a larger aging population due to birth control and abortion, it may not be long before our elders experience compulsory euthanasia.

REFLECTIONS

JUNE 18

2 John 5-6 HCSB

So now I urge you, dear lady—not as if I were writing you a new command, but one we have had from the beginning—that we love one another. And this is love: that we walk according to His commands. This is the command as you have heard it from the beginning: you must walk in love.

To love is to be like Jesus. To love is to do the Father's will and obey heaven's commands. To walk in love is to manifest what love is. Love is patient, kind, not envious, not boastful or conceited, not selfish, keeps no record of wrongs, is saddened by unrighteousness, rejoices in the truth, bears all things, believes, hopes, endures, never ends, and lays down its life (1 Cor. 13; 1 John 4:7-11). How then can abortion ever be the loving thing to do? Abortion isn't patient, it's hurried. Abortion isn't kind, it's cruel. Abortion is envious of those who fooled around and didn't suffer an unexpected pregnancy. Abortion boasts in a fundamental right to choose. Abortion puts one's self-will over the baby's. Abortion believes the baby is a punishment, a violation of one's body. Abortion is unconcerned with righteousness. Abortion exists on a lie and excludes the truth. Abortion won't bear the nine months of pregnancy. Abortion believes this is the best option for preserving personal freedom. Abortion hopes no one finds out. Abortion seeks not to endure, only to find that the act of abortion is hardly endurable. Abortion ends the life of a child. Abortion lays down the life of another!

PRAYER FOCUS: Jesus, I'm hurting over my abortion, please help me forgive myself and my partner. Lord, be gracious to me, the work of your own hands (Ps. 138:6-8). Be patient with me and kind to me. Jesus, show me that upon forgiveness you keep no record of my wrongs. Heal me, Lord, and fill me with hope as you make me new. Comfort me with the knowledge that I will be reunited with my child in heaven.

DID YOU KNOW? Post-abortion syndrome **(PAS)** can be experienced instantly by an individual or manifest years after an abortion. If you are struggling with the following symptoms, you may suffer from PAS. Symptoms include eating and sleeping disorders, panic attacks, depression, suicidal thoughts, anger, relational problems, sexual dysfunction, substance abuse, guilt, alienation, trouble bonding, reduced intimacy, low self-esteem, anxiety, feeling unforgivable, or helpless.[11] If this describes you, seek out help from your local pregnancy center or church, and know that God loves you. Meditate on these verses: Psalm 30:11-12; 68:19-20; 103:11-12; 130; 147:3; Micah 7:18-19; Romans 8, especially verses 1 and 31-39; 1 Peter 2:24; 5:7; and Jude 24-25. The following organizations can assist you: Ramah International, 941-473-2188, *www.ramahinternational.org*; Care Net, 1-800-395-HELP, *www.optionline.org*.

JUNE 19

Psalm 103:8-12 HCSB

The LORD is compassionate and gracious, slow to anger and rich in faithful love. He will not always accuse us or be angry forever. He has not dealt with us as our sins deserve or repaid us according to our offenses. For as high as the heavens are above the earth, so great is His faithful love toward those who fear Him. As far as the east is from the west, so far has He removed our transgressions from us.

God knows all our sins and weaknesses and yet he loves us. We can confess our sins to him for he is longing to forgive us. His love restores us. God is slow to anger, and when he is angry, it doesn't last for long. Jesus came to bear our sins. He didn't come to punish us according to what we deserve, but rather to absorb the punishment for us. He loves us! This is why he instructs us to live in his counsel, because his wisdom protects and blesses us. Despite our sins, we are still the object of the Lord's affections. Our burdens and failures should be given over to the Lord because he cares for us. As the psalmist has said, "Cast your burden on the Lord, and He will sustain you; He will never allow the righteous to be shaken" (Ps. 55:22 HCSB). When we trust God with our past we will discover how far he removes our sins from the present.

PRAYER FOCUS: Lord, I give you my sins today. Nail them to the cross and liberate me from their memory. I give you all that I am and all that I can be. Make me a new creature in Christ Jesus (2 Cor. 5:17) and cleanse me and create a new spirit within me (Ezek. 36:26-27; Ps. 51:9-11).

DID YOU KNOW? David wrote the fifty-first psalm after committing adultery with Bathsheba and arranging for the certain death of her husband in battle.[12] Yet David knew God intimately, and he knew the value of confession and repentance.

REFLECTIONS

JUNE
20

Isaiah 61:1-4 NKJV

The Spirit of the Lord God is upon Me, because the LORD has anointed Me to preach good tidings to the poor; He has sent Me to heal the brokenhearted, to proclaim liberty to the captives, and the opening of the prison to those who are bound; to proclaim the acceptable year of the LORD, and the day of vengeance of our God; to comfort all who mourn, to console those who mourn in Zion, to give them beauty for ashes, the oil of joy for mourning, the garment of praise for the spirit of heaviness; that they may be called trees of righteousness, the planting of the LORD, that He may be glorified. And they shall rebuild the old ruins, they shall raise up the former desolations, and they shall repair the ruined cities, the desolations of many generations.

Jesus read these words of Isaiah to the men in the Nazareth synagogue, recorded in the gospel of Luke (4:16-21). What better description of his ministry could be given than that Jesus was anointed to preach good tidings, to heal the brokenhearted, to proclaim liberty and the acceptable year of the Lord? His ministry was to the poor, to those caught in despair, and to those crushed in spirit. Jesus liberated all of us from sin and death. With a word, he delivered those who were in bondage and shackled by sin. He proclaimed boldly that the kingdom of God had come, and he talked of his return. He comforted the sick, the sad, the grief-stricken, and the lonely. Jesus gave everyone hope instead of hopelessness, joy instead of despair, and inspiration instead of discouragement. Perhaps the greatest thing about the Lord's ministry was not what Jesus did for people, but how he transformed them. Those who met the Messiah went on to rebuild, repair, and restore what had been lost. Have we been transformed by Jesus? It's not too late to reach out to him and be changed by the Master.

PRAYER FOCUS: Jesus, I want to exchange ashes for beauty and mourning for joy. I want to explode in praise as you lift my heaviness. Water the desert areas of my life and replenish the desolation of my soul. Make me into a force for good in my generation.

DID YOU KNOW? The name "Isaiah" literally means "Yahweh Is Salvation." The *Spirit-Filled Life Bible*, NKJV, wrote this in the introduction to Isaiah, "The Book of Isaiah is directly quoted twenty-one times in the New Testament and attributed in each case to the prophet Isaiah."[13]

REFLECTIONS

JUNE 21

Ezra 4:4-5 ESV

Then the people of the land discouraged the people of Judah and made them afraid to build and bribed counselors against them to frustrate their purpose, all the days of Cyrus king of Persia, even until the reign of Darius king of Persia.

Those of us who have gone down to pray or rescue at abortion facilities know there is opposition and discouragement from the people of the land. We are glared at, intimidated, and cursed. As unpleasant as this is, our biggest obstacle is found in the pro-abortion groups that lobby Washington and our state governments. These groups bribe our representatives with millions of dollars to impact policy and gain a favorable climate for abortion. Opposition always comes when treading on enemy territory. We need to be patient, strong, and courageous, never giving in to intimidation or fear. Our cause is just and our Lord is able to give us the victory. Remember what the apostle Paul told us: "Let us not grow weary of doing good, for in due season we will reap, if we do not give up" (Gal. 6:9 ESV). Despite the opposition they faced, and besides getting sidetracked by their personal affairs, the people of Judah ultimately rebuilt the temple—with the Lord's help.

PRAYER FOCUS: Lord, help me stand my ground in the midst of discouragement and attacks. Keep me focused on the task at hand and the high stakes of not remaining vigilant. Help us in the battle, Lord, for we have few resources and at times very little strength. Do not let our enemies triumph over us.

DID YOU KNOW? Based on the dates of King Cyrus' rule and King Darius' rule, it is estimated that the people of Judah were opposed for about twenty years.[14] The pro-life effort has been frustrated for more than double this amount of time. Still, the greatest hindrance to our movement may not be the opposition, but the blindness and the apathy of the church.

REFLECTIONS

JUNE 22

Ruth 2:11-12 NASB

Boaz replied to her, "All that you have done for your mother-in-law after the death of your husband has been fully reported to me, and how you left your father and your mother and the land of your birth, and came to a people that you did not previously know. May the Lord reward your work, and your wages be full from the Lord, the God of Israel, under whose wings you have come to seek refuge."

God is pleased when we reach beyond ourselves and our circumstances to help others. After the death of her husband, Ruth could have wallowed in her own grief and returned home with her sister-in-law. Instead, she chose to honor her husband and take care of his mother. Leaving behind what was familiar, she took a chance on loving her neighbor and a people yet unknown. As Ruth loved, she in turn was loved and discovered a new fulfillment among the people she served. The Lord rewards those who follow in his footsteps and love others. Ruth's faithful service led to her marriage to Boaz, honor among God's people, and the conception of a son who turned out to be the grandfather of King David.

PRAYER FOCUS: Lord, I thank you that no matter what I face, it's not the end of the story. You, O Lord, can do more than I think is possible or imagine (Eph. 3:20). Jesus, help me place you and your people first, trusting you to care for my needs. I am excited about the good you can bring out of my circumstances.

DID YOU KNOW? The name Ruth means "friendship."[15] Appreciate your friends today, for they are gifts from God! I hope you will always be friendly to others and enjoy many friendships.

REFLECTIONS

JUNE 23

1 Kings 10:9 HCSB

May Yahweh your God be praised! He delighted in you and put you on the throne of Israel, because of the LORD's eternal love for Israel. He has made you king to carry out justice and righteousness.

When she visited King Solomon, the queen of Sheba said, "May Yahweh your God be praised!" The Bible tells us that Solomon was the wisest man on earth (1 Kings 4:29-34). God gave Solomon the gift of wisdom and discernment, and the queen correctly perceived that he had been raised to the ultimate position of authority to bless the people. God wanted his people to have the best available wisdom and understanding in government because he loved them and desired good things for them. Thus, God powerfully equipped their king for service. For a leader to serve God well, he must conduct his affairs with integrity and maintain justice for all the people. A king's primary responsibility is to set righteous standards and implement them with justice. Jesus, the ultimate King, will, out of his eternal love, carry out justice for all people when he returns in his glorious righteousness.

PRAYER FOCUS: Lord, I ask you to bless our president and his cabinet. Grant them wisdom and the courage to do what is best for their people. If they are not following you and protecting the sanctity of human life, change their hearts and transform their minds so they can clearly see the humanity of the preborn. God, raise up government leaders who will make it their personal mission to restore personhood to the preborn and grant them equal protection under the law.

DID YOU KNOW? American presidents have a long history of calling on God for guidance and direction in leading our nation. During his inaugural address, Dwight D. Eisenhower prayed, "Almighty God . . . Give us, we pray, the power to discern clearly right from wrong, and allow all our words and actions to be governed thereby, and by the laws of this land. Especially we pray that our concern shall be for all the people regardless of station, race, or calling."[16]

REFLECTIONS

JUNE 24

2 Kings 18:5-7 NIV

Hezekiah trusted in the Lord, the God of Israel. There was no one like him among all the kings of Judah, either before him or after him. He held fast to the Lord and did not cease to follow him; he kept the commands the Lord had given Moses. And the Lord was with him; he was successful in whatever he undertook.

What was the key to Hezekiah's success? What made him stand out from all the kings of Judah? Hezekiah trusted in the Lord, the God of Israel. He was diligent in following the Lord and never ceased trusting Almighty God. Hezekiah based his leadership on the commands of Scripture, giving his government a firm foundation. God's commands are not intended to restrict our freedom or burden us but are put in place for our benefit and betterment. If we will yield to the Lord and follow his ways, we will be blessed in whatever we do. The key to success in leadership or anything else is following God. When we apply the wisdom of God to our finances, relationships, marriages, businesses, child-rearing, or whatever, we will succeed. Following God allows us to live our best possible life now and enjoy a remarkably joy-filled eternity.

PRAYER FOCUS: God, I desire to walk in your ways and follow your commands. Teach me how to walk in obedience, and help me understand that your desire is to bless me and your way of living is best for me. Keep me from temptation and grant me the wisdom to consult you and your Word before I take action.

DID YOU KNOW? Hezekiah succeeded in prolonging his earthly life and reign. Because of his obedience, he curried great favor with God—so much so that when Hezekiah was on his deathbed, he asked for healing, and the Lord granted his request (2 Kings 20:1-6).

REFLECTIONS

JUNE 25

2 Peter 1:16-21 NASB

For we did not follow cleverly devised tales when we made known to you the power and coming of our Lord Jesus Christ, but we were eyewitnesses of His majesty. For when He received honor and glory from God the Father, such an utterance as this was made to Him by the Majestic Glory, 'This is My beloved Son with whom I am well-pleased'—and we ourselves heard this utterance made from heaven when we were with Him on the holy mountain. So we have the prophetic word made more sure, to which you do well to pay attention as to a lamp shining in a dark place, until the day dawns and the morning star arises in your hearts. But know this first of all, that no prophecy of Scripture is a matter of one's own interpretation, for no prophecy was ever made by an act of human will, but men moved by the Holy Spirit spoke from God.

In his second letter, Peter tells us that we can trust the Bible to be the authoritative Word of God. The New Testament is not a collection of fairy tales or clever stories, but the result of eyewitness testimony and personal experience with Jesus. When the Holy Spirit descended on the apostles during the Day of Pentecost, he brought all things to their remembrance (Acts 1:1-8, 12-14; 2; John 14:25-26; 16:7-15). Likewise, Peter affirms that the Old Testament and its prophecies were the direct result of the Holy Spirit and not the intentions of men. Even though the Bible was penned by many authors, it was written by One God, and we can confidently place our trust in it. Many critics of the Bible get tripped up on the supernatural elements of the book because they do not approach it with faith. As Paul said, "A natural man does not accept the things of the Spirit of God, for they are foolishness to him; and he cannot understand them, because they are spiritually appraised" (1 Cor. 2:14 NASB). Believing is seeing. When one understands that God created the universe and all things, it is not difficult to believe he could part the Red Sea, raise the dead, sustain a man in the belly of a whale, or load two of every animal on an ark.

PRAYER FOCUS: God, fill me with your Holy Spirit and blow afresh on me all truth. Lead me by your Word and increase my ability to perceive its treasure.

DID YOU KNOW? Peter's name means "rock,"[17] but even Peter looked to the Rock of Ages (Deut. 32:4, 18; Ps. 61:2; 95:1; Isa. 26:4; Rom. 9:33)!

REFLECTIONS

JUNE 26

Hosea 4:1-3 ESV

Hear the word of the Lord, O children of Israel, for the Lord has a controversy with the inhabitants of the land. There is no faithfulness or steadfast love, and no knowledge of God in the land; there is swearing, lying, murder, stealing, and committing adultery; they break all bounds, and bloodshed follows bloodshed. Therefore, the land mourns, and all who dwell in it languish, and also the beasts of the field and the birds of the heavens, and even the fish of the sea are taken away.

∞

The more things change, the more they stay the same. Every generation deals with disobedience and sin, but when the sins of the people reach an apex, the land begins to mourn. Human sin can have a dramatic effect on the rest of God's creation. Our disobedience and poor stewardship can lead to crop devastation, ecological difficulties, and species extinction. Regrettably, all the sins listed in God's charge are occurring with increasing frequency in America today. Just look at our overcrowded prisons, frequent lawsuits, corporate corruption, divorces, drug trafficking, and abortion, not to mention the increasing immorality depicted in our movies and television shows. What is the remedy to this problem? The remedy lies in our knowledge of God, steadfast love, and faithfulness. Will we live out the call to love God and our neighbor? If we will return to God, love his people, and remain faithful to his commands, we can save our children and our land!

PRAYER FOCUS: God, increase our reverence for you and help us treat everything you have made with love and respect. Stir our spirits to return to you before the collective weight of our sin is so great that everything in the land suffers.

DID YOU KNOW? A typical twenty-six-week-old fetus is around nine to ten inches in length and weighs just over two pounds. Peter Tallack wrote, "By week twenty-six, the baby's parents may get a pleasant surprise: It is now possible to hear her heartbeat just by putting an ear to the mother's abdomen."[18]

REFLECTIONS

JUNE 27

2 Corinthians 4:17-18 NKJV

For our light affliction, which is but for a moment, is working for us a far more exceeding and eternal weight of glory, while we do not look at the things which are seen, but at the things which are not seen. For the things which are seen are temporary, but the things which are not seen are eternal.

Paul was able to look past his current afflictions and hardships to the eternal weight of glory—the purpose and reward for his struggle. Paul knew that the "now" is only for a moment, a temporary stop in a greater journey. He also knew the things one does with God and for the good of people is all that will matter in eternity. Where is our mindset today? Is it on the cares of this world—our finances, health, and career—or is it on the things of God? There is only one way to transcend our circumstances, and that is to surrender to God and live for his glory and the betterment of our fellow human beings. For the things that can afflict us, things like our unpaid mortgage, job loss, and divorce, are only temporary, but God and the people he has made are eternal.

PRAYER FOCUS: O Eternal God, from everlasting to everlasting, please rekindle afresh eternity in my heart. I know you have "made everything beautiful in its time," and that you have "put eternity in their hearts . . . I know that nothing is better for them than to rejoice, and to do good in their lives" (Eccles. 3:11-12 NKJV). Give me eyes to see the unseen and look past the giants in the land. Teach me to walk as I take the first step toward loving you and your people.

DID YOU KNOW? The child in the womb, whom you cannot see, is just as eternal as you and me. Every day God welcomes home thousands of aborted children. One wonders what is said between Creator and child. Conceivably, the Almighty could say, "Welcome home, my child. I'm sorry your earthly life was cut short, but I'm so glad you are here with me."

REFLECTIONS

JUNE 28

Psalm 71:5-6, 17-18 ESV

For you, O Lord, are my hope, my trust, O LORD, from my youth. Upon you I have leaned from before my birth; you are he who took me from my mother's womb. My praise is continually of you. . . . O God, from my youth you have taught me, and I still proclaim your wondrous deeds. So even to old age and gray hairs, O God, do not forsake me, until I proclaim your might to another generation, your power to all those to come.

Have we trusted Christ from our youth? Have we learned from him and do we still proclaim his wondrous deeds? If so, God has granted us a privileged position in the Kingdom. Our job yesterday, today, and tomorrow is to remain steadfast to what we have been taught and declare it to others. God desires to use every person's story as a witness, not just the stories of those who have been radically changed. There is great power in the testimony of a reformed drug addict, or a homosexual who found victory in Christ, but there is also great power in a life of faith born early and continued throughout the challenges of a human life span. God wants to use our steadfast faith to impact and encourage the next generation. In every stage or season of life, God has a plan and a purpose for our lives. He wants us to impact people by our good works and lead them to the Father. God's love for each one of us has never waned from before we were born to our old age. It has always been constant, and it will always be constant. Praise him for his good deeds and his wonderful love towards us!

PRAYER FOCUS: God, I am thankful that you are always with me. Show me that my age is not a determiner of my effectiveness or worth. Lord, use me when I am young and when I am old. Give me the strength to remain faithful and do your will.

DID YOU KNOW? Fanny Crosby, the famous Christian hymnist who wrote over eight thousand hymns, lived to be ninety-four years old.[19] Fanny was blinded shortly after birth, and from her youth until old age grew in the counsel of God. Three of her best known hymns are "Blessed Assurance," "To God be the Glory," and "Safe in the Arms of Jesus." Truly, Jesus was her story and her song, and she praised her Savior all the day long!

REFLECTIONS

JUNE 29

Genesis 20:17-18 HCSB

Then Abraham prayed to God, and God healed Abimelech, his wife, and his female slaves so that they could bear children, for the LORD had completely closed all the wombs in Abimelech's household on account of Sarah, Abraham's wife.

The twentieth chapter of the book of Genesis provides us with great proof that God is in direct control of reproduction. Abraham's and Sarah's encounter with Abimelech, king of Gerar, tell us much about God's dominion over life in the womb. Abraham said, "There is absolutely no fear of God in this place. They will kill me because of my wife" (Gen. 20:11 HCSB). Abraham was afraid that the native people would kill him if they knew Sarah was his wife, and then they would take her for their own. So while he introduced Sarah as his sister, he convinced Sarah to refer to him as her brother. When Abimelech noticed the beauty of Sarah, he sent for her and made her his wife. God, however, intended to bring the promised seed through Abraham and Sarah with the birth of Isaac. Therefore, as a precaution, the Lord rendered infertile the entire house of Abimelech, as well as Abimelech himself, so that his line would end if he did not obey God. God then visited Abimelech in a dream and told him about Sarah's real identity and how to set things right, which included returning Sarah to Abraham (Gen. 20:4-7). These verses make it clear that God is in direct control of fertility, conception, and life in the womb.

PRAYER FOCUS: God, thank you for being in control and for not allowing your plans to be thwarted by the fears and foolishness of your people. Lord, teach me to submit to your plan for my family, whether it is adoption, eventual conception, marriage without children, or the single life (1 Cor. 7:8-9).

DID YOU KNOW? Abraham and Sarah (Gen. 17:15-21), Jacob and Rachel (Gen. 30:22-24), Elkanah and Hannah (1 Sam. 1:5-20), and Zechariah and Elizabeth (Luke 1:7-16) all had trouble with fertility. If you are having trouble conceiving, study these stories and ask God to reveal to you his will for your family. Pray that he will give you direction, patience, and his peace, as you discover his will.

REFLECTIONS

JUNE 30

Philippians 2:3-11 NASB

Do nothing from selfishness or empty conceit, but with humility of mind regard one another as more important than yourselves; do not merely look out for your own personal interests, but also for the interests of others. Have this attitude in yourselves which was also in Christ Jesus, who, although He existed in the form of God, did not regard equality with God a thing to be grasped, but emptied Himself, taking the form of a bond-servant, and being made in the likeness of men. Being found in appearance as a man, He humbled Himself by becoming obedient to the point of death, even death on a cross. For this reason also, God highly exalted Him, and bestowed on Him the name which is above every name, so that at the name of Jesus every knee will bow, of those who are in heaven and on earth and under the earth, and that every tongue will confess that Jesus Christ is Lord, to the glory of God the Father.

Jesus is our great example in all things, but especially in the area of humility. The God of the universe humbled himself by becoming a man in order to pay the price for human sin. His sacrifice alone reconciled sinful men and women to the Father. Jesus was humble and selfless to the point of ultimate sacrificial love, enduring unjust punishment and a cruel death on a cross. While admitting that none of us will ever be equal with Christ, we need to strive to imitate him in our thoughts, words, and actions. We need to treat our brothers and sisters as better than ourselves, and put their needs ahead of our own. Humility, like so many virtues, is a process one grows in. My life has had its fair share of selfishness, pride, and the pursuit of personal welfare. But God has been abundantly gracious to me as I have journeyed towards becoming more humble and less self-focused. Find a way to serve others, and God will gradually transform your life from a self-focused perspective to a God-focused and others-focused perspective.

PRAYER FOCUS: God, I confess that Jesus Christ is Lord for your glory. I thank you, Father, that Jesus was so humble and loving that he willingly gave up the throne to die for me. I am mystified by your goodness and grace. Lord, be patient with me as I grow in humility. Teach me how to become more like you.

DID YOU KNOW? Scripture says "the man Moses was very humble, more than any man who was on the face of the earth" (Num. 12:3 NASB).

REFLECTIONS

_____

_____

_____

_____

_____

_____

_____

_____

July

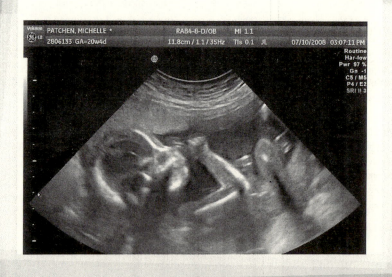

TWENTY-FOUR WEEKS GESTATION

JULY 1

Acts 3:2-6 NKJV

And a certain man lame from his mother's womb was carried, whom they laid daily at the gate of the temple which is called Beautiful, to ask alms from those who entered the temple; who, seeing Peter and John about to go into the temple, asked for alms. And fixing his eyes on him, with John, Peter said, "Look at us." So he gave them his attention, expecting to receive something from them. Then Peter said, "Silver and gold I do not have, but what I do have I give you: In the name of Jesus Christ of Nazareth, rise up and walk."

It is not always easy to see past our circumstances and trust God. Concerning the man at the temple gate, what good can come from a life of disability and begging? For starters, healing and the glorification of God, followed by the salvation faith of many people who were affected by the word and the sight of this healing testimony. Acts 4:4 says that "many of those who heard the word believed; and the number of the men came to be about five thousand" (NKJV). The disabled man also provided an opportunity for the apostles to demonstrate the love of God by reaching out to a neighbor and helping the weak. Forty years of disability led to the eternal salvation and healing of many men (Acts 4:22). Often we don't know why God allows certain hardships, but we can always trust his plan and believe he knows best (John 9:1-23; Acts 14:8-17). And we know that "all things work together for good to those who love God, to those who are the called according to His purpose" (Rom. 8:28 NKJV) and in God's good timing. We must never believe that because a person is disabled in the womb that their life is without purpose or meaning. God knows how they were formed and he intends it for good.

PRAYER FOCUS: God, teach us to see what you see and grant us an eternal perspective in the midst of difficult times. Lord, give us grace in our disappointment and keep our hearts open to your counsel. Teach us contentment, and teach us to believe we can do all things through Christ who strengthens us (Phil. 4:11-13).

DID YOU KNOW? The abortion industry preys upon the disabled. In her book *Secret Sin: When God's People Choose Abortion*, Mary Comm wrote, "In America, more than eighty percent of the babies diagnosed prenatally with Down syndrome are aborted."[1]

REFLECTIONS

_____

_____

_____

_____

JULY 2

1 Thessalonians 2:7-8, 11-12 ESV

But we were gentle among you, like a nursing mother taking care of her own children. So, being affectionately desirous of you, we were ready to share with you not only the gospel of God but also our own selves, because you had become very dear to us. . . . For you know how, like a father with his own children, we exhorted each one of you and encouraged you and charged you to walk in a manner worthy of God, who calls you into his own kingdom and glory.

I thank God that I grew up in a home with two loving parents who cared for me and gave me every opportunity to experience the love of Jesus. Though flawed and imperfect, my parents did their best to train me in God's wisdom while providing me with numerous discoveries and adventures. Their hard work, perseverance, and love made me a better person. I would not enjoy the blessings and fulfillment I have today if it were not for their care and sacrifice. The apostle Paul was right to use a family model in describing how he and his fellow missionaries had treated the faithful in Thessalonica. For it is often in the family, in those we are closest to, that we see the love of God and the love of our neighbor displayed. God designed us to love and be loved, and the best training ground for experiencing this is the home.

PRAYER FOCUS: Lord Jesus, I thank you for giving me a mom and a dad who loved me and guided me. Help me to be there for my children and be the best parent I can be. Jesus, I pray you would comfort those who didn't have a good home life. Father, be the parent to them that they never had and show them how to parent from your example.

DID YOU KNOW? Theodore Roosevelt once wrote, "Alone of human beings the good and wise mother stands on a plane of equal honor with the bravest soldier; for she has gladly gone down to the brink of the chasm of darkness to bring back the children in whose hands rests the future of the years."[2]

REFLECTIONS

JULY 3

Psalm 72:18-19 NKJV

Blessed be the LORD God, the God of Israel, who only does wondrous things! And blessed be His glorious name forever! And let the whole earth be filled with His glory. Amen and Amen.

∞

God's glory hovered over the waters at the beginning of creation. It covered Mount Sinai when he delivered the Ten Commandments. It visited Mary and conceived in her a Son. It dripped from a rugged cross at Calvary, and rolled away a stone revealing an empty tomb. God's glory blew through the Upper Room, filling the apostles with the Holy Spirit. One day, God's glory will ride on the clouds to judge the quick and the dead and render justice to all. "The heavens declare the glory of God; and the firmament shows His handiwork" (Ps. 19:1 NKJV). All creation speaks of God's greatness. As one created in his image, I praise the Great Eternal God. Let the whole earth praise him, for one day "at the name of Jesus every knee will bow" and "every tongue will confess that Jesus Christ is Lord, to the glory of God the Father" (Phil. 2:10-11 NASB).

PRAYER FOCUS: "Yahweh, our Lord, how magnificent is Your name throughout the earth! You have covered the heavens with Your majesty" (Ps. 8:1 HCSB). "Who is this King of glory? The Lord, strong and mighty, the Lord, mighty in battle. Lift up your heads, you gates! Rise up, ancient doors! Then the King of glory will come in. Who is He, this King of glory? The Lord of Hosts, He is the King of glory. Selah" (Ps. 24:8-10 HCSB). "May the glory of the Lord endure forever; may the Lord rejoice in His works" (Ps. 104:31 HCSB).

DID YOU KNOW? The *American Heritage Dictionary* defines *glory* as "exalted honor, praise, or distinction accorded by common consent; something that brings honor or renown; a highly praiseworthy asset; adoration, praise, and thanksgiving offered in worship; the splendor and bliss of heaven; a height of achievement."[3]

REFLECTIONS

JULY 4

Psalm 2:10-12 NIV

Therefore, you kings, be wise; be warned, you rulers of the earth. Serve the LORD with fear and rejoice with trembling. Kiss the Son, lest he be angry and you be destroyed in your way, for his wrath can flare up in a moment. Blessed are all who take refuge in him.

Kings, dictators, presidents, premiers, prime ministers, and those in positions of authority would do well to realize whom they serve. For God is the King of kings and Lord of lords. All those who govern should seek the Lord's wisdom in their affairs and conduct themselves with a reverential awe of God. All of us from small to great will give an account to the Lord, but those in positions of authority over people and nations will most certainly be responsible for much more. In the midst of their free will, rulers need to remember who sits on the throne of heaven! Leaders who take refuge in God will be protected, and their people will be blessed.

PRAYER FOCUS: God, it is a great privilege to lead your people. Help me to honor you and govern rightly if I am presented with the opportunity to lead. Lord, bless, protect, guide, and strengthen our leaders and those who serve in public office. May they be men and women of integrity, humility, and grace. Keep them grounded in your Word and your principles.

DID YOU KNOW? John Adams, America's second president, and Thomas Jefferson, America's third president, both died on this day in 1826, fifty years after the signing of the Declaration of Independence. Carved on the mantel in the state dining room is this prayer written by John Adams: "I pray to Heaven to bestow the best of Blessings on this House and all that shall hereafter inhabit it . . . May none but honest and wise men ever rule under this roof."[4]

REFLECTIONS

JULY 5

John 4:13-14 HCSB

Jesus said, "Everyone who drinks from this water will get thirsty again. But whoever drinks from the water that I will give him will never get thirsty again—ever! In fact, the water I will give him will become a well of water springing up within him for eternal life."

∞

Jesus spoke these words to the Samaritan woman at the well. She had been married five different times and was now living with her sixth male companion, who was not her husband. Instead of seeing her as a sinful person who had made bad choices, Jesus saw her as a daughter who needed his indwelling presence. Jesus cared for her and desired that she experience his life-giving Spirit. Jesus' heart's desire is to bless his children and give them abundant life both now and forever. Life is the essence of Christ, and if we are to be like our Lord, we must nourish and protect life, not destroy it. All who have not yet tasted the Water of Life can come and surrender to Jesus.

PRAYER FOCUS: Jesus, you are entirely good and I desire to know you more fully. Give me a hunger and a thirst for a deeper relationship with you. Satisfy my soul with your Word, your Spirit, and your presence. Lord, help us see that life is sacred and meant to be lived with you for all eternity.

DID YOU KNOW? In his book *The Righteous: The Unsung Heroes of the Holocaust,* author Martin Gilbert tells the stories of those extraordinary beautiful souls who helped hide and recue Jews during that horrific time. The following excerpt is part of an account given by David Prital concerning a Ukrainian Baptist who helped him: "With tears in his eyes, he comforted me and he invited me to his house. Together we entered his house and I understood instantly that I had met a wonderful person. 'God brought an important guest to our house,' he said to his wife. 'We should thank God for this blessing.' They kneeled down and I heard a wonderful prayer coming out of their pure and simple hearts, not written in a single prayer book. I heard a song addressed to God, thanking God for the opportunity to meet a son of Israel in these crazy days. They asked God to help those who managed to stay alive hiding in the fields and in the woods. Was it a dream? Was it possible that such people still existed in the world? They stopped praying and we sat down at the table for a meal, which was enjoyable. Before the meal, the master of the house read a chapter from the Bible. Here it is, I thought, this is the big secret. It is this eternal book that raised their morality to such unbelievable heights. It is this very book that filled their hearts with love for the Jews."[5] Obviously, the water that sprang forth from these Ukrainian peasants was the Water of Life!

JULY 6

2 Chronicles 20:12-17 NASB

"O our God, will You not judge them? For we are powerless before this great multitude who are coming against us; nor do we know what to do, but our eyes are on You." All Judah was standing before the LORD, with their infants, their wives and their children. Then in the midst of the assembly the Spirit of the LORD came upon Jahaziel the son of Zechariah . . . and he said, "Listen, all Judah and the inhabitants of Jerusalem and King Jehoshaphat: thus says the LORD to you, 'Do not fear or be dismayed because of this great multitude, for the battle is not yours but God's. Tomorrow go down against them. Behold, they will come up by the ascent of Ziz, and you will find them at the end of the valley in front of the wilderness of Jeruel. You need not fight in this battle; station yourselves, stand and see the salvation of the LORD on your behalf, O Judah and Jerusalem.' Do not fear or be dismayed; tomorrow go out to face them, for the LORD is with you."

Jehoshaphat and the people of Judah were facing imminent attack from a multitude of enemies. A report came to Jehoshaphat that "a great multitude is coming against you from beyond the sea" (2 Chron. 20:1-2 NASB). King Jehoshaphat, looking at sure destruction, cried out to the Lord with prayer and fasting. He called a national fast and prayed before the assembly of Judah (20:3-10). After the Lord spoke through Jahaziel, Jehoshaphat and the whole nation praised the Lord before, during, and after the battle (20:18-23, 27-29). Just like the people of Judah, we need to realize that the battle to abolish abortion belongs to the Lord! God will provide mighty victories and deliverances when we corporately fast, pray, and praise. If we will humble ourselves, ask for the victory, and praise God, we will see this atrocity of abortion fall. Many groups, like 40 Days for Life and Bound for Life, are already answering God's call to pray and fast for the ending of abortion. It is time for the men, women, children, and infants of the church to join these groups in this pursuit. When the church is united, abortion will collapse!

PRAYER FOCUS: God, unite the body of Christ in the purpose of putting an end to abortion. Help us attain equal protection for the preborn. Lord, teach us how to corporately fast, pray, and praise effectively. Do not let the enemy triumph over you or your church!

DID YOU KNOW? James W. Goll has written an insightful book about intercessory prayer inspired by the Moravian prayer movement of the eighteenth and nineteenth centuries. Read *The Lost Art of Intercession* and apply Goll's teaching to your prayer efforts.

REFLECTIONS

JULY 7

Romans 8:31-39 NKJV

If God is for us, who can be against us? He who did not spare His own Son, but delivered Him up for us all, how shall He not with Him also freely give us all things? Who shall bring a charge against God's elect? It is God who justifies. Who is he who condemns? It is Christ who died, and furthermore is also risen, who is even at the right hand of God, who also makes intercession for us. Who shall separate us from the love of Christ? Shall tribulation, or distress, or persecution, or famine, or nakedness, or peril, or sword? As it is written: "For Your sake we are killed all day long; we are accounted as sheep for the slaughter." Yet in all these things we are more than conquerors through Him who loved us. For I am persuaded that neither death nor life, nor angels nor principalities nor powers, nor things present nor things to come, nor height nor depth, nor any other created thing, shall be able to separate us from the love of God which is in Christ Jesus our Lord.

Hallelujah! What security we have in Jesus. This Bible passage, more than any other, has been a comfort to me over the years. In times of sin and discouragement, despair and loneliness, loss and failure, and joy and prosperity, the love of Christ and its eternal unquenchable flame has arrested my heart. In all of life's trials and tribulations, I am more than a conqueror because Christ Jesus loved me and gave himself as a ransom for my life. I praise you, Almighty God, because you loved me and my neighbors before any of us loved you. The Spirit and the bride say, "'Come!' And let him who hears say, 'Come!' And let him who thirsts come. Whoever desires, let him take the water of life freely" (Rev. 22:17 NKJV). Taste and see the goodness of God in the land of the living.

PRAYER FOCUS: Holy Anointed One, I praise you because of your gifts to me. "Oh, give thanks to the Lord, for He is good! For His mercy endures forever. Let the redeemed of the Lord say so, whom He has redeemed from the hand of the enemy" (Ps. 107:1-2 NKJV). Jesus, bathe me in your love that is beyond measure and without limit.

DID YOU KNOW? The forty-three verses in Psalm 107 speak powerfully about deliverance. Read the psalm and give thanks for the goodness and loving-kindness of the Lord. For anyone having trouble believing God can forgive them for their sins, C. H. Spurgeon's *All of Grace* is must reading. In it he wrote, "The Law is for the self-righteous, to humble their pride; the Gospel is for the lost, to remove their despair."[6]

REFLECTIONS

JULY 8

Galatians 5:14 HCSB

For the entire law is fulfilled in one statement: Love your neighbor as yourself.

Love manifests itself internally and as a result creates a self-directed life of obedience. Love writes its laws on one's heart (John 15:3-17; Rom. 10:3-12). Love does not harm its neighbor, but considers others better than one's self. If we love our neighbor, we won't steal from him. If we love our neighbor, we won't seduce his wife or her husband. If we love our neighbor, we won't cheat them in business. If we love our neighbor, we won't abort our child. The extent we are consumed by God's love will be the extent we love others. Love, and we will be loved; forgive, and we will be forgiven. Give, and it will be given unto us. Jesus said, "Don't assume that I came to destroy the Law or the Prophets. I did not come to destroy but to fulfill" (Matt. 5:17 HCSB). Christ's love did just that. Rest in Jesus, for he accomplished what we could never accomplish. Freed, we can now go in his love and love others.

PRAYER FOCUS: Jesus, your love for me boggles the mind. I am overwhelmed by your passion and grace for all humankind. Fill my heart with your love so that it spills over onto all your people. Worthy is the Lamb of God to receive praise and honor and glory forever!

DID YOU KNOW? By the twenty-eighth week of a pregnancy, a baby's eyes are sensitive to light and their inner ear has developed enough to hear a variety of sounds produced outside the womb. In fact, their ears have been able to pick up and understand sounds since the twentieth week.[7]

REFLECTIONS

JULY 9

Isaiah 42:5-6 ESV

Thus says God, the Lord, who created the heavens and stretched them out, who spread out the earth and what comes from it, who gives breath to the people on it and spirit to those who walk in it: "I am the Lord; I have called you in righteousness; I will take you by the hand and keep you; I will give you as a covenant for the people, a light for the nations."

∞

Often in Scripture God establishes credibility for his claims and prophecy by referencing the mighty works he has already performed. In the verses preceding today's Scripture, God prophesies through Isaiah the coming of his servant Jesus. We read, "Behold my servant, whom I uphold, my chosen, in whom my soul delights; I have put my Spirit upon him; he will bring forth justice to the nations. He will not cry aloud or lift up his voice, or make it heard in the street; a bruised reed he will not break, and a faintly burning wick he will not quench; he will faithfully bring forth justice. He will not grow faint or be discouraged till he has established justice in the earth; and the coastlands wait for his law" (Isa. 42:1-4 ESV). God's chosen servant will come in gentleness and establish justice for all the earth. How can we know the promise will come to pass? God says we can trust this because the One who created the heavens and the earth gives us his word. The One who created Jupiter and Mars and everything on Earth has declared it. The One who created our spirits and gives us life-sustaining breath has all power and authority to make his words come true. As prophecy is fulfilled, it makes the Word of God even more dependable. The Light of the World entered human history over two thousand years ago, and he wants us to share his light with others. It's time we shed God's light on abortion and dispense with this horrible specter of modern society.

PRAYER FOCUS: Creator of the universe, thank you that your Word is trustworthy and dependable. God, help me to see the overwhelming proof for the sacredness of human life written throughout Holy Scripture. Increase my reverence and awe for you as I discover and marvel at the things you have made. Jesus, take me by the hand and keep me!

DID YOU KNOW? Pastor Louie Giglio, in his "Passion Talk Series," has an excellent video on creation called *How Great Is Our God*. Get this forty-minute talk about the great God of the universe at *268generation.com*.

REFLECTIONS

JULY
10

Ruth 4:13-17 NASB

So Boaz took Ruth, and she became his wife, and he went in to her. And the LORD enabled her to conceive, and she gave birth to a son. Then the women said to Naomi, "Blessed is the Lord who has not left you without a redeemer today, and may his name become famous in Israel. May he also be to you a restorer of life and a sustainer of your old age; for your daughter-in-law, who loves you and is better to you than seven sons, has given birth to him." Then Naomi took the child and laid him in her lap, and became his nurse. The neighbor women gave him a name, saying, "A son has been born to Naomi!" So they named him Obed. He is the father of Jesse, the father of David.

Ruth had been married to Mahlon (Ruth 1:4-5; 4:10), Naomi's son, for ten years before she journeyed to Bethlehem and met Boaz. Mahlon and Ruth, as well as Chilion and Orpah, had failed to conceive children during their marriages. Before Boaz consummated the marriage to Ruth, the elders and the people who witnessed the marriage asked the Lord to bless Ruth and make her fertile like Rachel and Leah (Gen. 29:32-35; 30:22-24; Ruth 4:11). God answered their prayer and enabled Ruth to conceive Obed, the grandfather of King David, thus restoring to Naomi the family legacy she had lost with the death of her husband and two sons. God mightily blessed both women because of their love and faithfulness to each other, giving them a glorious posterity. We often forget that abortion affects many different people into many generations of the family. What inexpressible joy must have been Naomi's as she held her grandchild for the first time. Every conception is precious and valuable and some impact the future of all human beings.

PRAYER FOCUS: God, I marvel at the restorative plans you have for your people and how you bring good out of bad events. Lord, I pray for husbands and wives who have lost a spouse that you would comfort them and bring them peace. Lead them to a new relationship. Father, if it is your will, I pray for those couples who are having difficulty conceiving that you would open the womb and bless them with children.

DID YOU KNOW? The power of prayer offered by the Lord's servants, elders, and people can be very effective. If you are having trouble conceiving or need prayer for any reason, read James 5:14-18: "Is anyone among you sick? Then he must call for the elders of the church and they are to pray over him, anointing him with oil in the name of the Lord; and the prayer offered in faith will restore the one who is sick, and the Lord will raise him up, and if he has committed sins, they will be forgiven him. Therefore, confess your sins to one another, and pray for one another so that you may be healed. The effective prayer of a righteous man can accomplish much. Elijah was a man with a nature like ours, and he prayed earnestly that it would not rain, and it did not rain on the earth for three years and six months. Then he prayed again, and the sky poured rain and the earth produced its fruit" (NASB).

JULY 11

Ephesians 2:13-16 NKJV

But now in Christ Jesus you who once were far off have been brought near by the blood of Christ. For He Himself is our peace, who has made both one, and has broken down the middle wall of separation, having abolished in His flesh the enmity, that is, the law of commandments contained in ordinances, so as to create in Himself one new man from the two, thus making peace, and that He might reconcile them both to God in one body through the cross, thereby putting to death the enmity.

Jesus' work of redemption on the cross has given all people the opportunity to become part of God's family. Jesus brought together those who were not initially his chosen, and those who were his chosen through his all-sufficient atoning blood. Paul is explaining how Jesus died for all people, not just the Jews. Christ has broken down the middle wall of separation. Jesus shed his blood for the redemption of all people regardless of race, gender, development, function, or nationality. Now, "There is neither Jew nor Greek, there is neither slave nor free, there is neither male nor female; for you are all one in Christ Jesus" (Gal. 3:28 NKJV). Everything about Jesus is life-giving and life-sustaining. His holy, pure, innocent, and righteous blood secured our adoption for all time if we place our trust in him. Life is in the blood (Deut. 12:23; John 6:53-54). Whether one is far or near, God wants us all to wash our sins in the blood of the Lamb.

PRAYER FOCUS: Thank you, Jesus, for providing the final sacrifice of atonement so I can be reconciled to my Father. I am grateful that no one is excluded from redemption and that all people can find peace in you.

DID YOU KNOW? Abraham Lincoln referenced Mark 3:25 during his 1858 Republican Convention acceptance speech when he said, "A house divided against itself cannot stand. I believe this Government cannot endure permanently half slave and half free."[8] Likewise, the church in America cannot overcome abortion if it is divided between pro-choice and pro-life. A united church walking in the revealed light of Scripture will go a long way in ending this atrocity (1 John 1:5-7).

REFLECTIONS

JULY
12

Ezekiel 7:23-25 NIV

Prepare chains, because the land is full of bloodshed and the city is full of violence. I will bring the most wicked of the nations to take possession of their houses; I will put an end to the pride of the mighty, and their sanctuaries will be desecrated. When terror comes, they will seek peace, but there will be none.

When a nation's corporate sin reaches its peak and all the inhabitants of the land—from the priest to the king to the people—are engaged in wickedness, God brings judgment. Israel was practicing idolatry, murder, and wickedness that exceeded the nations around them, nations God had warned them not to follow or emulate (Ezek. 5:7-9). The judgments of God are often horrible and intense, but so is the sin that brought on the judgment. God frequently judges people according to their own standard of wickedness or depravity. He said, "The king will mourn, the prince will be clothed with despair, and the hands of the people of the land will tremble. I will deal with them according to their conduct, and by their own standards I will judge them. Then they will know that I am the Lord" (Ezek. 7:27 NIV). One of the main sins nations will be judged for is the shedding of blood, especially innocent blood. God revealed to Israel that life was in the blood, and that it was sacred. God is a life-giver, and to destroy what he has made in his image is particularly offensive to him. How long can we violate the sanctity of human life through abortion and avoid the wrath of God? We must repent and take action against this offense to the Lord of Life. Either that, or we will eventually suffer the fate of Israel, Nineveh, and Sodom.

PRAYER FOCUS: Holy God, forgive us for the offense of killing our babies before they are even born. Many of us do not know what we have done, and others have willfully sinned against you. O Lord, except our plea of contrition and allow us to make amends by fighting against the evils of sexual immorality and abortion. God, your goodness to our nation in the midst of this infant holocaust is beyond my ability to comprehend. When I look at our culpability and the weight of our sin, your grace and goodness seem overwhelming. God, there is none like you; please awaken your church to the plight of the least of these in the womb, and allow us to help and heal those wounded by abortion.

DID YOU KNOW? Women who undergo an abortion may experience heavy bleeding, uterine perforation, bladder injuries, bowel injuries, sepsis, comas, or death.[9] Abortion not only kills children, it hurts women both physically and psychologically. For a graphic, intense discussion of abortion malpractice and abuse against women, read *Lime 5* by Mark Crutcher.

JULY 13

Romans 9:10-12 ESV

And not only so, but also when Rebekah had conceived children by one man, our forefather Isaac, though they were not yet born and had done nothing either good or bad—in order that God's purpose of election might continue, not because of works but because of him who calls—she was told, "The older will serve the younger."

∞

In this text in Romans Paul uses the conception story of Jacob and Esau to prove his point about God's sovereignty in election and calling (Gen. 25:21-26). But I am struck by what his statement conveys about the innocence of the preborn. Certainly, as David pointed out in Psalm 51:5 ("Behold, I was brought forth in iniquity, and in sin did my mother conceive me" ESV), we are all born under original sin as a result of the fall. Beyond this, however, it appears that the preborn, having done nothing good or bad, are in a state of innocence that is greater than all the rest of humanity, save infants. God clearly rewards innocence and cares for the rights of the innocent (Exod. 23:7; 1 Sam. 19:5; Dan. 6:22; Jonah 1:14; Matt. 27:3-4). Abortion, then, is even more appalling to God, given the innocence of the victim. God's Word issues a stern warning to anyone who would take the life of his innocents: "Cursed be anyone who takes a bribe to shed innocent blood" (Deut. 27:25 ESV). Those involved with the profiteering of abortion must repent and stop taking bribes against the innocent. God will forgive the sins of those who repent and seek to do what is right (1 John 1:9; Rom. 6:1-2; Ps. 15).

PRAYER FOCUS: God, forgive us for how we have treated the innocent, weak, and vulnerable children in the womb. Lord, convict the abortionist and all who profit from this deadly practice about the harm they are doing to your women, men, children, and society. Bring restoration and healing to their lives as they begin walking in revealed truth and newness of life.

DID YOU KNOW? Abortion is a very lucrative business. In her book *Blood Money*, Carol Everett wrote, "The abortion business, like all other businesses, has its cycles. January is a good month; February is ok.... By March we were back on track, and I believed my ten thousand dollar a month income was a safe bet. On March 2, 1982, I rewarded myself and bought my new Toronado, as planned. Harvey gave the dealership a statement saying I had earned seventy thousand dollars in 1981."[10]

REFLECTIONS

JULY 14

Deuteronomy 10:17-19 NKJV

For the L ORD your God is God of gods and Lord of lords, the great God, mighty and awesome, who shows no partiality nor takes a bribe. He administers justice for the fatherless and the widow, and loves the stranger, giving him food and clothing. Therefore love the stranger, for you were strangers in the land of Egypt.

Our God is magnificent, unmatched, mighty, and just! He is completely fair and impossible to bribe. The Lord looks after the downtrodden, and he renders justice to the fatherless and those without an advocate. Best of all, he loves the stranger and the alien. Our God calls us to be imitators of who he is and do the things he does. We are to help the weak, defend the fatherless, care for the widow, seek justice, deal fairly, and love the stranger. Who in our culture is a bigger stranger than the preborn? The preborn are completely unknown to us as they develop in the hidden world of the womb. Our culture cruelly denies them the same basic rights that the rest of us enjoy. Often, we treat them as if they are unwelcome and completely foreign in our land. This is not the way anyone should act—and it is especially not the way the church should act. We should love our unknown brothers and sisters in the womb with the same love God had toward us when we were strangers to his family. Just as the Israelites were strangers in Egypt, we were strangers to a Holy God because of our sin. And yet he reached out to us and invited us to dine with him as his adopted children (Rom. 5:8; Eph. 2:17-19).

PRAYER FOCUS: Lord, since you have commissioned me to love, I ask for the power to love before I'm loved, reaching out to the strangers around me. Give me the passion and the drive to champion justice in the face of injustice. Teach me your ways that I might walk in them. Jesus, guide me by your Holy Spirit and temper my actions with grace and truth.

DID YOU KNOW? *Webster's Compact Dictionary* defines the word *stranger* as "a person who is unknown; a new arrival to a place, town, social gathering, a person who is unfamiliar with or ignorant of something."[11]

REFLECTIONS

JULY 15

John 10:10-15 NASB

The thief comes only to steal and kill and destroy; I came that they may have life, and have it abundantly. I am the good shepherd; the good shepherd lays down His life for the sheep. He who is a hired hand, and not a shepherd, who is not the owner of the sheep, sees the wolf coming, and leaves the sheep and flees, and the wolf snatches them and scatters them. He flees because he is a hired hand and is not concerned about the sheep. I am the good shepherd, and I know My own and My own know Me, even as the Father knows Me and I know the Father; and I lay down My life for the sheep.

This passage lays out the supernatural opinions of Jesus and the Devil concerning God's children and abortion. Men and women, it should be noted, can yield their services to either party and become instruments of good or evil. Regarding abortion, the thief comes to steal, kill, and destroy. First, he comes to steal the blessing of children from the parents (Ps. 127:3-5). Second, he comes to kill the child in the womb before that child can fulfill God's purposes; Satan hates God and what is made in God's image (Gen. 1:26-27; 3:11-15; Exod. 1:15-22; Job 1:6-22; Jer. 31:15; Matt. 2:13-18; Mark 4:13-15; Luke 13:15-16; Acts 26:14-18; 1 Thess. 2:17-20; Rev. 12:1-12). Third, he comes to destroy the parent's life afterward through guilt, shame, lies, accusations, and the incitement of self-loathing (Job 2:3-5; Zech. 3:1-4; Rev. 12:10). Jesus, on the other hand, is the Good Shepherd who gave us life in the flesh and is always offering us new life in the spirit. He owns the sheep, for we are created in his image. He knows us and loves us with a pure and holy love. His desire is for all of us to be saved and blessed (Deut. 7:8-10; Ps. 36:5-9; Lam. 3:22-24; Luke 15:4-10; 1 Tim. 2:3-6). The Devil seeks to kill and destroy people in hopes that they and others will curse and abandon God, while Jesus lays down his own life so that others might be saved. What a friend we have in Jesus.

PRAYER FOCUS: Jesus, minister to me your truth and your righteousness. Shepherd me and guide me in this life. Help me see through the schemes of the Devil and walk in your light. Thank you, Lord, for caring for all life, including me.

DID YOU KNOW? In his biography of George Müller, A. T. Pierson wrote, "The taunt was sublimely true: 'He saved others, Himself He cannot save'; it was *because* he saved others that He could not save Himself. The seed must give up its own life for the sake of the crop; and he who will be life to others must, like his Lord, consent to die."[12]

REFLECTIONS

JULY 16

1 Corinthians 15:54-58 HCSB

When this corruptible is clothed with incorruptibility, and this mortal is clothed with immortality, then the saying that is written will take place: Death has been swallowed up in victory. Death, where is your victory? Death, where is your sting? Now the sting of death is sin, and the power of sin is the law. But thanks be to God, who gives us the victory through our Lord Jesus Christ! Therefore, my dear brothers, be steadfast, immovable, always excelling in the Lord's work, knowing that your labor in the Lord is not in vain.

"The last enemy to be abolished is death" (1 Cor. 15:26 HCSB). Through his work on the cross Christ has brought the victory over death near. It can be had today when one places faith and trust in the Lord Jesus Christ. When we do, we experience the liberating joy that comes from knowing that all our sins have been forgotten as we trust in the provision of our Savior. "It is I who sweep away your transgressions for My own sake and remember your sins no more" (Isa. 43:25 HCSB). Those who place their faith and trust in Christ can rest in the peace of knowing one's final destiny is eternal fellowship with the Father, the Son, and the Holy Spirit. Jesus said, "I assure you: Anyone who hears My word and believes Him who sent Me has eternal life and will not come under judgment but has passed from death to life" (John 5:24 HCSB). "Death, where is your victory?" It has been swallowed up by the blood of the Lamb! Therefore, as new believers and elder saints our aim should be to walk in the counsel of God, remaining steadfast, immovable in our faith, throwing off everything that hinders, as we continue in the Lord's work, knowing our eternity is secure and our present is for God's glory (Heb. 12:1).

PRAYER FOCUS: Jesus, thank you for overcoming the great enemy of death and leading me beside the still waters of life. God, uphold me with your outstretched arm and bring me safely into your kingdom. Lord, keep me ever-mindful of your work and the harvest of souls that need your love and forgiveness. Allow me to be a light in the midst of darkness, full of grace and truth.

DID YOU KNOW? *The American Heritage Dictionary of the English Language* defines victory as: "1. Final and complete defeat of the enemy in a military engagement. 2. Any successful struggle against an opponent or obstacle. 3. The state of having triumphed."[13] Jesus' work on the cross is a completely finished work as he himself testified from the cross: "'It is finished!' Then bowing His head, He gave up His spirit" (John 19:30 HCSB).

REFLECTIONS

JULY 17

Isaiah 10:1-3 NIV

Woe to those who make unjust laws, to those who issue oppressive decrees, to deprive the poor of their rights and withhold justice from the oppressed of my people, making widows their prey and robbing the fatherless. What will you do on the day of reckoning, when disaster comes from afar? To whom will you run for help? Where will you leave your riches?

∞

God is a God of justice. In Deuteronomy 16:20, Moses, speaking of the appointment of judges, said, "Follow justice and justice alone, so that you may live and possess the land the Lord your God is giving you" (NIV). God will not take lightly the offenses of men serving in governments, courts, and legislatures who pervert justice and deny the rights of the oppressed and fatherless. How will those who championed or supported immense evils such as slavery, the Holocaust, and abortion fare before their Maker when they are called to account for their actions? No amount of money or influence will save them when they appear before the High Court of Heaven. Both the public servant and the average citizen would do well to follow Abraham Lincoln's basic creed: "Stand with anybody that stands right. Stand with him while he is right and part with him when he goes wrong."[14] Those who stand with God stand right!

PRAYER FOCUS: God, bless and protect the men and women who serve our country from the bench and in the legislature. Give them the courage and the moral compass to do what is right regardless of political pressure.

DID YOU KNOW? John F. Kennedy won the Pulitzer Prize for his book *Profiles in Courage*. Kennedy's book is an examination of eight U.S. Senators and their political courage in the face of opposition and unpopularity. Kennedy wrote these perceptive words on page one: "A nation which has forgotten the quality of courage which in the past has been brought to public life is not as likely to insist upon or reward that quality in its chosen leaders today—and in fact we have forgotten."[15]

REFLECTIONS

JULY 18

Psalm 9:7-12 HCSB

But the L‍ord sits enthroned forever; He has established His throne for judgment. He judges the world with righteousness; He executes judgment on the nations with fairness. The L‍ord is a refuge for the oppressed, a refuge in times of trouble. Those who know Your name trust in You because You have not abandoned those who seek You, Yahweh. Sing to the L‍ord, who dwells in Zion; proclaim His deeds among the nations. For the One who seeks an accounting for bloodshed remembers them; He does not forget the cry of the afflicted.

∞

Judgment is not a popular subject or something we typically like to think about. But judgment is a real part of life on earth and in heaven. God cannot render justice without judgment. When we see a mass genocide or a young child suffer from unimaginable physical and emotional abuse, our hearts cry out for justice. When a criminal walks free or a company defrauds its loyal employees, our anger is stirred, and we cry out for justice. God has established his throne for judgment, and the foundations of it are righteousness and justice (Ps. 89:14). When God renders justice, it is far superior to our attempts at justice. He judges in perfect truth, holiness, purity, grace, righteousness, and fairness. God judges as One with all the facts and perfect perception. He is a refuge for the poor, the weak, the needy, the widow, the orphan, the afflicted, and the fatherless. God will not abandon those who place their trust in him and seek refuge in the shadow of his wings. At the Last Judgment there will be an accounting for abortion, and the sooner we repent the better off we will be.

PRAYER FOCUS: Judge of all the earth, forgive us our transgressions and teach us to pursue justice with all our might. Forgive us for oppressing your preborn children and lying to their parents! Give us the courage and the passion to pursue righteousness and justice in all we do. Help our nation perceive the injustice of abortion.

DID YOU KNOW? Recent research indicates that young people are more opposed to abortion than their parents' generation. In Randy Alcorn's *Why Prolife*, he states, "A recent Gallup survey of teenagers found that seventy-two percent believe abortion is morally wrong. Only nineteen percent believe abortion should be legal in all circumstances, compared to twenty-six percent of adults. About thirty-two percent of teens, compared to seventeen percent of adults, thought abortion should never be permitted."[16] The survivors of abortion are beginning to discover the truth.

REFLECTIONS

JULY 19

Mark 9:40-42 ESV

For the one who is not against us is for us. For truly, I say to you, whoever gives you a cup of water to drink because you belong to Christ will by no means lose his reward. Whoever causes one of these little ones who believe in me to sin, it would be better for him if a great millstone were hung around his neck and he were thrown into the sea.

In these three verses from the gospel of Mark, we have three great lessons taught by Jesus. First, the unity of the body and the realization that we are many members of it should be foremost in our minds when dealing with unfamiliar brothers. If they glorify Christ and are working toward the same ends, we should count them as brothers and encourage them in their work. How much more effective would the body of Christ be if we stopped criticizing each other and focused on our common mission to love God and our neighbor? Second, the smallest act of goodness and charity is honored by God and rewarded. God is pleased when we do the right thing and help others. Third, those who cause others to sin, especially those in the faith, will be subject to severe punishment before Almighty God. Woe to the abortion counselor, pornography vendor, drug dealer, or anyone who encourages sinful behavior. In a similar passage from the gospel of Luke, Jesus adds a fourth important ingredient for right living: forgiveness. He said, "If your brother sins, rebuke him, and if he repents, forgive him, and if he sins against you seven times in the day, and turns to you seven times, saying, 'I repent,' you must forgive him" (Luke 17:3-4 ESV). If we are causing others to sin, the Lord will forgive us if we sincerely repent and stop doing it. Once forgiven, we need to forgive others. We all need forgiveness, and therefore it behooves us to forgive our neighbor.

PRAYER FOCUS: God, bring unity to your body. Give us a heart for lost and hurting people. Empower us to do the good works you have set before us. Help us to be careful not to cause our brothers to sin or stumble. Give us a hunger and a thirst for righteousness. Forgive us, Lord, as we forgive others and show us how blessed it is to forgive.

DID YOU KNOW? Christians are being snared by abortion. Randy Alcorn writes, "Forty-three percent of women obtaining abortions identify themselves as Protestant, and twenty-seven percent identify themselves as Catholic. So two-thirds of America's abortions are obtained by those with a Christian affiliation."[17] These sad statistics indicate how pervasive abortion is in the church. Believers must repent and change their own behavior before helping the nation (Judges 2:1-4).

JULY 20

Ecclesiastes 7:20 NASB

Indeed, there is not a righteous man on earth who continually does good and who never sins.

∞

There are truly righteous and good people in the world, but none of them are without transgression, especially when one ponders the requirements of the law and the inclusion of the thoughts of the heart. To the extent that we truly know someone is the extent to which we can verify this truth. Paul affirmed the sinfulness of all human beings in Romans 3.

> What shall we conclude then? Are we any better? Not at all! We have already made the charge that Jews and Gentiles alike are all under sin. As it is written: "There is no one righteous, not even one; there is no one who understands, no one who seeks God. All have turned away, they have together become worthless; there is no one who does good, not even one" (3:9-12 NIV).

All the externals could be spotless, but the human heart would tell a different tale. Jeremiah wrote, "The heart is more deceitful than all else and is desperately sick; who can understand it?" (Jer. 17:9 NASB). Learn from pastors and teachers, respect those in authority, emulate those of strong character and faith, but don't put them on a pedestal. There is only One righteous enough to be put on a pedestal (Ps. 11:7; Isa. 53:11; Acts 3:14; 1 Pet. 3:18; Rev. 15:3-4). Only Jesus can ascend the Lord's holy hill (Ps. 2:6-7; 24:1-4; 1 Pet. 2:22). We may, as an extension of his righteousness ascend with him, but we will not ascend without him.

PRAYER FOCUS: Lord, help us to understand that no matter how righteous and good we are, we still need your righteousness if we are to stand before Almighty God. Holy Spirit, teach us not to boast, but to serve.

DID YOU KNOW? Isaiah and Job were both overwhelmed by God's righteousness and his presence (Isa. 6:1-6; Job 42:1-6). Job 1:1 tells us that Job was blameless, God fearing, and a man who avoided evil. Job 42:5-6 reads, "I have heard of You by the hearing of the ear; But now my eye sees You; therefore I retract, and I repent in dust and ashes" (NASB). What does the revelation of God's presence do to one's concept of righteousness and holiness when one comes face-to-face with God? Stop looking for perfect people and instead discover the perfect Christ!

JULY 21

2 Corinthians 5:17-21 NKJV

Therefore, if anyone is in Christ, he is a new creation; old things have passed away; behold, all things have become new. Now all things are of God, who has reconciled us to Himself through Jesus Christ, and has given us the ministry of reconciliation, that is, that God was in Christ reconciling the world to Himself, not imputing their trespasses to them, and has committed to us the word of reconciliation. Now then, we are ambassadors for Christ, as though God were pleading through us: we implore you on Christ's behalf, be reconciled to God. For He made Him who knew no sin to be sin for us, that we might become the righteousness of God in Him.

When we place our faith in Jesus as the ransom for our sins, we are indwelt by the Holy Spirit and become new creations (John 14:12-17). As new creations we now have all the power and resources necessary to grow in Christ, resist sin, and love others. To the depth and extent that we pursue God we will experience maturity, victory over the old sin nature, and the fullness of love in this earthly life. The apostle Paul tells us that because we have now experienced the reconciliation of Christ, we can minister reconciliation to our fellow human beings. As those who have "become the righteousness of God in Him," we need to reach out to our neighbors with grace and truth, helping them see their need for God so that they too can become reconciled to God through the atonement of Jesus, the Lamb of God.

PRAYER FOCUS: Thank you, Jesus, that my admission into heaven does not depend on my righteousness, but upon yours. Lord, help me become more righteous and good as I grow in my relationship with you. Fill me with your wisdom and knowledge. No matter how much fruit I bear, help me remember that without you I can do nothing. Give me the courage to be your ambassador and love your people as you have loved me.

DID YOU KNOW? *The American Heritage Dictionary of the English Language* defines *righteous* as "meeting the standards of what is right and just; morally right; guiltless."[18]

REFLECTIONS

JULY 22

Psalm 40:4-5 ESV

Blessed is the man who makes the LORD his trust, who does not turn to the proud, to those who go astray after a lie! You have multiplied, O LORD my God, your wondrous deeds and your thoughts toward us; none can compare with you! I will proclaim and tell of them, yet they are more than can be told.

Blessed are they who do not put confidence in their own accomplishments or in the deceitful ways of the world, but in the Almighty God! Blessed are the men and women who place trust in the faithfulness and the promises of God. When we place our trust in the Lord he will multiply his wondrous deeds and his thoughts towards us. In our darkest hour and in our greatest joys, we will be able to say that none compares with God. We will receive more than we can ever fathom by making the Lord our trust. If we have already made the Lord our trust, we must proclaim his name and his wonderful deeds.

PRAYER FOCUS: God, thank you for the blessings of life and eternity with Christ your Son and our Lord. I adore you. Jesus, thank you for the blessing of children, and for the blessings of family and friends. Holy Spirit, thank you for blessing me with joy and peace. Multiply your wondrous deeds in my life. Draw near to me as I draw near to you (James 4:8).

DID YOU KNOW? Fetal surgery is being performed on babies in the second and third trimesters. These surgeries are performed in the womb and then sutured, allowing the mother to deliver her child healthier later in the pregnancy. Over the last twenty-five years, these surgeries have been performed to treat urinary tract obstruction, hernia of the diaphragm, twin-to-twin transfusion syndrome, and spina bifida.[19]

REFLECTIONS

JULY 23

1 John 2:15-17 NIV

Do not love the world or anything in the world. If anyone loves the world, the love of the Father is not in him. For everything in the world—the cravings of sinful man, the lust of his eyes and the boasting of what he has and does—comes not from the Father but from the world. The world and its desires pass away, but the man who does the will of God lives forever.

We need to seek the things of God or we will inevitably turn to the cares and concerns of this world. Focusing on the world often causes us to miss the Father and his love. To seek the things of God, we need to ask him to give us the eyes to see and the ears to hear what the Spirit is doing and saying. Additionally, we need to saturate ourselves with the Word of God and seek always to view life from an eternal perspective. It's interesting that two of the examples of worldliness given by John—the lust of the eyes and proud boasting—many times lead to the sin of abortion. Quite frequently, abortion is the second sin committed after the lust of the flesh has led to sexual immorality. Abortion owes much of its prominence to an increasingly sexual culture. Thus abortion is often the solution we choose to avoid the responsibility of parenting instead of facing our impurity, poor self-control, and lust. Pride is another huge reason we abort. We don't want people discovering our sin or the sins of our children, so we attempt to cover it up through abortion. In order to keep up appearances and maintain our boast of a good family, we hide the truth and harm our child or grandchild. We trade God's morality for human pride and cave in to the fear of what others might think, never contemplating God's perspective and the ultimate reality of his final judgment. Brothers and sisters, if we will heed God's counsel and pray often for the Holy Spirit to guide us, we will avoid most sins and keep from compounding our transgressions.

PRAYER FOCUS: God, I desire to make you my delight and my passion. Help me see worldly things for what they are and always see life with spiritual perception. Lord, mature me so that I can be in the world but not of it. Increase my desire to do your will and surrender myself to you.

DID YOU KNOW? John was the only apostle who didn't die a martyr's death.[20] He was also an eyewitness to the crucifixion, the empty tomb, and the second coming (John 19:25-27; 20:1-10; Rev. 1:1-3; 9-11).

REFLECTIONS

JULY 24

Psalm 62:5-8 HCSB

Rest in God alone, my soul, for my hope comes from Him. He alone is my rock and my salvation, my stronghold; I will not be shaken. My salvation and glory depend on God, my strong rock. My refuge is in God. Trust in Him at all times, you people; pour out your hearts before Him. God is our refuge. Selah.

Our hope is in God and God alone! Have we taken refuge in God and placed our faith in his sufficiency? Hebrews 11:6 says, "Without faith it is impossible to please God, for the one who draws near to Him must believe that He exists and rewards those who seek Him" (HCSB). Understand that God is our rock, the stronghold of our lives. We must trust in him at all times—never lose faith or trust in God and his power. It is no longer we who live, but Christ who lives in us, as the apostle Paul said: "I no longer live, but Christ lives in me. The life I now live in the body, I live by faith in the Son of God, who loved me and gave Himself for me" (Gal. 2:20 HCSB). We are not righteous enough, but Christ is! We are sinful and unworthy, but he is sinless and worthy. God's glory is increased by the weakness of his vessel and the level of transformation and power he displays in it. The battle belongs not to the strong or the swift or the learned, but to those who place their trust in the Lord.

PRAYER FOCUS: God, from this day forward I seek to be hidden in you. Teach me to lean upon your promises and trust in you with all my heart, soul, mind, and strength. I will not be shaken in my faith that you can redeem me. My salvation and glory depend on you. Thank you, Jesus, that you came for sinners. This sinner trusts in you!

DID YOU KNOW? At the cross, Jesus made a public spectacle of our supernatural enemies and the power of sin. Paul wrote, "When you were dead in trespasses and in the uncircumcision of your flesh, He made you alive with Him and forgave us all our trespasses. He erased the certificate of debt, with its obligations, that was against us and opposed to us, and has taken it out of the way by nailing it to the cross. He disarmed the rulers and authorities and disgraced them publicly; He triumphed over them by Him" (Col. 2:13-15 HCSB).

REFLECTIONS

_____

_____

_____

_____

JULY 25

2 Peter 1:3-11 HCSB

His divine power has given us everything required for life and godliness through the knowledge of Him who called us by His own glory and goodness. By these He has given us very great and precious promises, so that through them you may share in the divine nature, escaping the corruption that is in the world because of evil desires. For this very reason, make every effort to supplement your faith with goodness, goodness with knowledge, knowledge with self-control, self-control with endurance, endurance with godliness, godliness with brotherly affection, and brotherly affection with love. For if these qualities are yours and are increasing, they will keep you from being useless or unfruitful in the knowledge of our Lord Jesus Christ. The person who lacks these things is blind and shortsighted, and has forgotten the cleansing from his past sins. Therefore, brothers, make every effort to confirm your calling and election, because if you do these things you will never stumble. For in this way, entry into the eternal kingdom of our Lord and Savior Jesus Christ will be richly supplied to you.

We gain the righteousness of Christ through our faith in him. But why should we be concerned with righteousness at all? We should be concerned because our goal as Christ's disciples is to become more and more like our Savior. Upon our confession of faith, Christ's power is available to us by the working of the Holy Spirit. We must constantly seek to supplement our faith with his wisdom and power so we can excel at righteousness and good works. In this text from the first chapter of Second Peter, the author is encouraging us to work out in God. We often spend a great deal of time making sure our physical bodies are in shape, or making sure our vocational training is complete, but how much time do we spend cultivating our spiritual life? We need to spend time pursuing the things of God so we will be fit for service. Just as the firefighter needs to be in shape to fight the fire, we need to be in good spiritual shape to accomplish the tasks God has for us.

PRAYER FOCUS: God, increase my desire to spend time with you and cultivate a strong spiritual life. Lord, awaken me to the fact that after conversion my mission is to serve. Help me discover my spiritual gifts and put them to use for the benefit of your Kingdom and your people.

DID YOU KNOW? George Müller started an orphan house in England that served over ten thousand orphans, and he accomplished this without any financial solicitation.[21] What he used instead was steadfast and prevailing prayer. Müller epitomized Paul's advice in 1 Thessalonians 5:17 on daily pursuing communion with God: "Pray constantly."

REFLECTIONS

JULY 26

1 Peter 3:13-17 NASB

Who is there to harm you if you prove zealous for what is good? But even if you should suffer for the sake of righteousness, you are blessed. And do not fear their intimidation, and do not be troubled, but sanctify Christ as Lord in your hearts, always being ready to make a defense to everyone who asks you to give an account for the hope that is in you, yet with gentleness and reverence; and keep a good conscience so that in the thing in which you are slandered, those who revile your good behavior in Christ will be put to shame. For it is better, if God should will it so, that you suffer for doing what is right rather than for doing what is wrong.

Security and refuge for Christians is in God. If we will walk in his ways and follow his commands, we will dwell in safety and enjoy good things. Even if suffering comes in our pursuit of justice for the preborn, we will be blessed and rewarded by the Lord. Jesus tells us, "Blessed are those who have been persecuted for the sake of righteousness, for theirs is the kingdom of heaven. Blessed are you when people insult you and persecute you, and falsely say all kinds of evil against you because of Me. Rejoice and be glad, for your reward in heaven is great; for in the same way they persecuted the prophets who were before you" (Matt. 5:10-12 NASB). It is good to honor God and help those in need. We must be zealous in our efforts to abolish abortion and help those affected by it, always being ready to give a defense of our faith in Christ or the biblical merits for defending his children from all manner of harm and violence. In our witness it is important to maintain humility and gentleness toward those we are trying to help, as well as a conscience that approves of both our words and our actions. We must never be afraid to do what is right and good. If we suffer for our efforts, we can take heart knowing it will bring God glory and advance the cause of the kingdom of heaven.

PRAYER FOCUS: Lord, give me a passion for doing what is good. Keep my mind set on you when storms come or persecution descends upon me. Jesus, give me patience in dealing with people and discernment in the words I speak, and help me mature in my walk with you to develop righteousness and good character.

DID YOU KNOW? Rebecca St. James, the popular Christian musician, was born on this date in 1977. She has written a book that encourages sexual abstinence before marriage called *Wait for Me: Rediscovering the Joy of Purity in Romance*. Sadly, Rebecca's birth country, Australia, has offered abortion since 1969 in some states and generally holds a fairly liberal abortion policy today.[22]

REFLECTIONS

_____

_____

_____

JULY 27

Jude 20-23 NIV

But you, dear friends, build yourselves up in your most holy faith and pray in the Holy Spirit. Keep yourselves in God's love as you wait for the mercy of our Lord Jesus Christ to bring you to eternal life. Be merciful to those who doubt; snatch others from the fire and save them; to others show mercy, mixed with fear—hating even the clothing stained by corrupted flesh.

If we as believers in Christ are to stand our ground in this worldly culture and accomplish the good works God has prepared for us, we must build up our faith. We can build up our faith by focusing our attention and thoughts on the things of God, including reading his Word, praying in the Spirit, and finding shelter in God's love and promises. As we build up our faith, God will bring us opportunities to serve and love his people. Our growing faith will naturally lead to evangelism and good works—good works that should be ministered to all people, both believers and non-believers— as Paul taught us: "Therefore, as we have opportunity, let us do good to all people, especially to those who belong to the family of believers" (Gal. 6:10 NIV). When we pursue justice for the preborn, volunteer at our local pregnancy resource center, or engage in sidewalk counsel at the abortion facility, we have the opportunity to save people both literally and spiritually. In the midst of helping God's people, we will have ample opportunity to share our faith, our testimony, and the reasons why we are defending life. This will spare some from physical death and lead others to new life in Christ. Jude goes on to exhort us to love God's people with discernment and caution, showing mercy to those who doubt and mercy to those trapped in sin, but remaining vigilant so that we are not dragged into the sins of the people we are trying to help. Jude further exhorts us to rescue those who are in great peril and in grave danger of destruction. While it is likely that Jude is speaking about rescuing those on the brink of spiritual bankruptcy from the fires of hell, it is interesting to note that many of the children sacrificed during Old Testament times were "passed through the fire" (2 Kings 23:10; 2 Chron. 33:1-6; Jer. 19:5).

PRAYER FOCUS: Lord, keep me ever mindful of how much you love me and all the people you have made. Help me be diligent in cultivating a spiritual relationship with you, so that I can minister effectively to others. Grant me wisdom and discernment when sharing my faith.

DID YOU KNOW? According to WORDsearch 8, the word *rescue* is used over eighty times in the NIV Bible.[23] See Genesis 37:21-22, Jeremiah 22:2-3, and Galatians 1:3-4 for a few examples.

JULY 28

1 Kings 18:1-4 NKJV

And it came to pass after many days that the word of the LORD came to Elijah, in the third year, saying, "Go, present yourself to Ahab, and I will send rain on the earth." So Elijah went to present himself to Ahab; and there was a severe famine in Samaria. And Ahab had called Obadiah, who was in charge of his house. (Now Obadiah feared the LORD greatly. For so it was, while Jezebel massacred the prophets of the LORD, that Obadiah had taken one hundred prophets and hidden them, fifty to a cave, and had fed them with bread and water.)

This chapter in the first book of Kings documents the showdown between Elijah and the false prophets of Baal. Elijah's epic confrontation and victory gains most of our attention, but it is here in this text where we find a great example of a godly man loving his neighbor and rescuing others from death. After three and a half years of drought and famine, Ahab sent his servant Obadiah out to find food for his livestock (1 Kings 18:5; James 5:17). At this point, the Holy Spirit breaks the narrative in the story to give us a glimpse at the character and accomplishments of Obadiah. Jezebel, the wicked wife of Ahab who influenced her husband to worship Baal (1 Kings 16:31), was murdering the prophets of Jehovah. Obadiah, having a close relationship to the king, had much to lose by protecting the prophets from Jezebel's tyranny and rage. He feared God, however, and knew he must protect God's people from murder and injustice. At great risk to himself, he hid one hundred prophets in two separate caves and made provision for their physical needs during their seclusion. Obadiah honored God by caring for his people immediately and indefinitely. Conversely, Ahab dishonored God by seeking to save his own livestock while the people of God were perishing.

PRAYER FOCUS: God, I'm thankful that you rescue and save. Lord, I'm available to you as a rescue resource, so give me the courage and the faith to do what is right even when it is difficult or scary. Show me how I can help rescue the preborn.

DID YOU KNOW? The name Obadiah means "one who serves Yahweh."[24]

REFLECTIONS

JULY 29

3 John 4-8 ESV

I have no greater joy than to hear that my children are walking in the truth. Beloved, it is a faithful thing you do in all your efforts for these brothers, strangers as they are, who testified to your love before the church. You will do well to send them on their journey in a manner worthy of God. For they have gone out for the sake of the name, accepting nothing from the Gentiles. Therefore we ought to support people like these, that we may be fellow workers for the truth.

John commends a fellow servant, Gaius, for his love and support of traveling Christian missionaries. We can't all go overseas and teach the gospel to foreign peoples. We can't all volunteer our time at a pregnancy center, spend our weekdays doing sidewalk counseling, adopt children, run a women's shelter, or provide lodging for pregnant women who are struggling financially but want to keep their baby. Nor can we all teach abstinence in schools, give fetal development presentations in churches, lead a post-abortive support group, or write letters to our congresspeople, the president, and the media. But we can support those who do. Those who answer the call and go out "for the sake of the name" need our support through prayer, encouragement, assistance, financial contributions, and helps (attending marches, mailing letters, voting correctly, signing petitions, and so on). We should never let the fact that we can't do everything keep us from doing something. We can always find a way to get involved in the fight for life and persevere as a fellow worker for the truth.

PRAYER FOCUS: Lord, help me fill a role in the battle for justice and the lives of preborn children. Show me how I can help wounded mothers, hurting fathers, devastated grandparents and siblings, and the least of these around me. If I have finances, let me use them for good. If I have time, let me offer it. If I have needed skills, let me render them. Jesus, show me the path you would have me walk and help me walk it.

DID YOU KNOW? John Wesley was a great giver as well as a great teacher and theologian. A. T. Pierson wrote in his biography of George Müller, "It reminds us of the career of John Wesley, whose simplicity and frugality of habits enabled him not only to limit his own expenditure to a very small sum, but whose Christian liberality and unselfishness prompted him to give all that he could thus save to purely benevolent objects. . . . It is calculated that in the course of his life he thus gave away at least thirty thousand pounds."[25]

REFLECTIONS

JULY 30

Hebrews 13:3-8 HCSB

Remember the prisoners, as though you were in prison with them, and the mistreated, as though you yourselves were suffering bodily. Marriage must be respected by all, and the marriage bed kept undefiled, because God will judge immoral people and adulterers. Your life should be free from the love of money. Be satisfied with what you have, for He Himself has said, I will never leave you or forsake you. Therefore, we may boldly say: The Lord is my helper; I will not be afraid. What can man do to me? Remember your leaders who have spoken God's word to you. As you carefully observe the outcome of their lives, imitate their faith. Jesus Christ is the same yesterday, today, and forever.

This beautiful exhortation by the author of Hebrews has much to say, but I want to focus on the main theme of godliness. In a few short sentences, the author has established the trustworthiness of God and called us to walk out the two great commandments. We can trust God and depend on him because he will never abandon us. He is the same in every season and at all times. We approach him with boldness and assurance, for he loves us. As a byproduct of God's love, we love (1 John 4:19). Our love for God and our neighbor grows as we mature in Christ. Love compels us to visit the prisoner, help the oppressed, pursue purity, abstain from excess, find contentment in God's provision, and honor those in authority. We are to imitate Christ and his faithful followers who have gone before us. What a comfort it is to know that as we pursue our Lord, he is the same yesterday, today, and forever!

PRAYER FOCUS: God, transform me with your love, presence, and power. Help me walk in a manner worthy of you, give me a desire to keep your commands out of respect for you, and help me love my neighbor as myself.

DID YOU KNOW? The same God who motivated Spurgeon to preach, Tozer to write, Lewis to imagine, Graham to witness, Wilberforce to serve, King to speak, ten Boom to rescue, and Müller to pray, lives in you.

REFLECTIONS

JULY
31

Proverbs 28:12-13 NIV

When the righteous triumph, there is great elation; but when the wicked rise to power, men go into hiding. He who conceals his sins does not prosper, but whoever confesses and renounces them finds mercy.

I long to celebrate the total eradication of abortion! What elation we will feel when this injustice is destroyed, and this historic violation of human rights and dignity is obliterated. How long will this tragedy persist? If those in power uphold wickedness and those without power tolerate it, resolving to do nothing, it will last indefinitely. All Christian believers should realize there is no gain in hiding the sin of abortion, or ignoring it as if it doesn't exist. Let's repent and bring it out into the open so we can find mercy and healing. We must be earnest, diligent, and ready to see justice done. For the sake of our children, grandchildren, wives, husbands, friends, and neighbors, let us echo the words of Amos and say, "Let justice roll on like a river, righteousness like a never-failing stream!" (Amos 5:24 NIV).

PRAYER FOCUS: Lord, I confess _____. I know I have not done enough to fight abortion and uphold the rights of preborn human beings. Show me how I can get involved and love these needy children, my brethren. I'm tired of concealing my sins. I give them to you, O Lord, and ask that you create a clean heart in me and renew a right spirit within me.

DID YOU KNOW? The story of William Wilberforce and the abolition of the British slave trade is now a major motion picture called *Amazing Grace* (2007). Watch it and feel the elation that comes when the righteous triumph. There is much to be learned from this impassioned story of the struggle for human rights and the dignity of all people.

REFLECTIONS

August

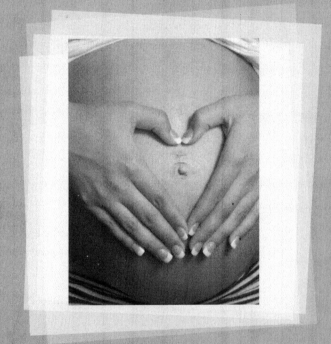

EXPECTATION

AUGUST 1

Ecclesiastes 11:4 NASB

He who watches the wind will not sow and he who looks at the clouds will not reap.

∞

Where is our focus? Are we looking at the latest trends or trying to catch the next wind of opportunity? Are we holding back for fear of uncertainty or are we looking at the building storm clouds and running for cover? It is easy to get distracted and turn our attention to the cares of this world and the mounting pressures in our lives. Distractibility is a major reason why so many of us fail to achieve all that God has for us and fail to advance the kingdom of God. What we behold is often what we become. Are we looking at the giant, the problem, the money, the time, the skills, or the great God who created the universe? We need to focus our attention on God and realize that with his help and guidance we cannot fail. The Israelite army saw Goliath and cowered at the ferociousness of his presence. But David saw God and the might of heaven's power. David knew the giant would fall because he opposed the people of God! When we put our confidence in God and go where he leads, we learn to believe what Jesus told us: "With people it is impossible, but not with God; for all things are possible with God" (Mark 10:27 NASB).

PRAYER FOCUS: God, train me to see you in any circumstance. Keep me steadfast and focused on you in everything I do. Help me trust in you forever (Isa. 26:3-4). Lord, help us see past the giant of abortion and know that with your help we can bring it to an end. Increase my faith to the point of a mustard seed so that I can watch the mountains move.

DID YOU KNOW? Irena Sendler, with the help of the Zegota organization, rescued 2,500 Jewish children from the Warsaw Ghetto during the Holocaust.[1] In 2007, at the age of ninety-seven, Miss Sendler was honored by the Polish parliament as a national heroine. Elzbieta Ficowska, who was six months old when she was rescued, read a letter written by Sendler that said, "Every child saved with my help and the help of all the wonderful secret messengers, who today are no longer living, is the justification of my existence on this Earth, and not a title to glory."[2] Watch Irena's moving story in the made-for-television movie, *The Courageous Heart of Irena Sendler*.

AUGUST 2

Jeremiah 1:11-12 ESV

And the word of the LORD came to me, saying, "Jeremiah, what do you see?" And I said, "I see an almond branch." Then the LORD said to me, "You have seen well, for I am watching over my word to perform it."

Did you know God still watches over his Word to perform it? If God says he will save, he will save. If he says he will deliver, he will deliver. If he says he will punish wickedness, he will punish wickedness. When God says he will protect the fatherless, that is exactly what he does. God watches over them both now and forever. God does exactly what he says, and he is faithful to what he has promised, good to all he has made, and abundantly merciful to those who ask for forgiveness. Consider the account of Abraham and Sarah: "In hope he believed against hope, that he should become the father of many nations, as he had been told, 'So shall your offspring be.' He did not weaken in faith when he considered his own body, which was as good as dead (since he was about a hundred years old), or when he considered the barrenness of Sarah's womb. No distrust made him waver concerning the promise of God, but he grew strong in his faith as he gave glory to God, fully convinced that God was able to do what he had promised" (Romans 4:18-21 ESV). Cling to the promises of God and know that he who promised is faithful!

PRAYER FOCUS: God, I thank you that your Word is true and that you will make sure to accomplish it both now and forever. Holy Spirit, speak to me through the Word and give me ears to hear what it is saying to me, my church, and the world. God, speak to me and encourage my faith to believe that you still speak today.

DID YOU KNOW? According to the *ESV Study Bible*, "The almond tree was the first tree to bud in the spring."[3] This native tree to the Middle East is a symbol of watchfulness and expectation.[4] We can expect God's words to come to pass, both now and in time.

REFLECTIONS

AUGUST 3

Numbers 12:6-8 HCSB

He said: "Listen to what I say: If there is a prophet among you from the LORD, I make Myself known to him in a vision; I speak with him in a dream. Not so with My servant Moses; he is faithful in all My household. I speak with him directly, openly, and not in riddles; he sees the form of the LORD. So why were you not afraid to speak against My servant Moses?"

In this passage from the Old Testament book of Numbers, God is rebuking Miriam and Aaron for speaking against Moses and challenging his authority. God affirms in these verses that he speaks through dreams, visions, and sometimes face-to-face. It appears, from this encounter, that the level of one's faithfulness may even determine the extent and manner in which one hears God. How often do we hear the voice of God? On more than one occasion, I have said, "God does not speak to me very often." But perhaps I should say, "I don't hear God speak very often." For God is always speaking, but it is clear to me that at times I have failed to listen for God or develop ears to hear what the Spirit is saying. The Bible says God speaks through creation (Rom. 1:19-21), the heavens (Ps. 19:1-4), angels (Luke 1:19), a still small voice (1 Kings 19:9-13), the Scriptures (Mark 12:10-11; 2 Tim. 3:16; 2 Pet. 1:20-21), other believers (Lev. 12:1-3; 1 Sam. 3:1-18; Acts 5:17-21; 1 Thess. 2:2-4), and the Holy Spirit (Mark 13:11; John 16:12-15). God has even spoken through a donkey (Num. 22:22-35)! The voice of God comes to us each day as we cultivate lives of obedience and faithfulness. When we practice being still before God we just might hear him more than we think.

PRAYER FOCUS: God, increase my expectation to hear from you and help me grow in discernment as I learn to separate your voice from my voice, the world's voice, and the Enemy's voice. Help me check everything I hear against your revealed Word. Lord, I long to know you as I am known and become more and more intimate with you.

DID YOU KNOW? Jack Deere, a former Dallas Theological Seminary professor, has written an insightful book on hearing the voice of God titled *Surprised by the Voice of God*.

REFLECTIONS

AUGUST 4

Leviticus 20:1-5 HCSB

The LORD spoke to Moses: "Say to the Israelites: Any Israelite or foreigner living in Israel who gives any of his children to Molech must be put to death; the people of the country are to stone him. I will turn against that man and cut him off from his people, because he gave his offspring to Molech, defiling My sanctuary and profaning My holy name. But if the people of the country look the other way when that man gives any of his children to Molech, and do not put him to death, then I will turn against that man and his family, and cut off from their people both him and all who follow him in prostituting themselves with Molech."

God is highly offended by child sacrifice and idolatry. To destroy one of God's created children is to profane his holy name and defile his sanctuary. Every single human being ever created is a potential sanctuary for the dwelling of the Holy Spirit. Paul affirms this truth in his first letter to the Corinthians: "Don't you know that your body is a sanctuary of the Holy Spirit who is in you, whom you have from God? You are not your own, for you were bought at a price. Therefore glorify God in your body" (1 Cor. 6:19-20 HCSB). Paul also refers to the church (the body of Christ) as God's sanctuary in 1 Corinthians 3:16-17. He writes, "Don't you yourselves know that you are God's sanctuary and that the Spirit of God lives in you? If anyone destroys God's sanctuary, God will destroy him; for God's sanctuary is holy, and that is what you are" (HCSB). In Leviticus 20:1-5, God applies his standard of conduct to both the Israelites and the foreigners who live in the land of Israel. All people need to stop the practice of abortion, but especially the church. If the church would stop hiding abortion, ignoring abortion, encouraging abortion, and committing abortion, the abortion industry would be devastated, and our nation would begin to heal. As Randy Alcorn said, "The abortion issue isn't about the church needing to speak to the world. It's about the church needing to speak to itself first, and then to the world."[5]

PRAYER FOCUS: God, forgive us for our ignorance and wickedness! Give us the courage to bring abortion out of the closet and into the light, so that people can be healed and saved from this devastating choice. Lord, transform our churches from places of shame to places of forgiveness and love.

DID YOU KNOW? The literal rendering of *children* and *offspring* in Leviticus chapter twenty is "seed."[6]

REFLECTIONS

AUGUST
5

Psalm 146 NKJV

Praise the LORD! Praise the LORD, O my soul! While I live I will praise the LORD; I will sing praises to my God while I have my being. Do not put your trust in princes, nor in a son of man, in whom there is no help. His spirit departs, he returns to his earth; in that very day his plans perish. Happy is he who has the God of Jacob for his help, whose hope is in the LORD his God, who made heaven and earth, the sea, and all that is in them; who keeps truth forever, who executes justice for the oppressed, who gives food to the hungry. The LORD gives freedom to the prisoners. The LORD opens the eyes of the blind; the LORD raises those who are bowed down; the LORD loves the righteous. The LORD watches over the strangers; He relieves the fatherless and widow; but the way of the wicked He turns upside down. The LORD shall reign forever—Your God, O Zion, to all generations. Praise the LORD!

Let us praise the Lord while we live! Meditating on this psalm and thinking of all the wisdom and truth it communicates will make us wise. We must trust in God alone and follow his advice and counsel. In the core of our beings we need to realize that the God of Jacob is the Maker of heaven and earth and all they contain. As we depend on God for our daily bread, let us never forget to praise him for his goodness and for all those things from which he has set us free. Let's trust the Lord to give us eyes to see, to exalt us at the proper time, and to increase our righteousness. As his hands and feet on this earth, all believers must partner with God in caring for the stranger, relieving the fatherless and widow, and turning abortion upside down!

PRAYER FOCUS: O God, there is none like you! You are worthy of all praise and respect. Help us to hear your heart for the preborn, the hurting, the weak, the poor, the fatherless, the needy, the stranger, and the lost.

DID YOU KNOW? By thirty-one weeks a baby in the womb weighs roughly four pounds and measures eleven inches long. A layer of fat is forming under their skin and their toenails that began growing in week fourteen are now complete.[7]

REFLECTIONS

AUGUST
6

2 Timothy 4:1-5 NASB

I solemnly charge you in the presence of God and of Christ Jesus, who is to judge the living and the dead, and by His appearing and His kingdom: preach the word; be ready in season and out of season; reprove, rebuke, exhort, with great patience and instruction. For the time will come when they will not endure sound doctrine; but wanting to have their ears tickled, they will accumulate for themselves teachers in accordance to their own desires, and will turn away their ears from the truth and will turn aside to myths. But you, be sober in all things, endure hardship, do the work of an evangelist, fulfill your ministry.

Shortly before his death, the apostle Paul wrote to his protégé Timothy to encourage him to preach the Word and hold fast to the truth. We need to hear this same advice today. We need to be ready to preach the Word of God when it is welcomed, as well as when it is shunned and opposed. Some of our contemporary churches and professing Christians don't believe in the inerrancy or infallibility of Scripture, the miracles of Jesus, the sanctity of human life, the existence of hell, or the supernatural. They pick and choose what they will believe or accept. If we are to walk with God, we must believe what he has revealed to us in his Word, and we must believe that the Bible is not deficient or compromised in any way. Surely, the Creator of the universe has the power to protect and sustain his message and make it plain and applicable to all who hear it. We need to be of sound mind, seeking God's wisdom in all matters, and we need to be a people able to endure hardship, present the gospel of salvation, and remain faithful to the call God has placed on our lives. As Paul told Timothy, "Be diligent to present yourself approved to God as a workman who does not need to be ashamed, accurately handling the word of truth" (2 Tim. 2:15 NASB).

PRAYER FOCUS: God, help me believe you and your Word and accept the things I cannot see. Lord, grant me revelation and wisdom with the areas of your Word that I don't understand or are hard for me to accept. Father, don't let my lack of experience or knowledge lead me to believe anything that is incompatible with what your Word teaches. Teach me instead the mystery of faith: "Now faith is the assurance of things hoped for, the conviction of things not seen" (Heb. 11:1 NASB).

DID YOU KNOW? The name *Timothy* means "honored of God" or "honoring God."[8] What better way to honor God, and receive honor from him, than to take him at his Word?

REFLECTIONS

AUGUST 7

Romans 15:13 NIV

May the God of hope fill you with all joy and peace as you trust in him, so that you may overflow with hope by the power of the Holy Spirit.

Believers, there is hope in God! If we are struggling to find deliverance, we must never give up hope as we trust God for it. If we are depressed, our trust should be placed in God as we wait for the joy of the Lord that comes through gaining his perspective. If we are grieving a loss, or lamenting the choices we have made, we can cry out to the Lord and ask the Holy Spirit to bring us peace. Our hope is in God both now and forever. Jesus came for us and he wants to bring us life. There is no need to settle for a counterfeit! We can take refuge in Almighty God and find what we need for this present moment and for all eternity. God's promises are for everyone—from the Jew to the Gentile, the sinner to the saint, the weak to the strong, the weary to the rested, the sick to the healthy, and the hurting to the whole. God wants us to taste and see that he is good by the power of the Holy Spirit. He wants us to overflow with hope! Where is our hope today? If it is not in God, what are we waiting for? Placing our trust in him begins an experience of more joy, peace, and hope.

PRAYER FOCUS: God, I am grateful that you have given me hope today and always through Jesus Christ. Bring me afresh the joy of my salvation and the hope of better days ahead. Lord, fill me with your joy, peace, and hope as I live each day. Give me a passion for you and for the things you love.

DID YOU KNOW? In Psalms 42 and 43, the psalmist reminds himself three times of the hope he has in God to deliver him from his pressing troubles: "Why are you downcast, O my soul? Why so disturbed within me? Put your hope in God, for I will yet praise him, my Savior and my God" (Ps. 42:5-6, 11; 43:5 NIV). Continue seeking refuge in God and you shall have it. As the writer of Hebrews told us: "Let us hold unswervingly to the hope we profess, for he who promised is faithful" (Heb. 10:23 NIV).

REFLECTIONS

AUGUST 8

John 11:21-27 NKJV

Then Martha said to Jesus, "Lord, if You had been here, my brother would not have died. But even now I know that whatever You ask of God, God will give You." Jesus said to her, "Your brother will rise again." Martha said to Him, "I know that he will rise again in the resurrection at the last day." Jesus said to her, "I am the resurrection and the life. He who believes in Me, though he may die, he shall live. And whoever lives and believes in Me shall never die. Do you believe this?" She said to Him, "Yes, Lord, I believe that You are the Christ, the Son of God, who is to come into the world."

This is a glorious truth! All who believe in Jesus will never die, but will pass from this life to the next wrapped in the sufficiency of his presence and glory. In Christ is the light and life of all humanity. Jesus is the source, sustenance, and resurrection of life. True life is found in Christ, who created all things at the beginning (John 1:1-4; Col. 1:15-20). As the giver of life, Jesus provides for both our physical and spiritual needs (Ps. 33:6-9; Matt. 4:4; 5:45; John 4:10-14; 6:35; 14:6-7). Jesus is the resurrection, for there is no other name given under heaven by which people can be saved (John 5:24-26; Acts 4:12). Jesus is the Good Shepherd (John 10:11), and the key to life is for his sheep to know his voice and follow him. We all must answer the question posed to Martha, "Do you believe this?" or Peter, "Who do you say that I am?" (Matt. 16:15-16). If we believe, we will receive and begin the greatest adventure of our lives.

PRAYER FOCUS: Jesus, I believe you are the Christ, the Son of the living God. Grant me the abundant life as I surrender to you and seek to do your will. Teach me to trust, love, forgive, and live for righteousness. Jesus, fill me with the Holy Spirit and use him to guide me into all truth.

DID YOU KNOW? C. S. Lewis, in his classic work *Mere Christianity*, wrote this about the claims of Christ and our subsequent decision: "A man who was merely a man and said the sort of things Jesus said would not be a great moral teacher. He would either be a lunatic—on a level with the man who says he is a poached egg—or else he would be the Devil of Hell. You must make your choice. Either this man was, and is, the Son of God: or else a madman or something worse. You can shut Him up for a fool, you can spit at Him and kill Him as a demon; or you can fall at His feet and call Him Lord and God, but let us not come with any patronizing nonsense about His being a great human teacher. He has not left that open to us. He did not intend to."[9]

REFLECTIONS

AUGUST 9

Genesis 9:4-7 NKJV

But you shall not eat flesh with its life, that is, its blood. Surely for your lifeblood I will demand a reckoning; from the hand of every beast I will require it, and from the hand of man. From the hand of every man's brother I will require the life of man. "Whoever sheds man's blood, by man his blood shall be shed; for in the image of God He made man. And as for you, be fruitful and multiply; bring forth abundantly in the earth and multiply in it."

These commands were given to Noah after the Great Flood. In them God reestablished the hierarchy of creation and the sacredness of human life (Gen. 9:1-6). God points out to Noah that the life of all flesh is in the blood and that it should be honored. In the case of humans, however, it is to be protected and cherished above all else. Anyone who violated this principle and murdered another person would be subject to death at the hands of other men, fulfilling the Mosaic standard of life for life. These verses clearly establish human preeminence in God's earthly creation, because all other created things are given into human hands for sustenance and management. People are above the rest of God's earthly creation because they are the only beings made in his image. Each and every human life is precious to God. God knows how many people the earth can sustain, and every child conceived by him has his blessing. He commanded Noah, his family, and us to be fruitful and multiply in abundance. This then is the horror of abortion, for it sheds the blood of innocent human beings who are made in the image of God, underpopulates the earth, and perpetuates violence.

PRAYER FOCUS: Jesus, transform our culture from one of death to life. Give us a love for children and a reverence for all living things. Show us how to cherish every life regardless of the conception circumstance. Help us to see that, as the Creator, you approve of every child conceived and have appointed them to life.

DID YOU KNOW? Abortion is dangerously reducing the world's population. Dr. John Willke claims, "In a developed nation, the average woman must bear 2.1 children (Mean Fertility Rate) in order to maintain a level population." Many Western nations are below this birth rate. Using Italy for an example, Dr. Willke states, "In 1993, there were 5,265 more Italians buried than were born. If this continues unchanged, within 100 years its population will shrink from 57 to 15 million, with half of those over 65 years old."[10]

REFLECTIONS

_____

_____

AUGUST
10

Proverbs 29:12-14 HCSB

If a ruler listens to lies, all his officials will be wicked. The poor and the oppressor have this in common: the LORD gives light to the eyes of both. A king who judges the poor with fairness—his throne will be established forever.

Presidents, congresspeople, and judges would do well to listen to the wisdom found in the Bible—especially Proverbs 29:12-14. If our leaders continue listening to lies from the pro-abortion lobby, Planned Parenthood, and pro-choice supporters, wickedness will permeate their governance and those who work in their administrations will be corrupt. A leader's primary responsibility is to protect the people of their nation. A leader oppressing the poor, or "the least of these," forgets their common heritage with the people, for God is the Maker of both and the Judge of all! On the other hand, a leader who is kind to the needy, fair to the poor, and pursues justice for all the people will be rewarded and blessed during their time of governance. Jesus' government is the complete fulfillment of a fair and just rule and it is a rule that has been established forever (Rev. 20:4-6; 22:3-5). As the prophet Isaiah foretold, "The dominion will be vast, and its prosperity will never end. He will reign on the throne of David and over his kingdom, to establish and sustain it with justice and righteousness from now on and forever. The zeal of the LORD of Hosts will accomplish this" (Isa. 9:7 HCSB).

PRAYER FOCUS: God, give our leaders the wisdom to follow your commands and principles so that all people may live in peace and be blessed. Lord, forgive our nation for its support of abortion and the destruction of your precious children. Change the hearts of those in government and the courts. Transform their hearts of stone into hearts of flesh and their heads of knowledge into heads of understanding.

DID YOU KNOW? Josiah is regarded in Scripture as a king who turned his ways to the Lord like no other. When Josiah was twenty-six years old, in the eighteenth year of his reign, his secretary and the high priest discovered the Book of the Law in the temple and read it to him (2 Kings 22:3-10). Josiah, upon hearing the Words of God, tore his robes and repented (2 Kings 22:11, 18-20). After that, he took action against the idolatry of the nation (2 Kings 23:3-20). 2 Kings 23:25 has this to say about Josiah and his accomplishments: "Before him there was no king like him who turned to the Lord with all his mind and with all his heart and with all his strength according to all the law of Moses, and no one like him arose after him" (HCSB).

AUGUST 11

1 Chronicles 25:4-6 NASB

Of Heman, the sons of Heman: Bukkiah, Mattaniah, Uzziel, Shebuel and Jerimoth, Hananiah, Hanani, Eliathah, Giddalti and Romamti-ezer, Joshbekashah, Mallothi, Hothir, Mahazioth. All these were the sons of Heman the king's seer to exalt him according to the words of God, for God gave fourteen sons and three daughters to Heman. All these were under the direction of their father to sing in the house of the LORD, with cymbals, harps and lyres, for the service of the house of God.

These verses focus our attention on Heman and his children, all of whom David set apart to prophesy and worship in the temple of God (1 Chron. 25:1). The fifth verse provides an excellent example of the blessing of children. God gave fourteen sons and three daughters to Heman, to exalt and bless him as a father. God also created them to offer worship to himself and bless the people of God through their gifts and talents as musicians. Every child is a gift from God (Ps. 127:3-5). The man and woman whose family is full of them is most certainly blessed (Ps. 128:3-4). Every person conceived has a purpose and a plan to fulfill. Some will please and praise God, some will honor their parents and bless them, and some will benefit their neighbors and the whole of society. But all are wanted, loved, and sent by Almighty God. If we have large families, praise God for his favor. None of us knows how many children God will send us, but every child is a gift to be treasured and loved with all our hearts.

PRAYER FOCUS: Lord, thank you for children and the gift of life. Forgive me if I have misunderstood the value and purpose of human life. God, help me yield my will to yours in the area of family, children, and pregnancy. Jesus, show me that you will help me provide for all the children you see fit to bless me with.

DID YOU KNOW? At least two modern American families have seventeen or more children: the Chernenko family of California has seventeen children, and the Duggar family of Arkansas has nineteen.[11] Both sets of parents describe their children as gifts.

REFLECTIONS

AUGUST 12

Genesis 18:25-26 NKJV

Far be it from You to do such a thing as this, to slay the righteous with the wicked, so that the righteous should be as the wicked; far be it from You! Shall not the Judge of all the earth do right?" So the LORD said, "If I find in Sodom fifty righteous within the city, then I will spare all the place for their sakes."

Because Abraham anticipated that God was about to bring judgment against Sodom and destroy it, he began pleading with God for the lives of the righteous in the city. Abraham plead with God by calling to mind the merits of his own nature. Abraham knew God was just and always did the right thing, so he appealed to God's own character as he made his plea for the people. As the Lord and Abraham spoke, eventually it was determined that God would spare the entire city, both wicked and righteous, if just ten righteous people could be found there. God promised, "I will not destroy it for the sake of ten" (Gen. 18:32 NKJV). Ultimately, God allowed for Lot and his daughters to be rescued before he destroyed Sodom. We see in this account, as we saw in the account of the Flood, that God brings supernatural judgment at the point where wickedness is at its height and righteousness is almost completely lacking. Therefore, God is good and just even in the midst of wickedness and depravity. For the sake of the righteous and the good of all, God allows us time to repent and turn from the sin of abortion and any other sins entangling us. As God's people on earth, we need to be like Abraham and cry out for God's mercy and goodness to prevail in the land so he will not have to destroy it.

PRAYER FOCUS: God, give me a passion to live righteously. Increase the number of righteous men and women who live in the land and give them a voice and a platform to effect godly change. Lord, increase my passion for people that I might plead for them and their needs.

DID YOU KNOW? Lou Engle began a corporate prayer ministry that pleads with God for the ending of abortion, a return to holiness by the church, and revival in America. Find out more about these stadium prayer gatherings at *www.thecall.com*.

REFLECTIONS

AUGUST 13

Hosea 9:10-11 ESV

Like grapes in the wilderness, I found Israel. Like the first fruit on the fig tree in its first season, I saw your fathers. But they came to Baal-peor and consecrated themselves to the thing of shame, and became detestable like the thing they loved. Ephraim's glory shall fly away like a bird—no birth, no pregnancy, no conception!

Speaking through the prophet Hosea, God pronounced judgment upon the nation of Israel for their idolatry, sexual immorality, and wickedness. Hosea harkens back to the beginning of the nation of Israel when God was delighted in them and their forefathers. The current generation, however, had played the harlot, mixing with the practices of Baal worship and engaging in depravity (Num. 25; Ps. 106:28-43). Israel's lust and passion for foreign gods had made them an abomination. The introduction to Hosea in the *ESV Study Bible* states the following about Baal worship: "Baal was the weather-god worshiped in Syria-Palestine, who had control over agriculture and fertility, rainfall and productivity. . . . one major aspect of Baalism touches on this prophet's message: the religions appeal to human sexuality (cf. Isa. 57:3-10). Other aspects—such as drunkenness, bestiality, human sacrifice, mutilations, and incest—may be discerned in the book, but Hosea understands the strength of Baalism's appeal to the sex drive by way of ritual prostitution."[12] As part of Israel's punishment, their fruitfulness and glory would cease. God declared they would no longer enjoy the fruitfulness of the womb and new life. In reverse order, the prophet encapsulates the entire journey of new life that will be withheld from them because of their disobedience and sin. It is interesting to note that the very things Israel sought from Baal became what God withheld from them: fertility and productivity.

PRAYER FOCUS: God, forgive me and my nation for our sexual immorality, lust, pornography, fornication, perversion, and adultery. Help us to reclaim our purity and walk in acceptable and godly sexual practices. God, forgive us for the lust and idolatry that have led to the modern-day holocaust of abortion.

DID YOU KNOW? The name *Ephraim* means "twice fruitful."[13] See Genesis 41:52.

REFLECTIONS

AUGUST
14

Colossians 2:9-14 NIV

For in Christ all the fullness of the Deity lives in bodily form, and you have been given fullness in Christ, who is the head over every power and authority. In him you were also circumcised, in the putting off of the sinful nature, not with a circumcision done by the hands of men but with the circumcision done by Christ, having been buried with him in baptism and raised with him through your faith in the power of God, who raised him from the dead. When you were dead in your sins and in the uncircumcision of your sinful nature, God made you alive with Christ. He forgave us all our sins, having canceled the written code, with its regulations, that was against us and that stood opposed to us; he took it away, nailing it to the cross.

Jesus' work on the cross is the definitive moment in human history! His death to atone for our sins is finished, complete, and entirely sufficient to rescue us from our bodies of sin and death. Nothing in all creation—"neither height nor depth, nor anything else in all creation, will be able to separate us from the love of God that is in Christ Jesus our Lord" (Rom. 8:39 NIV). If we have placed our lives in the hands of Jesus, we have been redeemed, not by human hands but by Almighty God, who has come in the flesh to pay our sin debt and set us free. Jesus came to bring that which was dead into new life. Jesus has forgiven our sins, satisfied the law where we could not, and settled our sin debt by nailing himself to the cross as payment in full. John said, "If the Son sets you free, you will be free indeed" (John 8:36 NIV). Paul explained it this way: "But the gift is not like the trespass. For if the many died by the trespass of the one man, how much more did God's grace and the gift that came by the grace of the one man, Jesus Christ, overflow to the many! Again, the gift of God is not like the result of the one man's sin: The judgment followed one sin and brought condemnation, but the gift followed many trespasses and brought justification. For if, by the trespass of the one man, death reigned through that one man, how much more will those who receive God's abundant provision of grace and of the gift of righteousness reign in life through the one man, Jesus Christ" (Rom. 5:15-17 NIV). No matter how far we have fallen or how long we have strayed, Jesus is able to bring us home if we will yet believe in him. All glory and honor belongs to the Lamb, for he was and is and is to come!

PRAYER FOCUS: Lord, you are worthy of all praise and my heart will sing of your goodness and mercy. You are my Daily Bread, my Prince of Peace, my Portion, my Defender, and my Deliverer. Jesus, stir up in me rivers of living water so that I might know the power of your love and your resurrection.

DID YOU KNOW? Jesus began his public ministry at around the age of thirty and gave his life for you and me three years later.[14] A ministry that spanned only three years changed the world. According to E. W. Bullinger in *Number in Scripture*, the number three represents divine perfection: "Hence the number three points us to what is real, essential, perfect, substantial, complete, and Divine."[15]

AUGUST 15

Hebrews 12:22-24 NASB

But you have come to Mount Zion and to the city of the living God, the heavenly Jerusalem, and to myriads of angels, to the general assembly and church of the firstborn who are enrolled in heaven, and to God, the Judge of all, and to the spirits of the righteous made perfect, and to Jesus, the mediator of a new covenant, and to the sprinkled blood, which speaks better than the blood of Abel.

The writer of Hebrews is contrasting the old covenant given at Mt. Sinai (Exod. 19:12-25; 20:1-21; Heb. 12:18-21) with the new covenant represented by Mt. Zion (Ps. 2:6; 1 Pet. 2:6; Rev. 14:1). We trust in no small thing when we place our faith in Jesus Christ. Our belief grants us fellowship forever with the living God, angels, the church, redeemed saints made perfect in righteousness, and Jesus. Our inclusion with Christ, the heavenly host, and the church is secure because of Christ's blood sacrifice on the cross which paid the ransom for our sins. His sacrifice speaks a better blood than any of the Old Testament sacrifices, including Abel's, which was the first to be documented in Scripture.[16] Abel's sacrifice was sufficient to atone for his own personal sin and was pleasing to the Lord (Gen. 4:3-4). Jesus' sacrifice, on the other hand, was perfect, holy, and sufficient to atone for the sins of the entire world (John 1:29; Heb. 9:15-28). Abel and Jesus were both unjustly murdered, but while Abel's blood cried out for justice because of Cain's action, Jesus' blood fulfilled and satisfied the Father's justice once and for all, allowing for the pardon of any Cain who repents. Jesus' blood indeed "speaks better than the blood of Abel."

PRAYER FOCUS: Jesus, I am overwhelmed by your love and sacrifice. Your love, O Lord, endures forever, and your faithfulness reaches to the skies (1 Chron. 16:34; Ps. 36:5). I'm so grateful you gave me life—twice! Jesus, take my life and use it for your glory.

DID YOU KNOW? Jesus was twelve years old when he first spoke in the temple (Luke 2:41-49). The number twelve is often associated with government and authority in Scripture. Some examples of this are: the twelve tribes of Israel (Gen. 49:1-28; Deut. 33); the twelve apostles (Matt. 10:1-10); Aaron's high priestly breastpiece with twelve stones (Exod. 28:15-29); Solomon's twelve deputies (1 Kings 4:7); Elisha's mantle while he was plowing with twelve pairs of oxen (1 Kings 19:19); the twelve thousand sealed from each of the tribes of Israel in tribulation (Rev. 7:4-8); and the New Jerusalem, with twelve gates and twelve angels (Rev. 21:10-14). Jesus came to govern, and the government will rest on his shoulders (Isa. 9:6-7; Matt. 12:28; Luke 4:43, John 19:3-22).

AUGUST 16

Luke 23:33-34 NKJV

And when they had come to the place called Calvary, there they crucified Him, and the criminals, one on the right hand and the other on the left. Then Jesus said, "Father, forgive them, for they do not know what they do." And they divided His garments and cast lots.

Jesus' first statement from the cross is powerful, asking God to forgive those who were about to kill him. Even as he suffered, bled, endured insults, and was spat upon, Jesus' heart was filled with compassion for his persecutors as he prayed for their forgiveness. The prophet Isaiah foresaw that all this would happen: "Therefore I will divide Him a portion with the great, and He shall divide the spoil with the strong, because He poured out His soul unto death, and He was numbered with the transgressors, and He bore the sin of many, and made intercession for the transgressors" (Isa. 53:12 NKJV). Under such circumstances, the natural inclination would be for one to consider vengeance, justice, and judgment. But Jesus sought always to help the lost and work for the good of all, even the wicked. This then is the power of our God and the beauty of our faith, to love in the midst of atrocity. How then should we treat abortionists like Warren Hern, George Tiller, or Susan Wicklund? How then are we to treat those who mock us, hurt us, cheat us, offend us, abuse us, and hate us? We are to forgive them and intercede for their healing, asking God to restore them to a right relationship with himself. Let me make one thing clear—forgiving is not condoning. Jesus did not say, "Father, I approve of what they are doing," or "Father, these men don't need forgiveness." Jesus understood better than anyone the difference between righteousness and wickedness, but his compassion worked for the salvation of all. Hatred, violence, and contention will not advance our fight for justice, but love, truth, forgiveness, and sacrifice will. Jesus did not come to kill, but to die for the sins of humanity.

PRAYER FOCUS: Father, forgive those who kill your children, for they do not fully know what they are doing. Nor do they know who you are! God, teach me how to love and forgive like Jesus, even if I am similarly abused (Acts 7:59-60). Lord, help me understand that it has not been given to me to judge or avenge, but that I am called to be like you, a sacrificial agent of love (Deut. 32:35-36, 41; Matt. 5:44; Luke 6:35-36; John 5:22; 8:1-11).

DID YOU KNOW? Warren Wiersbe has written a book entitled *The Cross of Jesus*, which is about the significance of the cross and Jesus' last words spoken upon it. In it he writes, "While our Lord was doing his greatest work on earth, dying for the sins of the world, he uttered some of his greatest words. These seven last words from the cross are windows that enable us to look into eternity and see the heart of the Savior and the heart of the gospel."[17]

AUGUST 17

Psalm 73:12-19 HCSB

Look at them—the wicked! They are always at ease, and they increase their wealth. Did I purify my heart and wash my hands in innocence for nothing? For I am afflicted all day long and punished every morning. If I had decided to say these things aloud, I would have betrayed Your people. When I tried to understand all this, it seemed hopeless until I entered God's sanctuary. Then I understood their destiny. Indeed, You put them in slippery places; You make them fall into ruin. How suddenly they become a desolation! They come to an end, swept away by terrors.

In this psalm, Asaph is trying to understand earthly inequity, injustice, and oppression. How can our oppressors be so blessed while we are suffering (Ps. 73:2-9, 13-14)? How can the wicked escape punishment for their crimes and be allowed to live in luxury? How could the Nazis enjoy the spoils of slave labor while they gassed Jewish families daily? Asaph pondered these things and meditated upon the things of God until he discovered the truth. We should not envy the wicked, we should pray for them. Meditate upon this psalm in God's Word and discover, just like Asaph, that life is eternal, and our experience on this earth is only the beginning. God's gift to the human race of free will allows for great acts of benevolence and righteousness, as well as great acts of wickedness and depravity. Even so, God is just and the punishment of the wicked for their choices will come upon them suddenly. When that happens, their illumination and terror will be great! If we have acted wickedly, we must repent and turn our ways to the Lord, for he cares for us. If we have held fast to the commands of God, we must continue and our reward will be great and our joy made full!

PRAYER FOCUS: God, help me to lean not on my own understanding, but upon yours. Lord, help me trust in your sovereignty. Help me see beyond this earthly life and death to the realm of eternity. Jesus, show me that how I live matters, and help me choose to do what is right.

DID YOU KNOW? The first word written in most English translations of the book of Psalms is "blessed." In the first two verses of Psalm 1, the Holy Spirit gives us two great principles for living a blessed life. "Blessed is the man who does not walk in the counsel of the wicked or stand in the way of sinners or sit in the seat of mockers. But his delight is in the law of the Lord, and on his law he meditates day and night" (NIV). First, the blessed person avoids wickedness and ungodly counsel during their life. Second, the blessed person meditates on God's Word day and night, finding in it all they need for life.

REFLECTIONS

AUGUST 18

Psalm 33:13-22 NIV

From heaven the Lord looks down and sees all mankind; from his dwelling place he watches all who live on earth—he who forms the hearts of all, who considers everything they do. No king is saved by the size of his army; no warrior escapes by his great strength. A horse is a vain hope for deliverance; despite all its great strength it cannot save. But the eyes of the Lord are on those who fear him, on those whose hope is in his unfailing love, to deliver them from death and keep them alive in famine. We wait in hope for the Lord; he is our help and our shield. In him our hearts rejoice, for we trust in his holy name. May your unfailing love rest upon us, O Lord, even as we put our hope in you.

To whom do we look for help? Upon whose strength do we rely? Are we placing our trust in wealth, strength, abilities, or associates? Or are we placing our trust in the Lord who forms the hearts of all, and the only One who is mighty to save? Only God can redeem and deliver; no amount of power, influence, achievement, or personal blessing can save us from the requirements of the law. If we have not placed faith in Jesus, what will we do when God rises up to judge and render justice upon the earth? No wealth will pay our debt. No army will have the power to defend us. No vessel will be sufficient to hasten our escape. We will stand and be judged upon our own merits. If our hope is not in Jesus and his shed blood of atonement, we will face the justice of God alone! Our hope is in the Lord and we wait for his deliverance. When we place our hope in God we discover all that God has for us in this earthly life and the next. But if we do not, we will be forever separated from the love of God and the majesty of his power.

PRAYER FOCUS: Jesus, my heart, which you formed, believes in you (Rom. 10:9-10). I ask you to be my hope, my shield, my strength, my help, and my deliverer! Lord, rest your unfailing love upon me and be gracious to me, both now and forever. I will sing of your praises forever because my hope and my salvation are in you.

DID YOU KNOW? According to *Firefly's World of Facts*, "your heart pumps 3,600 gallons (13,640 L) of blood around your body in a day. An average heartbeat rate of 70 beats a minute adds up to more than 100,000 beats a day."[18]

REFLECTIONS

AUGUST 19

Daniel 3:16-18 NASB

Shadrach, Meshach and Abed-nego replied to the king, "O Nebuchadnezzar, we do not need to give you an answer concerning this matter. If it be so, our God whom we serve is able to deliver us from the furnace of blazing fire; and He will deliver us out of your hand, O king. But even if He does not, let it be known to you, O king, that we are not going to serve your gods or worship the golden image that you have set up."

Joshua 24:15 says, "Choose for yourselves today whom you will serve . . . but as for me and my house, we will serve the Lord" (NASB). Everybody has to make up their own mind who they will serve. For Shadrach, Meshach, and Abed-nego, their choice was obvious; they chose to serve the living God. When King Nebuchadnezzar erected a ninety-foot statue that the province of Babylon was to worship at the sound of music, these three men refused because it violated the first commandment given to Moses to have no other gods before the God of Israel, and never to make or worship an idol (Exod. 20:3-6; Dan. 3:1-5). Long before their faith was put to the test, Shadrach, Meshach and Abed-nego knew where their allegiance lay and who it was they served. They knew it was better to serve God than human-made statues, and that God had the power to rescue them in this life or the next. Scripture makes it clear that we are to obey God first and people in authority second. When we are told it is acceptable to abort one's child, check first with God and see if he says it is acceptable. God did indeed rescue his faithful servants from the hottest fire King Nebuchadnezzar could throw them into (Dan. 3:24-27). God's rescue prompted the king to say, "There is no other god who is able to deliver in this way" (Dan. 3:29 NASB). Our obedience to God and the truth stands as a witness to all, even to kings.

PRAYER FOCUS: God, grant me the courage and the confidence to serve you even during the most adverse circumstances. Lord, I am thankful for the courageous examples of faith written in the pages of Scripture.

DID YOU KNOW? China's "family planning policy," known as the "one child policy," has resulted in a very low birth rate, many more male births than female, and reduced the population by an estimated three hundred million people. Zhao Bingli, vice minister of the State Family Planning Commission, said, "After thirty years of efforts, exponential population growth has been effectively controlled, and some three hundred million births have been prevented."[19]

REFLECTIONS

239

AUGUST 20

Job 2:9-10 ESV

Then his wife said to him, "Do you still hold fast your integrity? Curse God and die." But he said to her, "You speak as one of the foolish women would speak. Shall we receive good from God, and shall we not receive evil?" In all this Job did not sin with his lips.

Before Job's wife told her husband to "curse God and die," their ten children had been killed, their servants and livestock destroyed, and Job's health had been stripped from him (Job 1:12-22; 2:3-8). She spoke out of suffering and the sorrow of her soul, but Job would not allow her advice to be used as the final tool of the Devil for his destruction. Job knew that God was sovereign, and he trusted that the Sovereign had a reason and a plan for allowing this calamity, even if he could not see it. Make no mistake, Job was very oppressed by this attack and deeply troubled. He complained greatly (Job 3), was misunderstood and accused falsely by his friends (Job 8:2-9; 11:3-15), argued his case before God and his friends (Job 13:1-15; 40:1-5), and pleaded with God for relief (Job 16:15-22). There is no doubt that the Christian life is hard and difficult at times. We all face hardships, trials, temptations, loss, and wickedness as God allows us to experience both the good and evil that pervades this earthly existence. But like Job, we need to hold fast our integrity and place our trust in God, allowing him to do an even deeper work in us through suffering. Paul wrote, "For I consider that the sufferings of this present time are not worth comparing with the glory that is to be revealed to us" (Rom. 8:18 ESV). Job suffered on a level that few of us can identify with, or even imagine, but the result was a deeper faith in God and a greater revelation as to whom he served. Job said, "For I know that my Redeemer lives, and at the last he will stand upon the earth. And after my skin has been thus destroyed, yet in my flesh I shall see God, whom I shall see for myself, and my eyes shall behold, and not another. My heart faints within me!" (Job 19:25-27 ESV). In our suffering, we may question God, argue with him, plead with him, and complain to him, but we must never abandon our trust and faith in him, because our Redeemer is the only hope and assurance we have that our end will be better than our beginning (Job 42:7-17).

PRAYER FOCUS: God, grant me wisdom and endurance during times of suffering. Allow me to hold fast my faith in you and to see your light in the midst of deep darkness. Show me that I can rest in you, even in times of great wickedness, hardship, and death.

DID YOU KNOW? God was confident in Job's heart and fidelity before he allowed Satan to afflict him (Job 1:8).

AUGUST 21

Job 29:11-17 NIV

Whoever heard me spoke well of me, and those who saw me commended me, because I rescued the poor who cried for help, and the fatherless who had none to assist him. The man who was dying blessed me; I made the widow's heart sing. I put on righteousness as my clothing; justice was my robe and my turban. I was eyes to the blind and feet to the lame. I was a father to the needy; I took up the case of the stranger. I broke the fangs of the wicked and snatched the victims from their teeth.

Job, while giving his final defense to his friends, recounts his earlier days and the reasons why he was so revered in the land of Uz. This righteous man, whom the Holy Spirit described as "blameless and upright," was respected by all because he lived what he spoke (Job 1:1; 29:7-10). Job fulfilled, to the best of his ability, the two great commandments of loving God and loving his neighbors (Matt. 22:36-40). Job understood that the Father God supplied all his needs and, therefore, he ought to supply the needs of others. This moral man rescued the poor and the fatherless, helped the widow and the sick, and pursued righteousness and justice with passion. He assisted the blind and the handicapped, looked after the needy, and took up the defense of the stranger. Finally, Job took action against the wicked and rescued their victims whenever possible. If Job were alive today, he would speak out against abortion and try to rescue the preborn. It is time for Christians to stand up and be counted, to live what we believe, or abortion will continue to harm our neighbors and flourish in our land.

PRAYER FOCUS: God, give us the courage of Job, the heart of Job, and the wisdom of Job that we might fulfill the calling you have given us. Lord, forgive us for legalized abortion and make its horror known throughout the church and the nations. God, send forth deliverers who will reap a harvest of life and peace in our nation.

DID YOU KNOW? "At thirty-three weeks, just over eight months, the baby may recognize a piece of music and even jump in time to it," according to Peter Tallack.[20]

REFLECTIONS

241

AUGUST
22

Exodus 1:22 HCSB

Pharaoh then commanded all his people: "You must throw every son born to the Hebrews into the Nile, but let every daughter live."

The Enemy is always trying to incite us to kill others and destroy the good things of God before they can come and bless the people. Immediately after this decree by Pharaoh, we read the story of Moses' rescue from the water and God's providential placement of him in the hands of Pharaoh's daughter (Exod. 2:1-10). Even as Satan and his band of disciples kill countless innocents, God's mighty plans for deliverance prevail! Moses' parents showed great courage as they hid their son from the Egyptians for the first three months after his birth. But when they could no longer guarantee their son's safety, his mother placed him in a basket and lowered him gently into the reeds along the banks of the Nile. As Pharaoh's daughter was bathing in the river, she found the child and took compassion on him, arranging unwittingly for his own mother to nurse him until he could join her in the palace. God began his deliverance of Israel with the tears of a child, "When she opened it, she saw the child—a little boy, crying. She felt sorry for him and said, 'This is one of the Hebrew boys'" (Exod. 2:6 HCSB). How great is our loss yearly, weekly, daily, hourly, and moment to moment from legalized abortion? Still, God's plans will prevail and his deliverers will come!

PRAYER FOCUS: God, send us the Moses of the pro-life movement. Bring forth your men, women, and children who will fight for the removal of abortion and the establishment of justice for all, both born and preborn. God, grant them favor with our government and fill them with a passion for life and a purpose that cannot be shaken.

DID YOU KNOW? Pharaoh's idea to discriminate based on the sex of the child is not a thing of the past. It is happening in the world today. Alcorn states in *Why Prolife*, "In Bombay, of eight thousand amniocentesis tests indicating the babies were female, all but one of the girls were killed by abortion." In another study of ninety-nine American mothers who were informed early of the sex of their child using amniocentesis, the results were as follows: "Only one mother elected to abort her boy, while twenty-nine elected to abort their girls."[21]

REFLECTIONS

AUGUST 23

2 Corinthians 9:6-8 NIV

Remember this: Whoever sows sparingly will also reap sparingly, and whoever sows generously will also reap generously. Each man should give what he has decided in his heart to give, not reluctantly or under compulsion, for God loves a cheerful giver. And God is able to make all grace abound to you, so that in all things at all times, having all that you need, you will abound in every good work.

One of the greatest things about the Christian life is the opportunity to be like our Savior! Jesus is the greatest giver. The Lord gave up his heavenly throne and became a man so he could give his life as a ransom for the sins of the world (Matt. 20:28; Phil. 2:5-8). He created the universe and this marvelous planet for us to enjoy (Col. 1:16). After he commissioned the Twelve, Jesus said, "Heal the sick, raise the dead, cleanse those who have leprosy, drive out demons. Freely you have received, freely give" (Matt. 10:8 NIV). Each of us has received so much from our Lord. How could we not be excited to give to his people and further his Kingdom work on earth? When we give we are simply being good stewards of what God has already blessed us with (1 Chron. 29:14). We should be excited to support pro-life ministries, pregnancy resource centers, adoption agencies, churches, missionaries, and anyone who is serving and loving God's people. When we give with a cheerful and expectant heart, God will increase our awareness of his grace, and he will make sure we have all we need and improve our ability to contribute more abundantly to every good work.

PRAYER FOCUS: God, teach me to understand that all wealth and ability comes from you. Help me use my physical and financial resources to bless others and set the captives free. God, thank you for all the good gifts you have given me already (James 1:17). Use me, Lord, as an instrument of your righteousness on earth.

DID YOU KNOW? The apostle Paul said, "In everything I did, I showed you that by this kind of hard work we must help the weak, remembering the words the Lord Jesus himself said: 'It is more blessed to give than to receive'" (Acts 20:35 NIV). George Müller, who gave 81,000 pounds over his life of ministry, said, "My aim never was, how much I could obtain, but rather how much I could give."[22]

REFLECTIONS

AUGUST 24

Colossians 3:1-4 NASB

Therefore if you have been raised up with Christ, keep seeking the things above, where Christ is, seated at the right hand of God. Set your mind on the things above, not on the things that are on earth. For you have died and your life is hidden with Christ in God. When Christ, who is our life, is revealed, then you also will be revealed with Him in glory.

As the redeemed who are hidden in Christ, Christians should always be seeking the things of God. In the third chapter of his letter to the Colossians, Paul contrasts the ways of the earth (lying, greed, sexual immorality, anger) with the ways of God (compassion, kindness, humility, forgiveness). But Paul doesn't stop there—the Christian life is more than following a code of moral conduct. The key is Colossians 3:14-17: "Beyond all these things put on love, which is the perfect bond of unity. Let the peace of Christ rule in your hearts, to which indeed you were called in one body; and be thankful. Let the word of Christ richly dwell within you, with all wisdom teaching and admonishing one another with psalms and hymns and spiritual songs, singing with thankfulness in your hearts to God. Whatever you do in word or deed, do all in the name of the Lord Jesus, giving thanks through Him to God the Father" (NASB). We are to follow the words of Christ, who is himself the Word (John 1:1). What better way to set our minds on the things above than to set our minds on the One who has already been revealed from above and is yet to be revealed in all his fullness? Christ is our life, our sustenance, our daily bread, and the closer we walk with him, the greater his heart and character will be revealed in us. To understand his mission and how we are a part of that mission (Matt. 28:19-20; Luke 4:18-21; John 3:16-17), we must abide with him and discover the supreme goal of a redeemed life—to love his Father and feed his sheep (Matt. 22:34-37; John 13:34-35; 21:15-17).

PRAYER FOCUS: Lord, thank you for loving me fully. Jesus, give me a passion for people, young and old, born and preborn, sick and well, lost and redeemed, lovely and unlovely. Grow my love more and more in real knowledge and discernment (Phil. 1:9).

DID YOU KNOW? Benjamin Rush, a signer of the Declaration of Independence, was a prominent doctor, educator, and abolitionist. He once said, "The Gospel of Jesus Christ prescribes the wisest rules for just conduct in every situation of life."[23]

REFLECTIONS

AUGUST 25

Psalm 50:14-15 NKJV

Offer to God thanksgiving, and pay your vows to the Most High. Call upon Me in the day of trouble; I will deliver you, and you shall glorify Me.

Does God have our hearts today? Prior to these verses in Psalm 50, God declared the insufficiency of the sacrificial system to fully satisfy him. God's love cannot be bought and his favor cannot be purchased; therefore, the Most High desires a personal relationship with us more than he desires sacrifice. The Lord doesn't want ritualistic believers. He wants worshipful believers. His love is a gift that he wants us to willingly give back to him. God desires our heartfelt gratitude and appreciation for who he is and what he has done for us. He wants us to call on him in good times and bad, and to know him even as we are known. God wants us to experience his love as he rescues us from trouble and provides for all our needs. In return, the Lord desires that we honor him, revere him, and cry "Abba, Father!" God doesn't want our money, our time, or our lives; God wants us to *desire* to give him our money, our time, and our lives. We should give thanks to the Lord and love him because he first loved us.

PRAYER FOCUS: Light of the World, shine on me and reveal all that I have to be thankful for. Illuminate your goodness and grace in my life. Overwhelm my heart with your love for me. Show me wonderful things and bring me to my knees in worship of who you are. Lead me beside still waters and cleanse my soul, and give me peace as I give you all of me.

DID YOU KNOW? The worship group Watermark recorded the majority of their songs for the album *A Grateful People* live on this day in 2005. Nathan and Christy Nockels, the leaders of the group, have experienced the loss of two children during their ten years plus of music ministry, and yet their music is an experience of worship and gratitude.[24]

REFLECTIONS

AUGUST 26

Psalm 90:10-12 HCSB

Our lives last seventy years or, if we are strong, eighty years. Even the best of them are struggle and sorrow; indeed, they pass quickly and we fly away. Who understands the power of Your anger? Your wrath matches the fear that is due You. Teach us to number our days carefully so that we may develop wisdom in our hearts.

Earthly life is short and full of trouble, and the wisest among us count each day as precious. If we serve God and seek to do his will, our lives will be full and blessed, no matter how long they are. The brevity of our earthly life is due to sin and the universal consequence of Adam and Eve's fall from grace in the Garden of Eden. God's original plan for them was life indefinite (Gen. 2:15-17; 3:19-22), but the length of human life was greatly shortened after the Fall and reduced again after the Flood (compare Genesis chapter five with Genesis chapter eleven). Today, our earthly life span is very similar to the accounting of the psalmist: "Our lives last seventy years or, if we are strong, eighty years." While people sometimes live to be over one hundred, it is very easy to identify with an approximate life span of seventy to eighty years on earth. Anything shorter is considered premature or heartbreaking, especially in the case of infants, children, adolescents, and young adults. Therefore, the wise place their faith in Jesus, for how much more heartbreaking is a short sinful life on earth followed by separation from our Creator for eternity? Life on earth is precious and it should not be taken away by anyone, but life with Christ is forever and we should seek to help all people discover it.

> *For God loved the world in this way: He gave His One and Only Son, so that everyone who believes in Him will not perish but have eternal life. For God did not send His Son into the world that He might condemn the world, but that the world might be saved through Him. Anyone who believes in Him is not condemned, but anyone who does not believe is already condemned, because he has not believed in the name of the One and Only Son of God. (John 3:16-18 HCSB).*

PRAYER FOCUS: God, continue to mature me in love and respect for you. I am in awe of who you are and what you have blessed me with in this life. Lord, teach me to number my days and use them for your glory and purposes. Give me a heart of understanding and gratitude, with eyes to see the needs of your people. Bring me to the Bible during every season of my life and teach me from its deep wisdom.

DID YOU KNOW? Methuselah has the longest recorded life span in the Bible at 969 years of age (Gen. 5:27).

AUGUST 27

Isaiah 57:1-2 NIV

The righteous perish, and no one ponders it in his heart; devout men are taken away, and no one understands that the righteous are taken away to be spared from evil. Those who walk uprightly enter into peace; they find rest as they lie in death.

When people of the Kingdom die, it can appear to be counterproductive to the kingdom work of God. But God in his sovereignty knows what is needed for the servant as well as the body of Christ at large. Perhaps it's time for new leadership, and the removal of the righteous one or ones expedites this process. At times, the body needs correction in the form of judgment. Sometimes, the one who sows is removed to make way for the one who waters in order for the harvest to begin. In predicting his own death, Jesus said, "I tell you the truth, unless a kernel of wheat falls to the ground and dies, it remains only a single seed. But if it dies, it produces many seeds" (John 12:24 NIV). Whatever the reason, if the righteous and upright die early or full of age, they can be confident they will rest in peace because their hope is in the great eternal God. Where is our hope today? Is it in this life or is it in the Giver of this life? When we put faith in the One who has conquered the grave, we will have peace even as we lie in death. God's timing is perfect for he sees the unseen, the future, and every possible angle or purpose. When it comes to the death of his servants, we can trust that their death, like all things, is in his control. Looking through the window of revealed truth, one can see that the righteous are spared from the toil of future evil days as they find rest in the arms of their beloved Savior.

PRAYER FOCUS: God, increase my awareness of eternity and my perception of life beyond the grave. Teach me that this present life is full of purpose and meaning regardless of its duration. Help me understand the value of human life and the benefits of respecting every single human person you have created. Thank you, Lord, for giving me cherished relationships and providing me with peace and hope during times of loss.

DID YOU KNOW? According to the Centers for Disease Control and Prevention, more than two million Americans have died each year for the past twenty years recorded.[25] The loss we feel when those closest to us die can be overwhelming. If you find yourself grieving a loss, I recommend the following books as helpful resources for understanding and coping with loss: *The Dawn of Hope* by Eldyn Simons, *A Grace Disguised* by Jerry Sittser, *Safe in the Arms of God* by John MacArthur, and *Gone, But Not Lost* by David Wiersbe.

AUGUST 28

Matthew 10:28-31 NKJV

And do not fear those who kill the body but cannot kill the soul. But rather fear Him who is able to destroy both soul and body in hell. Are not two sparrows sold for a copper coin? And not one of them falls to the ground apart from your Father's will. But the very hairs of your head are all numbered. Do not fear therefore; you are of more value than many sparrows.

Knowing they would face persecution, ostracism, and martyrdom, Jesus told his disciples not to fear those who could kill the body. He knew in order for them to face the trials to come they would need to know with whom their security rests, how much they are valued, and who holds the future. God is the One with the power, ability, and love necessary to sustain us in all things, even death. The God who maintains the universe and our solar system in perfect order watches over us. He waters the earth and provides for every creature he has made from conception to death. The Father's love and care for his entire creation is continually evident, and yet he cares for people more than anything else. He has individually numbered our hairs and created this earth with all its beauty, complexity, and sustenance for our management and provision. Nothing in the universe is more important to God than we are. We can rest in God's great love for us and be content in the knowledge that Jesus is supreme, both now and forever. When we seek wisdom, an eternal perspective, and God's love, we will overcome our fears and achieve all God has for us in this life and the next.

PRAYER FOCUS: Father, I am in awe of you. Mature me and help me cultivate a heart of wisdom and understanding. Lord, walk beside me in every circumstance and give me David's confidence (Ps. 23:4-6). Jesus, I am so grateful for your love. Grant me your presence in good times and bad.

DID YOU KNOW? The Earth is the ideal habitat for humanity and several other creatures. Hugh Ross, in his *More Than a Theory*, wrote this about our marvelous planet: "Even if the observable universe contains as many planets as stars, about 50 billion trillion, the possibility (without invoking divine miracles) for the existence of just one planet with the required conditions for advanced life falls below 1 in 10^{1000}. Stated another way, the probability from a nontheistic perspective of finding a body anywhere in the observable universe with the necessary conditions to support advanced life is at least 10^{850} times more remote than the possibility that a blindfolded person could pick out a single marked electron randomly shuffled into a tightly packed pile of electrons that fills the entire universe, on the first try."[26]

AUGUST 29

Genesis 25:21-24 ESV

And Isaac prayed to the Lord for his wife, because she was barren. And the Lord granted his prayer, and Rebekah his wife conceived. The children struggled together within her, and she said, "If it is thus, why is this happening to me?" So she went to inquire of the Lord. And the Lord said to her, "Two nations are in your womb, and two peoples from within you shall be divided; the one shall be stronger than the other, the older shall serve the younger." When her days to give birth were completed, behold, there were twins in her womb.

Couples having trouble conceiving can pray to the Lord to ask him to open the womb and give them the desire of their hearts. Perhaps he will bless them with children and grant their prayer. At the very least, dialogue with God leads to a better understanding of his present will in each of our lives. In Rebekah's case, God chose to open her womb with twin boys. Notice how the Scriptures refer to the developing babies as children—not tissues, blobs, cells, embryos, fetuses, preborn, unborn, or any other term people like to use for children in the womb. The twin boys needed time to develop, but they already had personal and national destinies to fulfill (Gen. 25:23). Each one of us is uniquely created with a purpose and a destiny that only we can fulfill. Every life has the potential to reproduce new life, and as a result the loss of any one life can affect endless generations to come. In the case of Jacob and Esau, entire nations would have been affected had one or both boys been lost in the womb.

PRAYER FOCUS: God, the biblical evidence that life begins at conception is strong and overwhelming. Help me cope with the sorrow I feel over the tragedy of abortion. I pray and weep for the doctors who slaughter endless generations before their lives begin. Jesus, forgive all those fathers who have walked away from their pregnant partners, or the mothers who have chosen to destroy their children. Holy Spirit, comfort all the children lost to abortion, children who will never see an earthly sunset, exchange vows, or hold their firstborn. God, forgive us for we do not know what we do.

DID YOU KNOW? A baby's ability to suck from the breast is fully developed by thirty-five weeks. Peter Tallack wrote, "Ultrasound scans have shown that as soon as thumb-sucking begins, a baby tends to show a clear preference for either the left or right thumb. This left- or right-handedness, which stays with the baby for life, develops in the womb rather than in early childhood, as previously thought."[27]

REFLECTIONS

AUGUST 30

Proverbs 17:22 NASB

A joyful heart is good medicine, but a broken spirit dries up the bones.

It's easy to lose our joy as we grapple with abortion. The tragedy is so large and pervasive that it is easy to become overwhelmed and forget the goodness of God. In our brokenness over this sin, we should not allow our own spirits to be broken. Rather, we can come to the God of all hope and let him fill us with his presence and his life-giving joy. Ponder how good God has been to us, our friends, and our nation during this dark and difficult time. Let the joy of the Lord renew our strength and calm our soul. No matter how things appear, we know God is on the throne and that he is good! When we meditate on Scripture and let his truth refuel our tanks and set us free, we can "be joyful in hope, patient in affliction, faithful in prayer" (Rom. 12:12 NIV). With a joyful heart we can celebrate and embrace life as we overcome evil with good. And we can laugh and love and let the medicine of God heal us every day!

PRAYER FOCUS: Jesus, give me your peace and your patience as I walk through difficult times and face overwhelming realities. Take my hand and let me know you are in control. Lord, work all things together for the good of those who love you, and grant me joy, health, and life as I seek to serve you and the kingdom of heaven.

DID YOU KNOW? Modern medical science has begun studying the role a positive mental state plays in a person's physical health. In 2004, a USA TODAY article written by Sharon Jayson titled "Power of a Super Attitude" reported that the National Institute of Health gave forty-four grants to researchers who were evaluating optimism and its health benefit. The article included this quote: "'Mind-body medicine is now scientifically proven,' says Herbert Benson, a cardiologist and associate professor of medicine at Harvard Medical School, who is considered a pioneer in the field. 'There are literally thousands of articles on how the mind and brain affect the body.'"[28] Scientific discoveries affirm what God told us long ago: a joyful heart is good medicine.

REFLECTIONS

AUGUST
31

Acts 8:29-35 NIV

The Spirit told Philip, "Go to that chariot and stay near it." Then Philip ran up to the chariot and heard the man reading Isaiah the prophet. "Do you understand what you are reading?" Philip asked. "How can I," he said, "unless someone explains it to me?" So he invited Philip to come up and sit with him. The eunuch was reading this passage of Scripture: "He was led like a sheep to the slaughter, and as a lamb before the shearer is silent, so he did not open his mouth. In his humiliation he was deprived of justice. Who can speak of his descendants? For his life was taken from the earth." The eunuch asked Philip, "Tell me, please, who is the prophet talking about, himself or someone else?" Then Philip began with that very passage of Scripture and told him the good news about Jesus.

Philip was ministering to a large group of people and having tremendous success when the Spirit called him away to witness to a lone individual (Acts 8:5-8, 26). Philip was sensitive to the Spirit, obedient, giving, and equipped. If we all lived like Philip, the power of God working through us would be extraordinary! The good news is: each one of us can be like Philip. We can seek God with our whole heart and then follow wherever he leads. We can ask God to help us cultivate the heart and faith of Philip. If we do, we won't miss God's divine appointments in our lives. Being sensitive to the Spirit and God's Word will allow us to develop faithfulness and courage. Our journey, like Philip's, will bear fruit when we submit to God's will, check our own agendas at the door, enrich ourselves with the Word (know it), and seek the Spirit's leading equipping us with the tools and insights necessary to assist others as they search for the truth of God. If we are persistent and patient in our efforts to obtain these qualities, God will bring about a good result. In time, they will prove invaluable to our witness for Christ and our ministry to others.

PRAYER FOCUS: Lord, give me ears to hear the Spirit and the resolve to obey your leading. Show me your will and help me to not get in the way of it. Jesus, I'm making myself available to you, so please direct me to whatever work you have for me.

DID YOU KNOW? The humiliation of Christ, prophesied in Isaiah 53:7-8 and quoted in today's passage (Acts 8:32-33) has strong parallels to the experience of an aborted child: "The eunuch was reading this passage of Scripture: 'He was led like a sheep to the slaughter, and as a lamb before the shearer is silent, so he did not open his mouth. In his humiliation he was deprived of justice. Who can speak of his descendants? For his life was taken from the earth.'" Like Jesus, the victims of abortion are led to the slaughter, silent before their execution, unjustly treated, deprived of earthly descendants, and have their lives taken for no offense of their own.

REFLECTIONS

September

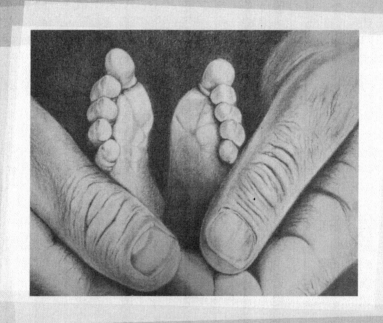

BIRTH

SEPTEMBER 1

Romans 12:17-19 HCSB

Do not repay anyone evil for evil. Try to do what is honorable in everyone's eyes. If possible, on your part, live at peace with everyone. Friends, do not avenge yourselves; instead, leave room for His wrath. For it is written: Vengeance belongs to Me; I will repay, says the Lord.

Sadly, the late-term abortionist George Tiller was murdered on May 31, 2009, by Scott Roeder. After this happened I read an article where a man said that pro-life groups should applaud the murder of Tiller if in fact they believe abortion to be murder. He said that if they condemn the act, it only belies the reality that the taking of Tiller's life and that of the preborn are not equal. This argument makes no sense because if one values all life from conception forward, then one would naturally value Tiller's life as much as his victims. This does not mean, of course, that one condones Tiller's occupation, lifestyle, or choices. That is something a Christian, or anyone else who values human life, could never do. Nor does it mean that one should not seek justice for the preborn. I only hope that Tiller repented of his sins before his passing from this world to the next. For we will all stand before a just and holy God, one who said, "Vengeance belongs to Me; I will repay, says the Lord." The continued effort to establish the personhood of the preborn and provide justice for all our citizens should never stop until victory is achieved. We must never forget, however, that those who escape justice here will not escape justice at the judgment seat of Christ. Therefore, live at peace with everyone and overcome evil with good.

PRAYER FOCUS: Jesus, forgive George Tiller for the people he destroyed and murdered and forgive Scott Roeder for murdering Tiller. Lord, when I am discouraged by injustice, show me that justice waits with you. Let me bring life, peace, and truth wherever I go. Fill my mind with the knowledge that you have overcome the darkness, and let the only death I'm involved with be my own in its appointed time, or when you give me the opportunity to lay it down for the good of another.

DID YOU KNOW? In 2005, Christin Gilbert, a nineteen-year-old woman, was killed by George Tiller's abortion facility due to sepsis and cardiac arrest following the abortion of her twenty-eight-week-old child.[1]

REFLECTIONS

SEPTEMBER 2

Isaiah 55:9-11 NKJV

For as the heavens are higher than the earth, so are My ways higher than your ways, and My thoughts than your thoughts. For as the rain comes down, and the snow from heaven, and do not return there, but water the earth, and make it bring forth and bud, that it may give seed to the sower and bread to the eater, so shall My word be that goes forth from My mouth; it shall not return to Me void, but it shall accomplish what I please, and it shall prosper in the thing for which I sent it.

The Spirit first directed me to these verses in Isaiah when I was standing on a sidewalk in front of an abortion facility trying to rescue men, women, and children from the devastating choice of abortion. I always bring my Bible with me when I go to pray and offer assistance to the people consenting to abortion. One day, as person after person declined my offer of help, I grew frustrated and restless. So, I prayed to God and asked him what I could do to be more effective. The Spirit impressed on my mind Isaiah 55:9-11. After I read the verses, the Spirit instructed me to read God's Word for it would not return void. From that time forward, I have sought to read Scripture aloud whenever I am at an abortion facility. Over time, I have seen it lift the spirits of fellow believers as they pray, sidewalk counsel, or protest. I have seen it bring people together and soften doctrinal differences. I have seen it arrest the conscience of pro-abortion and pro-choice people. Best of all, I've seen it change hearts and minds and save children. Perhaps the greatest impact has been how the Word of God has ministered to me and made me a better person. Never underestimate the supernatural power of God's Word to prepare the soil and ready the harvest!

PRAYER FOCUS: Lord, show me it is not what I can do but what you can do that counts. Give me fresh wisdom and insight into how to use the spiritual tools you have already given me in my service for your Kingdom. Refresh me with your life-giving Word!

DID YOU KNOW? Moses commanded that the law of God be read aloud to all the people of Israel every seven years (Deut. 31:9-13). Notice how the Word of God is beneficial for everyone to hear, especially the children.

REFLECTIONS

SEPTEMBER 3

Mark 10:6-9 NKJV

But from the beginning of the creation, God "made them male and female." "For this reason a man shall leave his father and mother and be joined to his wife, and the two shall become one flesh"; so then they are no longer two, but one flesh. Therefore what God has joined together, let not man separate.

When the Pharisees asked Jesus about the legality of divorce, his response was recorded in the gospel of Mark 10:6-9. He said that from the very beginning God made the human race male and female and blessed the office of marriage. God views marriage as sacred, a holy union where the two individuals spiritually and intimately become one flesh. This joining is a powerful bond and should be revered by all. Obviously, divorce, sexual immorality, fornication, or adultery can destroy or weaken this bond and lead to great difficulties in life. We need to strive for purity before, during, and after marriage in all seasons of life. The author of Hebrews wrote, "Marriage is honorable among all, and the bed undefiled; but fornicators and adulterers God will judge" (Heb. 13:4 NKJV). Sex is a blessing from God to be enjoyed in marriage for the benefit of those joined by God. If man should not separate those joined in marriage, how much more so those conceived by God's divine will?

PRAYER FOCUS: God, help me gain control over my sexual desires and impulses. Give me discernment and wisdom in this highly sexual culture about what to engage in or watch. Jesus, forgive me when I stumble and fill me with your hope and peace as I contemplate the day of my ultimate deliverance from sin. Lord, bless my marriage, or my future marriage, with purity, love, and joy.

DID YOU KNOW? Research indicates that people who are married tend to experience greater financial security, sexual satisfaction, and health than those who remain single or cohabitate.[2]

REFLECTIONS

SEPTEMBER 4

Malachi 2:15 NIV

Has not the Lord made them one? In flesh and spirit they are his. And why one? Because he was seeking godly offspring. So guard yourself in your spirit, and do not break faith with the wife of your youth.

God knew from the beginning it was not good for man to be alone, so he created a suitable mate for Adam when he made Eve (Gen. 2:18-24). God created every human being with an innate desire for intimacy and fellowship. One of the greatest ways this is satisfied on earth is through healthy marriage and family. Through these crucial institutions we learn about sharing, giving, caring, loyalty, patience, boundaries, perseverance, laughter, love, and much more. God not only provides for many of our greatest needs through marriage and family, He also uses them to teach us about his own character and love for us. Being part of a healthy marriage or family is excellent training for the ultimate relationship one can have: a relationship with God. For it is in our walk with God that we experience the height of intimacy and fellowship. It naturally follows then that one of God's great purposes for marriage is children, family, and the perpetuation of more marriages and families. We need to guard our spirits and remain faithful in marriage so that we can raise children who are sensitive to intimacy and fellowship, children who are prepared to take the hand of their Maker and walk with him.

PRAYER FOCUS: God, grow me in gratitude and appreciation for my beloved. Help me see your love for me in the mate you provided for me. Spirit, help me guard my spirit and remain faithful to my spouse in every season of life. Lord, if you see fit to bless us with children, give us the strength, wisdom, and knowledge to raise them in your ways, so that when they are old, they will not depart from you.

DID YOU KNOW? The U.S. Department of Health and Human Services provides a list of the benefits of a healthy marriage on their Administration for Children and Families website *www.acf.hhs.gov/index.html*. Some of the benefits listed for children are better physical and emotional health, decreased chance for divorce when they marry, less likelihood of abusing drugs or contracting a sexual disease, less likelihood of being raised in poverty, and a higher likelihood of having academic success or going to college.[3]

SEPTEMBER 5

Galatians 1:11-16 NASB

For I would have you know, brethren, that the gospel which was preached by me is not according to man. For I neither received it from man, nor was I taught it, but I received it through a revelation of Jesus Christ. For you have heard of my former manner of life in Judaism, how I used to persecute the church of God beyond measure and tried to destroy it; and I was advancing in Judaism beyond many of my contemporaries among my countrymen, being more extremely zealous for my ancestral traditions. But when God, who had set me apart even from my mother's womb and called me through His grace, was pleased to reveal His Son in me so that I might preach Him among the Gentiles, I did not immediately consult with flesh and blood.

It is comforting to know the gospel is not according to human traditions and insights but rather by the direct revelation of Jesus Christ. There is never any reason for us to lose heart when facing those opposed to Christ and his gospel, for perhaps their Damascus experience still awaits, as the apostle Paul's did. We should pray diligently for those who oppose us that they too will have a revelation of Jesus Christ and that he would awaken their conscience and inform their mind. As Paul continues to clarify his qualifications for apostolic authority, notice where he traces his personhood and calling: to the womb! Like Jeremiah and John the Baptist before him, Paul understood that his commissioning was from conception. This shouts loudly that life is sacred and full of purpose from the very beginning of the joining of sperm and egg!

PRAYER FOCUS: Jesus, I pray for all those who stand opposed to your Word, the pro-life movement, and the truth that life begins at conception. Open their eyes, Lord, and give them a discerning spirit. Help Christians rightly divide the Word of Truth. Bring us out of mere, ideological faith to achieve real, living faith so we can impact the culture and end abortion.

DID YOU KNOW? The brain is the first organ to form in the womb. Peter Tallack wrote, "In just over nine months our baby's brain has grown around 100 billion neurons, with 100 trillion connections. Although it was the first organ to form, it is the last to be completed. Unlike most organs, which are virtually complete by day 50, the brain becomes more and more complex throughout pregnancy—and will keep on developing long after birth."[4]

REFLECTIONS

SEPTEMBER 6

Nahum 1:3 ESV

The Lord is slow to anger and great in power, and the Lord will by no means clear the guilty. His way is in whirlwind and storm, and the clouds are the dust of his feet.

∞

Regrettably, our nation has allowed abortion for the past forty-three years at the state level and thirty-seven years at the national level. This practice has led to the eradication of more than fifty million natural-preborn U.S. citizens! Surely, God is slow to anger; otherwise, our nation would have been dealt with by now. But he is also great in power and will not clear the guilty without satisfying justice. Without our full repentance and Christ's acceptable payment for all sin, we will pay for our personal and national sins with overwhelming horror as the verdict is read and our sentence pronounced. How long will we defy the living God and assume he is either unconcerned about our behavior or without power to do anything about it? We will discover in an instant just how mighty, awesome, and dreadful our Creator is. As Sodom and Gomorrah fell, so shall we fall if we do not take heed and repent of our iniquity and turn back to the living God, revering him and what he has made. God is beyond description, all-powerful, perfectly just, and utterly holy. His way is the whirlwind and storm, and clouds are the dust of his feet.

PRAYER FOCUS: God, I repent before you and confess that I have failed to fear you and hold you in awe. I have failed to grasp the magnitude of your person and the awesome power you wield. Words cannot describe how grateful I am that you are slow to anger and patient with sinners, of which I am one. Jesus, forgive me for my many sins and wrap me in your righteousness. Forgive me and my nation for abortion and help us to overcome the darkness before you rise up and justly judge this nation for her slaughter of the innocents.

DID YOU KNOW? The voice of the Lord can break cedars, shake the wilderness, and strip the forests bare (Ps. 29). In the preface of his famous work *The Knowledge of the Holy*, A.W. Tozer wrote, "The Church has surrendered her once lofty concept of God and has substituted for it one so low, so ignoble, as to be utterly unworthy of thinking, worshiping men. This she has not done deliberately, but little by little and without her knowledge; and her very unawareness only makes her situation all the more tragic."[5] Perhaps today's low view of the created stems from our continued low view of the Creator. Tozer's beautifully written book enhances one's view of God and the majesty of his power.

SEPTEMBER 7

Zechariah 7:9-13 NKJV

Thus says the LORD of hosts: "Execute true justice, show mercy and compassion everyone to his brother. Do not oppress the widow or the fatherless, the alien or the poor. Let none of you plan evil in his heart against his brother." But they refused to heed, shrugged their shoulders, and stopped their ears so that they could not hear. Yes, they made their hearts like flint, refusing to hear the law and the words which the LORD of hosts had sent by His Spirit through the former prophets. Thus great wrath came from the LORD of hosts. Therefore it happened, that just as He proclaimed and they would not hear, so they called out and I would not listen, says the LORD of hosts.

The people of Judah sent Sherezer and some men to the priests to determine if they should continue to fast now that the temple was being rebuilt. The Lord's first response, issued through Zechariah, was to challenge the men about the attitude of their hearts when they fasted (Zech. 7:5-7). God wants our hearts more than our practices. Next, Zechariah relayed the words in our passage to remind the men why the people went into captivity in the first place. They made their hearts like flint and refused to perform true justice, but God wanted his people to champion justice, extend mercy, and refrain from oppression. What happens when God's people stiffen their necks, shrug their shoulders, and cover their ears, pursuing their own ends and ignoring the will of God? The result was disaster as judgment and wrath came upon them. Furthermore, when they cried out for help, the Lord responded as they deserved and chose not to listen to their pleas. It is time for the body of Christ to listen to what the Word of God says about abortion and stop shrugging our shoulders! How can we in the church expect God to listen to us or bless us when we continue participating in and allowing abortion in our land? We desperately need to turn our hearts to the Father and stop the oppression of his children.

PRAYER FOCUS: God, help me fast with right motives, applying my whole heart to your will. I know you want my heart more than anything else. Teach me to surrender to your will in all areas, but especially in the area of loving my neighbor. Lord, even though we don't deserve it, listen to our pleas to end abortion. Please God, set the children on abortion's death row free.

DID YOU KNOW? Dietrich Bonhoeffer, a German Protestant theologian, was executed at Flossenburg concentration camp on April 9, 1945, for his resistance against the policies and practices of Hitler.[6] Bonhoeffer was one of the few voices from the church to speak out against the atrocities of Nazism. When will the modern church find her voice against abortion? Will she take up the call, or to her shame leave it to a small group of voices crying in the wilderness, like Bonhoeffer?

SEPTEMBER 8

Revelation 3:14-19 ESV

And to the angel of the church in Laodicea write: "The words of the Amen, the faithful and true witness, the beginning of God's creation. I know your works: you are neither cold nor hot. Would that you were either cold or hot! So, because you are lukewarm, and neither hot nor cold, I will spit you out of my mouth. For you say, I am rich, I have prospered, and I need nothing, not realizing that you are wretched, pitiable, poor, blind, and naked. I counsel you to buy from me gold refined by fire, so that you may be rich, and white garments so that you may clothe yourself and the shame of your nakedness may not be seen, and salve to anoint your eyes, so that you may see. Those whom I love, I reprove and discipline, so be zealous and repent."

These words were spoken by Jesus in his revelation recorded by John. They clearly apply to the Laodicean church, but the condition and heart of the Laodicean church can be found anywhere in any age. No matter when, who, or where the Laodicean church is, one thing is clear: She is a church marked by unawareness and blindness. No doubt, the church today is unaware of many important things, but when it comes to the area of abortion this is painfully evident. A great many of our denominations, pastors, and laity are lukewarm about abortion. This is the worst of all conditions, for the apathy and indifference of it leads one to falsehood and stagnation. The lukewarm position in the abortion debate is the pro-choice position. It is time to decide if we are cold (pro-abortion), lukewarm (pro-choice), or hot (pro-life). To be undecided, indifferent, apathetic, or afraid to offend—or anything other than pro-life—is to vote for death and miss the mark of Romans 13:8-10:

> *Owe no one anything, except to love each other, for the one who loves another has fulfilled the law. For the commandments, "You shall not commit adultery, You shall not murder, You shall not steal, You shall not covet," and any other commandment, are summed up in this word: "You shall love your neighbor as yourself." Love does no wrong to a neighbor; therefore love is the fulfilling of the law (ESV).*

PRAYER FOCUS: Jesus, forgive me and your people for our many sins. Awaken us, Lord! Make me, my church, and my nation hot for the things of God. Help us to see what we haven't seen and to do what we haven't done in the cause of life. Let us help the fatherless, weak, poor, oppressed, and least of these regardless of age, gender, stage of development, or function.

DID YOU KNOW? Christian theologian R. C. Sproul has written a book about abortion titled *Abortion: A Rational Look at an Emotional Issue*. In it he said, "Sadly, the organized church—more than any other institution apart from the Supreme Court—has neglected its duty to inform the public conscience."[7]

REFLECTIONS

SEPTEMBER 9

Isaiah 14:12-15 ESV

How you are fallen from heaven, O Day Star, son of Dawn! How you are cut down to the ground, you who laid the nations low! You said in your heart, "I will ascend to heaven; above the stars of God I will set my throne on high; I will sit on the mount of assembly in the far reaches of the north; I will ascend above the heights of the clouds; I will make myself like the Most High." But you are brought down to Sheol, to the far reaches of the pit.

Scholars disagree whether these verses apply solely to the king of Babylon, or to both the king of Babylon and Satan, the archenemy of God. Regardless, the illustration of ultimate pride and arrogance is staggering. Pride is a deadly sin because it hastens our separation from God. In the end, only one can be exalted and worshiped—the Creator God! Pride seeks to do its own will and glorify itself. Pride says, "My will be done," not "Thy will be done." Pride then is the opposite of humility, and consequently this sin is at the very heart of abortion. Instead of being humbled by God's selection of us to care for new life and submitting to his will, we rebel and substitute our will for his. Choosing not to be inconvenienced or burdened, we terminate the child, failing to understand that separation from God will lead us to trouble in this earthly life, and perhaps into the pit of hell in the next life if we fail to reconnect with God. If we have never confessed and renounced our abortion, we need to do so and find healing and grace in the arms of Jesus. If we are thinking about having an abortion or facilitating one, we need to humble ourselves and choose life! If we find ourselves or our partner pregnant, celebrate it, for God has chosen us to take part in one of his greatest miracles: *new life*.

PRAYER FOCUS: Jesus, I confess _____ to you and ask for your forgiveness and healing. Lord, protect me from the Enemy and his appeal to my pride and selfishness. God, I am glad you are going to cast the Great Deceiver into the lake of fire and sulfur for his crimes against you and your children (Rev. 20:10). Holy One, Lord Most High, you stand far above all things! Grow me in understanding, humility, and grace as I journey with you.

DID YOU KNOW? Lucifer is Latin for "daystar" or "morning star."[8] The New King James Version of the Bible translates Isaiah 14:12 as, "How you are fallen from heaven, O Lucifer, son of the morning!"

REFLECTIONS

261

SEPTEMBER 10

Psalm 25:4-7 NIV

Show me your ways, O LORD, teach me your paths; guide me in your truth and teach me, for you are God my Savior, and my hope is in you all day long. Remember, O LORD, your great mercy and love, for they are from of old. Remember not the sins of my youth and my rebellious ways; according to your love remember me, for you are good, O LORD.

If and when we are haunted by sin, overcome with guilt, filled with sorrow, desperate, and hopeless, we do not need to fear for God is good and his mercies are new every morning. The prophet Jeremiah put it this way: "Because of the Lord's great love we are not consumed, for his compassions never fail. They are new every morning; great is your faithfulness" (Lam. 3:22-23 NIV). Because God is a rescuer and a Savior, we can cry out to him today, asking him to wipe away our tears and teach us his ways. No sin of our youth or rebellion we have walked in is too much for God to cleanse and overcome. God loves us deeply, passionately, and he wants to give us hope and rest. We can lay our burdens at his feet and taste the goodness of God in the land of the living. God is not given to mood or circumstance. His mercy and love are integral—part and parcel—to his eternal nature. He longs to be merciful to all of us.

PRAYER FOCUS: Today's prayer comes from *The Knowledge of the Holy*, by A. W. Tozer: "Holy Father, Thy wisdom excites our admiration, Thy power fills us with fear, Thy omnipresence turns every spot of earth into holy ground; but how shall we thank Thee enough for Thy mercy which comes down to the lowest part of our need to give us beauty for ashes, the oil of joy for mourning, and for the spirit of heaviness a garment of praise? We bless and magnify Thy mercy, through Jesus Christ our Lord. Amen."[9]

DID YOU KNOW? While dying on the cross, Jesus revealed his abundant mercy in two tangible acts. First, to his persecutors, when Jesus prayed to the Father for their forgiveness (Luke 23:33-37). Second, to the thief, when upon his acknowledgment of truth, Jesus granted eternal life (Luke 23:39-43).

REFLECTIONS

SEPTEMBER 11

Deuteronomy 27:24-25
HCSB

"The one who secretly kills his neighbor is cursed." And all the people will say, "Amen!" "The one who accepts a bribe to kill an innocent person is cursed." And all the people will say, "Amen!"

September 11, 2001, was a terrible day in American history. It was a day marked by the mass murder of over six thousand innocent people. A little fewer than half of the deaths were at the hands of terrorists in New York, Virginia, and Pennsylvania, while a little more than half of the deaths were at the hands of abortionists and private citizens sprinkled throughout the fifty states. As the nation watched in horror while the Twin Towers fell, scarcely anyone perceived that day's slaughter of innocent children in the womb. Sadly, abortion has become so accepted and routine that almost no one ponders it. Whether we kill the innocent in secret or publically for the bribe of false heavenly rewards achieved through martyrdom, we become cursed! We open the door for evil to enter our lives when we engage in detestable practices. Many a person can attest to the destruction they have experienced following a decision to sin. Murder is never the answer to one's frustration or difficulties. If we have already murdered the innocent through abortion or anything else, we must repent and unload our curse on the One who was cursed for our redemption. Paul wrote in Galatians, "Christ has redeemed us from the curse of the law by becoming a curse for us, because it is written: Everyone who is hung on a tree is cursed" (Gal. 3:13 HCSB).

PRAYER FOCUS: Jesus, I weep for all those whose lives are cut short by violence and murder. I am in awe of your mercy and grace when I consider your willingness to forgive our sins, especially when those sins hurt others. Jesus, show me that following you helps me avoid sin. Lord, I'm turning from my past and present sins and giving them to you. Please set me free. Thank you, Jesus, that you are a rescuer!

DID YOU KNOW? Four hundred and three rescue workers (firefighters, paramedics, and police) were killed on 9/11 as they rescued and attempted to rescue people inside the World Trade Center Towers.[10]

REFLECTIONS

SEPTEMBER 12

Psalm 68:19-20 NIV

Praise be to the Lord, to God our Savior, who daily bears our burdens. Our God is a God who saves; from the Sovereign LORD comes escape from death.

We all need Jesus because every day comes with new trouble, challenges, and opportunities to sin. The burdens of this life can overwhelm us as we face the death of a child, the loss of a job, the pain of divorce, the weight of sin, the difficulties of parenting, the struggle of addiction, the aftermath of abortion, the emptiness of loneliness, and many other difficult things. Each day brings fresh temptations in the opportunities to lust, lie, indulge, covet, gossip, lash out in anger, withhold forgiveness, judge, and become proud. The list of things we can fall into is endless. Day by day, we need a burden-bearer. We need a deliverer, a Savior. In a word, we need Jesus. No one else has paid our sin debt and died for us. No one else has defeated our enemies (Eph. 6:12; Col. 2:15). No one else is seated at the right hand of the Father interceding for us. And no one else can save! If we have not placed our trust in Jesus, who else are we going to place it in? If we have fallen, who else can restore us? Where can we go? We can bring our burdens and our sins to the Lord Jesus. Whether it's the first time or the millionth time, only Jesus can save. From the Sovereign Lord comes escape from death, both today and tomorrow and forever. Hallelujah!

PRAYER FOCUS: "For troubles without number surround me; my sins have overtaken me, and I cannot see. They are more than the hairs of my head, and my heart fails within me. Be pleased, O LORD, to save me; O LORD, come quickly to help me" (Ps. 40:12-13 NIV). "I love you, O LORD, my strength. The LORD is my rock, my fortress and my deliverer; my God is my rock, in whom I take refuge. He is my shield and the horn of my salvation, my stronghold. I call to the LORD, who is worthy of praise, and I am saved from my enemies" (Ps. 18:1-3 NIV).

DID YOU KNOW? Eddie James has musically reproduced Lou Engle's prayer to end abortion in his song "Lou's Prayer." Get a copy of his CD, *LIFE*, at *ejworship.org* and let the Holy Spirit wash over you.

REFLECTIONS

SEPTEMBER 13

Luke 23:27-31 NASB

And following Him was a large crowd of the people, and of women who were mourning and lamenting Him. But Jesus turning to them said, "Daughters of Jerusalem, stop weeping for Me, but weep for yourselves and for your children. For behold, the days are coming when they will say, 'Blessed are the barren, and the wombs that never bore, and the breasts that never nursed.' Then they will begin to say to the mountains, 'Fall on us,' and to the hills, 'Cover us.' For if they do these things when the tree is green, what will happen when it is dry?"

On his way to his final execution site, Jesus spoke these amazing words to some mourning women in Jerusalem. When one considers great wars, holocausts, genocides, human trafficking, and abortion, one can see what Jesus might have meant when he said, "If they do these things when the tree is green, what will happen when it is dry?" If this is so, it's time to weep for ourselves and our children because human wickedness is growing. The days are coming when evil will overtake everything and precipitate Christ's return. Yet perhaps lost in this powerful statement of Jesus is his affirmation of the value of human life when he said, "Daughters of Jerusalem, stop weeping for Me, but weep for yourselves and for your children." He knew one of the most devastating things in life is experiencing the suffering and death of our children. So great is the agony that some will even envy those who have never experienced the blessing of children. Life is a most precious gift, and to see that gift taken prematurely from our children is overwhelmingly sad. How ironic that Jesus spoke these words as the Father prepared to watch his blameless Son die for the sins of the world. How long will we devalue human life and treat it as something to be discarded? When will we realize the tree is dry and begin to water it?

PRAYER FOCUS: Heavenly Father, you are the light and your Son is the life. Teach us to cherish the gift of life, freely given by you, and vow to respect and protect it from this day forth. Father, help us bear our deepest losses, for we are not alone because you have been there, too.

DID YOU KNOW? Some scholars see in the Luke 23:27-31 passage a prediction of the coming fall of Jerusalem in AD 70 (Luke 13:34-35; 19:41-44), while other scholars see a prediction of the judgments at end of the age (Rev. 6:15-16).

REFLECTIONS

SEPTEMBER 14

John 3:4-10 HCSB

"But how can anyone be born when he is old?" Nicodemus asked Him. "Can he enter his mother's womb a second time and be born?" Jesus answered, "I assure you: Unless someone is born of water and the Spirit, he cannot enter the kingdom of God. Whatever is born of the flesh is flesh, and whatever is born of the Spirit is spirit. Do not be amazed that I told you that you must be born again. The wind blows where it pleases, and you hear its sound, but you don't know where it comes from or where it is going. So it is with everyone born of the Spirit." "How can these things be?" asked Nicodemus. "Are you a teacher of Israel and don't know these things?" Jesus replied.

No one can know everything. Like Nicodemus, we all experience blindness and lack of understanding at times. So where do we go when we have questions or when we're confused? I hope our first answer is Jesus and his Word. In the pages of Scripture we find all the wisdom, knowledge, love, and grace we need to be successful in this life. However, before we can understand the deep things of Scripture, we must believe in Jesus. The writer of Hebrews says, "Now without faith it is impossible to please God, for the one who draws near to Him must believe that He exists and rewards those who seek Him" (Heb. 11:6 HCSB). The first step to getting our questions resolved and understanding God better is to be born of the Spirit through faith in Jesus Christ. Once we are indwelt by the Holy Spirit, he will guide us into all truth (John 16:13), truth like Jesus taught Nicodemus that life in the flesh begins in the water of the womb, but life in the Spirit begins when we place our faith in him.

PRAYER FOCUS: Jesus, today I affirm my belief in your death of atonement for my sins and your resurrection from the dead. Send me the Holy Spirit to guide me in the truth. Lord, I love your Word. Teach me from it as I meditate upon it. Thank you, God, that you are a teacher who teaches me what's best for me.

DID YOU KNOW? Jesus taught using both words and actions, but his greatest lessons were demonstrations (Luke 6:27-37; 23:32-43; John 2:18-22; 13:13-15).

REFLECTIONS

SEPTEMBER 15

1 Samuel 1:27-28 ESV

"For this child I prayed, and the LORD has granted me my petition that I made to him. Therefore I have lent him to the LORD. As long as he lives, he is lent to the LORD." And he worshiped the LORD there.

Samuel, the great prophet of Israel who was instrumental to both Saul and David, was the answer to a barren woman's anguished prayer. Samuel's mother, Hannah, was barren and suffered humiliation from her husband's second wife because of her condition (1 Sam. 1:2-8). In the ancient world, and certainly in the Israelite culture, it was considered a curse to be barren.[11] Bearing children was a role and a privilege wives longed for, to produce an heir and a heritage for their husbands. Hannah knew that God alone had the power over life and death. It was only with God's help that she would conceive and bear children (1 Sam. 2:5-8; Ps. 113:9). Therefore, Hannah made her request to the Lord with fervent prayer. She prayed to the Maker of heaven and earth, the Creator of life, the God who opens and closes the womb to give her a child. She prayed, "O Lord of hosts, if you will indeed look on the affliction of your servant and remember me and not forget your servant, but will give to your servant a son, then I will give him to the Lord all the days of his life, and no razor shall touch his head" (1 Sam. 1:11 ESV). Hannah vowed to give back to the Lord the child he had given her if he would open her womb. After the Lord granted her request and the child had been weaned, that's exactly what she did (1 Sam. 1:19-28). Samuel became a blessing to the entire nation because one woman knew the value of children.

PRAYER FOCUS: Lord, none of us know how we will impact our families, communities, nations, and neighbors, but we know that we were not created without intention and purpose. God, guide me in the direction you would have me go and help me fulfill my purpose in life. Lord, I am grateful you answer prayer. Jesus, today I ask you for _____.

DID YOU KNOW? After thirty-eight weeks in the womb, a baby who started out as a single cell is now around fourteen inches long and weighs about seven pounds.[12]

REFLECTIONS

267

SEPTEMBER 16

2 Thessalonians 2:15-17 HCSB

Therefore, brothers, stand firm and hold to the traditions you were taught, either by our message or by our letter. May our Lord Jesus Christ Himself and God our Father, who has loved us and given us eternal encouragement and good hope by grace, encourage your hearts and strengthen you in every good work and word.

Let us stand firm today in the truths of Scripture. Let us hold fast those things we were taught by others in the faith that align with what Scripture teaches. The Bible is constantly under attack in our culture, and there are many who try to marginalize, undermine, alter, or eradicate it. But instead of moving away from the Bible, we need to get to know the Word of God so that we can examine what we are taught and prove it to be true or false. It is important to know what we believe and why we believe it. The Bible teaches that abortion is a sin and contrary to God's will. God's people need to stop engaging in abortion and start working to abolish it. We can be encouraged today that the God of grace will be with us as we work through our sin of abortion or try to achieve justice for the preborn. If we work in the pro-life movement, a pregnancy resource center, post-abortion counseling, the adoption industry, an unwed mother's home, a women's shelter, or other areas of Christian ministry, God will strengthen us in the good work we are doing. And as we continue championing the truth, God will bless us as we bless others. God never tires of bringing hope to the hopeless and love to the unloved and forgotten, and neither should we.

PRAYER FOCUS: God, I am grateful for pastors, teachers, theologians, and biblical scholars who help me understand your Word better and how it applies to my life. I am also thankful for pro-lifers, missionaries, and ministry organizations that love and help your people. Give me strength today to share your Word and your truth with others who don't know it. Lord, prepare good works for me and help me accomplish them.

DID YOU KNOW? Focus on the Family has developed a small group curriculum titled "The Truth Project" to help people discover the truth of God. This resource helps us examine truth and develop a biblical worldview. For more information, visit *www.thetruthproject.org*.

REFLECTIONS

_____

_____

_____

268

SEPTEMBER 17

Psalm 106:36-41 ESV

They served their idols, which became a snare to them. They sacrificed their sons and their daughters to the demons; they poured out innocent blood, the blood of their sons and daughters, whom they sacrificed to the idols of Canaan, and the land was polluted with blood. Thus they became unclean by their acts, and played the whore in their deeds. Then the anger of the LORD was kindled against his people, and he abhorred his heritage; he gave them into the hand of the nations, so that those who hated them ruled over them.

Psalm 106 is a synopsis of Israel's rebellious history, the consequences of their sin, and God's ultimate restoration. One of Israel's worst sins was their worship of pagan gods and the practice of child sacrifice. God was so outraged at these that he abhorred his chosen people and lifted their hedge of protection, allowing the surrounding nations to rule over them. The Israelites became defiled through idolatry and the shedding of innocent blood. As a result, the whole nation became unclean and fell into darkness. Our nation is headed down the same path the Israelites chose to follow with Canaan. Many have abandoned the belief that the God of the Bible is the only God, believing instead there are many paths to salvation and enlightenment. Additionally, we have allowed abortion on demand, polluting the nation with innocent blood. Idolatry and the taking of innocent life inevitably lead to moral free fall and bondage. How long will it take the church and our nation to realize the desperate nature of our condition? Will we turn to the Lord and repent, or will we be consumed by our enemies?

PRAYER FOCUS: Lord, wake us up from our slumber and our denial of the evil we are engaged in. Jesus, hear our cries for help and deliver us from this mighty grip of relativism and death. Unleash your Spirit on the church and give us a renewed reverence for you and a desire to set the oppressed free!

DID YOU KNOW? On this day in 1862, the single bloodiest day of fighting in the Civil War occurred at Sharpsburg, Maryland, during the battle of Antietam. Some of the fiercest fighting took place at the Sunken Lane, later called "Bloody Lane," because of the incredible loss of life. Approximately three thousand Union soldiers and twenty-five hundred Confederate soldiers were killed, wounded, or missing once the fighting for the Sunken Lane had ended.[13] Tragically, this casualty total is eclipsed every two days by legalized abortion in the United States.

REFLECTIONS

SEPTEMBER 18

Isaiah 1:13-17 NKJV

Bring no more futile sacrifices; incense is an abomination to Me. The New Moons, the Sabbaths, and the calling of assemblies—I cannot endure iniquity and the sacred meeting. Your New Moons and your appointed feasts My soul hates; they are a trouble to Me, I am weary of bearing them. When you spread out your hands, I will hide My eyes from you; even though you make many prayers, I will not hear. Your hands are full of blood. Wash yourselves, make yourselves clean; put away the evil of your doings from before My eyes. Cease to do evil, learn to do good; seek justice, rebuke the oppressor; defend the fatherless, plead for the widow.

The prophet Isaiah spoke these words to the religious people of Judah who failed to perceive their woeful condition before God. All their religious ceremonies and pious practices angered God because they failed to practice the weightier matters of the law in their daily lives, such as justice, mercy, and faith. In his time, Jesus told the scribes and Pharisees, "Woe to you, scribes and Pharisees, hypocrites! For you pay tithe of mint and anise and cummin, and have neglected the weightier matters of the law: justice and mercy and faith. These you ought to have done, without leaving the others undone" (Matt. 23:23 NKJV). So great was the Judeans' rebellion that God stopped listening to their prayers. Certainly, the people of Judah were involved in many sins, but the Holy Spirit illuminates one sin in particular as a reason why their prayers went unanswered: the shedding of blood. God was very clear when he said, "I will not hear. Your hands are full of blood." When the people of God are involved in bloodshed, they are in a desperate state of separation from God. Only by turning from the wrong they have done and starting to work toward the opposite of their sin will they repair the breach and renew their fellowship with the Father. Abortion has filled our hands with blood through our tolerance of it even if we have not personally participated in it. We must wash ourselves through repentance, drive out the practice of abortion from among us, and then work diligently in the nation to stop the practice altogether. God wants us to love him and all his human creation. It's time for the body of Christ to do what is good by seeking justice, rebuking the abortionist, defending the preborn, and pleading for the healing of the nation!

PRAYER FOCUS: Father, forgive the church for failing to recognize the seriousness of abortion. Lord, heal those in your body who have committed the sin of abortion and the sin of tolerating abortion, and give them the courage to help others avoid their mistake. Holy Spirit, bring abortion out of the dark in our churches, so that we can forgive and heal those who've fallen victim to it and teach others to avoid it. Lord, anoint your pastors and teachers to share the truth about abortion in love, equipping their flock to undertake the responsibility of ending it.

DID YOU KNOW? Approximately 250,000 abortions are obtained yearly in America by self-described Christian members of the church.[14]

SEPTEMBER 19

Isaiah 1:18-20 NKJV

"Come now, and let us reason together," says the LORD, "Though your sins are like scarlet, they shall be as white as snow; though they are red like crimson, they shall be as wool. If you are willing and obedient, you shall eat the good of the land; but if you refuse and rebel, you shall be devoured by the sword; for the mouth of the LORD has spoken."

Just as God called out to the house of Judah, asking them to shun evil and pursue social justice, he calls out to the contemporary church regarding abortion. Will we stand in agreement with God's Word on the subject of abortion and refuse to participate in it, or will we allow it to continue? Will we compromise God's truth, encourage abortion, affirm that abortion is a woman's right, and sacrifice our children? Though we are covered in iniquity and great is our sin, God is ready to forgive us and wash away our guilt if we will choose life and champion justice for the least of these. The choice is ours. We can turn from abortion and fight until it is illegal in our land, or we can compromise the truth of God and willingly allow more than a million people to die every year in this country alone because of our apathy, indifference, and rebellion.

PRAYER FOCUS: Lord, raise up an army of believers who will fight for the rights of the preborn and against this atrocious violation of human rights and dignity. Jesus, bring your body to repentance, forgiveness, and life. Make us a people who will not tolerate abortion and its continued practice in our land.

DID YOU KNOW? John Wesley wrote a letter to encourage William Wilberforce during his fight to abolish slavery in England. I pray Wesley's letter will encourage us in our fight to abolish abortion as well.

My dear sir,

Unless the Divine power has raised you up as Athanasius contra mundum, I do not see how you can go through your glorious enterprise in opposing that execrable villainy, which is the scandal of religion, of England, and of human nature. Unless God has raised you up for this very thing, you will be worn out by the opposition of men and devils, but if God is for you who can be against you? Are all of them together stronger than God? Oh, be not weary of well-doing. Go in the name of God, and in the power of His might, till even American slavery, the vilest that ever saw the sun, shall vanish away before it. That He that has guided you from your youth up may continue to strengthen in this and all things, is the prayer of your affectionate servant, John Wesley.[15]

SEPTEMBER
20

Deuteronomy 21:1-9 ESV

If in the land that the LORD your God is giving you to possess someone is found slain, lying in the open country, and it is not known who killed him, then your elders and your judges shall come out, and they shall measure the distance to the surrounding cities. And the elders of the city that is nearest to the slain man shall take a heifer that has never been worked and that has not pulled in a yoke. And the elders of that city shall bring the heifer down to a valley with running water, which is neither plowed nor sown, and shall break the heifer's neck there in the valley. Then the priests, the sons of Levi, shall come forward, for the LORD your God has chosen them to minister to him and to bless in the name of the LORD, and by their word every dispute and every assault shall be settled. And all the elders of that city nearest to the slain man shall wash their hands over the heifer whose neck was broken in the valley, and they shall testify, 'Our hands did not shed this blood, nor did our eyes see it shed. Accept atonement, O LORD, for your people Israel, whom you have redeemed, and do not set the guilt of innocent blood in the midst of your people Israel, so that their blood guilt be atoned for.' So you shall purge the guilt of innocent blood from your midst, when you do what is right in the sight of the LORD.

Blood is so sacred to God that when innocent blood was shed his law instructed the nation of Israel to follow this practice when they encountered an unsolved murder. The community closest to the body was charged with the responsibility to perform the ceremony and purify the land. Every day in America our cities shed the blood of the innocent through abortion, and very few of our citizens cry out to the Lord for forgiveness and cleansing because of our communal sin. As the people of God, we need to pray and repent often for the sin of abortion, asking God to forgive our communities and nation for this ongoing practice. We need to cry out today to the One who provides escape from death. And we need to pray for God's mercy and power to be unleashed on the land so we can begin healing from this iniquity!

PRAYER FOCUS: Father, forgive me and my nation for the sin of murder, the shedding of innocent blood. Turn us from a culture that freely allows the shedding of blood to one that provides life and safety for all its citizens. Lord, I beg you to intervene on behalf of the preborn. Only by the Holy Spirit working through your people can we bring an end to this staggering national condition.

DID YOU KNOW? Some Bible commentators believe that Pilate symbolically referred to this practice of the Jews recorded in Deuteronomy when he washed his hands before Jesus' death on the cross: "So when Pilate saw that he was gaining nothing, but rather that a riot was beginning, he took water and washed his hands before the crowd, saying, 'I am innocent of this man's blood; see to it yourselves.' And all the people answered, 'His blood be on us and on our children!'" (Matt. 27:24-25 ESV).[16]

REFLECTIONS

272

SEPTEMBER 21

Matthew 6:25-27 NASB

For this reason I say to you, do not be worried about your life, as to what you will eat or what you will drink; nor for your body, as to what you will put on. Is not life more than food, and the body more than clothing? Look at the birds of the air, that they do not sow, nor reap nor gather into barns, and yet your heavenly Father feeds them. Are you not worth much more than they? And who of you by being worried can add a single hour to his life?

Jesus gave this illustration on the cure for worry during the Sermon on the Mount to help his listeners understand their inherent value to God and how they can trust him with all things. Trusting in our Father God to provide for our needs is a far better strategy than worrying about our food, shelter, and finances. The sovereign Lord has dominion over all things and he loves us. Anxiety doesn't help obtain or solve anything; it is an empty pursuit. God, however, being the source of all things, has unlimited resources at his disposal to meet our specific needs. Every day the world turns, God meets the needs of the universe at large and the earth in particular. Many people argue that it is selfish for a family to have several children because of the strain it puts on the environment through greater depletion of resources and overpopulation. In their fear, they fail to grasp that God is in control of the care and maintenance of the universe. Do not be deceived; the Creator knows how many people our planet can sustain. He is in control of life and death, nature, and the cosmos. Humankind certainly has a role to play regarding the planet's stewardship, and our behavior can impact the environment. But we cannot control God's will any more than we can control the brightness of the sun or when conception occurs. Every child God sends is part of his plan. Since God is good and has supreme knowledge of our needs, shouldn't we trust him and stop worrying about overpopulation and depleted resources?

PRAYER FOCUS: Maker of heaven and earth, speak to my heart today and allow me to realize that you are in control of all things and able to meet my needs. Lord, teach me not to worry and instead to trust in you. Nothing is impossible for you. Every being you have created you can provide for. Thank you, Lord, for providing for my needs, especially the ones I take for granted.

DID YOU KNOW? The world's resources are more than adequate to meet our needs. John and Barbara Willke stated, "The U.S. now uses less than half the land for farming that it did in the 1920s, even though there are now nearly 200 million more mouths to feed."[17]

SEPTEMBER 22

Proverbs 15:28 NKJV

The heart of the righteous studies how to answer, but the mouth of the wicked pours forth evil.

How do we answer our critics? How do we respond to our culture when it questions or opposes our convictions? We answer with the Word of God, preparing ourselves through study and education to give a defense of our beliefs (Col. 4:5-6; 1 Pet. 3:15). In order to bolster the faith of other believers and defend our views and beliefs to those outside the faith, we must understand our convictions and the substance of them. While the Scriptures are the best source for truth and foundation, it never hurts to consult the insights of other believers, scholars, or verified facts pertaining to particular issues. I suggest we all become readers of Christian apologetics on occasion. These are books on how to defend Christianity, and they keep our minds engaged, equip us for witnessing, and strengthen our faith. C. S. Lewis' *Mere Christianity*, Lee Strobel's *The Case for Christ*, and R. C. Sproul's *Defending Your Faith* would be good books to start with. Another one with many contributors, including Charles Colson, Leonard G. Goss, Norman Geisler, John W. Montgomery, J.P. Moreland, and Ravi Zacharias, is *Who Made God?: And Answers to Over 100 Other Tough Questions of Faith*. That book collects helpful articles from *The Apologetics Study Bible*. Study Bibles and commentaries can also be valuable tools in strengthening one's faith and confirming what we believe. As with all things, we must check what we read against Scripture and ask the Holy Spirit to be our guide as we search for the truth.

PRAYER FOCUS: Lord of Life, you say that "a soft answer turns away wrath, but a harsh word stirs up anger" (Prov. 15:1 NKJV). Help me to know your truth and share it in a spirit of gentleness and compassion. Give me a mind that understands your truth and a heart that can receive it. Lord, teach me from your deep wisdom and allow me to assist others in their search for truth.

DID YOU KNOW? Scott Klusendorf has written a short book on how to defend the pro-life position titled *Pro-Life 101: A Step-by-Step Guide to Making Your Case Persuasively*. The following quote from his book perfectly illustrates Proverbs 15:28: "During an HBO special, comedian Roseanne Barr told the audience: 'You know who else I can't stand is them people that are antiabortion. . . . I hate them. They're ugly, old, geeky, hideous men. They just don't want nobody to have an abortion, cause they want you to keep spitting out kids so they can molest them.'" Klusendorf uses this quote as an example of an "ad hominem" fallacy, where instead of talking to the point at issue one attacks an opponent.[18]

SEPTEMBER 23

Exodus 20:16 NIV

You shall not give false testimony against your neighbor.

∽

Many of the Ten Commandments are violated by the act of abortion, but perhaps the violation of the ninth commandment has contributed more than any other to its ongoing acceptance. The preborn are continually denied the rights of personhood and citizenship because of an abundance of false testimony—lies motivated by the Enemy and accepted by an all-too-willing public! One of the greatest ways to harm God's children, our neighbors, is to lie about them and to them. Satan is the father of lies. The gospel of John says that Satan was a "murderer from the beginning, not holding to the truth, for there is no truth in him. When he lies, he speaks his native language, for he is a liar and the father of lies" (John 8:44 NIV). Satan would like nothing more than for us to continue believing that some children aren't wanted, or that the population is too big, or that the *baby* is part of a woman's body, or that the *child* conceived in rape is an added victimization, or that a mother's health is in jeopardy when she's pregnant, or that abortion is a private matter, or that our freedom to choose supersedes another's freedom to live, or that tolerance is more important than justice or truth. We must combat falsehood with the truth (Eph. 4:25). We must address the lies of abortion with Scripture, science, embryology, logic, ultrasound technology, observation, personal testimony, and common sense. Every year in our nation a quarter of our newest neighbors are destroyed because of these ongoing lies. The body of Christ must stand up with God for truth, and bring this atrocity to a halt once and for all!

PRAYER FOCUS: God, wake up the body of Christ, your church, and give us a passion for truth and life. Help us see through the lies of the Enemy at all times, whether they are directed at us or our neighbors. Lord, protect those who are post-abortive from the lie that they can't be forgiven, and protect your church from the lie that abortion is too big and too accepted to be stopped. God, grant us wisdom, patience, persistence, compassion, guidance and love as we fight for every life you create.

DID YOU KNOW? The framers of the U.S. Constitution had preborn children in mind when they wrote it. Look closely at the following words from the Preamble, "*We the people* of the United States, in Order to form a more perfect Union, establish Justice, insure domestic Tranquility, provide for the common defense, promote the general Welfare, and secure the Blessings of Liberty to ourselves and our *Posterity*, do ordain and establish this Constitution for the United States of America."[19]

SEPTEMBER 24

Acts 15:18 NKJV

Known to God from eternity
are all His works.

The apostle James made this statement after referring to the prophet Amos as proof that God was indeed calling the Gentiles as well as the Jews into his kingdom (Amos 9:11-15; Acts 15:13-17). While James is primarily referring to the foreknowledge of God in including the Gentiles in his plan of salvation, I want to focus on a secondary observation that some might miss. Look again at the words of James, and ponder that from eternity God has known all his works and the purposes for each. Every created thing and being is made with a purpose to fulfill; thus, it is wanted and valued by God. No one in all creation is left out. All people are created and desired by God (1 Kings 8:38-43; Job 12:9-10; Isa. 45:11-12; Col. 1:16). Perhaps nowhere is this better understood than in the famous verse from the gospel of John: "For God so loved the world that He gave His only begotten Son, that whoever believes in Him should not perish but have everlasting life" (John 3:16 NKJV). Obviously, the words "world" and "whoever" refer to all people. Every living person on the planet is wanted by God, whether they are a newly formed zygote or one hundred years old. Don't let the world tell us we are unwanted, because the Maker of the universe says just the opposite!

PRAYER FOCUS: God, show me clearly how the Enemy continually perverts your truth as he tries to destroy me and keep me from you. Lord, I am glad that no matter how I was conceived or where I live or what I do, you want me to become your adopted child. Holy Spirit, flood my heart with a strong sense of worth today and show me that I am of incredible value to you.

DID YOU KNOW? *Webster's Compact Dictionary* defines *wanted* as "sought after."[20]

REFLECTIONS

SEPTEMBER 25

Isaiah 49:1 NASB

Listen to Me, O islands, and pay attention, you peoples from afar. The LORD called Me from the womb; from the body of My mother He named Me.

∞

One of the greatest lies circulating today in the abortion debate is the notion that the baby is part of the mother's body. When we learn that "The Lord called Me from the womb; from the body of My mother He named Me," we can plainly see that this notion is completely false. First, to be called and named, the preborn baby must be a person. Second, to be from the body of its mother means the baby cannot be a part of it. If babies were a part of their mother's bodies, like the heart or the brain, then one could not be independent of the other at any point. The origination point of someone or their location does not make them an integral or permanent part of that location. Patients in a hospital may live inside the building for a period of time until they are well, but that does not make them a permanent part of the hospital or an integral part of its function. Further, the Bible states in Genesis 15:4, 2 Samuel 7:12, and Psalm 132:11 that offspring also comes from the body of the father. Human offspring has never originated from only one body but from two, with each parent contributing twenty-three chromosomes to the zygote. Randy Alcorn further exposed this falsehood that the baby is part of the mother's body when he wrote, "A Chinese zygote implanted in a Swedish woman will always be Chinese, not Swedish, because his identity is based on his genetic code, not that of the body in which he resides."[21] The truth is that the baby is inside the mother's body but not part of it. Each child is made by God—biologically originating from their mother's and father's bodies at conception, bearing a unique genetic code unlike any other human being.

PRAYER FOCUS: Jesus, forgive us for cheapening life by using language that misleads and undermines the sanctity of every individual you have created. Lord, expose the lies of the Enemy so that we can be delivered from the bondage of abortion.

DID YOU KNOW? "Your baby's sex is determined at the moment he or she is conceived. Of the 46 chromosomes that make up your baby's genetic material, two chromosomes called sex chromosomes—one from your egg and one from your partner's sperm—determine your baby's sex. A woman's eggs contain only X sex chromosomes. A man's sperm, however, may contain either an X or Y sex chromosome. If, at the instant of fertilization, a sperm with an X sex chromosome meets your egg, your baby will be a girl (XX). If a sperm containing a Y sex chromosome joins up with your egg, your baby will be a boy (XY). It's always the father's genetic contribution that determines the sex of the baby," states the Mayo Clinic.[22] Gender is proof that more than one body is involved in a pregnancy.

SEPTEMBER 26

Deuteronomy 30:19-20
NASB

I call heaven and earth to witness against you today, that I have set before you life and death, the blessing and the curse. So choose life in order that you may live, you and your descendants, by loving the Lord your God, by obeying His voice, and by holding fast to Him; for this is your life and the length of your days.

∞

Who chooses when life begins? Is it society, the father, the mother, or the child in the womb? The answer is none of them. God alone chooses when life begins. Life and death is a choice best left to God for only he controls them (Deut. 32:39; 1 Sam. 2:6). Life precedes choice. In order to choose, one must be a created living being who is *allowed* to choose. A healthy society makes laws to protect people from things like abortion. The whole reason an individual becomes part of any society is to provide themselves with security and equal opportunity. Though restrictive, laws grant the greatest amount of freedom to all citizens by imposing limits on total freedom. Restricting the speed I drive allows all people to enjoy the benefits of driving under better safety, including me. An individual's right to choose is necessarily limited when it endangers another person's right to choose. In the final analysis, then, I'm free to speed, but I don't have the right to speed, and if I'm caught, I'll face the just penalty of the law. Just laws don't abolish choice; they augment it. However, laws begin to break down when equality of choice is restricted and given only to certain groups or people. If only women have to obey the speed limit, it jeopardizes the safety of everyone on the road and undermines the law. This is precisely what abortion does and why it is so detrimental to society. Abortion allows mothers the choice to kill while denying fathers of preborn babies the choice to raise them and by denying developing babies themselves the choice to live. God's laws trump man's laws and place the ultimate limits and consequences on human choice. From the beginning, God has given humans free will and choice within limits (Gen. 2:8-17). God has given us his truth and shown us the right path to follow, but the choice to follow God is up to us. If we will love him, obey him, and cling to him, we will have abundant life.

PRAYER FOCUS: God, thank you for choosing to create me and love me, giving me the choice to love you back. Help us to see that life and death are in your hands and not intended for us to decide. Lord, drive the practice of abortion from your church and make your people wholly devoted to cherishing life.

DID YOU KNOW? During the 1858 Lincoln-Douglas debates, Lincoln said, "When Judge Douglas says that whoever, or whatever community, wants slaves, they have a right to have them, he is perfectly logical if there is nothing wrong in the institution; but if you admit that it is wrong, he cannot logically say that anybody has a right to do wrong."[23]

SEPTEMBER 27

Psalm 119:115-117 NASB

Depart from me, evildoers, that I may observe the commandments of my God. Sustain me according to Your word, that I may live; and do not let me be ashamed of my hope. Uphold me that I may be safe, that I may have regard for Your statutes continually.

God is our hope, our refuge, our daily bread. Press into God and lean on him and his Word in times of trouble or difficulty. Ask the Lord to intervene during tough times, giving us the courage we need to face an unexpected pregnancy, financial hardship, or any troubling time. Trust in the Lord and he will see us through the storms of life, carrying us to safety. One of the ways God keeps us safe is by keeping us from evildoers and their counsel, sowing his Word into our hearts so that we can recognize what is true from what is false. The lies justifying abortion are many and we must season our hearts with the truth in God's Word so that we can recognize the Archenemy's attempts to deceive us. If we realize that safety only comes when we obey God's commands and principles, we are far less likely to fall for the argument that abortion is safe now that it is legal. We will understand that only by pursuing purity and cherishing life will we keep our bodies and the bodies of our children safe. Abortion is never safe for developing children and often physically and psychologically damaging to the expectant mother and father. Post-abortive men and women are subject to depression, self-mutilation, suicide, and a host of other problems following an abortion. When struggling or when afraid, we can seek out the counsel of God to help us remain abstinent, carry our baby to term, choose adoption, or face single parenthood. No matter what our circumstances, God will sustain us and give us hope if we reach out to him.

PRAYER FOCUS: God, teach me your Word that I might benefit from your wisdom and avoid many mistakes. Help me to believe that "he who listens to me shall live securely and will be at ease from the dread of evil" (Prov. 1:33 NASB). Lord, when I do sin or make mistakes, help me understand that turning to you for guidance can keep me from compounding my errors and help me make good choices going forward. Jesus, reassure me that you love me and that you will help me no matter what I have done or what I face.

DID YOU KNOW? As of September 3, 2010, over 340 women have died during legal abortion procedures or from complications following an abortion since 1973 in the United States.[24] Go to *www.lifedynamics.com* and click on The Blackmun Wall for more information.

SEPTEMBER
28

1 Corinthians 10:24 ESV

Let no one seek his own good, but the good of his neighbor.

Some will argue that abortion is acceptable because the preborn baby could not survive outside its mother's womb and is therefore not viable. The problem with this argument is that it is irrelevant. No one expects a baby to survive by itself or develop independent from its mother and father or caregiver. No single baby in the history of the world has accomplished this. This is like requiring every child under the age of two to provide independently for its own welfare. Without someone providing food, shelter, clothing, medical care, and security, very few, if any, two-year-olds would survive. All developing babies in the womb are viable until nature, sickness, or man kills them. The viability argument is a smokescreen designed to assuage human guilt and deflect attention away from what abortion actually does, which is kill a developing child! Life is paramount. It's the starting point for all things. No gift is greater or more necessary to the human experience than life. The real question is, will we make sacrifices for the good of our children? Will we put the needs of new life before our career, finances, reputation, figure, or personal plans? At the core of Christianity is sacrifice for another. Jesus sacrificed for sinful humankind; the disciple's sacrificed for the early church; missionaries have and still sacrifice for the unsaved and the hurting all over the world. Every good parent knows what it is to sacrifice for their child by giving of their sleep, time, money, independence, and so on. Our Christian charity compels us to seek the good of our neighbors both inside and outside the womb. If we will look beyond ourselves, we will see that our tiny developing neighbors need our help, love, and protection, not our arrogant superiority.

PRAYER FOCUS: Lord, help us to see that without life nothing else matters or is even possible. Jesus, give me a heart for your children and my neighbors that places their needs above my wants. Increase my discernment and help me see readily the lies of the Devil. God, educate your church so completely on abortion that no single Christian believes abortion is all right to engage in or is willing to allow abortion to go unopposed in society.

DID YOU KNOW? Thousands of premature babies survive early birth every year and many go on to live normal, healthy lives. Some of these children have been born as early as twenty or twenty-one weeks gestation, weighing no more than ten or twelve ounces.[25]

SEPTEMBER 29

Luke 6:22 HCSB

You are blessed when people hate you, when they exclude you, insult you, and slander your name as evil because of the Son of Man.

Christians are often hated for communicating the truth of God, and there is no misunderstanding why. When Christians take a stand based on moral convictions, they will often hear statements like, "Don't impose your morality on me," or "You can't legislate morality." But this manages to miss the point. When we are communicating God's truth to others, we are not expressing our own morality but rather God's morality as revealed through the Bible (Ps. 119:160). Frankly, if we don't tell others about God's ways, who will? And to call attention to moral evils is not imposing morality on anyone. Instead, it is informing our neighbors that God offers them a better choice than the one they are making. Choosing to follow God will benefit them in this life and the next, for sinner and saint alike will face God's judgment (Matt. 12:36-37; Rev. 20:12-13). As for legislating morality, both God and society have no problem with this. Just take a look at biblical law (Deut. 22; 23; Matt. 5:19-48) and the U.S. penal code. Our nation has laws against murder, perjury, rape, statutory rape, public indecency, polygamy, prostitution, drug trafficking, drug possession, drunk driving, and so on. Society is safer and better for all people when some moral limits are placed on human behavior. Laws cannot stop all murders or all abortions because people are free moral agents, but they can limit the total number, punish the violators, and make society safer and more civil for the majority.

PRAYER FOCUS: God, I appreciate that you've given us standards and moral guidelines to live by. Help us see that placing moral limits on society is an excellent way to ensure general freedom and protect each individual. Lord, help me obey your commands and principles even when the rest of society does not.

DID YOU KNOW? In 1993, after several decades of liberal abortion policy, the Polish Parliament passed a law restricting abortion in all but a few cases. Detractors said that illegal abortions would skyrocket and, as a result, many women would be injured or killed. Dr. Willke shares the following statistics from Poland to refute this prediction: In 1980 there were 138,000 total abortions; in 2000 there were 138 total abortions. Deaths due to pregnancy, birth and confinement in 1991 amounted to 70; in 1997, deaths due to pregnancy, birth and confinement were 24. In 1990 there were 19 neonatal deaths in every 1,000 live births; in 1999 there were 9 neonatal deaths in every 1,000 live births. In 1999 there were 99 illegal abortions in Poland.[26]

SEPTEMBER 30

Matthew 28:18-20 ESV

And Jesus came and said to them, "All authority in heaven and on earth has been given to me. Go therefore and make disciples of all nations, baptizing them in the name of the Father and of the Son and of the Holy Spirit, teaching them to observe all that I have commanded you. And behold, I am with you always, to the end of the age."

∞

Matthew closes his gospel with these words of Jesus commissioning his disciples to accomplish the supreme calling of a redeemed life—called the Great Commission, which is the redemption and instruction of others. In today's climate of political correctness and tolerance for all things regardless of their truth, morality, or destructive potential, some in the church have lost the courage and boldness necessary to fulfill the Great Commission. The world does not need our tolerance—they need Jesus and his truth! The world needs to see our brokenness over sin and feel the hope that we profess in Christ. Do we hurt for the hurting, bleed for the bleeding, and love the unlovely? Or are we too inwardly focused to see and feel the needs of the lost and the dying? Our stand on abortion isn't just a political position or an ideological stance; it's an opportunity to fulfill the two great commandments and walk out the Great Commission (Matt. 22:34-40). There is plenty of opportunity for evangelism when we are ministering forgiveness to the post-abortive, or pleading with individuals at the abortion facility to let their baby live. Jesus and his love for all humankind leap off the Bible's pages when we are sharing what God's Word has to say about abortion. When we take a pregnant woman into our home or pay her medical expenses, many opportunities arise to offer salvation and talk about our faith. Adopting a child slated for abortion provides a tremendous opportunity to demonstrate the gospel to the child and society. We need to sit at the feet of Jesus and receive (Luke 10:38-41), but after we have received, we need to go and do (Matt. 10:1-10)!

PRAYER FOCUS: Jesus, the harvest is plentiful, but the workers are few (Luke 10:1-3). Equip me for service and embolden me to help your people who are lost in the darkness. Give me strength when I am weak; grace when I sin; restoration when I repent; courage when I am afraid; gentleness when I am confronted; love when I am unloved; and compassion where there is none.

DID YOU KNOW? In the early years of legalized abortion a Catholic priest at a Colorado abortion facility would stand against the outside wall of the waiting room and weep audibly for the people inside. Because of his intercession, many inside were moved to the point of choosing life for their baby. When will the church share his brokenness over abortion?

October

CHILDREN'S CHILDREN

OCTOBER 1

Proverbs 17:6 NIV

Children's children are a crown to the aged, and parents are the pride of their children.

∞

Family is a reward, a legacy, and a blessing from God. Children need good elderly role models, and the elderly need the energy, curiosity, and wonder of children. Distressingly, the deadly sins of abortion and euthanasia seek to destroy these bookends of the family. Satan wants nothing more than to deprive children of good role models and to deprive good role models of children to mentor. If we will value all life from conception to undetermined death, our land will be blessed and our heritage made secure. While Proverbs 17:6 clearly speaks of the value of every family member from preborn to old age, it also speaks of the dynamic between the children of God and their heavenly Father. All of God's children are a crown to the Ancient of Days, just as God is the pride of his people, his sons and daughters. There is none like our Father, for he is entirely good and his mercies endure forever. His sacrifice for the life of the world and his great love for the least of these and the hurting takes my breath away. The most amazing thing, however, is that as we delight in God, he delights in us. If we are one of God's adopted children, we must never forget to praise him, worship him, and tell him how awestruck we are to be his son or daughter. If we are not one of God's adopted children, we can ask him to adopt us. The apostle Paul showed the way: "If you confess with your mouth, 'Jesus is Lord,' and believe in your heart that God raised him from the dead, you will be saved" (Rom. 10:9 NIV).

PRAYER FOCUS: Father God, I'm proud to be your child and I am grateful for my earthly and heavenly families. I love you, Lord. Hear me as I sing your praises. Lift your voice and sing "Isn't He" by John Wimber: Isn't he/beautiful, isn't he; Isn't he/Prince of Peace, isn't he; Isn't he/Son of God/, isn't he; Isn't He/wonderful, isn't he; Isn't he/Counselor, isn't he; Isn't he/Almighty God, isn't He; isn't He, isn't He....[1] Continue this meditative praise inserting other attributes of God, for example holy, pure, righteous, life-giving, good to me, loving, merciful, forgiving, and so on.

DID YOU KNOW? Babies at birth have accomplished the miraculous. Listen to Peter Tallack summarize their achievements: "She has gone from egg, to embryo, to fetus, to trillions of cells of newborn baby. Protected by her mother and following her own unique set of genetic instructions, she has grown a face, arms, eyes, and legs. She has a brain and nervous system to control her body, stomach, and intestines to digest food, and a heart to pump blood. She has learned to breathe, to hear, to feed, to remember, and to tell her parents when she is hungry, tired, happy, or in pain—all before being born."[2]

OCTOBER 2

Hosea 14:9 HCSB

Let whoever is wise understand these things, and whoever is insightful recognize them. For the ways of the LORD are right, and the righteous walk in them, but the rebellious stumble in them.

Hosea concludes his book of prophesy with these words that apply not only to Hosea's teaching, but to the whole Bible, for in the pages of Scripture we discover God's revealed ways. In order to become like our Savior and grow in righteousness, we must learn the ways of God and then walk them out. Certainly one of God's ways is the way of life. He is the living God who planted the tree of life and provides rivers of living water to all who believe. He is the Creator of everything who sent his Son to give us life in abundance. As God's people on earth, we need to encourage life, promote life, defend life, protect life, cherish life, and save life. Abortion needs to become unthinkable to the believer and unheard of in the church. We need to be intentional in our efforts to help believers and nonbelievers choose life over death and raise their children instead of discarding them. We also need to work diligently toward the ending of legalized abortion in our nation. The righteous need to walk in God's living ways or we will continue stumbling in our churches, and our nation will slip into greater and greater rebellion. Take to heart the things communicated in this devotional and begin acting upon them. Speak out, speak up, and take action. Life is the foundation from which all other things proceed. Isn't it time we fight for it?

PRAYER FOCUS: God, lead us to your Word when we face complex social problems or when we're unsure of the truth. Holy Spirit, fill us with the wisdom and the knowledge to know what to do for the hurting and the lost who see abortion as their best or only option. Lord, increase our illumination and understanding of the preciousness of life in the church. Drive abortion from your church so that Christians can be powerful and effective in driving it from the nation.

DID YOU KNOW? God instructed Hosea to marry an adulterous wife and raise children with her to demonstrate his faithfulness to the unfaithful (Hosea 1-3). No matter how far you have strayed from the Lord's ways, it's never too late to return to him and taste the power of his redeeming love. Hosea's very name means "salvation" or "deliverance," testifying to God's goodness and his desire for all people to be set free.[3]

OCTOBER 3

Proverbs 21:6-7 HCSB

Making a fortune through a lying tongue is a vanishing mist, a pursuit of death. The violence of the wicked sweeps them away because they refuse to act justly.

Why do abortion proponents defend the act of child-killing so vigorously? Why do they lobby so hard on Capitol Hill? One answer is money. Abortion is big business in America and around the world. A fortune can be made by performing abortions, selling abortions, and running abortion facilities. Dr. John C. Willke gives an example of how lucrative abortion can be: "We have a letter from Shepel Management, Inc. in Brookline, MA soliciting a physician 'to perform abortions.' It states, 'This is a part time position requiring either a morning or an afternoon a week. It is an opportunity to earn upwards of $70,000 a year.'"[4] The lies surrounding abortion are much easier to promote when there is fortune to be made—but at what cost? After placing her faith in Jesus and leaving the abortion industry, Carol Everett recalled her emotions following a devotional time in which she read Psalm 139 for the first time: "I was convinced I had been killing babies. The words that really got me were these: 'Your eyes saw my unformed substance, and in Your book all the days of my life were written, before they ever took shape, when as yet there was none of them' (Ps. 139:16). I remembered holding those little babies' bodies in my hand as I cleaned the instruments. I specifically remembered that each of them had intestines—yes, some threadlike—but, they all had intestines. I remembered wondering why God gave them intestines if He knew they were going to be aborted. I knew now God intended for each of the 35,001 babies to live, each one that I had helped abort. The weight of my sin became very heavy, but I remembered 1 John 1:9."[5] Fortunately, Carol repented, received forgiveness, and turned her sorrow into the pursuit of justice. But what about all the other abortionists and abortion supporters who have not?

PRAYER FOCUS: God, forgive the people who work in the abortion industry. Shower your grace upon them and allow them to discover the truth, like Carol. Lord, lead them out of the darkness and into the light so that they can shed experiential light on the horrors of abortion and help our nation turn from this deadly practice.

DID YOU KNOW? Planned Parenthood made thirty-four percent of their $1 billion revenue for the year ending June 30, 2008, from the government and twenty-four percent from private contributions.[6] If your state provides tax support for abortion, find out how you can legally oppose this and stop it. Contact Stop International, a division of American Life League, for more information (*www.all.org/stopp/*). If you are a corporate or individual donor to Planned Parenthood, or any other abortion provider, it's time to rethink your donation!

OCTOBER 4

1 Timothy 6:17-19 NKJV

Command those who are rich in this present age not to be haughty, nor to trust in uncertain riches but in the living God, who gives us richly all things to enjoy. Let them do good, that they be rich in good works, ready to give, willing to share, storing up for themselves a good foundation for the time to come, that they may lay hold on eternal life.

Whether we are the poorest of the poor or the richest of the rich, our trust should be in the living God. Apart from him we have nothing, for he is the Maker, Sustainer, and Giver of all things. God freely and richly gives us all things to enjoy. How often in the storms of life do we forget his mighty provision? God gives us life, breath, food, water, amazing bodies, sunshine, rain, family, friends, children, health, and a host of other wonderful things. We should do good things for others because God does so many good things for us. Those with financial means should use the resources God has placed at their disposal to further God's kingdom and care for his people. Money can help pay for a pregnant woman's medical bills, routine checkups, or prenatal vitamins. Financial grants or gifts could make it more affordable for couples without great wealth to adopt. Every pro-life group in the nation could use additional financial support. Buying clothing, cribs, and baby gear for new moms or parents can give them a leg up on providing for their child. When we have the means, it is up to us to help the poor, the weak, the fatherless, the destitute, and the needy. God will bless us with treasures in heaven as we bless the least of these with treasures on earth.

PRAYER FOCUS: God, give me eyes to see the needs of people around me and a heart of compassion for the hurting, poor, and needy. Lord, turn me into a cheerful giver who is ready, able, and excited to give without strings attached. Jesus, I trust you more than my money. Use my earthly treasure for your heavenly work and give me discernment about when, where, how much, and to whom to give.

DID YOU KNOW? President John F. Kennedy designated the first Monday in October as Child Health Day. Proclamation 3487, designating Child Health Day, begins with these words, "WHEREAS children are our Nation's most priceless resource and most cherished responsibility; and WHEREAS it is essential that boys and girls of our Nation be given a good start in life by the fostering of their emotional, physical, and spiritual well-being so that in future years each may achieve his full potential for a productive and satisfying life."[7] Agreeing with President Kennedy, let's put our money and our efforts toward ending abortion, which is the greatest threat to our children's health.

OCTOBER 5

1 Chronicles 29:11-12 ESV

Yours, O LORD, is the greatness and the power and the glory and the victory and the majesty, for all that is in the heavens and in the earth is yours. Yours is the kingdom, O LORD, and you are exalted as head above all. Both riches and honor come from you, and you rule over all. In your hand are power and might, and in your hand it is to make great and to give strength to all.

The Lord reigns! Nothing can match Almighty God. His beauty is beyond compare. His power is supreme. His glory and majesty are breathtaking. His rule is just, and everything that has been made comes from his hands. All our possessions and everything we rely upon and use are provided by the Lord, the Maker of heaven and earth. David understood that when we give to God we simply give back to him a portion of what we have already been lavishly given. He said to God, "all this abundance that we have . . . comes from your hand and is all your own" (1 Chron. 29:14-17). Wealth and esteem that last come from God. It is sad and shortsighted when we place economics over justice, or personal gain over the needs of the oppressed. If we will honor God and take care of his people, fulfilling the weightier matters of the law, including justice and mercy and faithfulness (Matt. 23:23), he will take care of us and pour out a blessing we cannot imagine—a blessing until there is no more need (Mal. 3:10). Paul affirmed this truth when he wrote these words of gratitude to the Philippians for their support: "And my God will supply every need of yours according to his riches in glory in Christ Jesus" (Phil. 4:19 ESV). In all things we must give because it has been given to us.

PRAYER FOCUS: God, increase my trust in you. Give me a passion to seek first your kingdom and your righteousness (Matt. 6:31-33). Lord, today I choose to support life because life has been given to me. Jesus, motivate the body of Christ to give love, forgiveness, money, and resources to others because you have given those things to us. Father, prepare our hearts for the great work of ending abortion and make us into great givers (2 Cor. 9:6-9).

DID YOU KNOW? Billy Graham once wrote, "Someone has said that our lives should resemble channels, not reservoirs. A reservoir stores water; a channel distributes it. God wants us to be channels of blessing to others."[8]

REFLECTIONS

OCTOBER 6

Proverbs 13:22 NASB

A good man leaves an inheritance to his children's children, and the wealth of the sinner is stored up for the righteous.

As one who has benefited greatly from family inheritance, I can attest to the rewards of hard work, wise planning, and good financial stewardship by my grandfather. He was truly a good man, and his financial legacy is still working to produce good in my life and in the lives of others through my family. Still, there is more to an inheritance than money. Paul wrote in Titus 3:4-7, "When the kindness of God our Savior and His love for mankind appeared, He saved us, not on the basis of deeds which we have done in righteousness, but according to His mercy, by the washing of regeneration and renewing by the Holy Spirit, whom He poured out upon us richly through Jesus Christ our Savior, so that being justified by His grace we would be made heirs according to the hope of eternal life" (NASB). My grandfather's faith, integrity, marital example, work ethic, and love were a far greater inheritance to me than the money he left. What kind of an inheritance do we want to leave our children and their children after them? Do we want to leave a legacy that values life and fights for justice, or do we want to leave them with the impression that the needs of the oppressed don't matter and that the supreme goal of life is personal gratification? My grandfather was born in a generation where sacrifice for another was an esteemed value and I, for one, am grateful.

PRAYER FOCUS: God, I thank you for the legacy of my parents and grandparents and the good examples they set for me. Lord, bless them and be good to them. Thank you for being an even better role model than they, and that regardless of the job they did, be it good or bad, I can turn to you for direction and guidance in my life. Jesus, help me leave a lasting godly inheritance to my children and my children's children.

DID YOU KNOW? In his book *Answering the Call*, John Ensor devoted an entire chapter to historical examples of God's people defending life. In it he cites this quote from Ignatius Loyola (1491-1556): "Life is God's most precious gift. Abortion . . . is not merely an awful tyranny, it is a smear against the integrity of God as well. Suffer as we must, even die if need be, such rebellion against heaven must not be free to run its terrible courses."[9] What a legacy God has given us through the faithful.

OCTOBER 7

Leviticus 19:32 HCSB

You are to rise in the presence of the elderly and honor the old. Fear your God; I am Yahweh.

God loves us from the womb to the grave, and he cares about every stage of our life in between. The wisdom gained from those who have lived, loved, and lost can be immeasurable. God wants us to respect, honor, love, help, and cherish the elderly. If we are here today, it is only because a parent chose to allow us to be born, just as their parent before them chose the same. Without the hard work and unselfish love given by our parents and grandparents, many of us would not be the people we are today. God instructs us through his Word to "Honor your father and your mother, as the Lord your God has commanded you, so that you may live long and so that you may prosper in the land the Lord your God is giving you" (Deut. 5:16 HCSB). Honoring, respecting, and obeying our elders will enhance longevity and blessing during our life on this earth. We benefit from our elders' wisdom and provision when we submit to their authority. How much more so, when we submit to the authority of our greatest elder, the Ancient of Days? Everything God has communicated to us is for our benefit and betterment. When will we heed his advice on the important issues of abortion and euthanasia?

PRAYER FOCUS: God, thank you for the elderly and the wisdom, beauty, and care they bring to life. Show me how to be good to the elderly around me, and give me a servant's heart for the older generation to keep me mindful of the respect they are due. Jesus, bless my parents and grandparents. I love them and appreciate their love for me.

DID YOU KNOW? After years of tolerating the practice, the Netherlands became the first nation to legalize euthanasia in 2001.[10] John C. and Barbara H. Willke devote an entire chapter to euthanasia in their book, *Abortion Questions & Answers*. They provide an excellent chart comparing abortion and euthanasia showing, among other things, that both abortion and euthanasia argue the victim is unwanted and burdensome.[11]

REFLECTIONS

OCTOBER 8

Proverbs 19:18 NIV

Discipline your son, for in that there is hope; do not be a willing party to his death.

God expects parents to discipline their children when they are headed in the wrong direction. The home is the first place a child learns respect, manners, obedience, values, and God's ways. One of the primary responsibilities of a parent is to "train a child in the way he should go, and when he is old he will not turn from it" (Prov. 22:6 NIV). Parenting is difficult, as all parents know, and we need to pray often seeking the Holy Spirit's guidance in raising our children. Knowing they learn from our words and actions, we need to strive to provide consistent examples of love, compassion, grace, truth, and discipline in our homes. As we discipline, we need to keep our emotions in balance and discipline appropriately with measured physicality and discernment, not anger and wrath (Prov. 13:24). The goal of discipline is to instruct the child and mold better behavior for their immediate betterment and future benefit. We go too far when we desire to physically, emotionally, or spiritually hurt our children. When we err in discipline, we need to ask the Lord and our child for forgiveness. We should never be a willing party to their abuse or death! A parent's job is to love their children and guide them into God's ways with passionate affection, discipline, and encouragement. Resolve today to be a mom who nurtures, loves, instructs, and compassionately cares for her children, or a dad who protects, loves, disciplines, and encourages them.

PRAYER FOCUS: Father, give me insight and discernment when I am using corrective discipline with my child. Guard my tongue and keep the words I speak positive, encouraging, corrective, and wholesome. Holy Spirit, teach me from your Word the proper way to discipline and help me exercise good judgment when using any discipline method.

DID YOU KNOW? According to the department of Health and Human Services, in 2007, 794,000 children of the 5.8 million children referred to Child Protective Services agencies were determined to be victims of child abuse or neglect. Of those, an estimated 1,760 children died from child abuse or neglect, with more than 75% of the deaths occurring before the age of four.[12] When we fail to value life at any point, it becomes devalued at every point. We must strive to cherish and protect all our children, born or preborn.

OCTOBER 9

Daniel 2:22 NASB

It is He who reveals the profound and hidden things; He knows what is in the darkness, and the light dwells with Him.

Today is my birthday, and as I celebrate it I'm reminded of all the precious joys I've experienced in this life. The love of family, the joy of sports played with friends in my youth, intimate times with God, my beautiful bride, and the birth of my children are some of my life's highlights. What would I and others who love me have lost if my life had been cut short? Roughly nine months prior to my birth, I was conceived in my mother's womb despite the presence of an intrauterine birth control device (IUD). Her doctor, a couple of months before my conception, had replaced an older IUD with a new one that he failed to position properly. Unlike the condom, which creates a barrier between sperm and egg, the IUD does not prevent ovulation or conception in many cases, but instead causes inflammation of the endometrium (the mucous membrane lining the uterus), making it difficult for the newly formed child to implant in the uterus. In a 1980 article titled *"Medicine: IUD Debate," Time* magazine stated it this way: "Inserted into the uterus, they (IUD) cause a minor inflammation of the uterine lining that prevents the fertilized egg from implanting in the uterine wall after its journey through the fallopian tube."[13] My parents were completely uninformed and ignorant about the effects of the IUD they were using. Had God in his providence not made a way for me to be born, I could have been killed during my first week of life by this device that induces abortion. Many other contraceptives and birth control devices can interfere with life post-fertilization. It is imperative in our efforts to protect and cherish life that we research the effects of any contraceptive method we employ during marriage and prayerfully seek God's wisdom on the matter. If we discover we are using contraceptives that can be abortive, we should discontinue their use and ask God to grant us wisdom going forward (Ps. 19:12-13). If we are young, single, or unmarried, God calls us to sexual abstinence (Acts 21:25; Gal. 5:19; Eph. 5:3; 1 Thess. 4:3-4). Abstinence and purity protects all people from sexual diseases, unexpected pregnancy, and spiritual and emotional damage due to fornication before marriage. As Christians we must trust God with our sexuality; he will reward us with profound and hidden things. The light dwells with him, and he knows what's best for us and our future offspring.

PRAYER FOCUS: Thank you, God, for shedding light on the darkness and revealing hidden things. Grant me the fortitude, grace, and ability to remain abstinent until marriage. Lord, if it is within your will, give me a passion to have children during my marriage and grant me discernment concerning contraceptive use.

DID YOU KNOW? Alabama Physicians For Life, Inc. has excellent information about types of birth control and their effects, as well as their pros and cons. Go to *www.physiciansforlife.org* and click on Birth Control for more information. See also chapter 20 in *Abortion Questions & Answers*.

OCTOBER 10

Matthew 18:7 ESV

Woe to the world for temptations to sin! For it is necessary that temptations come, but woe to the one by whom the temptation comes!

There are so many things in this world contrary to the will of God, and temptation to sin abounds. Even though we are all responsible for our own actions and sins, God is not pleased with those who tempt others to stumble. As Christians, we need to prayerfully consider where we work and what we promote through our jobs and lives. Does our work honor God and help his people? Several years ago, without contemplating Matthew 18:7, I worked as a blackjack dealer in Las Vegas. While I seldom encouraged patrons to gamble, and never forced them to do so, I willingly collaborated with the casino and all that it represented by agreeing to work for them. Unless we are focused on God and immersed in his truth, we will fail to see how we are aiding the enemy in hurting others, believing that we are "just earning a pay check," or "simply providing for our family." Do we really need to run a provocative ad campaign? Why don't we provide comprehensive counseling to a pregnant client, including ultrasound and adoption services? Is all this nudity and profanity really necessary in our film? Is the mark-up on our product line just and fair? Are we working within budget and funding the right things with taxpayer money? No job or activity is perfect, but we should consider the impact we have on others and strive for integrity in all we do. Seeking our neighbor's good and living at peace with all pleases the Lord.

PRAYER FOCUS: Father, forgive me for causing others to stumble and participating in things that can potentially hurt or take advantage of them. Lord, grant me peace in my Christian liberty, but keep me aware that what is not a snare for me may be a snare for others. Help me guard against hurting them. And grant me discernment about my current job and whether or not you want me to continue in it.

DID YOU KNOW? The Devil is the greatest tempter of all. Read the gospels of Matthew (4:1-11) and Luke (4:1-13) and examine how Jesus withstood the temptation of the Evil One. We need to follow his example of prayer, fasting, and scriptural preparedness when we face various temptations, calling on Jesus to help us in the midst of our tempting. The Bible teaches us that "because he himself has suffered when tempted, he is able to help those who are being tempted" (Heb. 2:18 ESV).

OCTOBER 11

Jonah 3:5-10 NKJV

So the people of Nineveh believed God, proclaimed a fast, and put on sackcloth, from the greatest to the least of them. Then word came to the king of Nineveh; and he arose from his throne and laid aside his robe, covered himself with sackcloth and sat in ashes. And he caused it to be proclaimed and published throughout Nineveh by the decree of the king and his nobles, saying, "Let neither man nor beast, herd nor flock, taste anything; do not let them eat, or drink water. But let man and beast be covered with sackcloth, and cry mightily to God; yes, let every one turn from his evil way and from the violence that is in his hands. Who can tell if God will turn and relent, and turn away from His fierce anger, so that we may not perish?" Then God saw their works, that they turned from their evil way; and God relented from the disaster that He had said He would bring upon them, and He did not do it.

Corporate repentance is a powerful thing. When a whole group of people, from the greatest to the least, including the leadership, repents of their errors and wickedness, God often honors their repentance by restoring his blessing and removing any disasters he had purposed to bring against them in judgment. Just as individual repentance restores us to a good relationship with the Father, corporate repentance restores churches or nations to a healthy and proper relationship with the King of kings and Lord of lords. Repentance is a process that involves believing God and his revealed truth, humbling ourselves, seeking his forgiveness, and turning from the behavior or practice that is contrary to the divine will. If America will heed and believe what God has communicated about the dignity and value of all human life, we can avert much future sorrow in our nation. Let's admit our sin, seek forgiveness, and turn from the practice of abortion. Perhaps God will restore our country to her greatest ideals and allow her to become a light to the world, a shining city on a hill.

PRAYER FOCUS: God, your Scriptures are clear that life begins at conception, that each human being is fearfully and wonderfully made, that you are the Creator of the universe, and that every person is loved and desired by you. Lord, abortion is an abomination and a grievous sin against you, so please forgive me and my nation for our arrogance and sin. Lead us in the path of righteousness and help us create a constitutional amendment that protects all our citizens from zygote to undetermined death.

DID YOU KNOW? One of the main reasons Nineveh was in the crosshairs of judgment was their violent treatment of their fellow man (Jonah 3:8; see also Isa. 59:6-7).

REFLECTIONS

OCTOBER 12

Jonah 4:10-11 NKJV

But the Lord said, "You have had pity on the plant for which you have not labored, nor made it grow, which came up in a night and perished in a night. And should I not pity Nineveh, that great city, in which are more than one hundred and twenty thousand persons who cannot discern between their right hand and their left—and much livestock?"

∞

Jonah was a prophet of God who was given the mission to warn Nineveh of the consequences of her sin in hopes that the people would repent and choose a different path, God's path. But from the outset, Jonah didn't like his mission because he despised the Ninevites and their behavior (Jonah 1:1-3; 4:1-4). Perhaps Jonah had been personally touched by the violence of Nineveh and was unwilling to forgive them, or maybe in his zeal for God and his hatred of sin he manifested a loathing of sinners and an eager desire to see them punished. We may never know, but one thing is sure, Jonah had no love for wicked Nineveh and had forgotten God's great love for him during personal times of rebellion and wickedness. I believe this is precisely why God picked Jonah to deliver the message to Nineveh—to teach him afresh about redemption and the goodness of the God he served. After Nineveh repented and God accepted their contrition, Jonah's anger burned. He left the city and sat east of it. So God created a vine to shade him from the burning sun outside the city (Jonah 4:5-9). Almost as quickly as God had made the shade plant, he destroyed it with a worm that attacked the plant and made it wither, teaching Jonah a lesson about the value of things and people. We err in the same way as Jonah if we let our passion for justice and our hatred of abortion transform us into haters of lost people who do not fully understand what they are doing. Jesus never encouraged, applauded, or agreed with sinners, but he did love them. He loves everyone in darkness and wants to set them free.

PRAYER FOCUS: Jesus, I hate abortion and what it does to men, women, and children, but don't let me hate the people who are snared by it. Give me compassion for even the wickedest proponents of abortion. Lord, touch me with your heart of compassion for those who don't know your redemptive love or the right thing to do.

DID YOU KNOW? Several commentators observe that the total population of Nineveh was around 600,000 people, since the 120,000 persons mentioned in Jonah 4:10-11 who "cannot discern between their right hand and their left" were most likely little children.[14] God's heart has always gone out to the children and the little ones, even the children of the wicked. Jesus correspondingly taught us to have compassion for the lost and pray for our enemies and those who persecute us (Matt. 5:43-46).

OCTOBER 13

Deuteronomy 7:6-9 NKJV

For you are a holy people to the LORD your God; the LORD your God has chosen you to be a people for Himself, a special treasure above all the peoples on the face of the earth. The LORD did not set His love on you nor choose you because you were more in number than any other people, for you were the least of all peoples; but because the LORD loves you, and because He would keep the oath which He swore to your fathers, the LORD has brought you out with a mighty hand, and redeemed you from the house of bondage, from the hand of Pharaoh king of Egypt. Therefore know that the LORD your God, He is God, the faithful God who keeps covenant and mercy for a thousand generations with those who love Him and keep His commandments.

If we have committed our lives to Christ, we are privileged persons, chosen to be God's treasured possession. We are holy to the Lord and deeply loved by him. God did not choose us because we were wiser, purer, better, or more beautiful than others, but because he loved us. Jesus gave himself for all humankind, but only those who choose to love him back and receive his great gift of love will know eternal fellowship with him. When we trust Christ, we say *yes* to freedom and *no* to bondage. We rest in the knowledge that God is for us today; he is in our corner. We can feel his mighty hand and know that nothing is impossible with God directing our steps. When we're down or discouraged, we can take heart in the faithfulness of God, placing our faith in his power, knowing he is able to see us through any difficulty. Believers can delight in the Lord because his love and his mercy compel him to be good to us for endless generations!

PRAYER FOCUS: Father, help me love others the way you have loved me. Thank you, Lord Jesus, for choosing to love me from the foundation of the world (Matt. 25:34). Enrapture my soul with your goodness and beauty. Holy Spirit, pour over me the deep and abiding presence of your love.

DID YOU KNOW? Jesus said in Luke 12:34, "For where your treasure is, there your heart will be also" (NKJV). Pause for a moment and realize that you are God's treasure! God's greatest heart's desire is for you to become his adopted child through faith in Jesus Christ.

REFLECTIONS

OCTOBER 14

James 2:12-13 HCSB

Speak and act as those who will be judged by the law of freedom. For judgment is without mercy to the one who hasn't shown mercy. Mercy triumphs over judgment.

The apostle James encourages us to live free because we are free by the power of Christ living in us. Jesus came with grace and truth as he ministered to a lost world. But his greatest act of ministry was a demonstration of ultimate mercy as he willingly surrendered his life upon a humiliating cross to pay for the sins of limitless generations of lost people. Christ's mercy triumphed over the Father's just judgment for all who would believe and follow him. Following Christ involves more than intellectual belief; it requires loving God, pursuing God, and obeying God. Redeeming faith manifests itself in the works of Jesus. As we grow and mature, becoming more and more Christlike, we will reflect these works. The rescued becomes a rescuer; the forgiven becomes forgiving; the loved becomes a lover; the encouraged becomes an encourager; the receiver of truth becomes a defender of truth; the comforted becomes the comforter; the healed becomes a healer; the receiver of undeserved mercy becomes merciful. It is impossible to satisfy the justice of God without perfection, yet only the perfection of Christ can satisfy the Father's justice. We need to cling to Jesus and let his indwelling presence make us new. We need to walk with him, letting his power change us from the inside out. And we need to allow him to improve our character and atone for all the sins we cannot, because *mercy triumphs over judgment.*

PRAYER FOCUS: Merciful and faithful High Priest, I am so grateful you paid my sin debt and care for me like a Good Shepherd. Arrest my heart with your goodness and teach me your ways. Show me the path of life that I might follow you in all things (Ps. 16:11). Lord, help me to lean not on my own understanding, but on yours.

DID YOU KNOW? Mercy is an attribute of God. A. W. Tozer writes, "Both the Old and New Testaments proclaim the mercy of God, but the Old has more than four times as much to say about it as the New. We should banish from our minds forever the common but erroneous notion that justice and judgment characterize the God of Israel, while mercy and grace belong to the Lord of the Church. Actually there is in principle no difference between the Old Testament and the New."[15] Amen, "Jesus Christ is the same yesterday, today, and forever" (Heb. 13:8 HCSB).

OCTOBER
15

Matthew 18:21-22 NKJV

Then Peter came to Him and said, "Lord, how often shall my brother sin against me, and I forgive him? Up to seven times?" Jesus said to him, "I do not say to you, up to seven times, but up to seventy times seven."

Forgiveness does not come naturally or easily when we have been hurt by someone, especially a brother. Our natural instinct is to seek revenge, or be compensated in some way, for our injury. Peter sought to obtain a measuring stick by which he should offer forgiveness, but the Lord knew forgiveness was a necessary tool for obtaining the abundant life, and should be applied without limit. Warren Wiersbe wrote this about Peter's question: "Peter thought he was showing great faith and love when he offered to forgive at least seven times. After all, the rabbis taught that three times was sufficient. Our Lord's reply, 'Until seventy times seven' (490 times) must have startled Peter. Who could keep count for that many offenses? But that was exactly the point Jesus was making: Love 'keeps no record of wrongs' (1 Cor. 13:5 NIV). By the time we have forgiven a brother that many times, we are in the habit of forgiving."[16] As forgiven people, we must practice forgiveness (Matt. 6:14-15; Mark 11:24-25; Col. 3:13). Forgiveness flows out of awareness and humility. As we study God's Word and become aware of his standards for righteousness, we see how much we ourselves are in need of forgiveness. If we cultivate an attitude of humility before God and our neighbors, we will find it easier to forgive others when we're wronged.

PRAYER FOCUS: Lord, as you have forgiven me of so many offenses, sins, and errors, please help me to extend the same forgiveness to my neighbor. Help me cultivate the habit of forgiving. Make me slow to anger, quick to listen, and ready to forgive.

DID YOU KNOW? Debbie Morris, one of convicted killer Robert Willie's victims, has written a book titled *Forgiving the Dead Man Walking*. In it she writes, "People often ask, 'How do you feel about the death penalty now? Are you for or against it?' I still have ambivalent feelings. I've seen mankind's idea of ultimate justice; I have more faith in God's. And even God seems to put a higher priority on forgiveness than on justice. We don't sing 'Amazing Justice'; we sing 'Amazing Grace.' Does that mean I think a holy God would oppose the execution of a convicted murderer like Robert Willie? I don't know; I'm still wrestling with that question. But I do know this: Justice didn't do a thing to heal me. Forgiveness did."[17]

OCTOBER 16

Hosea 4:6 NIV

My people are destroyed from lack of knowledge. Because you have rejected knowledge, I also reject you as my priests; because you have ignored the law of your God, I also will ignore your children.

Much of the destruction we experience in our lives comes from a lack of knowledge about who God is, what he has taught us, and what he expects of us. We need to get to know God in spirit and in truth through worship, prayer, the study of his Word, and meditation on the things of God. Many times, however, our lack of knowledge does not come from ignorance, effort, or inexperience, but a rejection of knowledge. We often neglect or conveniently forget the knowledge and wisdom of God when we are pursuing sin. The willful distortion or omission of God's truth can have devastating consequences for us and our children. Nothing can be more devastating to a body of believers than when the leadership of shepherds chooses not to inform the people about God's ways—or worse yet, when they lead them into sin by falsehood, improper teaching, or wayward conduct. There is much the body of Christ does not know about the sanctity of human life and abortion because many pastors, priests, and teachers neglect to educate the church about it adequately or on a regular basis. Our national leaders and professionals have also contributed to a lack of knowledge concerning abortion. Many of our politicians, doctors, educators, and members of the mass media suppress or omit the truth about fetal development, ultrasound evidence, embryology, post-abortion syndrome, abortion complications, and the number of maternal deaths following abortion procedures. It's time for those in positions of leadership who know God's truth and who understand the medical, scientific, and evidential truth about the horror of abortion to step forward and lead. If they don't, God's people will continue to be destroyed from lack of knowledge.

PRAYER FOCUS: Lord of Life, raise up leaders to champion life in every arena and at every level. Holy Spirit, encourage existing leaders to preach, teach, and instruct their people concerning the dignity and value of human life from conception forward. Jesus, lead those who are not teaching the truth about life and abortion to repentance and a new commitment to educating their flock about this critical truth.

DID YOU KNOW? *Bella*, a 2007 movie about love, hope, and adoption, received the People's Choice Award at the Toronto Film Festival.[18] Rent this moving film and discover how one man's knowledge of the preciousness of life and the benefits of adoption moved him to care for a neighbor in distress. Watch this story and see the good that can come from loving your neighbor.

OCTOBER 17

Mark 13:31 NASB

Heaven and earth will pass away, but My words will not pass away.

~

Here, Jesus testifies to the preeminence of his words. The majesty and glory of creation does not compare to the eternal power of God's words (Col. 1:18). His words carry ultimate authority and truth, for he is the Word made flesh (John 1:14). Jesus' words and the words of all Scripture are living and active (Matt. 5:17; Heb. 4:12). Even in judgment, Jesus is inseparable from his words (Rev. 19:13). Nothing will stand the test of time except the words of God! "Heaven and earth will pass away, but My words will not pass away." We must live by God's words, meditate upon them, love them, and remember them, for they are the healing of the nations and the source of life. The Bible assures us that Jesus can make us new creations (2 Cor. 5:17; Rev. 21:5-6). We can trust God and know he meant what he said when he answered the expert in the law's question: "And He said to him, 'What is written in the Law? How does it read to you?' And he answered, 'You shall love the Lord your God with all your heart, and with all your soul, and with all your strength, and with all your mind; and your neighbor as yourself.' And He said to him, 'You have answered correctly; do this and you will live'" (Luke 10:26-28 NASB).

PRAYER FOCUS: Word of Life, fall afresh on me. Give me beauty for ashes and the oil of joy for mourning. Lead me beside still waters and give me rest as I trust in you. Take not your Holy Spirit from me but restore to me the joy of my salvation. Teach me to love you and my neighbor, both now and forever, the way you first loved me.

DID YOU KNOW? The apostle John used the Greek word *logos* for the title "Word" referring to Christ in three of his five books (John 1:1, 14; 1 John 1:1; Rev. 19:13). Elmer Towns wrote the following about John's usage: "Scholars debate whether John borrowed the term *logos* from the Greeks or the Jews. If the term is Greek, there may be numerous philosophical implications. If the term is Hebrew, John may be making reference to the wisdom of God personified (Proverbs, especially chapters 5—8). Probably John calls Jesus 'the Word of God' because this phrase is used over 1200 times in the Old Testament to refer to the revelation or message of God, as in the phrase, 'the Word of God came to . . .' Jesus Christ was the message, meaning, or communication from God to men. Jesus was everything the written and spoken Word of the Lord was in the Old Testament. Jesus is, therefore, the expression, revelation, and communication of the Lord. He is both the incarnate and inspired Word."[19]

OCTOBER 18

Joshua 7:10-12 NKJV

So the LORD said to Joshua: "Get up! Why do you lie thus on your face? Israel has sinned, and they have also transgressed My covenant which I commanded them. For they have even taken some of the accursed things, and have both stolen and deceived; and they have also put it among their own stuff. Therefore the children of Israel could not stand before their enemies, but turned their backs before their enemies, because they have become doomed to destruction. Neither will I be with you anymore, unless you destroy the accursed from among you."

∞

Joshua was lamenting before God the defeat of his troops at Ai and asking God why this was happening to God's chosen people. God revealed that some of Joshua's men, whom he had warned not to take the accursed things, had in fact done so and had themselves now become accursed, weakening the whole nation (Josh. 6:18-19; 7:1-3). When we sin and refuse to confess it and repent, especially in the area we are sent to battle, we will become weak before our enemies and damage our whole mission. When Joshua and the Israelites obeyed God and did not turn to the right or the left, they experienced victory after victory. But when they coveted the very things God sent them to destroy, they became accursed and the whole nation became weak. We cannot effectively battle pornography, promiscuity, sexual perversion, fraud, corruption, drugs, abuse, abortion, or any other sin if we are in agreement with these sins or involved in them. God's most effective warriors are free of iniquity and obedient to God (2 Cor. 10:3-6). Out of love and compassion, they reach out to help others who are wounded in the battle or lost in darkness. Does this mean God cannot or will not use us in areas we have sinned? No, it simply means that to be effective, we must flee from sin, resist sin, and repent when we do sin. Following repentance and healing, God can and does use former sinners to combat sins in which they were once involved. We must do our best to walk in obedience and fulfill Hebrews 12:1, which says, "Therefore we also, since we are surrounded by so great a cloud of witnesses, let us lay aside every weight, and the sin which so easily ensnares us, and let us run with endurance the race that is set before us" (NKJV).

PRAYER FOCUS: Lord, deliver the church from our sins and prepare us for the supernatural battles ahead. Be with us as you were with David when he wrote, "Blessed be the Lord my Rock, who trains my hands for war, and my fingers for battle—my loving-kindness and my fortress, my high tower and my deliverer, my shield and the One in whom I take refuge" (Ps. 144:1-2 NKJV). Lord, purify the body of Christ so that we can be effective in spiritual battle.

DID YOU KNOW? Joshua allowed Achan to confess his sins and repent before he was put to death for those sins, giving him hope for eternal redemption (Josh. 7:19-21).

OCTOBER 19

Joshua 10:12-14 NKJV

Then Joshua spoke to the Lord in the day when the Lord delivered up the Amorites before the children of Israel, and he said in the sight of Israel: "Sun, stand still over Gibeon; and Moon, in the Valley of Aijalon." So the sun stood still, and the moon stopped, till the people had revenge upon their enemies. Is this not written in the Book of Jasher? So the sun stood still in the midst of heaven, and did not hasten to go down for about a whole day. And there has been no day like that, before it or after it, that the Lord heeded the voice of a man; for the Lord fought for Israel.

After Joshua and the nation of Israel purged the sin of Achan from their midst and renewed their covenant with the Lord, God performed supernatural miracles during their next major battle with the Amorites. In addition to the miracle of the sun standing still over Gibeon, God sent large hailstones that demolished the retreating enemy: "And it happened, as they fled before Israel and were on the descent of Beth Horon, that the Lord cast down large hailstones from heaven on them as far as Azekah, and they died. There were more who died from the hailstones than the children of Israel killed with the sword" (Josh. 10:11 NKJV). Joshua, sensing the Israelites needed more time to completely destroy and triumph over their enemy, asked the Lord to prolong the daylight so none could escape in the darkness. The great God of nature intervened, demonstrating once again the power he dispenses to an obedient, faithful people. If the corporate church will align with the truth of God and obediently follow his commands, the body of Christ can defeat the enemies of the preborn and drive out the darkness with a prolonged and illuminating light.

PRAYER FOCUS: Jesus, unite the body of Christ under your headship and give us a common understanding of both when life begins and its preciousness. Holy Spirit, forge a common spirit among the body to fight for justice and champion the rights of the least of these in the womb. Lord, do the miraculous in us and through us once again.

DID YOU KNOW? The Book of Jasher, referenced in the book of Joshua, was a poetry book. The *Spirit-Filled Life Bible* indicates that "the Book of Jasher was an ancient, classical book of poetry about Israel's heroes and exploits. It is also mentioned in 2 Samuel 1:18."[20] *Unger's Bible Dictionary* adds, "by some the Book of Jasher is supposed to have perished in the captivity."[21]

REFLECTIONS

OCTOBER 20

Judges 6:14-16 HCSB

The LORD turned to him and said, "Go in the strength you have and deliver Israel from the power of Midian. Am I not sending you?" He said to Him, "Please, Lord, how can I deliver Israel? Look, my family is the weakest in Manasseh, and I am the youngest in my father's house." "But I will be with you," the LORD said to him. "You will strike Midian down as if it were one man."

God has great compassion and he cares about the suffering of his people, even when their suffering is brought about by their own sin and disobedience (Judg. 6:1-12). God allowed Midian to be used as a means of corrective judgment against the people of Israel, but when the time came for deliverance, he raised up a mighty warrior from among them to save the people and end their oppression. That mighty warrior was Gideon. Gideon was weary from oppression and did not consider himself to be of any account. Furthermore, as he felt the Lord had abandoned Israel and given her over to Midian, he had very little faith in a delivering God (Judg. 6:13). God, however, saw something different in Gideon, for he knew the plans he had for him, and he was about to prove that nothing is impossible for the great God of Israel (Judg. 7:7-22). Even in the midst of darkness and despair, God gives us hope and light if we will look for it, wait for it, and pray for it. If God calls us to do something, we must go in the strength we have and do it. Realize that despite our limitations, fears, and faith, the strength we have is no small thing when that strength is provided by Almighty God!

PRAYER FOCUS: Lord, speak to me through your Word and the Holy Spirit concerning how you see me and what you want me to accomplish. Take my hand and guide me when I doubt, fear, or need a sign before I will believe. God, use me for your glory and the good of your people and the Kingdom.

DID YOU KNOW? God provided many supernatural signs (angels; fleeces) to help Gideon strengthen his faith and accomplish his mission. The last sign Gideon received before battle was a dream (Judg. 7:13-15). In *A Dream Come True* James Ryle gives us a biblical and practical guide to understanding dreams and visions. He furnishes this insightful quote from Charles Spurgeon: "O young men, if you have received a thought which dashes ahead of your times, hold to it and work at it till it comes to something. If you have dreamed a dream from the Lord, turn it over and over again till you are quite sure it is not steam from a heated brain, or smoke from hell. When it is clear to your own heart that it is fire from off God's altar—then work, and pray, and wait your time!"[22]

OCTOBER 21

Judges 6:30-32 HCSB

Then the men of the city said to Joash, "Bring out your son. He must die, because he tore down Baal's altar and cut down the Asherah pole beside it." But Joash said to all who stood against him, "Would you plead Baal's case for him? Would you save him? Whoever pleads his case will be put to death by morning! If he is a god, let him plead his own case, because someone tore down his altar." That day, Gideon's father called him Jerubbaal, saying, "Let Baal plead his case with him," because he tore down his altar.

Gideon's faithfulness to God allowed him and the Israelites to triumph over their enemies, but what did his faithfulness do for God's own people who were wayward? Consider the case of Joash, Gideon's father, who was an active worshiper of Baal (Judg. 6:25). After the faith-filled obedience his son displayed by destroying Baal's altar and the Asherah pole, he courageously stood up to the men of the city and challenged the false god he once had served (Judg. 6:25-32). As Christians, our faith, obedience, and courage matter. We can turn the hearts of our families, friends, and neighbors by the actions we take, allowing the Holy Spirit to minister to others through the revelations of God and the power he displays in us. Gideon didn't act without fear or caution, but he did obey the instructions of the Lord. And in the process, God used him to set his own father free. Once Joash was free, he found his courage and exposed further the falsehood of Baal to the men of the city. We serve a liberating God who not only destroys our enemies, but frees the captives and rescues our friends.

PRAYER FOCUS: Thank you, God, for warriors and deliverers like Joshua and Gideon, men who do the right thing and place their trust and lives in your hands. Lord, raise up mighty deliverers in the present and future generations to tackle the tough stronghold of abortion. Grant them your favor and protection as they face the Enemy.

DID YOU KNOW? Asherah was a Canaanite goddess of sexual perversion and brutality. Merrill Unger wrote this about her: "She and her colleagues specialized in sex and war and her shrines were temples of legalized vice. Her degraded cult offered a perpetual danger of pollution to Israel and must have sunk to sordid depths as lust and murder were glamorized in Canaanite religion."[23]

REFLECTIONS

OCTOBER 22

1 Kings 18:21 NASB

Elijah came near to all the people and said, "How long will you hesitate between two opinions? If the LORD is God, follow Him; but if Baal, follow him." But the people did not answer him a word.

The body of Christ faces a modern-day Mount Carmel as we grapple with the legalized atrocity of abortion. Whom will we serve and whom will we fight for during the battle? Will we fight with the modern-day prophets of Baal and Asherah, who continue participating in and allowing the killing of countless innocents? Or will we stand with Almighty God and proclaim the sacredness of human life throughout all its stages? How long will the body of Christ hesitate between two opinions? Will we put away compromise and the fear of offense, taking up the case of the least of these, even if we stand alone, or will we continue debating the matter and allowing the slaughter to continue? Or, to our shame, will we remain silent, unable to utter a word in defense of the preborn, never pursuing justice? Believers need to stand strong and make our voices heard. We must pray, fast, weep, and do whatever it takes, in love, to end this unthinkable, unimaginable national tragedy.

PRAYER FOCUS: Lord, today I pledge to resist abortion, fight abortion, and do whatever is in my power to abolish abortion from the body of Christ and the nation. I am convinced of the truth that life begins at conception and that you are the Author of it. I will do my best to promote truth and help my fellow man. Holy Spirit, give me courage at the ballot box, in the church, in society, and in the home because you alone are God, and it is to you alone that I will give an account.

DID YOU KNOW? Faithful Christians throughout history have stood up against oppression and evil. Consider this brief testimony from David Faber's book, *Because of Romek: A Holocaust Survivor's Memoir*: "Kapo Schmidt never hit the children, never yelled at them. He gave us as much rest time as he could, but when the belt moved we had to work. If the coal wasn't cleaned of stones, Schmidt would be punished, and some new Kapo put in his place. He and I became friends, and he told me why he was in Jawiszowice. 'I'm a Christian,' he said, 'and I know the Nazis are wrong. I couldn't keep my mouth shut, so here I am.'"[24] I greatly admire believers like Kapo Schmidt (Prov. 31:8; Heb. 13:3).

OCTOBER 23

2 Timothy 4:18-21 NASB

The Lord will rescue me from every evil deed, and will bring me safely to His heavenly kingdom; to Him be the glory forever and ever. Amen. Greet Prisca and Aquila, and the household of Onesiphorus. Erastus remained at Corinth, but Trophimus I left sick at Miletus. Make every effort to come before winter. Eubulus greets you, also Pudens and Linus and Claudia and all the brethren.

Paul, imprisoned by the Romans and anticipating his martyrdom, closes his letter to Timothy with thoughts of God's faithfulness and the people he loves (2 Tim. 4:6-8 NASB). Paul's letter is an exhortation to Timothy to remain strong in the faith and continue the ministry set before him according to the ways of God (2 Tim. 4:1-2). Paul's final words hold forth several great treasures. First, faith in God transcends all circumstance. God is faithful no matter what we face, and Paul's confidence that his Lord will provide for him both now and in eternity is unshakeable. Second, relationships with God and people are what matter most. Paul's love for the people of God with whom he has ministered is clearly evident. Third, the value and urgency of time in our relationships and ministries is not to be underestimated. Paul encourages Timothy to make great haste to come see him for one last time (2 Tim. 4:9, 21). Historically, we don't know if Timothy made it to Rome before Paul's death, but we do know the window of Timothy's opportunity was brief. In a classic sermon, "Come Before Winter," Clarence Macartney said, "Before winter or never! There are some things which will never be done unless they are done 'before winter.' The winter will come and the winter will pass, and the flowers of the springtime will deck the breast of the earth, and the graves of some of our opportunities, perhaps the grave of our dearest friend. There are golden gates wide open on this autumn day, but next October they will be forever shut. There are tides of opportunity running now at the flood. Next October they will be at the ebb. There are voices speaking today which a year from today will be silent. Before winter or never!"[25] The time to address God, relationships, and abortion is now, for tomorrow is uncertain and, even if it comes, it may be too late (Eph. 5:15-16).

PRAYER FOCUS: God, apply my heart to wisdom and show me what is truly important. Holy Spirit, give me a sense of urgency for the things that matter most. Lord, help me to make good use of my time.

DID YOU KNOW? Clarence Macartney, pastor of First Presbyterian Church in Pittsburgh, first preached his sermon in 1915 and thereafter every October for 30-plus years.[26] An audio copy of this sermon, narrated by Max McLean, is available from Ligonier Ministries by calling 1-800-435-4343. I strongly recommend you obtain a copy of this sermon and learn from its wisdom.

OCTOBER 24

Revelation 12:10-11 NASB

Then I heard a loud voice in heaven, saying, "Now the salvation, and the power, and the kingdom of our God and the authority of His Christ have come, for the accuser of our brethren has been thrown down, he who accuses them before our God day and night. And they overcame him because of the blood of the Lamb and because of the word of their testimony, and they did not love their life even when faced with death."

As Satan is cast out of heaven and loses his opportunity to continually accuse the people of God, those martyred in the great tribulation declare the victory that awaits their brethren who are about to be heavily persecuted and martyred. God, in his wisdom, will not spare or shield these devout believers from violence, brutality, degradation, humiliation, pain, suffering, and death, but he has promised them victory (Rev. 11:7; 13:7; 17:14; 21:1-7). True life is found in Christ and is lived beyond the grave (John 11:25-26). Enraptured by the knowledge of God and the love of Christ, these martyrs overcome the enemy by the blood of the Lamb and the word of their testimony. Not even persecution and death can break their faith in a loving, delivering, prayer-hearing God. While certainly most believers will never face such persecution and opposition to their faith, everyone who is in Christ throughout the ages has found victory through the blood of the Lamb and the word of their testimony. Christ's blood is that which washes us clean and satisfies God's holy justice, while our testimonial faith in his provision assures us of our salvation. These two things, then, are how we overcome Satan and his evil pursuits. We overcome the wicked one by the blood of Jesus and our testimony of faith, deliverance, truth, love, and grace. When we endeavor to face the enemy in any arena, we must shield ourselves from his accusations with the blood-atoning provision of Christ, and secure our victory with a testimony of grace and truth.

PRAYER FOCUS: Lamb of God, your blood so precious shed for me, nothing but your blood sets me free! Help me know your ways are true, and do my best to walk with you. Shame the Enemy where he stands, and defeat all his destructive plans. Lead me to love and let me know, that all will be obtained in heaven's glow.

DID YOU KNOW? Photojournalist Michael Clancy, whose work has been published in *The New York Times*, *Newsweek*, and *USA Today*, took a photograph in 1999 of a fetal surgery to correct spina bifida on a twenty-one-week-old baby that changed his life dramatically.[27] View this powerful photograph and read his testimony at *www.michaelclancy.com*.

OCTOBER 25

Genesis 4:7-12 NKJV

"If you do well, will you not be accepted? And if you do not do well, sin lies at the door. And its desire is for you, but you should rule over it." Now Cain talked with Abel his brother; and it came to pass, when they were in the field, that Cain rose up against Abel his brother and killed him. Then the LORD said to Cain, "Where is Abel your brother?" He said, "I do not know. Am I my brother's keeper?" And He said, "What have you done? The voice of your brother's blood cries out to Me from the ground. So now you are cursed from the earth, which has opened its mouth to receive your brother's blood from your hand. When you till the ground, it shall no longer yield its strength to you. A fugitive and a vagabond you shall be on the earth."

The righteous will lay down their lives for God and their neighbor, but the wicked who refuse to repent will often manifest great iniquity. Sin begins in the heart and then manifests itself in destructive acts against our family, friends, and neighbors. Cain was prideful, angry, irreverent, and unforgiving in his heart long before he murdered his brother. Shortly before Abel's death, while God had rejected Cain's offering because it was improper, he was willing to give Cain another chance and even tried to warn Cain about the dangers of continuing to walk in his sinful ways (Gen. 4:3-7). But Cain hardened his heart and refused to listen to God's advice to walk in humility, forgiveness, and right conduct. Just as God predicted, the sins of the heart did overtake Cain, resulting in the murder of his brother. Even after his brutal act, Cain had no remorse for what he had done and arrogantly responded to God's question by implying that he was not the guardian of his brother. Cain's heart had grown cold and loveless because of his sin and his refusal to repent. Abel's blood cried out for justice and, as a consequence of Cain's sins, Cain lost the presence of God, security, and fruitfulness in labor (Gen. 4:13-16). We reap great devastation when we choose to reject God's counsel and destroy our neighbor.

PRAYER FOCUS: God, help me choose love and not hate, forgiveness and not bitterness, reflection and not anger, life and not death, trust and not contempt. When I sin, help me be quick to repent so that my sins don't fester and cause additional harm to myself and others. And give me a heart of wisdom and a desire to walk in your ways.

DID YOU KNOW? The name *Abel* means "breath." *The Book of Bible Names* says this about the name: "Perhaps his name prophetically reflected the shortness of his life."[28] Ironically, nothing shortens life more than the act of abortion.

REFLECTIONS

OCTOBER 26

2 Kings 8:11-13 NIV

He stared at him with a fixed gaze until Hazael felt ashamed. Then the man of God began to weep. "Why is my lord weeping?" asked Hazael. "Because I know the harm you will do to the Israelites," he answered. "You will set fire to their fortified places, kill their young men with the sword, dash their little children to the ground, and rip open their pregnant women." Hazael said, "How could your servant, a mere dog, accomplish such a feat?" "The LORD has shown me that you will become king of Aram," answered Elisha.

During Elisha's visit to Damascus, Ben-Hadad, king of Aram, sent Hazael to determine if he would recover from his current illness (2 Kings 8:7-10). God revealed to Elisha that the king would indeed recover from his sickness, but that Hazael would take the king's life anyway (2 Kings 8:14-15). On hearing this news, wicked Hazael did not recoil in horror, but simply wondered how someone with his lowly position could accomplish such ascension to power. The wicked human heart is unconcerned with the plight and oppression of others; it only lives for itself and its selfish gain (Prov. 21:10). The man of God, however, understands oppression, injustice, and grief, and begins to weep for the victims of Hazael during his brutal time of governance. The depth of Hazael's depravity and wickedness is reflected in his victims, for he is about to murder his king, young men, little children, women, and preborn babies! If God did not value the life of innocent children developing in the womb, he would not have led the author, through the Holy Spirit, to mention that the women were pregnant. The wicked know no bounds, and what is sacred to God and his people becomes simply a nuisance in the way of their personal gain. Sharing Elisha's heartache, weep with me for all those destroyed or slaughtered by abortion!

PRAYER FOCUS: God, the heartache I feel over the tragedy of abortion in my nation and around the world is overwhelming. Record my tears of sorrow on your scrolls and minister your peace to me. Lord, forgive us, your people, and those who do not know you of this great offense. Turn our tears into action and move us to end this hideous practice!

DID YOU KNOW? Little is known about Hazael before he comes to power. The *ESV Study Bible* records this in its commentary notes: "The messenger Hazael enters the narrative mysteriously. Readers are not told his lineage, nor even his role (servant? officer?). He comes from nowhere—a mere 'dog,' as he puts it in 8:13. A fragmentary Assyrian text on a basalt statue of King Shalmaneser III refers to him similarly as the 'son of nobody,' doubtless reflecting lowly, nonroyal origins."[29]

OCTOBER 27

Job 39:1-2 HCSB

Do you know when mountain goats give birth? Have you watched the deer in labor? Can you count the months they are pregnant so you can know the time they give birth?

∞

These verses, among many others, were spoken to Job by God during Job's time of testing and affliction (Job 38:1-3). God was testing Job and challenging his knowledge of the creation in order to display the inequality that existed between them. Clearly, Job was overmatched from the outset (Job 38:4-21). Job learned firsthand through revelation and experience that the living God was more than he knew and deeper still than he could fathom. There is much to be learned and observed about God from his discourse with Job over the final five chapters of the book. I want to focus on Job 39:1-2, however, and what these verses tell us about the preciousness of life in the womb. It is clear from God's questions to Job that God is intimately aware of the gestation periods in his animal kingdom. God knows their exact times for gestation, labor, and birth (Ps. 29:9). He knows the inward parts of each creature and how they progress through their stages of development. God, in his providence, provides, manages, and cares for his creatures at all times from conception to death. The *ESV Study Bible* translates Job 39:2 as, "Can you number the months that they fulfill, and do you know the time when they give birth?" Every month in the journey of life is crucial to the animal's development and purpose. If God displays such care and intention over his animal kingdom, how much more so does he care for and love humans, the crown jewel of his creation (Matt. 6:26)?

PRAYER FOCUS: Lord, keep me mindful of how I treat your creation. Grant me the discernment and wisdom to be a good steward of the planet—its plants, animals, resources, and people. Show me how to care for the things you have given me dominion over (Gen. 1:26-29).

DID YOU KNOW? "Each year, about 130 million women around the world go through the complex cycle of pregnancy and birth. Our increasingly sophisticated understanding of the process has drastically reduced the risks for both mother and baby. Ironically, the one thing that allows us to understand the process—our large brains—is principally responsible for the difficulties of childbirth. Most mammals, with much smaller brains and heads, have a far easier time squeezing out their offspring. Their infants are also more advanced in survival terms than our helpless babies—often able to walk, feed, and escape from predators immediately after birth. For a human baby to do this, its mother would have to undergo a 21-month pregnancy and then give birth to a toddler," writes Peter Tallack.[30]

OCTOBER 28

Luke 1:41-44 ESV

And when Elizabeth heard the greeting of Mary, the baby leaped in her womb. And Elizabeth was filled with the Holy Spirit, and she exclaimed with a loud cry, "Blessed are you among women, and blessed is the fruit of your womb! And why is this granted to me that the mother of my Lord should come to me? For behold, when the sound of your greeting came to my ears, the baby in my womb leaped for joy."

From inside his mother's womb, John the Baptist was the first to express joy over the coming of his Lord. His leap in the womb and subsequent filling of the Holy Spirit enabled Elizabeth, also filled with the Spirit, to recognize the presence of her Lord inside Mary (Luke 1:15). We know from earlier in this chapter that Elizabeth was in the sixth month of pregnancy, making John roughly twenty-four to twenty-seven weeks gestation when this event took place (Luke 1:24, 36). It is harder to pinpoint the gestational age of Jesus from this passage, but we know that Mary was in the first trimester of her pregnancy and possibly very early in it (Luke 1:26-40). If Mary conceived around the time the angel departed and only needed a week or two to travel to Zechariah's house, then it stands to reason she may have been less than a month pregnant (Luke 1:38-39; 56-57), making the recognition of Jesus in his embryonic stage all the more miraculous. Regardless of the gestational age, what is clear is that both Jesus and John were considered persons before their birth despite their stage of development. Each possessed a clear purpose and calling from the very moment of their conception.

PRAYER FOCUS: Jesus, begotten by the Holy Spirit and conceived in Mary, thank you for coming to earth through the womb and partaking in every stage of human life so that you could fully identify with me. Sovereign Lord, thank you for the many testimonies throughout Scripture that life begins at conception, your own being the most important. God, teach me to value all life, especially my neighbors' and my own. Thank you for miracles and the greatest miracle of all, the gift of you.

DID YOU KNOW? The original Greek word used for *baby* in this passage from Luke is *brephos*. The word *brephos* is used in other New Testament passages for babies or young children outside the womb. According to *Strong's Exhaustive Concordance of the Bible*, Luke 2:12-16, Luke 18:15, Acts 7:19, 2 Timothy 3:15, and 1 Peter 2:2 all use *brephos* to describe little ones outside the womb.[31] The Scriptures make no distinction between babies inside or outside the womb because in the biblical view, life begins at conception.

OCTOBER 29

Luke 12:2-3 NASB

But there is nothing covered up that will not be revealed, and hidden that will not be known. Accordingly, whatever you have said in the dark will be heard in the light, and what you have whispered in the inner rooms will be proclaimed upon the housetops.

God's knowledge is perfect. Jesus tells us that nothing will be hidden or covered up before God. God possesses intimate knowledge of all things with perfect clarity, including the thoughts and attitudes of the heart. God will render a just verdict concerning us and those we have lived with because he remembers every event, thought, detail, and word. This reality brings with it both absolute accountability and absolute justice. On the one hand, we will be judged according to every action done and every word spoken (Eccles. 12:14; Matt. 12:36). On the other hand, we will be rewarded and vindicated by all our words and actions that helped people and glorified God (Ruth 2:11-12; 1 Sam. 24:3-19; Prov. 22:4; Matt. 5:12; 10:42; Luke 6:35; 12:8). Accountability and justice are good things, but they don't bring peace. Truth and justice alone will not set us free because we are all transgressors. Only Jesus, the Prince of Peace, can set us free because he blotted out our sins by satisfying God's justice through his shed blood of atonement. There is no such thing as a private or secret abortion, but there is such a thing as forgiveness and healing provided by a loving God.

PRAYER FOCUS: Father God, darkness is not dark to you. Your light illuminates all. Lord, I believe you love me in spite of my sins and that you paid my sin debt on the cross. Jesus, today I confess my sins to you, those willful and those I have failed to discern. Holy Spirit, illuminate your grace to me and deepen my dependence on you. Thank you, Jesus, for forgiving me my trespasses (1 John 1:9).

DID YOU KNOW? Luke was a physician (Col. 4:14). He shared in the mission work of Paul and was present with him during his final imprisonment in Rome (2 Tim. 4:11). I wonder how a physician would understand these words of Christ recorded in Luke 12:2-3, for a doctor reveals much that is hidden in order to heal a patient. Doctors often see what we do not and can discern an individual's state of health by examining seemingly hidden things.

REFLECTIONS

OCTOBER 30

Ephesians 5:7-11 ESV

Therefore do not become partners with them; for at one time you were darkness, but now you are light in the Lord. Walk as children of light (for the fruit of light is found in all that is good and right and true), and try to discern what is pleasing to the Lord. Take no part in the unfruitful works of darkness, but instead expose them.

∞

Believers are children of God and children of light. As redeemed men and women in the Lord, we should manifest the light. Our journey of faith should progressively turn from the ways of darkness, some of which Paul describes in Ephesians 5:3-7, to the ways of light. Those who walk in the light seek to do what is good, stand for what is right, and proclaim and defend what is true. We are fallen fleshly people, but we have been bought with a price and filled with the presence of Christ. We need to rely on the Word of God and the Holy Spirit to help us discern what is pleasing to the Lord, and then we need to do our best to walk in it through prayer, repentance, worship, meditation, and faith. Sin is a deadly cancer, and we must do all we can to wage war against it and refuse it in our lives. We will be the best we can be when we walk in obedience to God and shun the sins that so easily entangle us. As children of the light and ministers of the light, we must turn from darkness and expose the works of the Enemy that harm us and our neighbors.

PRAYER FOCUS: Father, you know the depth of my sins and the difficulty I have with them. Lord, I desire to please you with every area of my life. Come, Holy Spirit, deliver me from my sins—their temptation, their hold, and their memory. Jesus, teach me to walk in the light and help me feel your mercy as I allow your light to expose the darkness in me. As your light grows, diminish the instances of darkness in me and fade the memory of when I walked in darkness.

DID YOU KNOW? The abortion industry lied about the number of maternal deaths that occurred from illegal abortions before abortion on demand was legalized. Mark Crutcher wrote, "They [the abortion industry] used to claim that, before legalization, 5,000 to 10,000 women died each year from botched illegal abortions. In fact, some still throw these figures around. However, the American Medical Association (AMA) says that the figure for 1950 was 263 and that it had dropped to 119 by 1970. Even Planned Parenthood's research arm, the Alan Guttmacher Institute, published a graph showing that the number of induced abortion-related deaths fell from about 200 in 1965 to about 110 in 1967."[32] Praise God today for people who are working to expose unfruitful works of darkness, especially the darkness of the abortion industry.

OCTOBER 31

Galatians 2:20-21 NKJV

I have been crucified with Christ; it is no longer I who live, but Christ lives in me; and the life which I now live in the flesh I live by faith in the Son of God, who loved me and gave Himself for me. I do not set aside the grace of God; for if righteousness comes through the law, then Christ died in vain.

Christ alone is righteous, and it is his righteousness that covers the redeemed. "Nor is there salvation in any other, for there is no other name under heaven given among men by which we must be saved" (Acts 4:12 NKJV). Because our salvation does not remove us from this fleshly body until our days on the earth are complete, we must live by faith. We must live by faith that Christ died once for all, faith that the work is finished, faith that nothing can separate us from the love of God, and faith that his grace is sufficient. Paul wrote in Romans 1:16-17, "For I am not ashamed of the gospel of Christ, for it is the power of God to salvation for everyone who believes, for the Jew first and also for the Greek. For in it the righteousness of God is revealed from faith to faith; as it is written, 'The just shall live by faith'" (NKJV). What majesty and glory and honor belong to our King, for he ransomed us from death by his own blood while we were yet sinners! When the Enemy accuses us, when our sins overwhelm us, when life burdens us, when death visits us, we know that Christ is enough. No, he is more than enough!

PRAYER FOCUS: Worthy is the Lamb, worthy is the Lamb that was slain! Jesus, draw near to me and fill me with things that are too wonderful for me (Jer. 33:3). Show me the depth, height, and width of your love (Eph. 3:16-20). Lord of life, Lord of all, keep me always in your care and according to your righteousness bring me safely to the throne room of God.

DID YOU KNOW? The word *Christ* means "anointed one." Elmer Towns wrote this about Paul's frequent use of it: "At least forty-nine times in his Epistles, Paul uses the expression 'the/our Lord Jesus Christ,' bringing together the three primary names of Jesus. . . . 'Lord' is His title, 'Jesus' is His name, and 'Christ' is His office. Actually, 'Christ' is a favorite name of the Apostle Paul, and he uses it independently of the other titles some 211 times in his writings."[33]

REFLECTIONS

November

LEGACY

NOVEMBER 1

1 Thessalonians 2:13 NIV

And we also thank God continually because, when you received the word of God, which you heard from us, you accepted it not as the word of men, but as it actually is, the word of God, which is at work in you who believe.

God's Word is inspired, timeless, and dependable. Paul and the other New Testament writers knew their writing was not their own creation, but rather the inspired revelation of God written through them to his people. Will we accept God's Word today as true and divine? If we do, it will begin doing its work in our lives. Believing is seeing. If we trust the revelations of God communicated through the Bible, our lives will be blessed. God will transform us in his timing, using any combination of factors, because the Holy Spirit and his Word will be at work in us. This process may be gradual, rapid, or anything in between, but we will be aware of it. The deep knowledge and wisdom of the Bible is limitless and applicable to any problem, circumstance, question, or need we may have. This intimate manual from God is sufficient for all our life needs, and we can build our life upon its foundation. If we follow its teachings, we will never be lost or without a guide. Praise God for giving us his Son, the Holy Spirit, and his Word.

PRAYER FOCUS: Father God, I accept your Word as true and divine. Teach me from its deep wisdom and knowledge, and build my life upon it and sow it into my heart. Holy Spirit, guide me to its rivers of living water and transform the desert areas of my life. Lord Jesus, I trust your revelation that life begins at conception. I will stand for life whenever and wherever I have the opportunity. Thank you for truth and that your Word is truth (John 17:17).

DID YOU KNOW? The Greek word used for truth in John 17:17 is *aletheia*. The *ESV Study Bible* makes this comment about its use: "The Greek word is surprisingly not an adjective (meaning 'your word is true') but a noun (*aletheia*, 'truth'). This implies that God's Word does not simply conform to some other external standard of 'truth,' but that it is truth itself."[1]

REFLECTIONS

NOVEMBER 2

Psalm 33:6-9 HCSB

The heavens were made by the word of the Lord, and all the stars, by the breath of His mouth. He gathers the waters of the sea into a heap; He puts the depths into storehouses. Let the whole earth tremble before the Lord; let all the inhabitants of the world stand in awe of Him. For He spoke, and it came into being; He commanded, and it came into existence.

We serve a supernatural, powerful, amazing God! He created the universe with the vastness and grandeur it contains simply by speaking. To understand even a little about God is to be in awe of him. The majesty, preeminence, and strength of God revealed through Scripture and nature is overwhelming. It is only through ignorance or a diminished view of the Almighty that we can even begin to think we have a right to treat his creation without respect. All the stars, planets, angels, people, animals, and plants were created for God's pleasure and purposes. Nothing is like him. Nothing compares to him. He is the great I Am! The psalmist said, "When I observe Your heavens, the work of Your fingers, the moon and the stars, which You set in place, what is man that You remember him, the son of man that You look after him?" (Ps. 8:3-4 HCSB). For reasons known only to himself, and because of his great love, God made man in his image and called him brother. The writer of Hebrews wrote, "In bringing many sons to glory, it was fitting that God, for whom and through whom everything exists, should make the author of their salvation perfect through suffering. Both the one who makes men holy and those who are made holy are of the same family. So Jesus is not ashamed to call them brothers" (Heb. 2:10-11 NIV). We respect what God has made and give glory to him because he was, and is, and is to come.

PRAYER FOCUS: Today's prayer focus is the chorus from Mercy Me's song, "Word of God Speak." "Oh word of God speak / would You pour down like rain / Washing my eyes to see / Your majesty / To be still and know / That You're in this place / Please let me stay and rest / In Your holiness / Word of God speak" (*Spoken For* album).[2]

DID YOU KNOW? The first two chapters of Genesis are not the only places where the Bible discusses creation. Look at Job 9:4-10, Psalms 104 and 148, Proverbs 8:22-31, Isaiah 40, John 1:1-18, 1 Corinthians 15:35-57, and Hebrews 1:1-3.

REFLECTIONS

NOVEMBER 3

Ephesians 2:8-10 ESV

For by grace you have been saved through faith. And this is not your own doing; it is the gift of God, not a result of works, so that no one may boast. For we are his workmanship, created in Christ Jesus for good works, which God prepared beforehand, that we should walk in them.

Salvation is the product of faith realized through unearned and undeserved grace given to us by God. God in his grace has given us life on earth and life in heaven if we will accept by faith the gift of his Son as the sacrifice for our sins. The work is finished—a work we didn't share in or deserve, for it was our rebellion that put Jesus on the cross. God is a gift-giver, and most of his best gifts are given without our collaboration, in spite of our merits. I have done very little, if anything, to deserve the gifts of my wife, children, friends, and abilities. Certainly I have done nothing to merit the sweet sacrifice of my Savior. God didn't give himself for me because I am good, but because he is good. James wrote, "Every good gift and every perfect gift is from above, coming down from the Father of lights with whom there is no variation or shadow due to change" (James 1:17 ESV). Our story as Christians does not end at salvation because God, having adopted us through our faith, has good works for us to do, the works of loving him and loving our neighbor. How shall we repay the Lord for his marvelous goodness to us? We cannot repay him, but we can learn from him as our example in all things and become gift-givers ourselves. We can give the gift of ourselves to God and to others, doing the good works we can in service and love to our neighbors. We can walk in good works because God has been superbly good to us, and we can allow him to use us to bless others.

PRAYER FOCUS: Lord, thank you for your many gifts to me. I am overwhelmed by your goodness and grace. You are without a doubt the King of kings and Lord of lords! Who else would lay down his life for a lost sheep like me (John 10:11, 14)? Jesus, life is so precious. Help me cherish it always, and teach me my value as you fashion me into a gift-giver.

DID YOU KNOW? On this date in 1973, just ten months after the nationwide legalization of abortion, my wife was born. Had she been aborted, the void in my life would have been immeasurable, and I would have lost one of God's greatest gifts to me long before I knew her name.

NOVEMBER 4

Ephesians 1:3-7 NASB

Blessed be the God and Father of our Lord Jesus Christ, who has blessed us with every spiritual blessing in the heavenly places in Christ, just as He chose us in Him before the foundation of the world, that we would be holy and blameless before Him. In love He predestined us to adoption as sons through Jesus Christ to Himself, according to the kind intention of His will, to the praise of the glory of His grace, which He freely bestowed on us in the Beloved. In Him we have redemption through His blood, the forgiveness of our trespasses, according to the riches of His grace.

If we have placed our faith in Jesus Christ, we are no longer aliens or strangers to God. Instead, we have become his friends and have been adopted into the family as sons or daughters of God. Adoption holds a special place in the heart of God. He is eager to rescue all who come to him seeking adoption. Jesus loves and wants us so much that he willingly paid the ultimate price to secure our adoption. Surely, God looks with favor on anyone who follows his example and extends the gift of adoption to his created children. If we feel called to adopt one or more children during our time on earth, we should prayerfully consider it and follow wherever the Holy Spirit leads. Notice afresh the beginning of today's passage where Paul writes, *He chose us in Him before the foundation of the world.* In order to be chosen by God for adoption, we must exist in some form. Perhaps the real question facing us is not when life begins, but, rather, who has dominion over it? From a biological perspective, it is clear that human life begins at conception, but from a theological perspective, life seems to begin even before that—in the mind of God. French philosopher Rene Descartes once wrote, *Cogito ergo sum:* "I think, therefore I am." I submit, God thought, therefore we are! Life is God's gift, and it is far too precious for us to throw away.

PRAYER FOCUS: Father, I am deeply humbled you chose me and my fellow believers to be a part of your plan before the foundation of the world. Before you formed us in the womb, you knew us and the choice we would make to follow you. Father, I glory in you and your gracious spirit of adoption. I'm overwhelmed by the prospect that one day, face to face, you will call me your son/daughter.

DID YOU KNOW? Bethany Christian Services (1-800-bethany; *bethany.org*) is the largest adoption agency in the U.S.A., with over eighty locations. Bethany even offers embryo adoption through their Embryo Adoption Progam.[3]

REFLECTIONS

319

NOVEMBER 5

John 13:34-35 HCSB

I give you a new command: love one another. Just as I have loved you, you must also love one another. By this all people will know that you are My disciples, if you have love for one another.

Jesus gave his disciples a new command that was greater than all the others with the exception of loving God—to love one another as he had loved them. Love is the distinguishing mark of a disciple of Christ. As God's love takes root in our hearts and begins manifesting itself in us, we become ambassadors of his love. As we grow in spiritual maturity, we show forth the love we have received from God by loving others. Our love will express itself in tangible ways to our spouse, family, friends, neighbors, and strangers. We will become givers and encouragers; we will look for opportunities to serve and to help. We will give our finances and our time to those in need or distress while we forgive and do our best to keep no record of wrongs. And we will love because he first loved us. Love is the most powerful force in the universe and the best course to follow. Love is sacrificial because it seeks the good of another over the good of the self. It seeks not to be filled, but to fill. Love commits, endures, reaches out, bleeds, and gives up its life. Truly, to love like Christ is divine, but before we abandon all hope of loving like our Savior, we need to remember that he resides in us. The apostle Paul wrote to the church at Corinth that "these three remain: faith, hope, and love. But the greatest of these is love" (1 Cor. 13:13 HCSB). Our goal as followers of Christ is to love God and his people.

PRAYER FOCUS: "Now to Him who is able to do above and beyond all that we ask or think according to the power that works in us—to Him be glory in the church and in Christ Jesus to all generations, forever and ever. Amen" (Eph. 3:20-21 HCSB).

DID YOU KNOW? Nichole Nordeman, the contemporary Christian singer-songwriter, is a nine-time Dove Award winner.[4] Her song "Hold On," from the album *Brave*, is about the power of God's love to rescue us from any circumstance. It communicates a great truth when she sings, "To hang between two thieves in the darkness / Love must believe you are worth it."[5]

REFLECTIONS

NOVEMBER 6

Matthew 23:29-37 NKJV

Woe to you, scribes and Pharisees, hypocrites! Because you build the tombs of the prophets and adorn the monuments of the righteous, and say, "If we had lived in the days of our fathers, we would not have been partakers with them in the blood of the prophets." Therefore you are witnesses against yourselves that you are sons of those who murdered the prophets. Fill up, then, the measure of your fathers' guilt. Serpents, brood of vipers! How can you escape the condemnation of hell? Therefore, indeed, I send you prophets, wise men, and scribes: some of them you will kill and crucify, and some of them you will scourge in your synagogues and persecute from city to city, that on you may come all the righteous blood shed on the earth, from the blood of righteous Abel to the blood of Zechariah, son of Berechiah, whom you murdered between the temple and the altar. Assuredly, I say to you, all these things will come upon this generation. O Jerusalem, Jerusalem, the one who kills the prophets and stones those who are sent to her! How often I wanted to gather your children together, as a hen gathers her chicks under her wings, but you were not willing!

How often do we honor great men and then forget what made them great, or whom it was they served? The religious elite of Jesus' time were so lost and in darkness that they believed their righteousness exceeded their forefathers, even as they were about to murder the King of kings and his disciples after him. Jesus prophesied, as their words confirmed in Matthew 27:25, that their sins and the sins of their fathers would be visited on their own heads because they rejected the Messiah, their only source of atonement (Heb. 9:11-28). This did not bring joy to Jesus, but sorrow, because his heart was to save and not to lose even a single soul. Jesus wants to gather his children under his mighty wings in order to encircle them with his protection. Are we willing?

PRAYER FOCUS: God, forgive me, my forefathers, and my nation for the blood we have shed through injustice and abortion. Cleanse us, Lord, and save us, for we are a wayward and blind people.

DID YOU KNOW? According to The *ESV Study Bible*, "The interval from the blood of righteous Abel (Gen. 4:8-11) to the blood of Zechariah (2 Chron. 24:20-22) encompasses all of OT biblical history. Abel was the first person murdered in the OT and Zechariah is the last murdered, since 2 Chronicles (where the murder of Zechariah is recorded) is the last book in the Hebrew canon."[6]

REFLECTIONS

NOVEMBER 7

Leviticus 25:18-19 NIV

Follow my decrees and be careful to obey my laws, and you will live safely in the land. Then the land will yield its fruit, and you will eat your fill and live there in safety.

Whose advice are we going to follow? Are we going to base our life around the anointed words of God, or will we trust in human insights and philosophies? Moses told the people of Israel that safety, security, and confidence comes from trusting God and following his commands and principles. This holds true for both individuals and nations. When we walk in God's ways, we are blessed in abundance and enjoy safety, both temporally and eternally. To the degree we personally or collectively follow God is the degree we will experience personal and national blessing and safety. We all recognize the world can be a very brutal and violent place, but I contend it would be far less so if the majority of humankind was submitted to the lordship of Christ. After all, how different would our nation and world be if everyone loved their neighbor and considered them better than themselves?

PRAYER FOCUS: Father, I want all people to live safely and abundantly in the land. I understand the land belongs to you and that bloodshed pollutes the land (Lev. 25:23; Num. 35:33-34; Ps. 50:10-12). Lord, turn us back to your ways so that our land will become clean and the nation can prosper (Isa. 1:16-19).

DID YOU KNOW? God commanded the Israelites to rest the land every seven years, just as they were to rest from their labor once a week during the Sabbath (Exod. 20:8-11; Lev. 25:2-7). Everything of value needs rest, and the land is no different. Notice how amply God provides for the people during the Sabbath years (Lev. 25:20-22). God will be more than good to us when we trust his Word and obey his commands.

REFLECTIONS

NOVEMBER 8

Leviticus 19:15-18 HCSB

You must not act unjustly when deciding a case. Do not be partial to the poor or give preference to the rich; judge your neighbor fairly. You must not go about spreading slander among your people; you must not jeopardize your neighbor's life; I am Yahweh. You must not harbor hatred against your brother. Rebuke your neighbor directly, and you will not incur guilt because of him. Do not take revenge or bear a grudge against members of your community, but love your neighbor as yourself; I am Yahweh.

Leviticus chapter nineteen is a powerful chapter about holiness and God's expectations for his people to live in holiness. He told the Israelite community, "Be holy because I, Yahweh your God, am holy" (Lev. 19:2 HCSB). God cares about us, our fellow man, and how we treat each other. The applications to abortion from this passage are many. First, we should not be unjust when rendering judgments personally or in our courts. Abortion is a great injustice to our offspring and the future of our nation. Second, we should not show favoritism or partiality. Abortion favors the powerful over the weak and gives rights to one person while withholding them from another. Third, we should not slander others. Abortion slanders the preborn and lies about who they are. Fourth, we are not to jeopardize our neighbor's life. Abortion takes our neighbor's life. Fifth, we are not to hate our brothers in our heart. When pro-life people are unwilling to forgive and decide to take the lives of those with whom they disagree, they demonstrate a hate for their neighbor that stems from the heart. Sixth, we are called to rebuke our neighbor when he or she is in the wrong. If we remain silent about the horrors of abortion, we will share our neighbor's guilt and culpability for abortion. If we speak out and they refuse to listen, the blood of the preborn will be on their own head. Seventh, we are not called to revenge or bitterness, but to love.

PRAYER FOCUS: God, I am overwhelmed by what it means to be holy and I confess that I am not. You alone are holy. Holy Spirit, use your power in me to mold me and improve my holiness until I rest with you. Jesus, show me what it means to be your disciple and help me walk it out.

DID YOU KNOW? The *Spirit Filled Life Bible* communicates the following insight about the phrase "love your neighbor as yourself" in Leviticus 19:18: "The word 'love' (Hebrew *ahav*) could be understood as *esteem*. Love of one's neighbor begins with self-esteem. Then one esteems his neighbor."[7]

REFLECTIONS

NOVEMBER 9

Proverbs 14:31 NASB

He who oppresses the poor taunts his Maker, but he who is gracious to the needy honors Him.

∞

According to this proverb, when we oppress the poor we taunt the living God! We arrogantly suppose he won't or can't call us to account for our actions. We wrongly assume that those with power on earth rule. The philosophies of "might makes right" and "survival of the fittest" pervade our thinking. This sort of thinking may seem correct if we observe the way things operate on earth, but God conducts business much differently in heaven. In heaven, just as it will be on earth when he returns to reign, God conducts his affairs with righteousness and justice. At the Judgment, those who taunted God and oppressed his people will be punished for their crimes and arrogance. Those who have been gracious to the needy, weak, poor, and fatherless on earth will be rewarded and blessed by their heavenly Father. Abortion is a great form of oppression because it seeks to terminate a life before it matures, thus robbing the aborted individual of all they could accomplish or experience in the future. On the other hand, if we choose to allow life to mature after God has blessed us with it, we honor him and his will for our lives. Carrying a pregnancy to term is an opportunity to demonstrate our trust in God and partner with him in the miracle of new life.

PRAYER FOCUS: Father, help me see that abortion is one of the greatest forms of oppression the world has ever known. Jesus, forgive me for any past sins of oppression, those times when I willingly or unwillingly oppressed my neighbor. And please fashion in me a heart of compassion that longs to reach out and be gracious to others, especially the poor and the needy.

DID YOU KNOW? UNICEF estimates on their website that 24,000 children die every day from preventable causes (*www.unicefusa.org*). They define preventable causes as malaria and measles, unclean water poisoning, inadequate shelter, and malnutrition.[8] While these totals from poverty, disease, and hunger are staggering, they pale in comparison to the number of children lost in the world each day through abortion. Global abortion estimates exceed well over one hundred thousand children per day![9] Clearly, the greatest thing we could do to prevent the death of children would be to stop all abortion practices.

NOVEMBER 10

Matthew 6:33-34 NASB

But seek first His kingdom and His righteousness, and all these things will be added to you. So do not worry about tomorrow; for tomorrow will care for itself. Each day has enough trouble of its own.

How often do we put off God or the things closest to his heart in order to take care of our personal needs? Instead of putting his kingdom first, how many times do we want to finish a project at home or get our retirement portfolio in order before we address matters of faith? It's easy to get distracted trying to provide for our own welfare, but God wants us to know that his system of provision is different from ours. He wants us to seek his kingdom and his righteousness before anything else. God knows that in eternity the only thing that will matter is whether or not we chose to be covered by Jesus' righteousness and that we lovingly participated in the works of the kingdom. If we clothe ourselves with Christ and press into the things of the Kingdom, God will provide amply for all our needs. When God is our primary source and our provider, worry begins to slip away as we learn to rely on the Lord. Often we fail to rely on him because we've never taken advantage of an opportunity to trust him. The time to trust God is when he asks us to step out in faith. We will be amazed at where the adventure leads. But perhaps the main reason we fail to trust God is that we don't understand our value to him, or we wrongly believe we have no value because of our sins. Jesus, however, clearly established just how much God values us prior to instructing us to seek him (Matt. 6:25-32). When we begin to understand how deeply God values us, we will not only believe we can trust him, but we will come to expect his provision and depend on it. God wants to provide for everything we need, so why don't we let him by seeking first his kingdom and his righteousness?

PRAYER FOCUS: Holy Spirit, deepen my faith and trust in the Father. Lord, I believe that you deeply value and love me. Show me, as I seek you, that you can provide for everything I need, and be good to me as I journey toward maturity in my faith. God, bless your people with an abiding sense of their value to you.

DID YOU KNOW? Patrick Henry, the American patriot, stated the following in his will: "This is all the inheritance I can give to my dear family. The religion of Christ can give them one which will make them rich indeed."[10] Henry understood the provision of the Lord. Go to wallbuilders.com to read more excellent quotes from our nation's founders about Christ.

NOVEMBER 11

Genesis 45:4-7 ESV

So Joseph said to his brothers, "Come near to me, please." And they came near. And he said, "I am your brother, Joseph, whom you sold into Egypt. And now do not be distressed or angry with yourselves because you sold me here, for God sent me before you to preserve life. For the famine has been in the land these two years, and there are yet five years in which there will be neither plowing nor harvest. And God sent me before you to preserve for you a remnant on earth, and to keep alive for you many survivors."

Joseph must have wondered what God was up to at many points on his journey to fulfill the dreams God had given him. How could his spiritual dreams be fulfilled when he was sold to a traveling caravan by his brothers? How could they be fulfilled when he was languishing in prison for refusing the advances of Potiphar's wife (Gen. 37:5-8, 25-28; 39:6-20)? But the Sovereign Lord had a plan for Joseph's release, advancement, and prominence in the land of Egypt that would ultimately save many lives and fulfill his dreams beyond his wildest imagination. When we are called to do hard things and we can't see the road ahead, still we must trust that God is working all things together for our good. God never left Joseph's side. In the end, he brought him forth from all his afflictions to greatness, allowing him to assist many of his neighbors. The road of a deliverer is not an easy one, but it is worth the trip. There can be no greater calling than the calling to save lives. Life is priceless. If God has sent us to defend, protect, or preserve life, we must do it with all our might, because the lives we help save are worth it.

PRAYER FOCUS: God, help me to trust you even in dark times because you know the end from the beginning. Lord, use me to love my neighbor and champion life and liberty wherever I go. Jesus, when I face hard things, give me the courage and the strength to endure the trials that are set before me, and give me a forgiving heart like Joseph.

DID YOU KNOW? Veterans Day was originally called Armistice Day to commemorate the armistice between the Allied nations and Germany, which went into effect on the eleventh hour of the eleventh day of the eleventh month in 1918, signaling the end of World War One.[11] We call our veterans from WWII the greatest generation not just because they won the war, but because of the lives they saved. Consider this quote from an infantry soldier who endorsed David Faber's Holocaust memoir, *Because of Romek:* "David Faber was there; he lived it, and he described it. My division opened the gates of Dachau. I was there in 1945. I saw all the horror. I was just a 19 year old kid from Ohio, a private in a rifle company, an Italian Roman Catholic. Then I knew what I'd been fighting for."[12]

NOVEMBER 12

Ecclesiastes 9:4-6 NKJV

But for him who is joined to all the living there is hope, for a living dog is better than a dead lion. For the living know that they will die; but the dead know nothing, and they have no more reward, for the memory of them is forgotten. Also their love, their hatred, and their envy have now perished; nevermore will they have a share in anything done under the sun.

Death in this realm is a reality. It takes away everything a person can choose, accomplish, or experience in this world. The earlier death comes to a person, the greater the tragedy and the greater the number of lost opportunities. When society takes away an individual's right to live through abortion, it strips them of all subsequent choices. The pro-choice movement in America is really the anti-choice movement because they withhold choice from children in the womb by preferring the choice of those who have already left the womb. Clearly, life and one's maturity precede choice. The more mature a living being becomes, the greater the opportunity for choice. Life, once granted by God, is foundational to all things human, and therefore trumps all else, making the right to life a base natural right. In order to choose between chocolate and vanilla, one must be living. In order to choose marriage or celibacy, one must be living. In order to accept or reject Christ, one must be living. Solomon was right that it is better to be a living dog than a dead lion. Anyone who is allowed to live has opportunity and hope. When will we give all our preborn children opportunity and hope?

PRAYER FOCUS: Author of Life, illuminate the darkness and allow us to see the value of life even in its most formative stages. Lord, open our eyes to the fact that we all were or will be zygotes, embryos, fetuses, newborns, toddlers, children, adolescents, and adults. Holy Spirit, remove the veil breaking the abortion debate wide open with truth and grace!

DID YOU KNOW? Scott Klusendorf has written a new defense for the pro-life position titled *The Case for Life*. In it he writes, "Humans have value simply because they are human, not because of some acquired property that they may gain or lose during their lifetime. If you deny this, it's very difficult to account for fundamental human equality for anyone."[13]

REFLECTIONS

NOVEMBER 13

1 Kings 3:9-13 HCSB

"So give Your servant an obedient heart to judge Your people and to discern between good and evil. For who is able to judge this great people of Yours?" Now it pleased the Lord that Solomon had requested this. So God said to him, "Because you have requested this and did not ask for long life or riches for yourself, or the death of your enemies, but you asked discernment for yourself to understand justice, I will therefore do what you have asked. I will give you a wise and understanding heart, so that there has never been anyone like you before and never will be again. In addition, I will give you what you did not ask for: both riches and honor, so that no man in any kingdom will be your equal during your entire life."

As Solomon began his rule on the throne of his father David, the Lord appeared to him in a dream and said, "Ask. What should I give you?" (1 Kings 3:5 HCSB). In true humility, and knowing the tasks before him, Solomon asked for a discerning heart to govern the people through obedience and justice. Solomon knew well from his father's example that good leadership was founded upon obedience to God and the dissemination of justice to God's people. Solomon's request found favor with the Lord because it was focused on others instead of self-focused. God was pleased with the heart of Solomon and the start of his rule, so God took an already wise young ruler and made him the wisest man to ever live. God rewards us when we do the right things, care for others, and follow his commands and principles (Ruth 2:12; Ps. 19:11; 58:11; Matt. 10:42; Rev. 22:12). Notice also how the very things Solomon didn't ask for (wealth, honor, and prominence) God abundantly added to him (Prov. 22:4). In leadership, as in life, when we follow God and bless others, we in turn will be blessed. Sadly, Solomon did not always please the Lord or exercise his wisdom properly (1 Kings 11).

PRAYER FOCUS: Lord, give me a heart of wisdom and a desire to conduct my affairs with righteousness and justice. Thank you for the many examples of both good and poor leadership in the Bible. Teach me from the deep wisdom of Scripture all the things I need to know in order to live the abundant life.

DID YOU KNOW? Solomon's first act of wisdom was to decide the fate of a baby. Read 1 Kings 3:16-28 and see just how Solomon used his wisdom to administer justice.

REFLECTIONS

NOVEMBER 14

Psalm 145:8-12 HCSB

The Lord is gracious and compassionate, slow to anger and great in faithful love. The Lord is good to everyone; His compassion rests on all He has made. All You have made will thank You, Lord; the godly will praise You. They will speak of the glory of Your kingdom and will declare Your might, informing all people of Your mighty acts and of the glorious splendor of Your kingdom.

God is good! He is full of grace and compassion for humankind. His slowness to anger is abundantly clear when one considers the great demonstrations of human wickedness throughout the ages, or our own personal wickedness when compared to the requirements of the law. He made his faithful love manifest to us through the life, ministry, and death of his Son, who daily upholds all things by the word of his power (Heb. 1:3). God is good perpetually to the righteous and the wicked, not wanting any to perish, but all to come to the knowledge of Christ (Matt. 18:12-14; 2 Pet.3:9). Everyone will eventually praise him. One day every knee will bow and every tongue confess that Jesus is Lord (Rom. 14:11). But those of us who are clothed in Christ will bless, magnify, and extol our Redeemer! Out of gratitude to God for Christ's provision, we will tell of his marvelous deeds from generation to generation, imploring all people to come and find grace and provision through our Savior. "Both the Spirit and the bride say, 'Come!' Anyone who hears should say, 'Come!' And the one who is thirsty should come. Whoever desires should take the living water as a gift" (Rev. 22:17 HCSB). All can come to the cross of the Savior and let him give them joy, peace, rest, and freedom. Come and let Christ make us new!

PRAYER FOCUS: Thank you, Lord Jesus, for your compassion, grace, and faithful love. I will praise you at all times for your wonderful deeds to me and to all people. Jesus, lead me beside still waters and captivate my soul with your goodness. Holy Spirit, help me to take advantage of the opportunities I have to share the love of Christ and the gospel.

DID YOU KNOW? "The goodness of God is the drive behind all the blessings He daily bestows upon us. God created us because He felt good in His heart and He redeemed us for the same reason. Do good in Thy good pleasure unto us, O Lord. Act toward us not as we deserve but as it becomes Thee, being the God Thou art. So shall we have nothing to fear in this world or in that which is to come. Amen," wrote A.W. Tozer.[14]

REFLECTIONS

NOVEMBER 15

Psalm 110:5-6 NASB

The Lord is at Your right hand; He will shatter kings in the day of His wrath. He will judge among the nations, He will fill them with corpses, He will shatter the chief men over a broad country.

God is loving, patient, and good toward all he has made, but his justice demands an accounting that will one day be satisfied by the Son in judgment. When God's slowness to anger is gone and his patience with the wicked evaporates, he will send judgment upon the earth. Jesus is returning to bring judgment to the sons of men, just as his Father did in ancient times (Gen. 6:5-7). God's wrath is a mighty and fearful thing, and no one can endure it unless he cuts it short or saves them from it (Matt. 24). All who delight in wickedness and show no restraint must beware, for God is not mocked! People often look at the judgments of God in the Old Testament and surmise that he is cruel and brutal. But that is not true. Judgment that is just responds in kind. God's judgment brings upon the wicked what they have sown. Whatever destruction they sowed in life, God brings back on their own heads with equal measure—unless they repent, finding provision in the arms of the Redeemer. Capital punishment is not cruel or mean when the crime committed warrants such a sentence. Furthermore, God's verdict is not like ours, for we see through a glass darkly and can never know all the details with absolute certainty. But God has perfect illumination and total clarity as to the thoughts and attitudes of the heart. God's verdict is just, and he has entrusted all judgment to his Son, who is seated at his right hand in the heavenly places (John 5:21-27; Eph. 1:20). We need to trust him with our lives and receive his loving provision for our sin.

PRAYER FOCUS: Lord Jesus, your goodness boggles the mind and often causes us to forget the fear that is due you. Lord, help us to know you are more than a Redeemer, our Prince of Peace. You are a Son, a King, a Savior, a Lamb, a Lion, a Servant, a Judge, a Warrior, a Lover, a Friend, a Shepherd, a Conqueror, a Priest, and a Creator. You are God with us, the great I Am!

DID YOU KNOW? Psalm 110 is referred to often in the New Testament. The ESV *Study Bible* states the following: "This psalm is one of the most cited OT texts in the NT, with quotations or allusions appearing in the Gospels, Acts, the Pauline epistles, Hebrews, and the Petrine epistles."[15] Jesus himself quotes this psalm in Luke 20:41-44.

NOVEMBER 16

Isaiah 48:9-11 HCSB

I will delay My anger for the honor of My name, and I will restrain Myself for your benefit and for My praise, so that you will not be destroyed. Look, I have refined you, but not as silver; I have tested you in the furnace of affliction. I will act for My own sake, indeed, My own, for how can I be defiled? I will not give My glory to another.

God's goodness to all, his slowness to anger, and his patience with wickedness adds to his glory. God is worthy of praise and adoration because of his treatment of all people, especially the wicked. He delays his anger and wrath for our sake and for the increase of his glory. Life here is his gift to all of us, and through its afflictions, trials, triumphs, and joys God refines us and tests us to see if we will yield to his lordship or remain estranged from him in our sinfulness. He will not allow his name to be defiled, his reputation to be marred, or his chosen people to perish. When justice is satisfied, judgment is finished and the former earth has passed away, then God's glory will be firmly established and made manifest to all. In the end, only One can be glorified, only One can be praised. God will not share his glory with another, for he alone is holy, righteous, good, faithful, and true.

PRAYER FOCUS: God, I thank you that when I am afflicted because of my sins, you are willing to work for my good if I will yield to you and repent. Lord, use my trials, afflictions, and triumphs for your glory and the furtherance of your kingdom. Lord, bring an end to the oppression of abortion for your own sake and your eternal glory!

DID YOU KNOW? God's glory will light up the New Jerusalem created after the Judgment. John wrote in Revelation 21:23, "The city does not need the sun or the moon to shine on it, because God's glory illuminates it, and its lamp is the Lamb" (HCSB). Jesus will literally manifest what he already is: "I am the light of the world. Anyone who follows Me will never walk in the darkness but will have the light of life" (John 8:12 HCSB).

REFLECTIONS

NOVEMBER 17

2 Timothy 3:1-5 ESV

But understand this, that in the last days there will come times of difficulty. For people will be lovers of self, lovers of money, proud, arrogant, abusive, disobedient to their parents, ungrateful, unholy, heartless, unappeasable, slanderous, without self-control, brutal, not loving good, treacherous, reckless, swollen with conceit, lovers of pleasure rather than lovers of God, having the appearance of godliness, but denying its power. Avoid such people.

In his Second Epistle to Timothy, Paul wrote about the increasing depravity of man as the last days approach. He warned Timothy to be on the lookout for religious people who are yoked with all manner of sinfulness and self-love, people who practice the externals of religion but have no true heart-level faith or experience with the living God. All the undesirable actions in today's passage describe the prideful, self-focused life as opposed to the God-first, others-focused life. Warren Wiersbe described it like this: "God commands us to love Him supremely, and our neighbors as ourselves (Matt. 22:34-40); but if we love ourselves supremely, we will not love God or our neighbors. In this universe there is God, and there are people and things. We should worship God, love people, and use things. But if we start worshiping ourselves, we will ignore God and start loving things and using people. This is the formula for a miserable life; yet it characterizes many people today."[16] Since pride is at the heart of all sin, it is not surprising that many of the negative character traits Paul mentions relate to the act of abortion. As we journey toward the last days, God is calling out to his children and asking us to pursue him and the things closest to his heart. If our answer is *no* or *not now*, we will end up embracing the things of this world or, worse yet, an empty religion.

PRAYER FOCUS: Merciful Father, show me the path of life. Help me discern right from wrong and be aware of the needs of others around me. Forgive me for my pride and waywardness and draw me closer to you and your ways. Lord, love me so completely that I overflow with love for my neighbors, family, and friends.

DID YOU KNOW? The best way to break the world's hold is to trust in Jesus and read his Word. The apostle Paul wrote, "Do not be conformed to this world, but be transformed by the renewal of your mind, that by testing you may discern what is the will of God, what is good and acceptable and perfect" (Rom. 12:2 ESV). A.W. Tozer wrote, "The threefold purpose of the Bible is to inform, to inspire faith and to secure obedience. . . . The Holy Scriptures will do us good only as we present an open mind to be taught, a tender heart to believe and a surrendered will to obey."[17]

NOVEMBER 18

Isaiah 26:9-10 NASB

At night my soul longs for You, indeed, my spirit within me seeks You diligently; for when the earth experiences Your judgments the inhabitants of the world learn righteousness. Though the wicked is shown favor, he does not learn righteousness; he deals unjustly in the land of uprightness, and does not perceive the majesty of the LORD.

∞

Do we hunger for God? Are our hearts eager to discover the ways of Christ and the Kingdom? Or are we more concerned with the cares, troubles, and pleasures of this world? Often, God jolts us out of the ways of waywardness, complacency, and death. How? Through trials and judgments. We learn the ways of God and improve in righteousness when we experience his corrective discipline or rebuke. If we don't learn this, we will slide into greater depravity, wickedness, and deception. Wickedness begins and often increases due to a lack of awareness and perception of God. The wicked ignore the majesty of the Lord because they do not know him and they fail to perceive his favor in their lives. They are lost in the darkness. If they do not come to the light, their darkness will deepen until they are totally enveloped by it. Perpetual unending darkness is the tragedy of a life spent separated from God. When believers live in the light, they perceive the majesty of the Lord!

PRAYER FOCUS: Lord, show me the light and illuminate your ways that I might walk before you in a manner that pleases you and blesses your people. Help me perceive more and more of your majesty as I mature in my faith. Thank you, God, that you are patient with, and good to, the wicked. I pray whenever I or anyone else is trapped in darkness that we would escape its grasp and discover the light.

DID YOU KNOW? According to the WORDsearch 8 Bible software program, the NASB uses the word "darkness" 163 times and the word "light" 227 times.[18] Check out the following Scriptures that discuss and contrast light and darkness: Genesis 1:4; Job 38:19; Psalm 18:28; Isaiah 5:20; 9:2; 58:10; Micah 7:8; Matthew 4:16; John 1:5; 3:19; 8:12; 12:46; Acts 26:18; Romans 13:12; Ephesians 5:8; 1 Peter 2:9; and 1 John 1:5. Come to the Light and let him shatter the darkness (Ps. 107:10-16)!

REFLECTIONS

NOVEMBER 19

Jeremiah 17:5-8 NIV

This is what the Lord says: "Cursed is the one who trusts in man, who depends on flesh for his strength and whose heart turns away from the Lord. He will be like a bush in the wastelands; he will not see prosperity when it comes. He will dwell in the parched places of the desert, in a salt land where no one lives. But blessed is the man who trusts in the Lord, whose confidence is in him. He will be like a tree planted by the water that sends out its roots by the stream. It does not fear when heat comes; its leaves are always green. It has no worries in a year of drought and never fails to bear fruit.

No matter how learned or successful people are, apart from God they don't have the answers. When we trust in humans rather than God, we are settling for finite wisdom obtained through a foggy haze. Jesus said it best in the gospel of Mark: "What good is it for a man to gain the whole world, yet forfeit his soul?" (Mark 8:36 NIV). Conversely, to trust in the living God is to step into eternity and benefit from the wisdom and clarity of the Ancient of Days! The psalmist said, "In God, whose word I praise, in God I trust; I will not be afraid. What can mortal man do to me?" (Ps. 56:4 NIV). Our faith must be placed in God, and when it is, we will be like trees planted by rivers of living water! Let the Lord be our confidence as we enter the harvest—unshakeable, unbreakable, abiding in the joy of the Lord forever.

PRAYER FOCUS: Father, I trust you to lead me beside still waters and show me the path of life. Fill my heart and mind with your wisdom, love, and knowledge. Keep me from temptation and grant me a forgiving heart. Holy Spirit, lead me into all truth, setting me free from this body of flesh and death.

DID YOU KNOW? John Sammis, the Presbyterian pastor who wrote the classic Christian hymn "Trust and Obey," received the main words for the song from his friend Daniel Towner. Towner wrote down the words during a testimony given by a young man who attended one of D. L. Moody's services in Massachusetts. During the young man's brief testimony he apparently said, "I am not quite sure—but I am going to trust, and I am going to obey."[19]

REFLECTIONS

_____

_____

_____

_____

_____

NOVEMBER 20

1 Samuel 15:24-29 NASB

Then Saul said to Samuel, "I have sinned; I have indeed transgressed the command of the LORD and your words, because I feared the people and listened to their voice. Now therefore, please pardon my sin and return with me, that I may worship the LORD." But Samuel said to Saul, "I will not return with you; for you have rejected the word of the LORD, and the LORD has rejected you from being king over Israel." As Samuel turned to go, Saul seized the edge of his robe, and it tore. So Samuel said to him, "The LORD has torn the kingdom of Israel from you today and has given it to your neighbor, who is better than you. Also the Glory of Israel will not lie or change His mind; for He is not a man that He should change His mind."

The cost of disobeying the direct commands of God, whether for the fear of man or for any other excuse, can be extremely high. Saul knew the will of the Lord personally, through the prophet Samuel, and he knew expressly what God had commanded him to do (1 Sam. 15:1-3; Gen. 36:12; Exod. 17:8-16; Num. 24:20; Deut. 25:17-19). In his pride and the desire of his own heart to please the people rather than God, Saul altered the Lord's plan and did what was wise in his own eyes (1 Sam. 15:5-11). Instead of striking Amalek and utterly destroying all he had, Saul spared Agag and the best of the sheep, oxen, fatlings, and the lambs. For being unwilling to destroy them utterly, Saul's act of rebellion cost him the throne! If we have surrendered our life to Christ, God expects us to learn his counsel and walk in his ways. He knows what is best for us, his people, and everyone else. Whenever the Lord's will is expressly clear, we must trust him and follow wherever he leads. Just as Samuel reminded Saul that God keeps his word, the Bible reminds us of the same. If God brought judgment to Amalek, his whole tribe, and Saul, he will bring judgment to those who choose unrepentant sin over repentance and salvation. God does not lie, and when he says to love our neighbor, he means it. And when he says he is the Creator of all life, he is.

PRAYER FOCUS: God, teach us to fear you, and to know that your words and commands are not something to trifle with. Father, fill my heart with both love and respect for you. Holy Spirit, empower me to follow your ways to the best of my ability.

DID YOU KNOW? A.W. Tozer said that "the greatness of God rouses fear within us, but His goodness encourages us not to be afraid of Him. To fear and not be afraid—that is the paradox of faith."[20]

REFLECTIONS

NOVEMBER
21

Luke 12:43-48 NKJV

Blessed is that servant whom his master will find so doing when he comes. Truly, I say to you that he will make him ruler over all that he has. But if that servant says in his heart, "My master is delaying his coming," and begins to beat the male and female servants, and to eat and drink and be drunk, the master of that servant will come on a day when he is not looking for him, and at an hour when he is not aware, and will cut him in two and appoint him his portion with the unbelievers. And that servant who knew his master's will, and did not prepare himself or do according to his will, shall be beaten with many stripes. But he who did not know, yet committed things deserving of stripes, shall be beaten with few. For everyone to whom much is given, from him much will be required; and to whom much has been committed, of him they will ask the more.

Jesus informs us through this parable that we need to be actively pursuing and doing the will of God. We can't afford to be dull to the Spirit or complacent about the work of the Kingdom. The Lord will reward those who diligently press into God and seek to obey his leading. But he will also punish those who ignore him and put off the work of the Kingdom, or worse yet, those who instead of loving God's people and striving to make things better hurt God's people and engage in wickedness. We don't know when Jesus will return, but we do know a good portion of his revealed will through Scripture. In the strength and illumination we have, we need to go and do what the Spirit and the Word have placed on our hearts. America has been given much by God and, as a result, much is required of us. But the church in America has been given the most because we have the light of the Savior and his Word. If we are not already doing so, it is time to get busy serving God and his people, because much has been committed to us (Prov. 3:27-28).

PRAYER FOCUS: Lord, help us to see what is required of us and with joy in our hearts seek to do your will—not out of compulsion or fear, but out of respect and admiration for what you have already done for us. Jesus, lead us to love because we are loved, to serve because we have been served, to give because it has been given to us; and to work for the kingdom because you work in us.

DID YOU KNOW? America is one of the most blessed nations on earth. Consider our abundant coastal regions, our vast natural resources, our hospitable climates, our amazing Constitution, our freedoms of speech and religion, our Christian heritage, our prosperity, and our ingenuity.

REFLECTIONS

NOVEMBER 22

Acts 5:25-29 HCSB

Someone came and reported to them, "Look! The men you put in jail are standing in the temple complex and teaching the people." Then the commander went with the temple police and brought them in without force, because they were afraid the people might stone them. After they brought them in, they had them stand before the Sanhedrin, and the high priest asked, "Didn't we strictly order you not to teach in this name? And look, you have filled Jerusalem with your teaching and are determined to bring this man's blood on us!" But Peter and the apostles replied, "We must obey God rather than men."

hy were Peter and the other apostles in jail in the first place? They were in jail because they followed the authority of God before the authority of men. The apostles understood that they served God first and only then human institutions. They also knew that God's intention for any governing body was to be an instrument used to punish evil and protect and reward that which is good. Peter wrote, "Submit to every human authority because of the Lord, whether to the Emperor as the supreme authority or to governors as those sent out by him to punish those who do what is evil and to praise those who do what is good" (1 Pet. 2:13-14 HCSB). The Sanhedrin was doing just the opposite by withholding and blocking the message of the gospel from the people. As soldiers in God's army, we, like the apostles, need to understand the proper chain of command. We must obey God rather than men when men are in direct violation or conflict with the clear commands of Scripture. If God affirms that life begins at conception, the matter is settled, and it doesn't matter what men say or condone. We need to agree with God and work to inform all people of God's truth. God calls us to pursue justice and righteousness regardless of the opposition or the outcome.

PRAYER FOCUS: Father, keep me ever mindful that you are on the throne. Lord, give me the desire and the courage to obey you above all others. Help me understand that civil disobedience is in fact obedience to you when the disobedience in question agrees with your revealed will and demands action. Jesus, help me support those fighting for what you have illuminated is right.

DID YOU KNOW? Peter and the apostles were supernaturally released from prison prior to the confrontation described in Acts 5:25-29. "Then the high priest took action. He and all his colleagues, those who belonged to the party of the Sadducees, were filled with jealousy. So they arrested the apostles and put them in the city jail. But an angel of the Lord opened the doors of the jail during the night, brought them out, and said, 'Go and stand in the temple complex, and tell the people all about this life'" (Acts 5:17-20 HCSB). The miraculous often occurs when we obey God.

NOVEMBER 23

John 15:18-20 ESV

If the world hates you, know that it has hated me before it hated you. If you were of the world, the world would love you as its own; but because you are not of the world, but I chose you out of the world, therefore the world hates you. Remember the word that I said to you: "A servant is not greater than his master." If they persecuted me, they will also persecute you. If they kept my word, they will also keep yours.

Jesus spoke these words to his disciples during the Last Supper. Like his disciples, we should not be surprised when we face opposition and hatred from the world because of what we believe. The world does not understand the things of the Spirit and is usually immersed in the self-focused life, pursuing its own pleasures and desires. Our belief system of ultimate truth, divine standards, and accountability often flies in the face of the non-believer and even the religious. At times we can be viewed as a threat or a challenge to the way others live. Those with power in the world often turn their fear of encroachment by Christianity or their hatred of those who will not bow to their power into persecution. When Jesus said, "if the world hates you, know that it has hated me before it hated you," essentially he was saying that if we live like he did, we will be treated like he was. Some will love us, thank us, learn from us, and join us, while others will hate us, mock us, and persecute us for the stands we take and the lives we live. God did not call us to an easy road or a life of universal appreciation by our peers. He called us to himself as his redeemed sons and daughters, a chosen people asked to share the grace and truth of our heavenly Father with the rest of his creation. The road we travel may be lightly traveled, difficult, or tortuous, but it is filled with redemption, love, reward, and glory.

PRAYER FOCUS: Father, shelter me in your love and help me persevere when the world hates me. Strengthen me when I face various trials and persecutions. Lord, help me to be an effective ambassador of your love, truth, and grace to everyone I meet. Keep me from harming or hating others, and give me the courage to share my faith and make my beliefs known.

DID YOU KNOW? Stephen, one of seven godly servants chosen by the apostles to perform ministry duties, was the first martyr of the faith (Acts 6; 7). Before he converted, Paul, earlier known as Saul, condoned the murder of Stephen (Acts 7:58; 22:20).

REFLECTIONS

NOVEMBER 24

1 Peter 5:6-10 NIV

Humble yourselves, therefore, under God's mighty hand, that he may lift you up in due time. Cast all your anxiety on him because he cares for you. Be self-controlled and alert. Your enemy the devil prowls around like a roaring lion looking for someone to devour. Resist him, standing firm in the faith, because you know that your brothers throughout the world are undergoing the same kind of sufferings. And the God of all grace, who called you to his eternal glory in Christ, after you have suffered a little while, will himself restore you and make you strong, firm and steadfast.

∞

If we are to be successful, contributing members in the family of God, we need to be humble, trusting, self-controlled, and watchful. We need to develop and practice humility before God and our fellow believers. If we lay aside our pride and consider others as better than ourselves, we will listen more, love better, and achieve our goals more easily. As believers, we need not worry or fear because God holds us in the palm of his hand, and his care for us is unrelenting and consistent during any circumstance. The Christian who is intimately involved with God learns they can trust him at all times. One of the fruits of the Spirit is self-control, or the restraint we exercise over our own impulses. I believe the longer and deeper one walks with the Savior, the more self-control one obtains. In fact, we can measure our maturity in Christ by our level of self-control. When we exercise restraint over our natural motivations, we avoid many difficulties and sins. Peter also instructs the faithful to be watchful and alert because our Enemy the Devil is constantly about the task of deceiving and devouring us. As temptations arise, trials come, or persecutions escalate, we need to resist the Devil and cling to God. Our resistance involves standing firm in our faith as we use the weapons of prayer and the Scriptures to combat the Enemy. When the Evil One attacks us, we can go to the Scriptures and study the tactics of Jesus (Matt. 4; Luke 4; Eph. 6:10-18). If we suffer, we know we are not alone, and that God will triumph over our Enemy in his timing—and that he himself will restore us.

PRAYER FOCUS: Lord Jesus, I appreciate the wisdom of your Word. Minister your grace and peace to me when I face various trials, temptations, and persecutions. Holy Spirit, grow me in humility, trust, self-control, and watchfulness. Father, I place my confidence in you, knowing that whatever I face, you will be with me, guiding me in the paths of righteousness for your name's sake (Ps. 23).

DID YOU KNOW? *Satan* in the Hebrew means "adversary," and *devil* in the Greek means "accuser."[21]

REFLECTIONS

NOVEMBER 25

Ephesians 3:14-20 NASB

For this reason I bow my knees before the Father, from whom every family in heaven and on earth derives its name, that He would grant you, according to the riches of His glory, to be strengthened with power through His Spirit in the inner man, so that Christ may dwell in your hearts through faith; and that you, being rooted and grounded in love, may be able to comprehend with all the saints what is the breadth and length and height and depth, and to know the love of Christ which surpasses knowledge, that you may be filled up to all the fullness of God. Now to Him who is able to do far more abundantly beyond all that we ask or think, according to the power that works within us.

This Thanksgiving season, as we reflect back on God's many gifts, as we gather about the table in fellowship with family and friends, I pray we will be strengthened in our inner person and that we will feel the breadth and length and height and depth of Christ's love for us and our families. This Thanksgiving let us ask God to use his power that works in us to do far more abundantly beyond what we could ask or need this coming year. Let us thank him for life and ask him to give it to us in abundance as the future days and years roll by. During this time of family gathering and thankfulness, reflect back over all the times God has used family imagery or analogy in his Word, and how often the family unit of father, mother, and child is on the heart and mind of God. God is all about relationships and the close bond of family. Christians can cherish the fact that we are part of the Father's heavenly family and we should do whatever we can to love, cherish, and protect our other family here on earth.

PRAYER FOCUS: "Give thanks to the Lord, for He is good, for His lovingkindness is everlasting. Give thanks to the God of gods, for His lovingkindness is everlasting. Give thanks to the Lord of lords, for His lovingkindness is everlasting. To Him who alone does great wonders, for His lovingkindness is everlasting; to Him who made the heavens with skill, for His lovingkindness is everlasting; to Him who spread out the earth above the waters, for His lovingkindness is everlasting; to Him who made the great lights, for His lovingkindness is everlasting" (Ps. 136:1-7 NASB).

DID YOU KNOW? The holiday of Thanksgiving traces its origin to the early 1600s when the Plymouth Pilgrims shared a harvest festival with the Wampanoag Indians.[22] Abraham Lincoln first nationalized the holiday in 1863. It was observed on November 26 that year. Franklin D. Roosevelt issued a proclamation in 1942 designating the fourth Thursday in November as Thanksgiving Day.

REFLECTIONS

NOVEMBER 26

1 John 3:23-24 NKJV

And this is His commandment: that we should believe on the name of His Son Jesus Christ and love one another, as He gave us commandment. Now he who keeps His commandments abides in Him, and He in him. And by this we know that He abides in us, by the Spirit whom He has given us.

The apostle John here encapsulates the core of what it means to be a Christian: belief in the all-sufficient Son of God and the subsequent love of one's neighbor. When we are characterized by these two things, the Holy Spirit who resides in us will attest to it, confirming in our spirit our place in the family of God. The Spirit will instruct, encourage, and help us walk in God's ways, keeping his commandments. He will increase our hunger for the things of God and his Holy Word. As the Spirit's love dawns in our heart each day, he will give us a love for others born out of his great love for us. Often the Spirit testifies to our spirit that we are God's children, compelling us to come to our Father and abide in his Vine (John 15:4-5; Rom. 8:16). Out of the storehouse of our Father's love we express the riches of his love to others. The love we have received from the Father and the love we bestow on our neighbors is the passport to a joy-filled eternity. Walk in love, for that is how we were called and how the Spirit wants us to live. Melt in the love of God, the grace of Christ, and the abiding presence of the Holy Spirit. We abide in him and he abides in us!

PRAYER FOCUS: Spirit of the living God, reign in me and testify to the authenticity of my adoption in Christ. Lord, light a fire in me to love others the way I have been loved by you. Help me care for all your children, both created and adopted. Great God, I magnify your holy name and stand in awe of your unsearchable wisdom, knowledge, grace, and love (Rom. 5:6-11). Jesus, abide in me as I abide in you.

DID YOU KNOW? Mary Waalkes Verwys, a dedicated sidewalk counselor, has written a book about her conversations with God and her neighbors in front of her local abortion facility. Her intimate, poignant, and compelling book, *Wednesday Mourning: A Sidewalk Counselor's Journal of God's Grace in the Abortion Struggle*, gives a window into the heart of sidewalk counselors, their service to Christ, and their struggle for life. In it she writes, "Integral to this ministry as a counselor is my deep communication with God. I would never have the courage or perseverance to be in front of the clinics if He were not my Constant Companion. I share my conversations with Him because I always desire that every word I speak to a client, come from His heart. Thank you for being willing to come to the sidewalk with me today. I trust that God will open your heart to see that abortion is not an 'issue.' It is a heart-rending, life-altering decision that has left countless millions in our culture wounded for life."[23]

NOVEMBER 27

1 Timothy 2:1-8 ESV

First of all, then, I urge that supplications, prayers, intercessions, and thanksgivings be made for all people, for kings and all who are in high positions, that we may lead a peaceful and quiet life, godly and dignified in every way. This is good, and it is pleasing in the sight of God our Savior, who desires all people to be saved and to come to the knowledge of the truth. For there is one God, and there is one mediator between God and men, the man Christ Jesus, who gave himself as a ransom for all, which is the testimony given at the proper time. For this I was appointed a preacher and an apostle (I am telling the truth, I am not lying), a teacher of the Gentiles in faith and truth. I desire then that in every place the men should pray, lifting holy hands without anger or quarreling.

David wrote, "O Lord, I call upon you; hasten to me! Give ear to my voice when I call to you! Let my prayer be counted as incense before you, and the lifting up of my hands as the evening sacrifice!" (Ps. 141:1-2 ESV). Both Paul and David knew that prayer is essential to the abundant life and the gateway to power. As believers, we are called to pray reverently, earnestly, routinely, corporately, privately, faithfully, believingly, specifically, devotedly, fervently, persistently, expectantly, without ceasing, and in agreement with God's will. God wants us to pray for deliverance, healing, victory, salvation, social justice, and those in authority. He wants us to pray for our families, friends, neighbors, strangers, and for all people, that they would place their trust in the lone Mediator between God and man and come to the knowledge of the Truth. He asks us to pray without anger or quarreling, seeking his glory and his best for his children (Matt. 6:9-13; John 17). In short, God wants us to pray! He has called us to be worshipers, warriors, protectors, and intercessors. What will happen to abortion when we repent and pray?

PRAYER FOCUS: Father in heaven, holy and great is your name. Glorify your name on the earth and bring all people to the beautiful light of your Son. Provide for my needs today. Lord Jesus, forgive me for my sins, especially those of sexual impurity. Help me forgive others who sin against me, keep me from temptation, and deliver me and my neighbors from evil. For yours is the Kingdom and the power and the glory forever (Luke 11:1-13)!

DID YOU KNOW? The intercession of God's people is powerful and effective (James 5:16). Mary Verwys records a moving story about some grandmothers who started earnestly praying for her on her day of sidewalk counseling. The intercession of these faithful saints achieved the miraculous as divine interventions led to the local abortion facility's closure.[24]

REFLECTIONS

NOVEMBER 28

2 Corinthians 1:8-11 HCSB

For we don't want you to be unaware, brothers, of our affliction that took place in Asia: we were completely overwhelmed—beyond our strength—so that we even despaired of life. Indeed, we personally had a death sentence within ourselves, so that we would not trust in ourselves but in God who raises the dead. He has delivered us from such a terrible death, and He will deliver us. We have put our hope in Him that He will deliver us again while you join in helping us by your prayers. Then many will give thanks on our behalf for the gift that came to us through the prayers of many.

Our service to the Lord is not without hardship, trial, and turmoil. God has not promised us an easy time in this world or a life free of hardship, but he has promised us that we will never be alone. The writer of Hebrews put it this way: "Be satisfied with what you have, for He Himself has said, I will never leave you or forsake you" (13:5 HCSB). God is our Deliverer today, tomorrow, and forever. Whether we live or die, God will deliver us. Paul understood that trials and persecution forge trust, community, and prayer in the believer's life. When we are surrounded by enemies, suffering, and affliction, we call out to God and our fellow believers for help, praying at all times and eliciting prayer from the faithful. As our dependence upon God and his people grows, great power is released and our deliverance comes. God knew from the beginning it was not good for man to be alone. If we reach out to God and his people, we never will be. Take heart today that we are not alone and pray for God's people both far and near.

PRAYER FOCUS: Lord, I pray for my brothers and sisters all over the world who are suffering today as they do your work (Rom. 8:26-28). Flood their hearts with your assurance and love. Give them the strength to endure and the trust to lean upon you and not their own understanding. Holy Spirit, gather your people in groups all over the world to pray for the entire body of Christ and for your will to be done.

DID YOU KNOW? Jim Elliot, the twenty-eight-year-old Christian missionary who was murdered by the Auca Indians of Ecuador, wrote the following in his journal: "One of the great blessings of heaven is the appreciation of heaven on earth. He is no fool who gives what he cannot keep to gain what he cannot lose."[25] Local missionaries working in urban ministries or in the abortion struggle need our prayers and support every bit as much as foreign missionaries.

REFLECTIONS

NOVEMBER 29

Hebrews 10:12-14 ESV

But when Christ had offered for all time a single sacrifice for sins, he sat down at the right hand of God, waiting from that time until his enemies should be made a footstool for his feet. For by a single offering he has perfected for all time those who are being sanctified.

The work is finished. The Savior of the world has died for sinners and has risen again! Jesus is seated at the right hand of the Father interceding for all those who believe, and waiting until the day when his enemies are put under his feet and cast from his presence. Sin is a deadly cancer and the world is a difficult place, but the Good News is that Jesus has overcome the world and the Devil once for all. And if we have placed our faith in Christ, we have overcome the world with him. The life of the Christian believer is hidden in Christ, and he has made us perfect forever through his sacrifice of love. His righteous blood of atonement covers us while we are being made holy. There could be no better news! He who the Son sets free is free indeed (John 8:36; Rom. 8:31-35). Priests and animal blood could never fully atone for the wickedness of fallen man, but God Almighty can. And the Good News is he did! When we put our lives in Jesus' nail-scarred hands we feel the abundance of our heavenly Father's provision.

PRAYER FOCUS: Jesus, Lamb of God, I come empty-handed and receive what you have graciously given. I place my trust, my life, and my future in your all-sufficient hands. I know you will not fail me for I am your adopted child and you have called me friend. I cling to your name, Jesus, because there is no other name under heaven by which I can be saved (John 3:18; Acts 4:12; Phil. 2:9-10).

DID YOU KNOW? Just as our sins and bad deeds are not able to keep us out of heaven if we have trusted Christ, our good deeds and righteous acts are not enough to get us into heaven without Christ. Corrie ten Boom's aunt expressed this well, as her family was consoling her with all of her good deeds of service after the doctor had confirmed she had only a few weeks to live: "'Empty, empty!' she choked at last through her tears. 'How can we bring anything to God? What does He care for our little tricks and trinkets?' And then as we listened in disbelief she lowered her hands and, with tears still coursing down her face, whispered, 'Dear Jesus, I thank You that we must come with empty hands. I thank You that You have done all—all—on the cross, and that all we need in life or death is to be sure of this.'"[26]

NOVEMBER 30

Proverbs 3:27-31 NIV

Do not withhold good from those who deserve it, when it is in your power to act. Do not say to your neighbor, "Come back later; I'll give it tomorrow"—when you now have it with you. Do not plot harm against your neighbor, who lives trustfully near you. Do not accuse a man for no reason—when he has done you no harm. Do not envy a violent man or choose any of his ways.

∞

If every person in the church and our nation followed this advice not to withhold good and to do no harm, what would happen to the demand for abortion in our land? It would all but disappear! How can we withhold good from our offspring? Do we really believe the preborn don't deserve to live? Life can be hard and difficult, but it is not without its joys. Who would begrudge their children the opportunity to experience life and pursue their passions, dreams, and opportunities? If we can protect and nurture life, then we must do it. If we have love, resources, or time to give, then we must give them. Waiting won't help—we must act now! Today is all we have, for yesterday is past and tomorrow may never come (Luke 12:15-26). Our preborn neighbors live trustingly near us or in us, so how can we betray their trust? Why do we accuse the preborn by saying they are not viable, unable to feel pain, lacking self-awareness, or simply cellular tissue when they have done us no harm? Why do we choose the way of the violent man and abort our child? It is time to stop withholding good from those who deserve it and abolish abortion in our land.

PRAYER FOCUS: Jesus, help us to see that life is a gift from you and that you have graciously included us in this gift-giving process. Lord, strengthen the bond between mother and child and father and child. Holy Spirit, work mightily in our marriages and families to create strong and lasting bonds. Father, help us to sense and seize our daily opportunities to impact eternity and lay up treasure in heaven.

DID YOU KNOW? The opportunities God sets before us are rarely accomplished if we fail to act. In the book of Esther, we read, "For if you remain silent at this time, relief and deliverance for the Jews will arise from another place, but you and your father's family will perish. And who knows but that you have come to royal position for such a time as this?" (Esther 4:14 NIV). Esther acted on her opportunity to entreat the king and saved her people. Rahab had the opportunity to hide the spies and she acted. Wilberforce used his opportunities in parliament to advance the cause of justice and end slavery in Great Britain. Harriet Tubman seized her opportunity to help slaves through the Underground Railroad, saving many lives. God is looking for people who are firm in the faith and willing to take action (Ps. 27; 1 Cor. 16:13-14).

December

FUTURE GENERATIONS

DECEMBER 1

Psalm 59:1-5 NASB

Deliver me from my enemies, O my God; set me securely on high away from those who rise up against me. Deliver me from those who do iniquity and save me from men of bloodshed. For behold, they have set an ambush for my life; fierce men launch an attack against me, not for my transgression nor for my sin, O Lord, for no guilt of mine, they run and set themselves against me. Arouse Yourself to help me, and see! You, O Lord God of hosts, the God of Israel, awake to punish all the nations; do not be gracious to any who are treacherous in iniquity.

David wrote this plea for deliverance when Saul sent some men to watch his house and kill him (1 Sam. 19:11-18). If the preborn scheduled for abortion could write to us from the womb, these words of David—Deliver me from my enemies, O my God—might well be how they would express themselves. Like David, the child scheduled for abortion needs the supernatural deliverance of the Lord and the help of God's people. They need the intervention and help of their families, friends, and neighbors. As God used David's wife Michal, and his friend Jonathan, to help him escape from death (1 Sam. 19:1-17), the preborn need those people closest to their parents and the members of their community to intervene on their behalf, allowing God to use them as his instruments of rescue. Planned Parenthood and other abortionists have set an ambush for these innocent children in the womb. If the people of God and those closest to the preborn don't stand up for them and help them, who will? Until the day when God supernaturally intervenes and rescues his children from abortion, he has given us his Word, his Spirit, and his command to love our neighbor. Today as the Lord gives us opportunity, we must speak out on behalf of the preborn and assist a relative, friend, or neighbor in their escape from the ambush of abortion.

PRAYER FOCUS: Lord, I know you will deliver all your preborn children in your way and in your timing. I hope and pray your people will rise up and make every effort to stop this atrocious, murderous practice in our world before it becomes necessary to punish all the nations. Come, Lord Jesus, assist us as we assist your people.

DID YOU KNOW? God has supernaturally intervened on many occasions in the pro-life struggle. One such occasion is the life of Gianna Jessen. Read her miraculous story about how she survived a late-term saline abortion in her powerful and moving book, *Gianna: Aborted . . . and Lived to Tell About It*, by Jessica Shaver and Gianna Jessen.[1]

REFLECTIONS

347

DECEMBER 2

Psalm 6:8-10 ESV

Depart from me, all you workers of evil, for the LORD has heard the sound of my weeping. The LORD has heard my plea; the LORD accepts my prayer. All my enemies shall be ashamed and greatly troubled; they shall turn back and be put to shame in a moment.

I have previously compiled a Bible study entitled *Who Am I?* where I ask readers to rewrite Psalm 6:8-10 and to substitute "the preborn" for the words "me" and "my." Just as the psalmist cried out for deliverance, and just as we cry out in our distress, the preborn cry out as well. As I rewrite these verses with the substituted words, we can put ourselves in the position of a child who is about to be aborted: *Depart from the preborn, all you workers of evil, for the Lord has heard the sound of the preborn's weeping. The Lord has heard the preborn's plea; the Lord accepts the preborn's prayer. All the preborn's enemies shall be ashamed and greatly troubled; they shall turn back and be put to shame in a moment.* I believe all those who destroy the preborn will be greatly troubled and ashamed by their depravity in the moment of God's illumination. But I also believe God wants to turn them back from their wayward course and deliver them from darkness before it's too late. If we have been involved in abortion, we need to seek the Lord's forgiveness through repentance and remorse, and discover how Christ's one moment on the cross covers all our greatly troubling sins and shame. God is calling out to us, his people, asking us to be instruments of both rescue and healing in the abortion struggle. God surely hears the preborn, but do we? Oh Lord, give us ears to hear!

PRAYER FOCUS: Jesus, open our eyes and ears to the plight of the preborn. Help us to perceive that abortion damages us all. Give us beautiful babies for the ashes of abortion and the joy of children for the mourning of regrettable choices (Isa. 61:3).

DID YOU KNOW? Bernard Nathanson, a medical doctor who was instrumental in the early years of abortion legalization, and who personally performed thousands of abortions, changed his mind about the practice when he first began seeing babies in the womb via ultrasound. When he asked a colleague to tape an abortion using ultrasound, it changed both their lives as they saw the "silent scream" of the preborn. In his book, *The Hand of God*, he writes, "In 1984 I said to a friend of mine, who was doing fifteen or maybe twenty abortions a day, 'Look, do me a favor, Jay. Next Saturday, when you are doing all these abortions, put an ultrasound device on the mother and tape it for me.' He did, and when he looked at the tapes with me in the editing studio, he was so affected that he never did another abortion. I, though I had not done an abortion in five years, was shaken to the very roots of my soul by what I saw."[2]

DECEMBER 3

Proverbs 14:34 NIV

Righteousness exalts a nation, but sin is a disgrace to any people.

Just as personal sin and rebellion against the ways of God bring pain and disgrace to our lives, national sin and rebellion brings pain and disgrace to our country. America's history is one of both exaltation and disgrace. Americans rejoice in our country's righteous acts, such as the Bill of Rights, the defense of freedom during World War II, the emancipation of the slaves, women's suffrage, helping reestablish the current nation of Israel, the Civil Rights Act, rebuilding nations we were once at war with, and giving aid to people or nations hit by natural disasters, ravaged by disease, or devastated by poverty. But America has also had its share of disgraces. Consider chattel slavery, Native American abuses, Japanese internment, childhood sweat shops, segregation, and racism—to name just a few. But how and when will our nation recover from the willing destruction of our own children through abortion? Americans need to remember that our national conduct matters. When will we shed the disgrace of abortion and exalt in the righteous decision to grant all our citizens, born or preborn, the right to life, liberty, and the pursuit of happiness?

PRAYER FOCUS: God, help my nation see our waywardness and depravity, and give us discernment and eyes to see what abortion really is and what it really does. Lord, return us to a nation under God who places her trust and confidence in you and your Word. Jesus, heal the brokenhearted and our great national wounds as we move from death to life by removing the legalized practice of abortion.

DID YOU KNOW? The Thirteenth Amendment to the Constitution was ratified during the month of December in 1865. This amendment was the complete and final step in the abolition of slavery in the United States. It states in section one, "Neither slavery nor involuntary servitude, except as a punishment for crime whereof the party shall have been duly convicted, shall exist within the United States, or any place subject to their jurisdiction."[3] I hope and pray our nation doesn't wait as long to abolish legalized abortion from our land as it did to abolish slavery, or that the fight to achieve it isn't as costly as the Civil War.

DECEMBER 4

1 Samuel 17:32-36 NASB

David said to Saul, "Let no man's heart fail on account of him; your servant will go and fight with this Philistine." Then Saul said to David, "You are not able to go against this Philistine to fight with him; for you are but a youth while he has been a warrior from his youth." But David said to Saul, "Your servant was tending his father's sheep. When a lion or a bear came and took a lamb from the flock, I went out after him and attacked him, and rescued it from his mouth; and when he rose up against me, I seized him by his beard and struck him and killed him. Your servant has killed both the lion and the bear; and this uncircumcised Philistine will be like one of them, since he has taunted the armies of the living God."

The giant of abortion, supported by a host of demonic principalities and powers, is standing in the land and taunting the armies of the living God! Who will face this giant? Who has the courage to oppose him? Like David, we are facing an enemy with great resources, strength, and experience. But if we believe like David and rely upon God, our enemy is no match for us. "God is our refuge and strength, a very present help in trouble. Therefore we will not fear, though the earth should change and though the mountains slip into the heart of the sea; though its waters roar and foam, though the mountains quake at its swelling pride.... The Lord of hosts is with us; the God of Jacob is our stronghold" (Ps. 46:1-3, 7 NASB). Our status, rank, gender, and age does not matter, only our faith in the living God. The power of our enemy will melt in the presence of Almighty God and a believing people. When Saul doubted David's ability, David reminded Saul of all the past times God had been faithful in his life and used him to rescue the weak from the powerful. David's hope, faith, and confidence were in the great God of the universe! As we line up for battle and rush to meet the enemy, let us not forget our Stronghold, our ever-present help in times of trouble, and say with assurance this giant of abortion will fall like Goliath because it has taunted the armies of the living God (1 Sam. 17:45-50).

PRAYER FOCUS: Mighty God, give us the confidence of David as we fight for life. Remind us of all the times you have assisted us and delivered us in the past as we prepare for battle. Give us eyes to see that nothing and no one is a match for you, and, as those who are hidden in you, we are more than conquerors (Rom. 8:31-39).

DID YOU KNOW? David's friend Jonathan also had confidence in God's ability to defeat his enemies. He knew with David that the Lord is not restrained to save by many or by few. Read an account of Jonathan's faith and courage found in 1 Samuel 14:1-23.

REFLECTIONS

350

DECEMBER 5

1 Samuel 17:38-40 NASB

Then Saul clothed David with his garments and put a bronze helmet on his head, and he clothed him with armor. David girded his sword over his armor and tried to walk, for he had not tested them. So David said to Saul, "I cannot go with these, for I have not tested them." And David took them off. He took his stick in his hand and chose for himself five smooth stones from the brook, and put them in the shepherd's bag which he had, even in his pouch, and his sling was in his hand; and he approached the Philistine.

We cannot fight battles with unfamiliar weapons or skills we don't possess. David had not been trained to fight with swords and armor, but he had been trained to fight with a sling. In the battle to rescue the preborn and help their parents, there are many ways to fight, and many methods to try. A housewife isn't going to fight like a politician, and a politician isn't going to fight like a sidewalk counselor. A protest organizer isn't going to fight like a pastor. Even though we all fight differently, we still need to fight together. We can all vote for the highly motivated pro-life politician or ballot initiative. The pastor can help the sidewalk counselor recruit at their place of worship, while the sidewalk counselor, pastor, and housewife can join the protest organizer's event. We can all support our local pastors and encourage them in their pro-life teachings, messages, and efforts. Just as we don't all fight in the same venue or manner, we don't all possess the same opportunities or skills. If we have time or money, we should devote a considerable portion of it to pro-life work. If we have the ability to raise money, we should help pro-life organizations raise support and increase their budgets, or financially assist pro-life political candidates who are committed to Wilberforce-like efforts once they achieve power. If our gifts or skills are teaching, we should teach. If writing, then write; if networking, then network; if intercession, then we should pray and fast; if caregiving, then we should work at a pregnancy center or a home for mothers in need. If our gift is parenting, we should adopt. Whatever we can do, we must do it with all our might. We are to use our own unique skills and personality to bring God glory, love our neighbor, and engage in the battle for life. We just might have the missing piece of the puzzle.

PRAYER FOCUS: Father, help us to see that we are many members of one body and that while each of us has a separate function, we work best as a cohesive whole. Lord, unite the body of Christ and the pro-life movement so that we might be powerful and effective.

DID YOU KNOW? Colorado was the first state in America to bring the personhood of the preborn before the voters in 2008. Sadly, the measure didn't pass, but around a half-a-million voters did affirm that the preborn are persons from the moment of conception.[4] The personhood movement is growing, and several other states are gathering petition signatures to bring similar amendments before their voters. Go to *www.personhoodusa.com* for more information.

DECEMBER 6

Jeremiah 7:28-34 HCSB

You must therefore declare to them: This is the nation that would not listen to the voice of the LORD their God and would not accept discipline. Truth has perished—it has disappeared from their mouths. Cut off the hair of your sacred vow and throw it away. Raise up a dirge on the barren heights, for the LORD has rejected and abandoned the generation under His wrath. "For the Judeans have done what is evil in My sight." This is the LORD's declaration. "They have set up their detestable things in the house that is called by My name and defiled it. They have built the high places of Topheth in the Valley of Hinnom in order to burn their sons and daughters in the fire, a thing I did not command; I never entertained the thought. Therefore, take note! Days are coming"—the LORD's declaration—"when this place will no longer be called Topheth and the Valley of Hinnom, but the Valley of Slaughter. Topheth will become a cemetery, because there will be no other burial place. The corpses of these people will become food for the birds of the sky and for the wild animals of the land, with no one to scare them off. I will remove from the cities of Judah and the streets of Jerusalem the sound of joy and gladness and the voices of the groom and the bride, for the land will become a desolate waste."

Jeremiah was a prophet with a heavy mission. He was sent to God's people with a message of truth and sorrow, informing them that their hearts were far from the living God who they professed to serve, and that God's wrath was about to be poured out upon them. All of God's past efforts to bless them or discipline them had gone unheeded. They would not listen to God or his prophets, and Jeremiah was told they would not listen to him either (Jer. 7:27). Their idolatry, greed, oppression, and child-killing had reached the point of no return, and God was no longer willing to tolerate their wickedness. As we fight against the modern day idolatrous slaughter of innocent children called abortion, we must never forget the stakes of our mission. The spiritual and literal future of our nation and world depends on our repentance and cessation of the practice of abortion. If we do not return to the living God and walk in his ways, the days are coming when we will no longer be called the land of the free and the home of the brave—but the land of slaughter and desolation!

PRAYER FOCUS: Righteous Judge, we, the body of Christ, admit our guilt in allowing abortion to flourish in our land. Lord, we repent of our wickedness and ask for your forgiveness and help in turning first ourselves and then our nation back to your righteous ways. Jesus, we thank you for your undeserved grace during this dark time. Convict us of our sin, Lord, and show us afresh the path of life.

DID YOU KNOW? Archaeologists have discovered evidence of child sacrifice at Carthage. The *ESV Study Bible* records this in their footnotes for Jeremiah 7:31: "Archaeological excavations at Carthage, a Phoenician colony founded in the eighth century BC, include the charred remains of thousands of child sacrifices."[5]

REFLECTIONS

DECEMBER 7

Psalm 55:4-6 NKJV

My heart is severely pained within me, and the terrors of death have fallen upon me. Fearfulness and trembling have come upon me, and horror has overwhelmed me. So I said, "Oh, that I had wings like a dove! I would fly away and be at rest."

Why do we weep as we walk on the USS Arizona Memorial? Why do we stand in hushed silence as the waves break on the Normandy beaches? Why do we stare in horror at a pile of empty shoes in a Holocaust photograph? Is it because of the cruelty of our enemies? Yes, but it is much more than that. It is the immense gravity of the loss of life. We all feel it because we are alive, and at that moment, we recognize like at no other time the preciousness of life. God has placed a sense of time and justice in human hearts, and we intuitively recognize the tragedy of lives cut short, lives gone forever from the earth. Oh, what dreams they might have lived! How can we look so indifferently on abortion and fail to recognize how it affects us all? December 7, 1941, was the day of the attack on Pearl Harbor by Japanese imperial forces, a day President Roosevelt said would live in infamy. But that is not the only day that will live in infamy. When, O Lord, will we come to our senses and halt the holocaust of abortion?

PRAYER FOCUS: Lord, the living share a kindred fellowship of what it means to be alive, and in this fellowship lead us to a profound sense of the tragedy of abortion. Help us to admit our guilt and repent of this awful practice. Jesus, forgive us our trespass and lead us into the redemption of new life as we bring abortion to the ash heap of history.

DID YOU KNOW? Abraham Lincoln sent one of the most moving letters of consolation written during the Civil War. The letter's profound sense of the preciousness of life is what makes it memorable and powerful. His letter to Mrs. Bixby is as follows:

Dear Madam,
I have been shown in the files of the war Department a statement of the Adjutant General of Massachusetts, that you are the mother of five sons who have died gloriously on the field of battle. I feel how weak and fruitless must be any word of mine which should attempt to beguile you from the grief of a loss so overwhelming. But I cannot refrain from tendering to you the consolation that may be found in the thanks of the Republic they died to save. I pray that our Heavenly Father may assuage the anguish of your bereavement, and leave you only the cherished memory of the loved and lost, and the solemn pride that must be yours, to have laid so costly a sacrifice upon the altar of Freedom.
Yours, very sincerely and respectfully, A. Lincoln[6]

DECEMBER 8

Matthew 4:16 NKJV

The people who sat in darkness have seen a great light, and upon those who sat in the region and shadow of death Light has dawned.

Matthew records these words from Isaiah chapter nine at the beginning of Jesus' ministry. Not only did they fulfill Old Testament prophecy, but they also illuminated the truth of the work and ministry of the Messiah. Our Lord and Savior is a light-giver. He shines for all people to see, both then and now. He is our greatest hope, our most trusted advisor, our teacher, our redeemer, our friend. Jesus is the way, the truth, and the life! When we sit at his feet his Spirit and his Word instruct our lives. Until the light of Christ dawns in our hearts, we are people living in darkness, residing in the uncomfortable land of the shadow of death. How can we know the truth unless we know Jesus? We can't, until we come to the light of Christ and let his love illuminate our path. Only Jesus can satisfy the soul and meet human needs. We can't let the light pass us by—we must get up and walk with him for "God is light and in Him is no darkness at all" (1 John 1:5 NKJV).

PRAYER FOCUS: Light of Truth, guide me and lead me to your dwelling place and fill my heart and mind with your wisdom, grace, and love (Ps. 43:3). Lord, love me, teach me, convict me, and correct me that I might be a legitimate child of God. When I am lost or confused, shine your light on me that I might see the road ahead.

DID YOU KNOW? The deVeber Institute for Bioethics and Social Research in Ontario, Canada, has produced a book titled *Women's Health after Abortion: The Medical and Psychological Evidence* by Elizabeth Ring-Cassidy and Ian Gentles. The book highlights and exposes the health risks and medical complications arising from induced abortion. Their findings are gleaned from more than five hundred articles that have been printed in medical or other professional journals.[7] Anyone who believes abortion doesn't hurt women would do well to consult this resource. For more information, go to *www.deveber.org*.

REFLECTIONS

354

DECEMBER 9

Colossians 1:11-14 HCSB

May you be strengthened with all power, according to His glorious might, for all endurance and patience, with joy giving thanks to the Father, who has enabled you to share in the saints' inheritance in the light. He has rescued us from the domain of darkness and transferred us into the kingdom of the Son He loves. We have redemption, the forgiveness of sins, in Him.

∞

Paul's prayer for the church at Colossae is applicable and appropriate for all believers, but especially for those who work directly in the pro-life struggle. I pray similarly for all those who labor in the field for life. I pray they would be strengthened with all power in their efforts to rescue the preborn and enlighten, assist, and help their parents and society. I pray God provides everything they need according to his glorious might. May all those in the pro-life struggle be filled with God's Spirit and abound with endurance and patience during this marathon for life. May the joy of the Lord be their strength and may the lives they see saved and the souls God sets free be their passport to joy unspeakable! I pray those in the movement would abound in thankfulness to the Father who enables them to do this work and who brings them into the kingdom of light. May we remain grateful even in difficult times or when we experience little or no appreciation for our efforts. May we remember always that we rescue, sacrifice, and love because God first rescued, sacrificed, loved, and saved us. Lastly, I pray that all of God's children continually sense his glorious presence and know that he has rescued all of us from the domain of darkness and brought us into the kingdom of his Son, in whom we have redemption, the forgiveness of sins.

PRAYER FOCUS: Thank you, Father, for your glorious goodness to us. I am grateful for your Son, who is the preeminent, all-sufficient propitiation for our sin, our Mighty Deliverer and Redeemer. Lord, help us to not grow weary in well doing! Let us run the race with joy, endurance, patience, gratitude, freedom, and perseverance (Rom. 2:6-7; 1 Cor. 9:24; 15:58; Gal. 6:9; 2 Thess. 3:13; Heb. 12:1; James 2:8).

DID YOU KNOW? *The Pocket Oxford English Dictionary* defines the word "redeem" as (1) make up for the faults or bad aspects of; (2) save someone from sin or evil; (3) fulfill a promise; (4) regain possession of something in exchange for payment; (6) repay a debt.[8]

REFLECTIONS

DECEMBER 10

Numbers 11:11-14 NIV

He asked the LORD, "Why have you brought this trouble on your servant? What have I done to displease you that you put the burden of all these people on me? Did I conceive all these people? Did I give them birth? Why do you tell me to carry them in my arms, as a nurse carries an infant, to the land you promised on oath to their forefathers? Where can I get meat for all these people? They keep wailing to me, 'Give us meat to eat!' I cannot carry all these people by myself; the burden is too heavy for me."

∞

Even God's chosen servant Moses got discouraged and overwhelmed by the demands and the difficulties of the work God gave him. With God all things are possible, but when we take our eyes off of him, even for a moment, we can become overwhelmed. Still, in spite of Moses' complaint, the Lord found merit in his plea for help and sent him assistance from the camp (Num. 11:16-17). Our leaders need our help, and we need their help and the help of our brothers and sisters in Christ (Num. 11:27-29; Ps. 20:1-2; 2 Chron. 7:14; Gal. 6:2). While God can and does often accomplish his work through a small remnant, the goal should be to include all the people of God, whenever possible, so that all can share in the work and benefit from the transformation it brings about. The Word of God is amazing in its depth, and the many insights it can reveal to us from a single verse or passage is astounding. As it presents both the highs and the lows, the victories and the failures of God's people, it reveals hidden treasure and deep truths. Hidden in this complaint from Moses is the affirmation of God's gestational development cycle from conception to birth. Moses was not the only frustrated servant who affirmed that life begins in the womb (Job 3:1-17; Jer. 20:14-18). If we are not now engaged in the pro-life struggle, we should get involved; "The harvest is plentiful, but the workers are few. Ask the Lord of the harvest, therefore, to send out workers into his harvest field" (Luke 10:2 NIV).

PRAYER FOCUS: Lord Jesus, send us help from the sanctuary and bring forth our brothers and sisters to help us carry this burden for life (Ps. 20:1-2). Let us not love in word only but with truth and action (1 John 3:18). Lord, fill us with godly sorrow and prepare us for battle (2 Cor. 7:9-11).

DID YOU KNOW? 250,000 people showed up to support Martin Luther King, Jr. when he gave his famous "I Have a Dream" speech in Washington.[9] William Wilberforce presented an abolition petition before the members of Parliament that contained over eight hundred thousand signatures from the citizens of England, estimated to be around ten percent of the populace.[10] Every great leader needs the support of God and the people if they are to succeed.

DECEMBER 11

Philippians 1:9-14 ESV

And it is my prayer that your love may abound more and more, with knowledge and all discernment, so that you may approve what is excellent, and so be pure and blameless for the day of Christ, filled with the fruit of righteousness that comes through Jesus Christ, to the glory and praise of God. I want you to know, brothers, that what has happened to me has really served to advance the gospel, so that it has become known throughout the whole imperial guard and to all the rest that my imprisonment is for Christ. And most of the brothers, having become confident in the Lord by my imprisonment, are much more bold to speak the word without fear.

Even as Paul was in prison, he taught, encouraged, and strengthened his fellow believers through his actions and writing. Paul's prayer was that the people in Philippi would abound more and more in love, growing in knowledge and discernment as to the ways of God so that they could approve what is excellent. Love is the most important part of our Christian walk and witness, but when we couple love with knowledge and discernment, we will have our greatest impact on the lives of others. As believers we are to love others boldly as we walk in the ways of God. Our lives of faith bring God glory as we love others and accept a righteousness not of our own. After these words of equipping and prayer, Paul encourages the faithful to be bold and courageous as they advance the kingdom of God. Most people who get arrested seek to distance themselves from the charge against them, or they deny their involvement. Not so with Paul. He boldly took advantage of his opportunity to preach Christ crucified and resurrected to the very people who imprisoned him for sharing the Good News. Paul's courage invigorated his fellow laborers to preach more boldly and openly to the people. What a witness we can be to our captors and our supporters when we remain faithful to God during our difficult circumstances. If we press into Jesus during troubling times, God will accomplish some of his greatest work in us and through us.

PRAYER FOCUS: Lord, steel my courage and keep me focused on you when I face various trials and tribulations. Give me an eternal perspective to see the opportunities to advance your kingdom, even in the midst of adversity. Jesus, be my confidence, my fortress, my high tower, and my supply in the day of trouble.

DID YOU KNOW? The first group mentioned among those who will share in the second death in Revelation 21:8 is the cowardly. Joshua and Paul aren't the only ones called to have courage!

REFLECTIONS

DECEMBER 12

Mark 12:41-44 NASB

And He sat down opposite the treasury, and began observing how the people were putting money into the treasury; and many rich people were putting in large sums. A poor widow came and put in two small copper coins, which amount to a cent. Calling His disciples to Him, He said to them, "Truly I say to you, this poor widow put in more than all the contributors to the treasury; for they all put in out of their surplus, but she, out of her poverty, put in all she owned, all she had to live on."

Jesus used the offering of the widow to teach his disciples a lesson in sacrifice, trust, and faith. The widow demonstrated all three through her modest gift. First, she was willing to sacrifice to her very limits for the work of the Kingdom, for she gave all she had. Second, her willingness to place all she had to live on in the treasury demonstrated great trust in the living God to provide for her needs. She must have believed that man does not live by bread alone (Deut. 8:3; Luke 4:4). Third, she displayed extraordinary faith that God could use her small amount of money to accomplish his work. Perhaps this gesture of faith is the reason her story is recorded for us in Holy Scripture, because through it God is still using her example as a lesson for the body of Christ. The Master is still accomplishing his work through the widow's mite. We are all called to give out of our surplus, but when we give sacrificially, great power is released to accomplish the work of God. When we give with a generous, trusting, faith-filled heart, we will be amazed by what God will do.

PRAYER FOCUS: Jesus, I am inspired by the widow who out of her poverty cared for others. Help me see that it is possible to give regardless of means. Let us all love our neighbor, like the widow. Lord, the faith of your most humble servants is amazing and challenging. Teach me to depend completely on you and use the resources you have given me for the work of the Kingdom. Holy Spirit, help me be more mindful of my heavenly treasure than my earthly treasure.

DID YOU KNOW? The Bible says, "Pure and undefiled religion in the sight of our God and Father is this: to visit orphans and widows in their distress, and to keep oneself unstained by the world" (James 1:27 NASB).

REFLECTIONS

DECEMBER 13

Psalm 121 NASB

I will lift up my eyes to the mountains; from where shall my help come? My help comes from the LORD, who made heaven and earth. He will not allow your foot to slip; He who keeps you will not slumber. Behold, He who keeps Israel will neither slumber nor sleep. The LORD is your keeper; The LORD is your shade on your right hand. The sun will not smite you by day, nor the moon by night. The LORD will protect you from all evil; He will keep your soul. The LORD will guard your going out and your coming in from this time forth and forever.

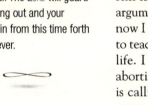

Each time my wife gave birth to one of our children, I purchased a Bible for them. As they came forth from the womb, I wanted them to have a firm foundation for life, the everlasting Word of God. Inside the cover I wrote them a personal note and selected a key verse or passage for their life. On this date, I chose Psalm 121 for my daughter, Brooke. I was keenly aware Brooke would need the Lord's help because she was born at twenty-nine weeks gestation, almost three months before her due date. Amidst all the travail and concern during her birth came a beautiful two pound, thirteen ounce baby girl. Her deep blue eyes and long fingers clearly evidenced her Creator, for she was fearfully and wonderfully made! During the next several weeks in a neonatal intensive care unit, I watched Brooke grow and develop in plain sight. As I marveled at her and prayed to God on her behalf, I began feeling the Father's concern for the millions of preborn babies who are threatened by abortion. The irrefutable living evidence of Brooke, who should still have been in the womb, destroyed every pro-abortion argument I had ever heard. At some level, I was blind, but now I could see! God dramatically used my daughter Brooke to teach me about the value and preciousness of every human life. I could no longer remain on the sidelines and allow abortion to go unchallenged. God was calling me and he is calling all Christians to rise up and speak for those who cannot speak for themselves.

PRAYER FOCUS: Lord, awaken your people to the truth of life in the womb! We don't all need a Brooke, but we do need a wake-up call. Give us eyes to see and ears to hear the children. Maker of heaven and earth, help us. Lord, do not slumber. Be our shade, protect us from all evil, and keep our souls, for we are the work of your hands, the people of your pasture.

DID YOU KNOW? Brooke died from illness on January 21, 2003, just hours before the thirtieth anniversary of *Roe v Wade*. God guarded her going out and her coming in during that time and forevermore!

REFLECTIONS

DECEMBER 14

Zechariah 3:1-5 NIV

Then he showed me Joshua the high priest standing before the angel of the Lord, and Satan standing at his right side to accuse him. The Lord said to Satan, "The Lord rebuke you, Satan! The Lord, who has chosen Jerusalem, rebuke you! Is not this man a burning stick snatched from the fire?" Now Joshua was dressed in filthy clothes as he stood before the angel. The angel said to those who were standing before him, "Take off his filthy clothes." Then he said to Joshua, "See, I have taken away your sin, and I will put rich garments on you." Then I said, "Put a clean turban on his head." So they put a clean turban on his head and clothed him, while the angel of the Lord stood by.

Who can make us clean? Who can change our dirty clothes and give us fresh garments (Isa. 64)? How will we answer our accuser when he points out our indulgence in pornography, our abortions, our gossip and slander, our dishonesty in business, our lies, our adultery, our fornication, our theft, our disrespect of parents and elders, our pride, our lust, our anger, our covetousness, or our idolatry? Just like Joshua and the nation he represented, we are lost and without hope unless we have an Advocate and a Savior (Isa. 61:10; 1 John 2:1-2). Thanks belong to God because he chose us before the foundation of the world, while we were yet sinners, to be his children. We are all burning branches snatched from the fire by the One who alone brings salvation (Ps. 62:1-2; Rom. 8:1-4, 33-34; 1 Thess. 5:9-10; Heb. 5:9-10). If we have placed our faith in Jesus, we need not fear, for the Lord has forgiven our sins, paid our debt, rebuked our accuser, and changed our clothes! Salvation is God's free gift, and with the gift comes partnership with Christ, pursuit of the good works prepared in advance, and many rewards to be garnered—and in this there is much work to be done.

PRAYER FOCUS: Lord, I am grateful you chose me and all my past, current, and future brothers and sisters in Christ to be your sons and daughters. Use us, Lord, to accomplish your purposes and bring many more people to your throne of grace.

DID YOU KNOW? Joshua's garments were rank as well as filthy. The *ESV Study Bible* records these words in their footnote for Zechariah 3:3: "Joshua was not merely clothed with filthy garments but, more precisely, clothed in garments soiled with excrement, which would automatically defile the wearer."[11] Fittingly, the name Joshua means "Jehovah saves."[12]

REFLECTIONS

DECEMBER 15

Joel 2:12-14 ESV

"Yet even now," declares the LORD, "return to me with all your heart, with fasting, with weeping, and with mourning; and rend your hearts and not your garments." Return to the LORD your God, for he is gracious and merciful, slow to anger, and abounding in steadfast love; and he relents over disaster. Who knows whether he will not turn and relent, and leave a blessing behind him, a grain offering and a drink offering for the LORD your God?

Is our personal and national wickedness too great to overcome? Is there no hope? Is it past the time to do the right things? No, our God is long-suffering, patient, and good to all. And he is speaking to us today, just as he spoke to the people of Judah and Jerusalem when he spoke through the prophet Joel: "Return to the Lord your God, for he is gracious and merciful, slow to anger, and abounding in steadfast love." Today, even now, God is calling us to repent and return to him with devoted hearts, with fasting, weeping, mourning, and with broken hearts over our individual and national sins. Let us cry out for mercy and grace as we ready our hearts to sacrificially love our neighbors and seek justice. If the body of Christ corporately repents, God may turn from his judgment upon the land and bless us and our nation. After all, he relents over disaster. He said, "If my people who are called by my name humble themselves, and pray and seek my face and turn from their wicked ways, then I will hear from heaven and will forgive their sin and heal their land" (2 Chron. 7:14 ESV). When the body of Christ repents, abortion will fall (Joel 2:16-20).

PRAYER FOCUS: God, make us thirsty for righteousness and return our culture to one that cherishes life. Father, return us to purity and passion and help us drive abortion from the church and the nation! Lord Jesus, I repent of _____. Specifically forgive the church of its sins of pride, idolatry, failing to love our neighbor, sexual impurity, unclean lips, critical spirits, cowardice, anger, and _____. Send us new wine that we, in the body of Christ, might delight in you and partner with you in the great work of abolishing abortion. May your glory be advanced and your people bettered during this effort.

DID YOU KNOW? The book of Joel is estimated to have been written between the ninth and the fourth centuries BC.[13] Like many biblical prophets, Joel wrote for his current generation and future audiences. God's "Yet even now" carries the same urgency for us today as it did for the people of Judah in ancient times. When one ponders the passage of time between then and now and the uncertain time remaining before the "Day of the Lord," one begins to taste the long-suffering nature of God. Make no mistake, whether we partner with God in the effort to end abortion or he rises up to end it in judgment, abortion will be overcome.

DECEMBER 16

Psalm 51:1-4 HCSB

Be gracious to me, God, according to Your faithful love; according to Your abundant compassion, blot out my rebellion. Wash away my guilt, and cleanse me from my sin. For I am conscious of my rebellion, and my sin is always before me. Against You—You alone—I have sinned and done this evil in Your sight. So You are right when You pass sentence; You are blameless when You judge.

Christ's work of atonement is finished and sufficient to cover all sin once for all. But our repentance of sin is an ongoing process by which we seek to keep close to God and remain in constant fellowship with him through confession. David composed this psalm of contrition after he coveted Uriah's wife Bathsheba, committed adultery with her, tried to deceive Uriah through furlough and dissipation, and ultimately arranged for Uriah's death in battle (2 Sam. 11; 12:1-15). David's sins hurt many people and greatly grieved God, but God accepted his plea for forgiveness because David repented in his inner man with a broken and contrite spirit (Ps. 51:17). David well understood that while his sins affected many people, it was ultimately God whom he had sinned against and to whom he would render an account for his actions. When we sin against God, we need to follow David's example and repent sincerely from our brokenness over our sins. Just like David, we need to appeal to God's grace, love, and compassion, asking him to intervene on our behalf and cleanse us, freely admitting our sins and God's full justification in passing judgment upon us because of them. Whatever our sins have been, are, or will be, they need to be brought before the Lord in humble repentance through contrite confession. Only then do we taste the freedom of soul that comes through restoration and grace.

PRAYER FOCUS: Lord, I am comforted to know that even your greatest servants struggled with sin and wrong decisions. I realize I am not alone in my struggles. But I also realize that what allowed David and others to grow and mature in their faith was repentance followed by a renewed urgency and intention to walk with you in obedience. Lord, be gracious, compassionate, and loving towards me, the work of your hands, by forgiving my sins and restoring to me the joy of your salvation. Cleanse me, God, and help me walk in greater obedience to you.

DID YOU KNOW? The very next verse in David's psalm of contrition traces his sinful nature and tendencies back to his conception in the womb. He writes, "Indeed, I was guilty when I was born; I was sinful when my mother conceived me" (Ps. 51:5 HCSB). The ESV *Study Bible* presents this in their footnotes for Psalm 51:5: "The idea is not that the act of conception was itself sinful, but (as the parallel first line shows) that each worshiper learns to trace his sinful tendencies to the very beginning of his existence—not only from birth but even before that, to conception."[14]

DECEMBER 17

Hebrews 4:14-16 NASB

Therefore, since we have a great high priest who has passed through the heavens, Jesus the Son of God, let us hold fast our confession. For we do not have a high priest who cannot sympathize with our weaknesses, but One who has been tempted in all things as we are, yet without sin. Therefore let us draw near with confidence to the throne of grace, so that we may receive mercy and find grace to help in time of need.

Jesus is our Savior, our King, our Lord, our Friend, and our High Priest. He is a Priest forever who daily bears our burdens, making everlasting intercession for us! Jesus' blood secured our redemption for all time, and he never loses those entrusted to him (John 17:12-20; 18:9; Phil. 1:6). Jesus passed through the heavens upon the completion of his sinless work of obedience and is seated at the right hand of the Father. He brings his knowledge and experience of being human and facing temptation in human form to bear upon his prayers and dealings with us, his children. Knowing Christ's love, sacrifice, and work on our behalf, we can come confidently, boldly, and expectantly to his throne of grace for help during any temptation, sin, or difficulty. For he loves us with an everlasting love and he who promised is faithful, authoritative, and competent to work all things together for the good of those who love God (Rom. 8:28). This is the Good News: Jesus who died and who was raised loves us, redeemed us, fights for us, and he will never let us down. Love never fails!

PRAYER FOCUS: O conquering King, perfect Priest, loving Friend, Lord of lords, Jesus, my righteousness. I exalt in you and your love for me. Holy, holy, holy, is the Lord God Almighty and worthy of praise, he who was and is and is to come (Rev. 4:8)! Jesus, overcome me with your love and sufficiency. I will tell of your love and your wonderful deeds from generation to generation. Be gracious to me, Jesus, in my times of need.

DID YOU KNOW? The writer of Hebrews goes to great lengths to establish that Jesus Christ is the Messiah—the Priest-King foretold in the order of Melchizedek (Gen. 14:14-20; Ps. 110:4; Heb. 5; 6; 7). In his argument, the author makes the point that the yet unborn priesthood of which Levi was the progenitor was in the loins of Abraham when he paid tithes to Melchizedek (Heb. 7:9-10; Gen. 29:34; Exod. 6:14-26; Num. 3:5-9; Deut. 10:8; 21:5). Life is in the blood, and the Bible often stresses the importance of bloodline in one's life. The question for us today is whose bloodline do we share? Adam's alone, or Adam's first and Christ's second through adoption? For just as in the bloodline of Adam all die, those adopted into the bloodline of Christ will live (John 17:12-21; 1 Cor. 15:20-22; 2 Cor. 5:17-21).

DECEMBER
18

Luke 7:37-48 NKJV

And behold, a woman in the city who was a sinner, when she knew that Jesus sat at the table in the Pharisee's house, brought an alabaster flask of fragrant oil, and stood at His feet behind Him weeping; and she began to wash His feet with her tears.... Now when the Pharisee who had invited Him saw this, he spoke to himself, saying, "This man, if He were a prophet, would know who and what manner of woman this is who is touching Him, for she is a sinner." And Jesus answered and said to him, "Simon, I have something to say to you." So he said, "Teacher, say it." "There was a certain creditor who had two debtors. One owed five hundred denarii, and the other fifty. And when they had nothing with which to repay, he freely forgave them both. Tell Me, therefore, which of them will love him more?" Simon answered and said, "I suppose the one whom he forgave more." And He said to him, "You have rightly judged." Then He turned to the woman and said to Simon, "Do you see this woman? I entered your house; you gave Me no water for My feet, but she has washed My feet with her tears and wiped them with the hair of her head. You gave Me no kiss, but this woman has not ceased to kiss My feet since the time I came in. You did not anoint My head with oil, but this woman has anointed My feet with fragrant oil. Therefore I say to you, her sins, which are many, are forgiven, for she loved much. But to whom little is forgiven, the same loves little." Then He said to her, "Your sins are forgiven."

Today's passage beautifully illustrates the greatness of Jesus, the power of forgiveness, the importance of love, and the emptiness of religion. The Pharisee was caught up in the externals of religion and through his self-righteous indignation failed to love either Jesus, his guest, or the broken woman at the Lord's feet. When laws, regulations, and performance are the sole guide, they won't bring transformation, freedom, or love, but a heavy chain. But when love, truth, grace, and forgiveness are experienced, transformation begins and burdens are released in joyful acts of love, service, and obedience. This sinful woman had been transformed by Jesus' love for her and out of her gratitude boldly loved her Savior. As the account demonstrates, Jesus is more concerned with what is in our hearts, how much we love him and others, and how far we've come out of the darkness than our past sins or their frequency. Whether we owe a little or a lot, only Jesus can pay our debt. Come and kiss the feet of Love and watch him make more of our lives than we or anyone else thought possible!

PRAYER FOCUS: Love me, Jesus, and I shall love others. Forgive me, Jesus, and I shall forgive others. Be kind to me, Jesus, and I shall be kind to others. Keep me, Jesus, and I shall never fall.

DID YOU KNOW? Fifty denarii was the equivalent of less than two months wages, while five hundred denarii equaled almost two years wages.[15]

REFLECTIONS

DECEMBER 19

Joel 3:21 NKJV

For I will acquit them of the guilt of bloodshed, whom I had not acquitted; For the LORD dwells in Zion.

The prophet Joel closes his book with the good news that God will ultimately acquit Judah and Jerusalem of their sins of bloodshed at the end of the age. If God is willing to forgive his chosen people for their idolatry and bloodshed, he is willing to forgive us for our transgressions and bloodshed. God is loving, kind, patient, and forgiving! Our heavenly Father is a redeemer to the very last, and he longs to be good to us. Abortion doesn't have to define us or be the end of our story. If we confess our sins, draw near to God, and let him be the definer of our lives, we will discover a purpose and a peace like no other. We can turn to God and allow him to be the writer of the rest of our story. With God all things are possible (Mark 10:27; Phil. 4:13). God can remove our personal and national sins and wash our stains away. The Lord Jesus can do a deep work in our hearts by turning fathers' and mothers' hearts to their children and their children's hearts to their fathers and mothers. And he can turn our churches' hearts to the children and our children's hearts to the churches.

PRAYER FOCUS: Lord, we entrust our past to you and place our future in your hands. We repent of the bloodshed of abortion and humbly ask you to make beauty out of ashes. Lord Jesus, transform our hearts personally, corporately, and nationally to respect and protect every life you have created from conception to the time appointed by you for the end of life. Thank you, God, that you forgive the sin of bloodshed and set the captives free!

DID YOU KNOW? Master's International School of Divinity, based in Evansville, Indiana, offers an online degree in Life-Issues Counseling. If you desire to work with women and men dealing with life issues, contact the school at 1-800-933-1445 or go online to *www.mdivs.edu*. This program is a great starting point for ministers, youth leaders, pregnancy resource directors and staff, counselors, or anyone who wants to become equipped to help people struggling with life decisions and post-abortion difficulties. If you would like to receive immediate confidential help in working through a past abortion, contact Ramah International at 941-473-2188 or go online to *www.ramahinternational.org*.

DECEMBER 20

1 Peter 1:18-23 NIV

For you know that it was not with perishable things such as silver or gold that you were redeemed from the empty way of life handed down to you from your forefathers, but with the precious blood of Christ, a lamb without blemish or defect. He was chosen before the creation of the world, but was revealed in these last times for your sake. Through him you believe in God, who raised him from the dead and glorified him, and so your faith and hope are in God. Now that you have purified yourselves by obeying the truth so that you have sincere love for your brothers, love one another deeply, from the heart. For you have been born again, not of perishable seed, but of imperishable, through the living and enduring word of God.

∞

God did not redeem us with the things he has made, but with his Son, the unmade eternal source of life! When Jesus redeems us, he makes us alive forever through his precious blood. Everything that has life, both flesh and spirit, derives its life from Jesus. "For by him all things were created: things in heaven and on earth, visible and invisible, whether thrones or powers or rulers or authorities; all things were created by him and for him. He is before all things, and in him all things hold together" (Col. 1:16-17 NIV). Jesus created us and filled us with living blood so we could live and love, but he died for us so that through his life-atoning blood our spirits could live with him in abundance for all eternity. Faith starts with Jesus, grows through hope and relationship, and ends with the Father and the realization of all hope (Heb. 11:1). When we place trust in Jesus and believe in him, our blood type changes from perishable to imperishable and we begin feeding off the living, pure, enduring Word of God. And God's Word purifies and changes us into lovers of God and lovers of his people. For when we are born again, we are born anew, and this time we share the blood of the Father and his Only Begotten!

PRAYER FOCUS: Lord of Life, speak to me and use your blood to set me free. Give me grace to walk with thee and take my rest beneath your tree. Show me things I do not know and use your Word to help me grow. Call your greatness to my mind whenever this life treats me unkind.

DID YOU KNOW? Jesus' sacrifice on the cross for all humankind set the bar for human worth and value immeasurably high. The *Spirit Filled Life Bible* has this in their commentary for 1 Peter 1:18-19: "The value of the human being can be inferred from the price paid to redeem man (John 3:16; 1 Cor. 6:20). God the Son, the Divine One through whom the worlds were created, became flesh and died for the sins of humanity. That He willingly shed His blood and died for us reveals not only the value of the human personality, but also the importance of salvation."[16]

REFLECTIONS

DECEMBER 21

1 John 4:10-11 HCSB

Love consists in this: not that we loved God, but that He loved us and sent His Son to be the propitiation for our sins. Dear friends, if God loved us in this way, we also must love one another.

God daily demonstrates his love for us in innumerable ways. But his greatest demonstration was through his Son, who gave his life as a ransom for every lost and wayward person. Jesus paid the debt of all sinners at Calvary because of his goodness and love for all people. He loves us more than anything else in all creation (Rom. 5:8; 2 Cor. 5:21). If we have experienced this love, we know it compels us to love others regardless of their merits or reciprocity. As John goes on to say in verse nineteen, "We love because He first loved us." As God pours his love into our hearts, we begin loving others, not out of obligation or duty, but out of compassion and grace because of the gratitude that resides in our spirits due to the abiding presence of God in our lives. The love of God transforms and arrests. Nothing compares to the love of God and the endless river of joy it produces in the human heart. When we receive God's love today, tomorrow we are fishers of men, healers of the broken, and lights in the midst of darkness.

PRAYER FOCUS: Lover of my soul, embrace me today and enrapture me with your great passion for me. Pour your love and grace so fully into my life that it spills out onto my neighbor. Jesus, teach me to cherish life, love others, forgive often, pray for my enemies, and delight always in you. Lord, I am grateful that you love me more than I can fathom and that I can always trust you to care for me.

DID YOU KNOW? The word *propitiation* (regaining someone's favor) is used only twice in the New Testament, and both times they are in the book of 1 John (1 John 2:2; 4:10). "The word describes Christ, through His sacrificial death, as appeasing the wrath of God on account of sin. It also pictures His death as expiatory, providing a covering for sin. By means of the atoning death of Christ, God can be merciful to the sinner who believes in Him, and reconciliation is effected."[17]

REFLECTIONS

DECEMBER 22

Luke 10:25-37 ESV

And behold, a lawyer stood up to put him to the test, saying, "Teacher, what shall I do to inherit eternal life?" He said to him, "What is written in the Law? How do you read it?" And he answered, "You shall love the Lord your God with all your heart and with all your soul and with all your strength and with all your mind, and your neighbor as yourself." And he said to him, "You have answered correctly; do this, and you will live." But he, desiring to justify himself, said to Jesus, "And who is my neighbor?" Jesus replied, "A man was going down from Jerusalem to Jericho, and he fell among robbers, who stripped him and beat him and departed, leaving him half dead. Now by chance a priest was going down that road, and when he saw him he passed by on the other side. So likewise a Levite, when he came to the place and saw him, passed by on the other side. But a Samaritan, as he journeyed, came to where he was, and when he saw him, he had compassion. He went to him and bound up his wounds, pouring on oil and wine. Then he set him on his own animal and brought him to an inn and took care of him. And the next day he took out two denarii and gave them to the innkeeper, saying, 'Take care of him, and whatever more you spend, I will repay you when I come back.' Which of these three, do you think, proved to be a neighbor to the man who fell among the robbers?" He said, "The one who showed him mercy." And Jesus said to him, "You go, and do likewise."

This very day abortion is robbing, hurting, wounding, and destroying lives in our church and community. Will we pass by on the road or will we intervene and bring help to the hurting, life to any who will accept it, and the love of Christ? How many men will be robbed of fatherhood, or how many women will agonize alone over the loss of their child? How many more children will die today without compassion and attempted rescue? Are we too busy, too self-righteous to associate with sinners in need, too tolerant to hear the cries of our preborn neighbors? Why did the priest and Levite pass by? Were they prejudiced, afraid, unconcerned, late, indifferent, hardened, ashamed, cowardly, or self-absorbed? Why did the Samaritan take action and help the stranger in need? Was it his goodness, courage, available time, training, status, or wealth? Or did he simply possess a love for his neighbor and an innate sense of the value of the human person? All of us are valuable. A disciple of Christ isn't just a worshiper or a learner; a disciple is a person of action motivated by the indwelling presence of Christ and his love. It is time for followers of Christ to take action and help the broken beside the road.

PRAYER FOCUS: Lord, when I see the broken or hear of their needs, give me the grace to get involved and help them. Jesus, give me a love for the lost, a passion for the hurting, and a desire to meet the needs I can when you give me opportunity.

DID YOU KNOW? John Ensor ends his book *Answering the Call* with an acronym for the word H.E.L.P. (Hold Each Life Precious).[18] His simple device is not only a clever tool of remembrance, but foundational to all godly ministry. When we hold each life precious, we begin to think and act like Jesus (Mark 10:43-45).

REFLECTIONS

DECEMBER 23

2 Corinthians 1:3-4 NASB

Blessed be the God and Father of our Lord Jesus Christ, the Father of mercies and God of all comfort, who comforts us in all our affliction so that we will be able to comfort those who are in any affliction with the comfort with which we ourselves are comforted by God.

The greatness of God is unsearchable. The books that have been written about his attributes and nature are many and no doubt incomplete. The love of God is rich, deep, powerful, and beyond description. The mercy and grace of God provide a never-ending river of sustenance affording the recipients great wonder, joy, and gratitude. The comfort of God is a necessity and a delight to the soul. God is spirit. In a spirit of prayer we can release our wounds, cares, sins, fears, frustrations, doubts, and turmoil to the Lord and let his Spirit minister comfort to us. The psalmist wrote, "In the multitude of my anxieties within me, Your comforts delight my soul" (Ps. 94:19 NKJV). God knows our heartaches, our choices, our pain, and our sins, and he longs to comfort us with his great forgiveness and love if we will bring our worries, sins, and failures to him. Peter told us to "humble yourselves under the mighty hand of God, that He may exalt you at the proper time, casting all your anxiety on Him, because He cares for you" (1 Pet. 5:6-7 NASB). If we are haunted by abortion, or any other thing, we can confess it to God and let him comfort us today. When we do, we experience in our spirit the words of Isaiah: "Shout for joy, O heavens! And rejoice, O earth! Break forth into joyful shouting, O mountains! For the Lord has comforted His people and will have compassion on His afflicted" (49:13 NASB). After the Holy Spirit has comforted us, we should not be surprised if he invites us to assist others in finding the comfort of God and receiving the healing they need.

PRAYER FOCUS: Great Comforter, show me the path of life and lead me in the way everlasting. Lord, I am overcome by _____. Take my burdens, hurt, and guilt away and leave me with the abiding sense of your great presence and love. Sing over me, God, and allow me to see myself the way you see me. Holy Spirit, blow a fresh wind on me today.

DID YOU KNOW? The Greek word used for *comfort* in 2 Corinthians 1:3-4 is *parakaleo*, from *paraklesis*, which means to call near, to invite, to beseech, to invoke by consolation. Similarly, one of the Hebrew words used for *comfort* in the Old Testament (Ps. 23:4) is *nacham*, which means to console, to give forth sighs, to pity.[19] God invites us to share our pain with him so he might weep with us and turn our despair into praise and joy.

DECEMBER 24

John 8:3-11 NIV

The teachers of the law and the Pharisees brought in a woman caught in adultery. They made her stand before the group and said to Jesus, "Teacher, this woman was caught in the act of adultery. In the Law Moses commanded us to stone such women. Now what do you say?" They were using this question as a trap, in order to have a basis for accusing him. But Jesus bent down and started to write on the ground with his finger. When they kept on questioning him, he straightened up and said to them, "If any one of you is without sin, let him be the first to throw a stone at her." Again he stooped down and wrote on the ground. At this, those who heard began to go away one at a time, the older ones first, until only Jesus was left, with the woman still standing there. Jesus straightened up and asked her, "Woman, where are they? Has no one condemned you?" "No one, sir," she said. "Then neither do I condemn you," Jesus declared. "Go now and leave your life of sin."

Only the Sinless can pass final, definitive judgment on God's greatest treasure, human beings. We are not asked to judge our neighbors, and we have not been granted the authority to do so (John 5:22; James 4:11-12). But as redeemed sinners, we have been asked to love our neighbors. And one aspect of loving our neighbors is to share God's truth with them, guiding them to his Word and ultimately to a relationship with Jesus. God desires that we help, warn, instruct, and guide our neighbors in his ways. He wants us to be followers of Christ who, like our Lord, bring hope and light through the combined presence of grace and truth. Jesus displayed great compassion and forgiveness for the woman caught in adultery, but he also affirmed the sinfulness of her condition when he advised her to leave behind the yoke of sin that sexual immorality had reaped in her life. Jesus knew that in order for her to be set free and live the abundant life, she needed forgiveness, truth, repentance, and restoration. We do no one a favor by neglecting to address sin under the guise of being nonjudgmental. The doctor who refuses to remove a cancerous lump because it will cause the patient some pain ultimately does his patient a disservice. Jesus loves us too much to leave us broken in his mercy; he wants to make us whole (Mark 6:56; Luke 4:16-21; 8:36; John 7:23). Let's partner with him and share his grace and truth without judgment to a lost and dying world.

PRAYER FOCUS: Jesus, you alone are the Judge of all people, and I humbly acknowledge it is not my domain or responsibility to render judgment upon anyone. Lord, help me love you and my neighbor to the best of my ability, always pointing to your truth, your grace, your ways, and your love as I relate to your children, the precious work of your hands.

DID YOU KNOW? The song "O Holy Night" was played during the first AM radio broadcast on this date in 1906 by Reginald Fessenden.[20] If you get the chance, listen to this classic song tonight and let the music and lyrics about the birth of Christ penetrate your soul. Celebrate the baby who changed the world!

DECEMBER 25

Isaiah 25:8-9 NASB

He will swallow up death for all time, and the Lord God will wipe tears away from all faces, and He will remove the reproach of His people from all the earth; for the LORD has spoken. And it will be said in that day, "Behold, this is our God for whom we have waited that He might save us. This is the LORD for whom we have waited; Let us rejoice and be glad in His salvation."

Today as we celebrate the Savior's birth, contemplate what he did, what he still does, and what he will ultimately do at the end of the earthly age. Jesus, born of a virgin in the most humble of circumstances, came to die. He came that we might have new life and life in all its fullness! Jesus is the Light of the World, the Prince of Peace, and the embodiment of God's good will towards men. He created us, loves us, cares for us, and died for us. Christmas is more than a holiday or a time of remembrance. It is the beginning of the end for the hateful Enemy of God. It is God with us, for us, and in us. "'O death, where is your victory? O death, where is your sting?' The sting of death is sin, and the power of sin is the law; but thanks be to God, who gives us the victory through our Lord Jesus Christ" (1 Cor. 15:55-57 NASB). What elation will be ours at the culmination of Christ's triumph, when the One we trusted and waited for is victorious! Behold, this is our God; we trusted in him and he saved us (Ps. 62:5-8; Rev. 21:3-6). Worthy is the Lamb!

PRAYER FOCUS: Lord Jesus, thank you for life and life abundant. Lord, I am deeply humbled by the knowledge that no one took your life from you, but that you willingly laid it down for a sinner like me. Jesus, there is none like you! You alone are worthy of all my praise, and I will delight daily in your salvation.

DID YOU KNOW? The Christmas classic *It's a Wonderful Life* is based on a short story written by Philip Van Doren Stern titled "The Greatest Gift." In 1943, Stern sent two hundred copies of his twenty-four-page short story to friends and family for Christmas, despite his unsuccessful attempts to publish. Three years later Frank Capra's production company, having bought the rights to the story, made the now classic film.[21] The movie's strong pro-life message is perfect for Christmas because the value of every human life is what Christmas is all about.

REFLECTIONS

DECEMBER 26

Matthew 25:31-36 ESV

When the Son of Man comes in his glory, and all the angels with him, then he will sit on his glorious throne. Before him will be gathered all the nations, and he will separate people one from another as a shepherd separates the sheep from the goats. And he will place the sheep on his right, but the goats on the left. Then the King will say to those on his right, "Come, you who are blessed by my Father, inherit the kingdom prepared for you from the foundation of the world. For I was hungry and you gave me food, I was thirsty and you gave me drink, I was a stranger and you welcomed me, I was naked and you clothed me, I was sick and you visited me, I was in prison and you came to me."

Jesus spoke these words to his disciples on the Mount of Olives concerning the end of the age. Remarkably in this passage about judgment between those who have chosen to follow God and those who have not, there is no mention of obvious sin or individual merit. No, instead the focus is on the love of one's neighbor and the people's concern for the least of these. The focus is on our display of Christ-like love and compassion for others. God wants us to live like he lived and follow his example. He wants us to do what he did. When the five thousand were hungry, he fed them with five loaves and two fish (Matt. 14:15-21). When the Israelites were thirsty, God brought forth water from a rock (Deut. 8:15). Jesus quenches the thirst of everyone who will accept his invitation to salvation (John 4:13-26; Rev. 22:17). God welcomes the stranger and makes provision for them (Lev. 19:33-34; Deut. 10:17-19; Rom. 5:6-10). He clothes the naked (Gen. 3:10, 21; Luke 8:26-35), visits and heals the sick (Matt. 14:14; Mark 5:21-43), and comforts, visits, and releases the prisoner (Gen. 39:20-21; Isa. 61:1; Acts 5:17-20; 12:6-11). At the end of the age, and at all times, Jesus is pleased with those people who love, serve, and sacrifice like their Savior.

PRAYER FOCUS: Jesus, help me to perceive the needs of others and, when I can, to meet those needs. Lord, grant me favor, wisdom, provision, and discernment as I address the needs around me. Father, assist me with everything I do through your Holy Spirit and prayer. Thank you, God, that in all things you are my example.

DID YOU KNOW? Corrie ten Boom is credited with saying, "The measure of a life . . . is not its duration, but its donation."[22] Clearly, the ten Booms loved their neighbors. Corrie records this prayer in *The Hiding Place*: "Lord Jesus, I offer myself for Your people. In any way. Any place. Any time."[23] What will the measure of our lives be? I pray that when our lives are complete, we will be counted among the sheep.

REFLECTIONS

DECEMBER 27

Matthew 25:37-40 ESV

Then the righteous will answer him, saying, "Lord, when did we see you hungry and feed you, or thirsty and give you drink? And when did we see you a stranger and welcome you, or naked and clothe you? And when did we see you sick or in prison and visit you?" And the King will answer them, "Truly, I say to you, as you did it to one of the least of these my brothers, you did it to me."

∞

The righteous, knowing they never personally did these things for Jesus and humbled by the knowledge that without Christ they fell well below the mark, ask when they did these things for Christ. So the King, in his response, clarifies that kindness, care, and love expressed to our fellow human beings is received by God as love for him, especially to those of the faith. When God chooses to conceive new life in a woman, he gives her and her partner a gift and a tremendous opportunity to love and care for the least of these. Certainly in the womb and throughout their lives, our children will be hungry, thirsty, naked, or in need of clothing, and potentially sick or in prison. By accepting and loving our preborn children, we also have the opportunity to care for the stranger. While our children share many attributes with us, they are also strangers who are unique and unknown to us and others, especially in the womb. Bearing, adopting, and raising children are ways for each of us to demonstrate our faith and trust in God and his plans for us. Loving the least of these certainly involves caring for our own children and families, but it goes beyond that to helping the needy, broken, wayward, and oppressed among us. When believers help others and stand up for preborn children by working toward the cessation of legalized abortion, we reflect the character of Christ and evidence his presence working within us to the glory of God.

PRAYER FOCUS: Jesus, human beings are a gift and a treasure. Help me to never forget the value of every person regardless of size, age, race, gender, ability, function, or location. Lord, give me a heart and a passion for the welfare of others both close to me and far away. Jesus, allow me to see you in your children and your children in you.

DID YOU KNOW? More and more Christian artists are engaging the culture through the popular media of movies. Films like *The Passion of the Christ*, *Facing the Giants*, *Fireproof*, and *Soul Surfer* have enjoyed success. If you haven't done so already, check out the films *Letters to God*, *To Save a Life*, and *October Baby*. Trust Christ—live for him—love what he loves, and one day upon his merits we will find ourselves humbled to be among his sheep.

DECEMBER 28

1 John 3:16-19 NIV

This is how we know what love is: Jesus Christ laid down his life for us. And we ought to lay down our lives for our brothers. If anyone has material possessions and sees his brother in need but has no pity on him, how can the love of God be in him? Dear children, let us not love with words or tongue but with actions and in truth. This then is how we know that we belong to the truth, and how we set our hearts at rest in his presence.

John, the apostle of love, said it best: we are to be like Jesus! Jesus died for us and if need be, we should lay down our lives for others whom God loves. The collective church has tremendous resources in man power and material goods, and our preborn neighbors have been in great need since 1967. How can we help them? What can we do to assist them in their distress? We can love them not just with words or tongue but with actions and the truth! We can tell everyone we know about the dignity of human life, fetal development, and the scriptural support for life's value from conception to the Lord's determined end. We can pursue pro-life ballot initiatives and vote in unison for pro-life legislation. No one who aligns himself with Christ should ever vote pro-choice or pro-abortion. James wrote, "Anyone, then, who knows the good he ought to do and doesn't do it, sins" (James 4:17 NIV). We can become educated and remain educated through pro-life books, organizations, and Internet resources. We can intercede, protest, counsel, and rescue at the abortion facility. We can assist and help the pregnant and post-abortive. We must pray, give, and mobilize the body of Christ for action. We can share the truth boldly in the public square through radio, television, the halls of government, the church, the schools, and on the Internet. If we seek God for guidance and search for opportunities to get involved, we can turn the tide in the battle and assist the Lord as he sets the captives free. Christians have to take action and keep taking action until the victory is won, setting our hearts at rest as we love the least of these, his children.

PRAYER FOCUS: Lord, make me a doer of your Word and not just a hearer only. Father, assist the body of Christ as we assist your people. Holy One, protect us, sustain us, love us, help us, embolden us, fight with us, and provide for us as we enter the fray. Holy Spirit, grant us peace, wisdom, and joy as we work for the good of our neighbors. Gracious Father, defeat the Enemy!

DID YOU KNOW? On this date in 1973, President Nixon signed the Endangered Species Act to protect certain species and the ecosystems they depend on. Upon signing the act Nixon said, "*Nothing is more priceless and more worthy of preservation than the rich array of animal life with which our country has been blessed.*"[24] Just eleven months earlier, our Supreme Court decided that human life was not worthy to be protected in the environment of the womb!

DECEMBER 29

Luke 18:1-8 ESV

And he told them a parable to the effect that they ought always to pray and not lose heart. He said, "In a certain city there was a judge who neither feared God nor respected man. And there was a widow in that city who kept coming to him and saying, 'Give me justice against my adversary.' For a while he refused, but afterward he said to himself, 'Though I neither fear God nor respect man, yet because this widow keeps bothering me, I will give her justice, so that she will not beat me down by her continual coming.' And the Lord said, 'Hear what the unrighteous judge says. And will not God give justice to his elect, who cry to him day and night? Will he delay long over them? I tell you, he will give justice to them speedily. Nevertheless, when the Son of Man comes, will he find faith on earth?'"

Jesus used this parable about the persistent widow to encourage his disciples that God would always be with them and answer their prayers for justice. Unlike the unjust judge, God cares for his children and sees to it that they receive justice. All we need to do is ask and believe! The Lord is telling us how to achieve social justice in an unjust world—one that is corrupted by sin and submitted to the flesh. We are to address any injustice we see through prevailing prayer and persistent action. The widow didn't just merely pray for relief and justice; rather, she sought it diligently and relentlessly. As we pursue justice for preborn babies, we must earnestly pray to our just Father for aid and victory and relentlessly pursue those in power, who may not fear God or respect people, until we receive justice. If we are pursuing legal and legislative change, we must not quit after one or two or three failed measures. No, we must continue until hearts are changed, votes are amassed, and victory is won. If we are praying, demonstrating, or rescuing at the abortion facility, we must not stop until we close the facility down or convince all their pregnant clients to choose life. If we are educating and equipping the church or the nation, we must not stop until our students are educated, motivated, and focused on the goal of overturning legalized abortion. Action is the key, but it will fizzle out and fade away without faith and prayer. God must be our ever-present supply or we fight in vain.

PRAYER FOCUS: Father, give us justice against our adversaries and set the hidden victims in the womb free! Lord, give us patience, self-control, energy, and doggedness as we fight for life and pursue equality for all people. Set the truth of human worth before us as we partner with you in bringing grace, truth, and love to the people.

DID YOU KNOW? The recent documentary film *Blood Money* is a powerful look at abortion in America from the pro-life perspective. Among the many clips in the film is a speech by Ronald Reagan in which he stated, "More than a decade ago, a Supreme Court decision literally wiped off the books of fifty states statutes protecting the rights of unborn children. Abortion on demand now takes the lives of up to one and a half million unborn children a year. Human life legislation ending this tragedy will someday pass the Congress, and you and I must never rest until it does."[25] Over two decades have passed since these words of Reagan and still we cannot rest!

DECEMBER 30

Colossians 3:12-17 NIV

Therefore, as God's chosen people, holy and dearly loved, clothe yourselves with compassion, kindness, humility, gentleness and patience. Bear with each other and forgive whatever grievances you may have against one another. Forgive as the Lord forgave you. And over all these virtues put on love, which binds them all together in perfect unity. Let the peace of Christ rule in your hearts, since as members of one body you were called to peace. And be thankful. Let the word of Christ dwell in you richly as you teach and admonish one another with all wisdom, and as you sing psalms, hymns and spiritual songs with gratitude in your hearts to God. And whatever you do, whether in word or deed, do it all in the name of the Lord Jesus, giving thanks to God the Father through him.

∞

As believers who go forth in this mission field to save lives, help our neighbors, and wake up society, we need to remember who we are and act accordingly. We are God's chosen people who are holy and dearly loved! We must walk with Christ and allow his Spirit to produce in us a harvest of peace and life. As the apostle Paul said, "The fruit of the Spirit is love, joy, peace, patience, kindness, goodness, faithfulness, gentleness and self-control. Against such things there is no law" (Gal. 5:22-23 NIV). Compassion, kindness, humility, gentleness, and patience should be the hallmark of all our efforts to bring the church and the nation back to life. Love and forgiveness must be the banner we carry and the approach we take with those who are wounded, hurting, confused, and lost. Moment to moment and even in our difficult times, we need to ask Christ for his peace so we can be ministers of peace. Each day as we journey through this valley, let us remain grateful to our God for his mercy, grace, provision, miracles, love, and fellowship. We must spend time in God's marvelous Word and allow it to direct our path, nourish our souls, and renew our mind. Finally, brothers and sisters, whatever we do in the cause for life, do it all in the name of Jesus, giving thanks to him who is able to do more than we think or ask, according to the power of God at work within us (Eph. 3:20).

PRAYER FOCUS: Jesus, you are wonderfully good! Holy Spirit, guide us into all truth and lead us in the way everlasting. Go before us, making a river in the desert, a way in the wilderness. Father, give us a broken heart for your children and a love for everyone you have made.

DID YOU KNOW? Jesus made us to love. How then can we not love now and for all eternity? In his sermon titled "The Drum Major Instinct," Martin Luther King, Jr. said it well: "Jesus gave us a new norm of greatness . . . he who is greatest among you shall be your servant. That's a new definition of greatness. And this morning, the thing I like about it: by giving that definition of greatness, it means that everybody can be great, because everybody can serve. You don't have to have a college degree to serve. You don't have to make your subject and your verb agree to serve. You don't have to know about Plato and Aristotle to serve. You don't have to know Einstein's theory of relativity to serve. You don't have to know the second theory of thermodynamics in physics to serve. *You only need a heart full of grace, a soul generated by love.* And you can be that servant."[26] Let us serve humanity with love regardless of their race, gender, size, ability, function, location, creed, or degree of development.

DECEMBER 31

Jude 24-25 NASB

Now to Him who is able to keep you from stumbling, and to make you stand in the presence of His glory blameless with great joy, to the only God our Savior, through Jesus Christ our Lord, be glory, majesty, dominion and authority, before all time and now and forever. Amen.

Think of it—God is able to keep us from stumbling and present us blameless in his presence with great joy! What grace and freedom we have in Jesus Christ our Lord! He who has all glory, majesty, dominion, and authority has declared us worthy, based on our faith and his righteousness. What a Savior and what a friend we have in Jesus. Fully persuaded by the Word and confident in our Savior, we can go forth in the glory of new life and love him and his children. Behold, "If anyone is in Christ, he is a new creature; the old things passed away; behold, new things have come. Now all these things are from God, who reconciled us to Himself through Christ and gave us the ministry of reconciliation, namely, that God was in Christ reconciling the world to Himself, not counting their trespasses against them, and He has committed to us the word of reconciliation. Therefore, we are ambassadors for Christ, as though God were making an appeal through us; we beg you on behalf of Christ, be reconciled to God. He made Him who knew no sin to be sin on our behalf, so that we might become the righteousness of God in Him" (2 Cor. 5:17-21 NASB). In 1963, Martin Luther King, Jr., stirred the nation with his "I Have a Dream" speech. In like manner, I hope this dream to abolish abortion has stirred my readers to judge our children not by the color of their skin or their journey in the womb, but according to the God who created them and by the future content of their character. Let the children live! Choose life, make a stand for life, and cherish life. Let them live, because love is for eternity!

PRAYER FOCUS: Jesus, your greatness and love are unmatched! Your sacrifice proves my worth, and your grace is as comforting as it is overwhelming. Lord, use my life for your glory and the good of your people. Holy Spirit, speak to me and bring me peace. Father, I pray that everyone would know your Word, hear your voice, and make you their greatest choice!

DID YOU KNOW? The name of Jesus and the word "life" occur together in over twenty-five verses in the New Testament.[27] Jesus said in the gospel of John, "I am the bread of life; he who comes to Me will not hunger, and he who believes in Me will never thirst" (John 6:35 NASB). Satisfaction is found in Jesus!

The Illustrator

Many thanks to Robin Coran for her efforts in providing the illustrations that depict the miracle of human development in the womb and add so much to this work. Robin is a tireless advocate for the preborn and the inherent value of every human life. To find out more about Robin and her artwork please visit her on Facebook or email her at *robin.coran@gmail.com*.

∞

The Author

Joel Patchen is the founder and president of Anna's Choice, LLC. Anna's Choice is a ministry that seeks to abolish abortion in America and the world by motivating the body of Christ to take action. We encourage you to check out our Website, *annaschoice.org*. Learn more about Anna's Choice, obtain other books by the author, or purchase the *Who Am I?* Bible study to lead in your church or small group. Joel lives in Colorado with his wife, Michelle. They have five children: three sons and two daughters, one of whom is in heaven. Look for *Letters to My Dad: Diary of a Preborn Daughter* on Amazon and discover the impact Brooke's life had on the author. Joel is available for teaching, speaking engagements, conferences, and sanctity of life events. To inquire about an appearance, please contact Anna's Choice at joel@annaschoice.org.

∞

Scripture Index

OLD TESTAMENT

Genesis 1:27-28 — January 5
Genesis 4:1 — February 5
Genesis 4:7-12 — October 25
Genesis 9:4-7 — August 9
Genesis 18:25-26 — August 12
Genesis 20:17-18 — June 29
Genesis 25:21-24 — August 29
Genesis 45:4-7 — November 11
Exodus 1:15-21 — April 11
Exodus 1:22 — August 22
Exodus 4:11-12 — March 4
Exodus 20:16 — September 23
Exodus 21:22-24 — April 30
Exodus 23:6-7 — March 21
Exodus 23:25-26 — March 9
Leviticus 17:11-14 — January 30
Leviticus 19:15-18 — November 8
Leviticus 19:32 — October 7
Leviticus 20:1-5 — August 4
Leviticus 25:18-19 — November 7
Numbers 11:11-14 — December 10
Numbers 12:6-8 — August 3
Numbers 35:33 — June 3
Deuteronomy 7:6-9 — October 13
Deuteronomy 8:17-18 — February 18
Deuteronomy 10:17-19 — July 14
Deuteronomy 21:1-9 — September 20
Deuteronomy 24:16-18 — February 6
Deuteronomy 27:24-25 — September 11
Deuteronomy 30:15-16 — April 19
Deuteronomy 30:19-20 — September 26
Deuteronomy 33:26-27 — April 20
Joshua 1:8-9 — May 30
Joshua 7:10-12 — October 18
Joshua 10:12-14 — October 19
Judges 6:14-16 — October 20
Judges 6:30-32 — October 21
Judges 13:2-5 — June 14
Ruth 2:11-12 — June 22
Ruth 4:13-17 — July 10

1 Samuel 1:27-28 — September 15
1 Samuel 15:24-29 — November 20
1 Samuel 17:32-36 — December 4
1 Samuel 17:38-40 — December 5
1 Samuel 26:23-25 — May 18
2 Samuel 14:14 — March 10
2 Samuel 22:31 — January 12
2 Samuel 23:2-4 — April 16
1 Kings 3:9-13 — November 13
1 Kings 10:9 — June 23
1 Kings 18:1-4 — July 28
1 Kings 18:21 — October 22
2 Kings 8:11-13 — October 26
2 Kings 18:5-7 — June 24
1 Chronicles 5:18-20 — June 6
1 Chronicles 25:4-6 — August 11
1 Chronicles 29:11-12 — October 5
2 Chronicles 7:13-14 — January 25
2 Chronicles 14:11 — March 7
2 Chronicles 20:12-17 — July 6
Ezra 4:4-5 — June 21
Nehemiah 9:26-28 — May 25
Esther 4:11-16 — May 29
Job 2:9-10 — August 20
Job 24:12 — January 17
Job 29:11-17 — August 21
Job 31:13-15 — May 15
Job 31:21-23 — May 24
Job 39:1-2 — October 27
Psalm 2:10-12 — July 4
Psalm 6:8-10 — December 2
Psalm 7:1-2 — May 14
Psalm 9:7-12 — July 18
Psalm 10:1-3 — April 3
Psalm 10:4-8 — April 4
Psalm 10:9-14 — April 5
Psalm 19:1-4 — March 18
Psalm 19:7-11 — February 26
Psalm 22:30-31 — May 8
Psalm 25:4-7 — September 10

Psalm 27:1 — March 1
Psalm 30:11-12 — February 7
Psalm 32:1-5 — March 15
Psalm 33:6-9 — November 2
Psalm 33:13-22 — August 18
Psalm 34:8 — April 2
Psalm 36:5-9 — May 26
Psalm 40:4-5 — July 22
Psalm 50:10-12 — April 9
Psalm 50:14-15 — August 25
Psalm 51:1-4 — December 16
Psalm 55:4-6 — December 7
Psalm 59:1-5 — December 1
Psalm 62:5-8 — July 24
Psalm 68:19-20 — September 12
Psalm 71:5-6, 17-18 — June 28
Psalm 72:18-19 — July 3
Psalm 73:12-19 — August 17
Psalm 76: 7-9 — March 30
Psalm 78:5-7 — May 1
Psalm 82:2-4 — February 9
Psalm 90:10-12 — August 26
Psalm 94:3-7 — March 6
Psalm 94:16 — March 24
Psalm 94:20-21 — April 10
Psalm 102:18-20 — February 1
Psalm 103:8-12 — June 19
Psalm 106:36-41 — September 17
Psalm 107:1-3 — March 23
Psalm 110:5-6 — November 15
Psalm 119:11 — April 7
Psalm 119:57-60 — April 17
Psalm 119:115-117 — September 27
Psalm 121 — December 13
Psalm 126:5-6 — January 26
Psalm 127:3 — January 6
Psalm 128 — April 27
Psalm 139:13-16 — January 2
Psalm 142:1-2 — January 18
Psalm 142:3-5 — January 19
Psalm 142:6-7 — January 20
Psalm 145:8-12 — November 14
Psalm 146 — August 5
Psalm 150 — June 16
Proverbs 3:27-31 — November 30
Proverbs 10:2 — May 20
Proverbs 12:6 — March 12
Proverbs 13:22 — October 6

Proverbs 14:25-27 — February 13
Proverbs 14:31 — November 9
Proverbs 14:34 — December 3
Proverbs 15:28 — September 22
Proverbs 17:6 — October 1
Proverbs 17:15 — January 24
Proverbs 17:22 — August 30
Proverbs 19:18 — October 8
Proverbs 19:9 — February 16
Proverbs 21:6-7 — October 3
Proverbs 22:2 — March 11
Proverbs 24:10-12 — February 10
Proverbs 28:12-13 — July 31
Proverbs 29:12-14 — August 10
Proverbs 31:8-9 — January 23
Ecclesiastes 7:20 — July 20
Ecclesiastes 9:4-6 — November 12
Ecclesiastes 11:4 — August 1
Ecclesiastes 11:5 — January 10
Song Of Songs 8:6-7 — February 14
Isaiah 1:13-17 — September 18
Isaiah 1:18-20 — September 19
Isaiah 5:20-23 — April 13
Isaiah 9:6-7 — January 13
Isaiah 10:1-3 — July 17
Isaiah 14:12-15 — September 9
Isaiah 25:8-9 — December 25
Isaiah 26:9-10 — November 18
Isaiah 42:5-6 — July 9
Isaiah 43:18-19 — February 25
Isaiah 45:9-12 — January 22
Isaiah 46:3-4 — January 1
Isaiah 48:9-11 — November 16
Isaiah 48:17-19 — January 31
Isaiah 49:1 — September 25
Isaiah 49:15-16 — March 3
Isaiah 54:10 — May 11
Isaiah 55:6-7 — May 3
Isaiah 55:9-11 — September 2
Isaiah 57:1-2 — August 27
Isaiah 58:2-4 — March 27
Isaiah 58:6-9 — March 28
Isaiah 61:1-4 — June 20
Isaiah 64:6-8 — March 25
Jeremiah 1:4-5 — February 23
Jeremiah 1:11-12 — August 2
Jeremiah 7:28-34 — December 6
Jeremiah 8:5-6 — May 2

Jeremiah 17:5-8 — November 19
Jeremiah 18:7-10 — March 29
Jeremiah 29:11 — March 8
Lamentations 2:19 — January 28
Lamentations 3:22-23 — March 5
Lamentations 3:48-50 — April 26
Ezekiel 7:23-25 — July 12
Ezekiel 16:20-22 — February 4
Ezekiel 18:30-32 — March 13
Ezekiel 22:29-30 — February 12
Daniel 2:22 — October 9
Daniel 3:16-18 — August 19
Daniel 9:4-6 — May 5
Daniel 9:8-11 — May 6
Daniel 9:17-19 — May 7
Hosea 4:1-3 — June 26
Hosea 4:6 — October 16
Hosea 9:10-11 — August 13
Hosea 14:9 — October 2
Joel 1:2-3 — June 17
Joel 2:12-14 — December 15
Joel 3:21 — December 19
Amos 5:14-15 — May 31
Obadiah 15 — June 2
Jonah 2:8 — June 15
Jonah 3:5-10 — October 11
Jonah 4:10-11 — October 12
Micah 6:8 — January 15
Micah 7:18-19 — January 11
Nahum 1:3 — September 6
Nahum 3:1 — March 20
Habakkuk 1:2-4 — May 16
Zephaniah 3:17 — May 17
Haggai 1:14-15 — June 10
Zechariah 3:1-5 — December 14
Zechariah 7:9-13 — September 7
Zechariah 8:16-17 — January 14
Malachi 2:15 — September 4
Malachi 4:5-6 — April 24

NEW TESTAMENT

Matthew 4:16 — December 8
Matthew 5:17-18 — May 9
Matthew 5:44-45 — January 29
Matthew 6:25-27 — September 21
Matthew 6:33-34 — November 10
Matthew 10:16-20 — May 28

Matthew 10:28-31 — August 28
Matthew 12:11-12 — February 3
Matthew 12:35-37 — March 31
Matthew 18:7 — October 10
Matthew 18:21-22 — October 15
Matthew 22:17-21 — February 17
Matthew 23:23-24 — May 13
Matthew 23:29-37 — November 6
Matthew 25:31-36 — December 26
Matthew 25:37-40 — December 27
Matthew 26:28 — March 22
Matthew 28:18-20 — September 30
Mark 5:35-36 — June 5
Mark 9:40-42 — July 19
Mark 10:6-9 — September 3
Mark 12:41-44 — December 12
Mark 13:31 — October 17
Luke 1:34-37 — April 8
Luke 1:41-44 — October 28
Luke 5:30-32 — March 14
Luke 6:22 — September 29
Luke 6:36-38 — April 6
Luke 7:37-48 — December 18
Luke 10:25-37 — December 22
Luke 11:46 — April 28
Luke 12:2-3 — October 29
Luke 12:6-7 — January 16
Luke 12:43-48 — November 21
Luke 18:1-8 — December 29
Luke 18:15-17 — April 25
Luke 19:4-10 — May 12
Luke 21:23-24 — May 10
Luke 23:27-31 — September 13
Luke 23:33-34 — August 16
John 3:4-10 — September 14
John 4:13-14 — July 5
John 5:24 — May 19
John 8:3-11 — December 24
John 8:44 — June 9
John 10:10-15 — July 15
John 11:21-27 — August 8
John 13:34-35 — November 5
John 14:5-6 — April 14
John 15:18-20 — November 23
Acts 2:38-39 — May 27
Acts 3:2-6 — July 1
Acts 5:25-29 — November 22
Acts 8:29-35 — August 31

Acts 10:34-35 — March 26
Acts 15:18 — September 24
Acts 17:24-28 — April 18
Romans 1:16-17 — April 21
Romans 1:19-20 — January 7
Romans 6:23 — February 2
Romans 8:31-39 — July 7
Romans 9:10-12 — July 13
Romans 12:17-19 — September 1
Romans 13:1, 6-7 — April 15
Romans 13:8-11 — January 27
Romans 15:1-4 — April 22
Romans 15:5-6 — February 15
Romans 15:13 — August 7
1 Corinthians 1:26-31 — June 11
1 Corinthians 10:24 — September 28
1 Corinthians 13:4-8 — January 21
1 Corinthians 15:54-58 — July 16
2 Corinthians 1:3-4 — December 23
2 Corinthians 1:8-11 — November 28
2 Corinthians 4:17-18 — June 27
2 Corinthians 5:17-21 — July 21
2 Corinthians 7:10-11 — February 11
2 Corinthians 9:6-8 — August 23
Galatians 1:11-16 — September 5
Galatians 2:20-21 — October 31
Galatians 5:14 — July 8
Galatians 6:9-10 — May 22
Ephesians 1:3-7 — November 4
Ephesians 2:8-10 — November 3
Ephesians 2:13-16 — July 11
Ephesians 3:14-20 — November 25
Ephesians 5:7-11 — October 30
Ephesians 6:10-13 — June 7
Ephesians 6:14-18 — June 8
Philippians 1:9-14 — December 11
Philippians 2:3-11 — June 30
Philippians 4:4-9 — June 12
Colossians 1:11-14 — December 9
Colossians 1:15-20 — January 8
Colossians 2:9-14 — August 14
Colossians 3:1-4 — August 24
Colossians 3:12-17 — December 30
Colossians 4:2-4 — February 8
1 Thessalonians 2:7-8, 11-12 — July 2
1 Thessalonians 2:13 — November 1
1 Thessalonians 5:14-15 — May 4
2 Thessalonians 1:6-9 — June 13

2 Thessalonians 2:15-17 — September 16
1 Timothy 2:1-8 — November 27
1 Timothy 4:4-5 — February 24
1 Timothy 4:7-8 — April 1
1 Timothy 6:17-19 — October 4
2 Timothy 1:7-10 — February 28
2 Timothy 3:1-5 — November 17
2 Timothy 3:16-17 — January 3
2 Timothy 4:1-5 — August 6
2 Timothy 4:18-21 — October 23
Titus 2:11-14 — June 1
Philemon 4-7 — April 23
Hebrews 2:14-17 — January 9
Hebrews 3:4 — January 4
Hebrews 4:12-13 — March 19
Hebrews 4:14-16 — December 17
Hebrews 6:10 — April 29
Hebrews 10:12-14 — November 29
Hebrews 12:22-24 — August 15
Hebrews 13:3-8 — July 30
James 1:12 — February 19
James 1:22-25 — February 27
James 2:12-13 — October 14
James 2:24-26 — February 21
James 5:5-6 — February 20
James 5:19-20 — May 23
1 Peter 1:18-23 — December 20
1 Peter 2:24 — March 17
1 Peter 3:13-17 — July 26
1 Peter 4:17-19 — May 21
1 Peter 5:6-10 — November 24
2 Peter 1:3-11 — July 25
2 Peter 1:16-21 — June 25
1 John 1:8-9 — March 16
1 John 2:15-17 — July 23
1 John 3:1 — March 2
1 John 3:16-19 — December 28
1 John 3:23-24 — November 26
1 John 4:7 — April 12
1 John 4:10-11 — December 21
2 John 5-6 — June 18
3 John 11 — June 4
3 John 4-8 — July 29
Jude 20-23 — July 27
Jude 24-25 — December 31
Revelation 3:14-19 — September 8
Revelation 4:11 — February 22
Revelation 12:10-11 — October 24

Notes

JANUARY

1. Randy Alcorn, *Why Pro-Life?* (Sandy, Ore.: Eternal Perspective Ministries, 2004), 28. See also R. Houwink, *Data: Mirrors of Science* (New York: American Elsevier Publishing, 1970), 104-190.
2. I owe much in this summary to Josh McDowell, *The New Evidence that Demands a Verdict* (Nashville, Tenn: Thomas Nelson Publishers, 1999), 4.
3. Russell Ash, *Firefly's World of Facts* (Buffalo, NY: Firefly Books, 2007), 203.
4. Peter Tallack, *In the Womb* (Washington, D.C.: National Geographic Society, 2006), 28.
5. The Globalist Quiz, "Child adoptions worldwide," *The Boston Globe*, July 8, 2007, www.boston.com/news/world/articles/2007/07/08/child_adoptions_worldwide/.
6. Michael Denton, *Evolution: A Theory in Crisis* (Chevy Chase, Md.: Adler & Adler Publishers, 1996), 162. See also Denton's description of the cell's complexity, 328-331.
7. Josh McDowell, *The New Evidence that Demands a Verdict* (Nashville, Tenn: Thomas Nelson Publishers, 1999), 164-202.
8. Tallack, 58, 86.
9. Ash, 41.
10. Elmer L. Towns, *The Names of Jesus* (Colorado Springs, Colo: Accent Publications, 1987), 145-167.
11. Merrill F. Unger, *Unger's Bible Dictionary*, third edition (Chicago: Moody Press, 1966), 717.
12. Craig Brian Larson and Brian Lowery, editors, *1001 Quotations That Connect: Timeless Wisdom for Preaching, Teaching, and Writing* (Grand Rapids, Mich: Zondervan, 2009), 78.
13. Author's own calculation based on a salary of $33,000,000 per year and 162 games played at three hours in length. See www.msn.foxsports.com/mlb/player/alex-rodriguez/85368.
14. Author's own calculation based on an abortion rate of 1.2 million babies per year. See www.abort73.com/abortion_facts/us_abortion_statistics.
15. Tallack, 50.
16. Guttmacher Institute in Brief, "Facts on Induced Abortion in the United States," the Alan Guttmacher Institute, May 2010, www.guttmacher.org/pubs/fb_induced_abortion.html.
17. John C. Willke and Barbara H. Willke, *Abortion Questions & Answers* (Cincinnati, Ohio: Hayes Publishing Company, 2003), 38-46.
18. William Shakespeare, *The Complete Works of William Shakespeare* (Avenel, N.J.: Gramercy Books, 1990), 1088.
19. Willke and Willke, 302.
20. Alcorn, 15.
21. WORDsearch 8. *Preaching Library*. Computer software. WORDsearch Corp., 2008. —Search in NIV for "love." Psalms and 1 John calculations based on number of occurring sections.
22. "woe." *Webster's Compact Dictionary*, 2001.
23. Alcorn, 79. Repeated in Sue Reily, "Life Uneasy for Women at Center of Abortion Ruling," *The Oregonian*, 9 May 1989, A2.
24. Salary.com, "Salary.com's 9th Annual Mom Salary Survey Reveals Stay-at-Home Moms Would Earn $122,732 in the U.S. and $135,661 in Canada," marketwire.

com, May 5, 2009, http://www.marketwire.
com/press-release/Salarycoms-9th-Annual-
Mom-Salary-Survey-Reveals-Stay-
Home-Moms-Would-Earn-122732-US-
NASDAQ-SLRY-984585.htm.

25 Religion of Founding Fathers, "Religious
Affiliation of the Founding Fathers of the
United States of America," Adherents.
com, November 4, 2005, www.adherents.
com/gov/Founding_Fathers_Religion.html.
(Signers who switched affiliation from
one denomination to another have been
counted twice in the tabulation).

26 Larry Schweikart and Michael Allen, A
Patriots History of the United States: From
Columbus's Great Discovery To The War On

Terror (New York: Penguin Group, 2004),
71.

27 John Ensor, Answering the Call (Colorado
Springs, Colo.: Focus on the Family,
2003), 21.

28 Carol Everett with Jack Shaw, Blood
Money (Sisters, Ore.: Multnomah Books,
1992), 69, 79-93, 176.

29 "neighbor." Webster's Compact Dictionary,
2001.

30 Tallack, 52.

31 Eddie James, Life. Compact disc. Fresh
Wine Records. Jacket lyrics.

32 Tallack, 36.

33 McDowell, 34.

FEBRUARY

1 Statistics, "Death Row Fact Sheet,"
Florida Department of Corrections,
accessed August 15, 2010, www.dc.state.
fl.us/oth/deathrow/index.html.

2 Tallack, 148.

3 Scott Klusendorf, Pro-Life 101: A Step-by-
Step Guide to Making Your Case Persuasively
(Signal Hill, Calif.: Stand to Reason Press,
2002), 12.

4 Willke and Willke, 150-156.

5 Sarah Peterson Hage, editor, The Book
of Bible Names (Wheaton, Ill.: Tyndale
House Publishers, 1997), 6, 14.

6 Ensor, 96. Repeated in, Frederica
Mathewes-Green, Real Choices: Offering
Practical, Life-Affirming Alternatives to
Abortion (Sisters, Ore.: Multnomah Books,
1994), 248, and David Reardon, Aborted
Women, Silent No More (Chicago: Loyola
University Press, 1997), xi.

7 John Newton, Out of the Depths (Grand
Rapids, Mich.: Kregel Publications, 2003,
revised and updated by Dennis Hillman),
149, 158.

8 Tallack, 148.

9 Key Facts at a Glance, "Number of
persons executed in the United States,
1930-2009," Bureau of Justice Statistics,
Statistical Tables, December 2009, http://

bjs.ojp.usdoj.gov/content/glance/tables/
exetab.cfm.

10 Women and the Death Penalty, "Eleven
females have been executed since
1976," Death Penalty Information
Center, accessed August 16, 2010, www.
deathpenaltyinfo.org/women-and-death-
penalty.

11 Willke and Willke, 53, 54.

12 Ibid., 82.

13 Be Mine, "Valentine's Day by the
Numbers," U.S. Census Bureau, 2007,
www.infoplease.com/spot/valcensus1.html.

14 Harold Evens, The American Century
(New York: Alfred A. Knopf, 1998), 314.

15 Willke and Willke, 374-377. See also
Schweikart and Allen, 530-532.

16 Annual Report 2007-2008, "Summary of
Services Delivered by Planned Parenthood
Affiliate Health Centers: Calendar Years
2006 and 2007," Planned Parenthood,
page 9 of 24, www.plannedparenthood.org/
files/AR08_vFinal.pdf.

17 Tallack, 144.

18 William Wilberforce, Real Christianity,
revised by Bob Beltz (Ventura, Calif: Regal
Books, 2006), 13.

19 Ensor, 18. Also, Alan Guttmacher
Institute, "Induced Abortion," Facts in

Brief, February 2002. This fact sheet says, "The data in this fact sheet are the most current available. Most are from research conducted by the Alan Guttmacher Institute. An additional source is the Centers for Disease Control and Prevention."

[20] Tallack, 56, 148.

[21] *Ibid.*, 56.

[22] Casting Crowns, *Lifesong*. Compact disc. Sony BMG Music Entertainment, 2005.

[23] David C. Reardon, Julie Makimaa, and Amy Sobie, *Victims and Victors: Speaking Out about their Pregnancies, Abortions, and Children Resulting from Sexual Assault* (Springfield, Ill.: Acorn Books, 2000), ix-x.

[24] Reardon, et al., 63.

[25] *Ibid.*, et al. x.

[26] Ash, 38.

[27] *Ibid.*, 230.

[28] Tallack, 60. Repeated in Alcorn, 33.

MARCH

[1] Thomas Euteneuer, "How Many Heisman Winners has Abortion Killed?" Spirit & Life—Human Life International, Volume 01, Number 96, December 14, 2007, www.hli.org/index.php?option=com_acajoom&act=mailing&task=view&listid=2&mailingid=47

[2] WORDsearch 8. *Preaching Library*. Computer software. WORDsearch Corp., 2008. —Search in NIV for "children." Genesis and Matthew calculations based on number of occurring sections.

[3] Alcorn, 43. Repeated in Jennifer Kabbany, "Abortion vs. Ultrasound," *Washington Times*, October 29, 2003.

[4] Willke and Willke, 208.

[5] C. H. Spurgeon, *All of Grace: An Earnest Word to those who are Seeking Salvation by the Lord Jesus Christ* (Chicago, Ill.: Moody Press, 2010), 32.

[6] WISQARS, "Leading Causes of Death Report," (report years 1981-1998 & 1999-2007) Office of Statistics and Programming, National Center for Injury Prevention and Control, Centers for Disease Control and Prevention, http://webappa.cdc.gov/cgibin/broker.exe?_service=v8prod&_server=app-v-ehip-wisq.cdc.gov&_port=5081&_sessionid=g5362apnL52&_program=wisqars.percents10.sas&age1=.&age2=.&agetext=AllAges&category=ALL&_debug=0

[7] Author's own calculation based on a conservative abortion estimate of 1.3 million abortions per year. See Willke, 130, 131.

[8] Ash, 92, 93.

[9] Tallack, 72, 148.

[10] History & Archaeology, "Ralph Abernathy (1926-1990)," *The New Georgia Encyclopedia*, April 27, 2004, http://www.georgiaencyclopedia.org/nge/Article.jsp?id=h-2736.

[11] Alcorn, 76. Repeated in Shettles and Rorvik, *Rites of Life* (Grand Rapids, Mich.: Zondervan, 1983), 129.

[12] Ash, 21.

[13] Thomas Dubay, S.M., *The Evidential Power of Beauty* (San Francisco: Ignatius Press, 1999), 139.

[14] McDowell, 4-5.

[15] For a complete description, see Tallack, 62.

[16] Facts on Induced Abortion Worldwide, "Worldwide Incidence and NOTES Trends," Guttmacher Institute, October 2009, www.guttmacher.org/pubs/fb_IAW.html.

[17] Tallack, 50.

[18] WORDsearch 8. *Preaching Library*. Computer software. WORDsearch Corp., 2008. —Search in NKJV for "good" + "goodness."

[19] Tallack, 72, 148.

[20] Ash, 162.

[21] Scott Klusendorf, *The Case for Life* (Wheaton, Ill.: Crossway Books, 2009), 83.

[22] "conception." *The Pocket Oxford English Dictionary, tenth edition*, 2005.

[23] "conception." *The American Heritage Dictionary of the English Language*, 1970.

APRIL

[1] April Fool's Day, "Taco Bell Buys the Liberty Bell," *New York Times*, April 1, 2010, www.nytimes.com/imagepages/2010/04/01/business/01basics_CA0.html. See also "Entry at Museum of Hoaxes," 2008, www.museumofhoaxes.com/hoax/Hoaxipedia/Taco_Liberty_Bell/.

[2] Ensor, 98-101.

[3] Corrie ten Boom, with Elizabeth and John Sherrill, *The Hiding Place* (Grand Rapids, Mich.: Chosen Books, 35th anniversary edition, 2006), 250.

[4] *The ESV Study Bible, English Standard Version* (Wheaton, Ill.: Crossway Bibles, 2008), 1093.

[5] Tallack, 78.

[6] WRI Features. "How many species are there?" World Resource Institute, accessed October 2008, http://archive.wri.org/newsroom/wrifeatures_text.cfm?ContentID=535.

[7] Derek Prince, *Shaping History Through Prayer and Fasting* (New Kensington, Pa.: Whitaker House, 2002), 11-13.

[8] "love." *Webster's Compact Dictionary*, 2001.

[9] Tallack, 86.

[10] Benjamin Hart, *Faith & Freedom* (Christian Defense Fund, 1997), 108.

[11] David Barton, "The Founding Fathers on Jesus, Christianity and the Bible," "George Washington," Wall Builders – Issues and Articles May 2008, www.wallbuilders.com/LIBissuesArticles.asp?id=8755#FN125. Repeated in, George Washington, *The Last Official Address of His Excellency George Washington to the Legislature of the United States* (Hartford: Hudson and Goodwin, 1783), 12; see also *The New Annual Register or General Repository of History, Politics, and Literature, for the Year 1783* (London: G. Robinson, 1784), 150.

[12] Wilberforce, 197.

[13] Tallack, 96.

[14] Library Factfiles, "The Oklahoma City Bombing," *The Indianapolis Star*, Updated: August 9, 2004, www2.indystar.com/library/factfiles/crime/national/1995/oklahoma_city_bombing/ok.html

[15] *The ESV Study Bible*, 378.

[16] Ibid., 2335. Repeated in, Eusebius, *Church History* 2.25; 3.1.

[17] Tallack, 87-88.

[18] Timeline: "Abortion History Timeline," National Right to Life, accessed August, 2010, www.nrlc.org/abortion/facts/abortiontimeline.html.

[19] Peggy Noonan, *When Character was King: A Story of Ronald Reagan* (New York: Viking Penguin, 2001), 327.

[20] Donald J. Mabry, "Letter from a Birmingham Jail," Historical Text Archive: Electronic History Resources, http://historicaltextarchive.com/sections.php?action=read&artid=40.

[21] Elisabeth Elliot, *Shadow of the Almighty: The Life and Testament of Jim Elliot* (New York: HarperCollins Publishers, 1979), 132.

[22] James Strong, *The New Strong's Exhaustive Concordance of the Bible* (Nashville, Tenn.: Thomas Nelson Publishers, 1990), 877.

[23] Adam Clarke, "Adam Clarke--Biography and Commentary," SwordSearcher Bible Software accessed November 2, 2010, www.swordsearcher.com/christian-authors/adam-clarke.html. Repeated in, *The New Schaff-Herzog Encyclopedia of Religious Knowledge*.

MAY

1. Tallack, 56, 94.
2. "Kyle Busch." *Biography Resource Center* (Detroit: Gale, 2006), Gale Biography in Context, Web. 10 Nov. 2010. "Sarah Elizabeth Hughes." *Notable Sports Figures*, Dana R. Barnes, editor (Detroit: Gale, 2004), Gale Biography in Context, Web. 10 Nov. 2010. "Kay Panabaker." *Contemporary Theatre, Film and Television*, Vol. 70. (Detroit: Gale, 2006), Gale Biography in Context, Web. 10 Nov. 2010. See also www.kaypanabaker.com.
3. James Daley, editor, *Great Speeches by African Americans* (Mineola, N.Y.: Dover Publications, 2006), 13, 21, 28.
4. Dorie McCullough Lawson, *Posterity: Letters of Great Americans to their Children* (New York: Broadway Books, 2004), 138, 139.
5. Guttmacher Institute in Brief, "Facts on Induced Abortion in the United States," The Alan Guttmacher Institute, May 2010, www.guttmacher.org/pubs/fb_induced_abortion.html.
6. Edward McKendree Bounds, *The Complete Works of E. M. Bounds—Power through Prayer* (WORDsearch Cross e-book, 2008), fourth chapter.
7. Unger, 247, 898-899. See also *The Holman Illustrated Study Bible, Holman Christian Standard Bible* (Nashville, Tenn.: Holman Bible Publishers, 2006), 704.
8. McDowell, 27.
9. Tallack, 94.
10. *Ibid.*, p. 80.
11. John Newton, "Faith—Spiritual Knowledge—Seeking—True Repentance," Sermon index.net accessed November 2, 2010, www.sermonindex.net/modules/articles/index.php?view=article&aid=11619
12. Wilberforce, 127.
13. Willke and Willke, 140-141.
14. Theodor Seuss Geisel, *Horton Hears a Who!* (New York: Random House, 1954), opening page.
15. Ginny Owens, "Biography," ginnyowens.com, accessed August, 2010, www.ginnyowens.com/about-ginny-owens/.
16. Robert J. Morgan, *Then Sings My Soul: 150 of the World's Greatest Hymn Stories* (Nashville, Tenn.: Thomas Nelson, 2003), 185. See also The Spafford Children's Center, http://spaffordcenter.org/id1.html.
17. Tallack, 104.
18. Unger, vii.
19. The Economic Impact of Abortion, "What do 40 million Lost Lives Mean?" National Right to Life handout: National Right to Life Educational Trust Fund, 12/00.
20. Tallack, 32.
21. Louis Bülow, "The Oscar Schindler Story," www.auschwitz.dk, accessed August 26, 2010, www.auschwitz.dk/id2.htm.
22. Willke and Willke, 238.
23. *Ibid.*, 49-50.
24. Ash, 36, 41, 44.
25. NCHS – FASTATS, "Leading Causes of Death," Centers for Disease Control and Prevention, accessed October 6, 2008, www.cdc.gov/nchs/fastats/lcod.htm.
26. Guttmacher Institute In Brief, "Facts on Induced Abortion in the United States," The Alan Guttmacher Institute, May 2010, www.guttmacher.org/pubs/fb_induced_abortion.html.
27. Evens, 500.
28. Annual Report 2007-2008, "Summary of Services Delivered by Planned Parenthood Affiliate Health Centers: Calendar Years 2006 and 2007," Planned Parenthood, pages 9, 18 of 24, www.plannedparenthood.org/files/AR08_vFinal.pdf.
29. Joni Eareckson-Tada, "SCI Hall of Fame > 2006 HOF Inductees," National Spinal Cord Injury Association, August 15, 2006, www.spinalcord.org/news.php?dep=9&page=74&list=982.

JUNE

1. Tallack, 104.
2. Ralph G. Newman, editor, *Lincoln for the Ages* (Garden City, N.Y.: Doubleday & Company, 1960), 330-331.
3. Top 100 Speeches, "Martin Luther King, Jr." "I've Been to the Mountaintop," American Rhetoric, accessed August 27, 2010, www.americanrhetoric.com/speeches/mlkivebeentothemountaintop.htm.
4. David C. Whitney and Robin Vaughn Whitney, *The American Presidents*, eighth edition (Pleasantville, N.Y.: The Reader's Digest Association, 1996), 267, 268, 272.
5. Stephen E. Ambrose, *D-Day, June 6, 1944: The Climactic Battle of World War II* (New York: Simon & Schuster, 1994), 303, 582.
6. Evens, 502-503.
7. David Barton, "George Washington, Thomas Jefferson and Slavery in Virginia," Wall Builders--Issues and Articles January 2000, 9. Repeated in, Thomas Jefferson, *Notes on the State of Virginia*, second edition (New York: M. L. & W. A. Davis, 1794), 240-242, Query XVIII.
8. Tallack, 149.
9. *The Spirit-Filled Life Bible, New King James Version* (Nashville, Tenn.: Thomas Nelson Publishers, 1991), 750.
10. *The ESV Study Bible*, 1646.
11. Willke and Willke, 49-59.
12. *The ESV Study Bible*, 999.
13. *The Spirit-Filled Life Bible*, 958.
14. *The ESV Study Bible*, 809.
15. Peterson Hage, 29.
16. Jack Countryman, *If My People... A 40-Day Prayer Guide for Our Nation* (Nashville, Tenn.: Thomas Nelson, 2008), Day 36—*Dwight D. Eisenhower*.
17. Peterson Hage, 48.
18. Tallack, 108-109.
19. Frances Jane Crosby, "Fanny Crosby," The Cyber Hymnal, accessed November 2, 2010, www.hymntime.com/tch/bio/c/r/o/crosby_fj.htm. See also Fanny J. Crosby, *Fanny J. Crosby: An Autobiography*, second edition (Peabody, Mass.: Hendrickson Publishers, 2008).

JULY

1. Mary Comm, *Secret Sin: When God's People Choose Abortion* (Garden City, N.Y.: Morgan James Publishing, 2007), 5.
2. In His Own Words, "Quotations from the speeches and other works of Theodore Roosevelt," Theodore Roosevelt Association accessed October 7, 2010, www.theodoreroosevelt.org/life/quotes.htm. Repeated in, Theodore Roosevelt, *The Great Adventure: Present-Day Studies in American Nationalism* (New York: Charles Scribner's Sons, 1918), 5
3. "glory." *The American Heritage Dictionary of the English Language*, 1970.
4. Whitney and Whitney, 25.
5. Martin Gilbert, *The Righteous: The Unsung Heroes of the Holocaust* (New York: Holt, 2004), 13.
6. Spurgeon, 32.
7. Tallack, 114, 118.
8. Whitney and Whitney, 134.
9. Mark Crutcher, *Lime 5* (Denton, Tex.: Life Dynamics, 1996), 11-82.
10. Everett with Shaw, 105-106.
11. "stranger." *Webster's Compact Dictionary*, 2001.
12. Arthur T. Pierson, *George Müller of Bristol: His Life of Prayer and Faith* (Grand Rapids, Mich.: Kregel Publications, 1999), 365.
13. "victory." *The American Heritage Dictionary of the English Language*, 1970.
14. Newman, 282.
15. John F. Kennedy, *Profiles in Courage* (New York: HarperCollins, 2000), 1.
16. Alcorn, 15. Repeated in, "Gallup: Seventy-Two Percent of Teens Say

Abortion Wrong," November 24, 2003, WorldNetDaily.com.

[17] Alcorn, 17. Repeated in, *Family Planning Perspectives*, July-August 1996, 12.

[18] "righteous." *The American Heritage Dictionary of the English Language*, 1970.

[19] Tallack, 112-113.

[20] John Foxe, *The New Foxe's Book of Martyrs*, updated by Harold J. Chadwick (North Brunswick, N.J.: Bridge-Logos Publishers, 1997), 10.

AUGUST

[1] Gilbert, 142.

[2] Lloyd de Vries, "Poland Honors Holocaust Hero," CBS News (AP) March 14, 2007, http://www.cbsnews.com/stories/2007/03/14/world/main2568540.shtml. See also Harry de Quetteville, "'Female Schindler' Irena Sendler, who saved thousands of Jewish children, dies," Telegraph.co.uk., accessed April 20, 2009, www.telegraph.co.uk/news/1948680/Female-Schindler-Irene-Sendler-who-saved-thousands-of-Jewish-children-dies.html.

[3] *The ESV Study Bible*, 1370.

[4] Unger, 1133.

[5] Alcorn, 17.

[6] Strong, 931.

[7] Tallack, 148-149.

[8] Peterson Hage, 52. See also Teresa Norman, *A World of Baby Names* (New York: Berkley Publishing Group, 1996), 73.

[9] C.S. Lewis, *Mere Christianity* (New York: Macmillan Publishing Company, 1960), 56.

[10] Willke and Willke, 286-287. Repeated in, Italy Birth Rate…, *Boston Globe*, July 31, 1994, 13, W. Montabono, "Italian Baby Boom Goes Bust," *Los Angeles Times*, June 24, 1994, A1 & A6.

[11] The Chernenko Family and The Duggar Family, "Large Families," Incredible Births, accessed August 31, 2010, www.incrediblebirths.com/large_families.html.

[21] Pierson, 301.

[22] Natasha Cica, "Abortion Law in Australia, Major Issues Summary," Law and Bills Digest Group 31 August 1998, www.aph.gov.au/library/pubs/rp/1998-99/99rp01.htm#major.

[23] WORDsearch 8. *Preaching Library*. Computer software. WORDsearch Corp., 2008. —Search in NIV for "rescue."

[24] *The ESV Study Bible*, 1677.

[25] Pierson, 297-298.

[12] *The ESV Study Bible*, 1620.

[13] *Ibid*, 123.

[14] *Ibid.*, 1809-1810.

[15] E. W. Bullinger, *Number in Scripture: Its Supernatural Design and Spiritual Significance* (Grand Rapids, Mich.: Kregel Publications, 1967), 108.

[16] Robert Jamieson, A.R. Fausset, and David Brown, *A Commentary: Critical, Experimental, and Practical on the Old and New Testaments* (Toledo, Ohio: Jerome B. Names & Co., 1884, WORDsearch CROSS e-book).

[17] Warren W. Wiersbe, *The Cross of Jesus: What His Words from Calvary Mean for Us* (Grand Rapids, Mich.: Baker Books, 1997), 50.

[18] Ash, 92.

[19] China Through A Lens, "Family Planning Law and China's Birth Control Situation," china.org.cn, accessed May 5, 2009, www.china.org.cn/english/2002/Oct/46138.htm. See also Alcorn, 60.

[20] Tallack, 124.

[21] Alcorn, 59-60. Repeated in, Jo McGowan, "In India They Abort Females," *Newsweek*, February 13, 1989. And *Medical World News*, December 1, 1975, 45. See also *Newsweek*, "Brave New Babies," February 1, 2004.

[22] Pierson, 298-299.

[23] David Barton, "The Founding Fathers on Jesus, Christianity and the Bible," "Benjamin Rush," Wall Builders –

Issues and Articles May 2008, www.
wallbuilders.com/LIBissuesArticles.
asp?id=8755#FN125. Repeated in,
Benjamin Rush, *The Autobiography of
Benjamin Rush*, George W. Corner, editor
(Princeton: Princeton University Press,
1948), pp. 165-166.

24 Watermark. *A Grateful People*. Compact
disc. Rocketown Records, 2006 jacket
notes.

25 Table 1, "Number of deaths, death rates,
and age-adjusted death rates, by race
and sex: United States, 1940, 1950,

1960, 1970, and 1980-2006," Centers for
Disease Control and Prevention, May
2, 2009, www.disastercenter.com/cdc/
Table_1_2006.html.

26 Hugh Ross, *More Than a Theory: Revealing
a Testable Model for Creation* (Grand
Rapids, Mich.: Baker Books, 2009), 112.

27 Tallack, 122.

28 Sharon Jayson, "Power of a Super
Attitude." *USA TODAY* October
12, 2004, www.usatoday.com/news/
health/2004-10-12-mind-body_x.htm.

SEPTEMBER

1 Bonnie Chernin Rogoff, "Who Cries
For Christin Gilbert?" *GOPUSA* June
8, 2009, www.gopusa.com/commentary/
brogoff/2009/br_06081.shtml.

2 Linda J. Waite, Maggie Gallagher,
*The Case For Marriage: Why Married
People Are Happier, Healthier, and Better
Off Financially* (New York: Broadway
Books, 2000), 47-64, 78-96, 97-109.
See also David Popenoe and Barabara
Dafoe Whitehead, "Ten Important
Research Findings on Marriage and
Choosing a Marriage Partner – Helpful
Facts for Young Adults," The National
Marriage Project November 2004,
www.virginia.edu/marriageproject/pdfs/
pubTenThingsYoungAdults.pdf.

3 Administration for Children and Families,
"The Healthy Marriage Initiative,"
"Benefits of Healthy Marriages," U.S.
Department of Health and Human
Services, accessed August 24, 2009, www.
acf.hhs.gov/healthymarriage/benefits/
index.html.

4 Tallack, 132.

5 Aiden Wilson Tozer, *The Knowledge of
the Holy* (New York: Harper Collins
Publishers, 1961), vii.

6 Dietrich Bonhoeffer, *The Cost of
Discipleship* (New York: Simon & Schuster,
first Touchstone edition, 1995), 22.

7 R. C. Sproul, *Abortion: A Rational Look
at an Emotional Issue* (Colorado Springs,

Colo.: NavPress, 1990), 151.

8 Wiersbe, Warren W., *The Bible
Exposition Commentary – The Prophets*
(Colorado Springs, Colo.: Victor, 2002).
WORD*search* CROSS e-book. 1. Babylon
(Isa. 13:1-14:23; 21:1-10). See also *The
Spirit-Filled Life Bible*, 981.

9 Tozer, 90.

10 9/11 by the Numbers, "Death, destruction,
charity, salvation, war, money, real estate,
spouses, babies, and other September 11
statistics," *New York Magazine*—nymag.
com, accessed September 1, 2009, www.
nymag.com/news/articles/wtc/1year/
numbers.htm.

11 Unger, 126.

12 Tallack, 133.

13 Bruce Catton, *The American Heritage
New History of the Civil War* (New York:
MetroBooks, 2001), 224-227.

14 Ensor, 21. See also Alcorn, 17.

15 Sproul, 149-150. Repeated in, Charles
Colson, *Kingdoms in Conflict* (Grand
Rapids, Mich.: Zondervan Publishing
House, 1987), 105.

16 See Albert Barnes, *Notes on the New
Testament Explanatory and Practical*, edited
by Robert Frew (WORD*search* CROSS
e-book); Adam Clarke, A *Commentary
and Critical Notes* (New York: Abingdon-
Cokesbury Press, 1826, WORD*search*
CROSS e-book); Warren W. Wiersbe,
Wiersbe's Expository Outlines – Wiersbe's

Expository Outlines on the Old Testament (Colorado Springs, Colo.: Victor, 1993, WORD*search* CROSS e-book).

17 Willke and Willke, 293. Repeated in *Washington Times*, editorial, 7-1-2001.

18 Klusendorf, 23. Repeated in, Paul Duncan, "The Pearls of Abortion," *Evangel*, January, 1995.

19 *The Constitution of the United States of America with the Declaration of Independence and the Articles of Confederation* (New York: Fall River Press, 2002), 37. The emphasis in the text is mine.

20 "wanted." *Webster's Compact Dictionary* 2001.

21 Alcorn, 38.

22 Roger Harms, M.D. and Myra Wick, M.D., Ph.D., medical editors, *Mayo Clinic Guide to a Healthy Pregnancy* (Intercourse, PA: Good Books, 2011), 86.

23 Abraham Lincoln, *Selected Speeches and Writings* (New York: Library of America, Vintage Books, 1992), 187.

24 Life Dynamics Inc., "The Blackmun Wall," lifedynamics.com, accessed September 3, 2010, www.lifedynamics. com/Pro-life_Group/Pro-choice_Women/. See also Mark Crutcher, *Lime 5* (Denton, Tex.: Life Dynamics Inc., 1996).

25 Willke and Willke, 98-99.

26 *Ibid*, 251-252.

OCTOBER

1 John Wimber, "Isn't He." 1980 Mercy/ Vineyard CCLI# 1541 worship archive, accessed September 28, 2009, www. worshiparchive.com/song/isnt-he.

2 Tallack, 146.

3 *The Spirit-Filled Life Bible*, 1256.

4 Willke and Willke, 338.

5 Everett with Shaw, 176.

6 Annual Report 2007-2008, "Summary of Services Delivered by Planned Parenthood Affiliate Health Centers: Calendar Years 2006 and 2007," Planned Parenthood, page 18 of 24, www.plannedparenthood. org/files/AR08_vFinal.pdf.

7 John T. Woolley, Gerhard Peters, "John F. Kennedy—Proclamation 3487--Child Health Day," The American Presidency Project [online]. Santa Barbara, Calif.: University of California, August 16, 1962, accessed October 1, 2009, www.presidency. ucsb.edu/ws/index.php?pid=24032.

8 Billy Graham, *Hope for Each Day* 2002 ed. (Nashville, Tenn.: J. Countryman/Thomas Nelson, 2002), 359.

9 Ensor, 106. Repeated in George Grant, *Third Time Around: The History of the Pro-Life Movement from the First Century to the Present* (Brentwood, Tenn.: Wolgemuth &

Hyatt, 1991), 59.

10 Carol J. Williams, "Netherlands OKs Assisted Suicide." *Los Angeles Times* April 11, 2001, http://articles.latimes.com/2001/ apr/11/news/mn-49567/3.

11 Willke and Willke, 232.

12 Administration for Children & Families, "Child Maltreatment 2007—Summary," U.S. Department of Health and Human Services, accessed October 7, 2009, www. acf.hhs.gov/programs/cb/pubs/cm07/ summary.htm.

13 "Medicine: I.U.D. Debate." *Time* May 26, 1980, www.time.com/time/magazine/ article/0,9171,951492-1,00.html.

14 See Adam Clarke, *A Commentary and Critical Notes* (New York: Abingdon-Cokesbury Press, 1826, WORD*search* CROSS e-book); Warren W. Wiersbe, *The Bible Exposition Commentary – History* (Colorado Springs, Colo.: Victor, 2003, WORD*search* CROSS e-book); Robert Jamieson, A.R. Fausset, and David Brown, *A Commentary: Critical, Experimental, and Practical on the Old and New Testaments* (Toledo, Ohio: Jerome B. Names & Co., 1884, WORD*search* CROSS e-book).

15 Tozer, 90-91.
16 Warren W. Wiersbe, *The Bible Exposition Commentary – New Testament, Volume 2* (Colorado Springs, Colo.: Victor, 2001, WORD*search* CROSS e-book — Forgiveness Matt. 18:21-35).
17 Debbie Morris, *Forgiving the Dead Man Walking* (Grand Rapids, Mich.: Zondervan Publishing House, 1998), 250-251.
18 Alejandro Monteverde, *Bella*, DVD, Lions Gate Entertainment, 2006, Metanoia Films, LLC. 91 min., jacket notes. See also www.bellamoviesite.com/site/#/film/awards/.
19 Towns, 102-103.
20 *The Spirit-Filled Life Bible*, 320.
21 Unger, 555.
22 James Ryle, *A Dream Come True* (Orlando, Fla.: Creation House, 1995), 172. Repeated in, Charles Spurgeon, *Metropolitan Tabernacle Pulpit* (Carlisle, Pa.: Banner of Truth, 1991), vol. 14, 217-228.
23 Unger, 412.
24 David Faber with Anna Vaisman & James D. Kitchen, *Because of Romek: A Holocaust Survivor's Memoir*, second edition (La Mesa, Calif.: Faber Press, 2006), 145-146.
25 Collections, "Come before winter," by Clarence Macartney, 1879-1957." Precept

Austin, page 3 of 8, accessed November 8, 2009, www.preceptaustin.org/come_before_winter.htm.
26 Bob Bauman, "A local word on the Word" *Lumina News* October 15, 2009, http://www.luminanews.com/article.asp?aid=5190&iid=188&sud=42 See also http://revitalizeyourchurch.blogspot.com/2005/08/come-before-winter.html.
27 Michael Clancy, "Story of the 'Fetal Hand Grasp' Photograph." Michaelclancy.com, accessed September 9, 2010, www.michaelclancy.com/story.html.
28 Peterson Hage, 5.
29 *The ESV Study Bible*, 658.
30 Tallack, 144.
31 Strong, 95, 189, 194, 531.
32 Crutcher, 131. Repeated in, Council on Scientific Affairs, American Medical Association, "Induced Termination of Pregnancy Before and After *Roe v. Wade*: Trends in the Mortality and Morbidity of Women," *Journal of the American Medical Association*, 12/9/92—"Abortion Providers Share Inner Conflicts," *The American Medical News*, 7/12/93—Rachel Benson Gold, *Abortion and Women's Health*, Alan Guttmacher Institute, 1990.
33 Towns, 31.

NOVEMBER

1 *The ESV Study Bible*, 2059.
2 Mercy Me, *Spoken For*. Compact disc. M2 Communications, LLC, 2002. Jacket notes.
3 Bethany Christian Services, "About Us," bethany.org accessed September 10, 2010, www.bethany.org/A55798/bethanywww.nsf/0/C232C8DA99A0BA8685256CF200083E24.
4 cbnmusic.com, "Nicole Nordeman," cbn.com, The Christian Broadcast Network, accessed September 10, 2010, www.cbn.com/cbnmusic/artists/nordeman_nichole.aspx.
5 Nicole Nordeman. *Brave*. Compact disc.

Sparrow Records, 2005. Jacket notes.
6 *The ESV Study Bible*, 1872.
7 *The Spirit-Filled Life Bible*, 172.
8 Believe in Zero, "No child should ever die from a preventable cause. Every day 24,000 do." UNICEF United States Fund accessed January 26, 2010, www.unicefusa.org/campaigns/believe-in-zero/.
9 Facts About Abortion, "Worldwide Abortion Statistics," Abort73.com, accessed September 10, 2010, www.abort73.com/abortion_facts/worldwide_abortion_statistics. — Author's own calculation based on the estimate of 42 million abortions per year.

10 David J. Vaughan. *Give Me Liberty: The Uncompromising Statesmanship of Patrick Henry* (Elkton, Md.: Highland Books, 1997), 186. Repeated in William Wirt Henry, *Patrick Henry: Life, Correspondence and Speeches* (Harrisonberg, Va.: Sprinkle Publications, 1993 [1891]), 2:631.

11 "History of Veterans Day," United States Department of Veterans Affairs, accessed January 27, 2010, www1.va.gov/opa/vetsday/vetdayhistory.asp.

12 Sam S. Platamone, Member K Company. 222nd Infantry 42nd Infantry Rainbow Division, U.S. Army, Liberators of Dachau. Faber with Vaisman and Kitchen, back cover.

13 Klusendorf, 49.

14 Tozer, 82.

15 *The ESV Study Bible*, 1084.

16 Warren W. Wiersbe, *The Bible Exposition Commentary – New Testament, Volume 2* (Colorado Springs, Colo.: Victor, 2001, WORDsearch CROSS e-book.—Turn Away from the False (2 Tim. 3:1-9).

17 Aiden Wilson Tozer, compiled by Marilynne E. Foster, *Tozer on the Holy Spirit* (Camp Hill, Pa.: Wing Spread Publishers, 2000), September 19.

18 WORDsearch 8. *Preaching Library*.

Computer software. WORDsearch Corp., 2008. Search in NASB for "darkness" and "light,"—number of occurrences.

19 Hymn History, "Trust and Obey," Open Bible Institute & Theological Seminary, accessed February 8, 2010, www.invitationtochrist.org/trust_and_obey.htm. See also Robert J. Morgan, *Then Sings My Soul: 150 of the World's Greatest Hymn Stories* (Nashville, Tenn.: Thomas Nelson, 2003), 221.

20 Tozer, 84.

21 Unger, 263, 972.

22 "Thanksgiving Day." *Encyclopædia Britannica*, 2010. Encyclopædia Britannica Online, accessed February 19, 2010, www.britannica.com/EBchecked/topic/590003/Thanksgiving-Day.

23 Mary Waalkes Verwys, *Wednesday Mourning: A Sidewalk Counselor's Journal of God's Grace in the Abortion Struggle* (Grand Rapids, Mich.: Roberts Publishing, 2003), 8.

24 *Ibid.*, 72-75.

25 Elliot, 108.

26 Corrie ten Boom, with Elizabeth and John Sherrill, *The Hiding Place* (Grand Rapids, Mich.: Chosen Books, 2006), 55.

DECEMBER

1 Jessica Shaver and Gianna Jessen, *Gianna: Aborted . . . and Lived to Tell About It* (Wheaton, Ill.: Tyndale House Publishers, 1995).

2 Bernard N. Nathanson, *The Hand of God: A Journey from Death to Life by the Abortion Doctor who Changed His Mind* (Washington, D.C.: Regnery Publishing, Inc., 2001), 140-141.

3 *The Constitution of the United States of America with the Declaration of Independence and the Articles of Confederation*, 67.

4 "Amendment 48: 'Personhood' issue crushed" *The Gazette* –gazette.com

November 4, 2008, www.gazette.com/articles/amendment-42820-headline-text.html.

5 *The ESV Study Bible*, 1388.

6 Abraham Lincoln, *Great Speeches Abraham Lincoln*, with historical notes by John Grafton (New York: Dover Publications, 1991), 105.

7 Elizabeth Ring-Cassidy and Ian Gentles, *Women's Health After Abortion: The Medical and Psychological Evidence*, second edition (Toronto, Ontario, Canada: deVeber Institute, 2003), 2-4.

8 "redeem." *The Pocket Oxford English Dictionary*, tenth edition, 2005.

9 Evens, 464.

10 "The Abolition of Slavery and 'The Better Hour,' William Wilberforce and the Clapham Group," Wilberforce Central, accessed September 22, 2010, www.wilberforcecentral.org/wfc/Wilberforce/index.htm.

11 *The ESV Study Bible*, 1755.

12 Peterson Hage, 21.

13 *The ESV Study Bible*, 1643.

14 *Ibid.*, 1000.

15 *Ibid.*, 1966.

16 *The Spirit-Filled Life Bible*, 1908.

17 *Ibid.*, 1932.

18 Ensor, 127.

19 Strong, *Exhaustive Concordance*, 212.—Greek Dictionary, 77.

20 Helen M. Fessenden, *Fessenden Builder of Tomorrows* (New York: Coward-McCann, 1940), 153-154.

21 Philip Van Doren Stern, *The Greatest Gift* (New York, NY: Viking Penguin, 1996).

22 Craig Brian Larson and Brian Lowery, ed. *1001 Quotations that Connect: Timeless Wisdom for Preaching, Teaching, and Writing* (Grand Rapids, Mich.: Zondervan, 2009), 305.

23 ten Boom, with Sherrill, 90.

24 Office of Protected Resources, "Endangered Species Act (ESA)," U.S. National Oceanic and Atmospheric Administration (NOAA) Fisheries, accessed September 23, 2010, http://www.nmfs.noaa.gov/pr/laws/esa/.

25 David K. Kyle. *Blood Money: The Business of Abortion*. DVD. TAH.LLC, 2010. www.bloodmoneyfilm.com. See also Ronald Reagan's "Evil Empire Speech," presented at the National Association of Evangelicals in Orlando, Florida, March 8, 1983. National Center, accessed December 8, 2010, www.nationalcenter.org/ReaganEvilEmpire1983.html.

26 Martin Luther King, Jr., "The Drum Major Instinct," Martin Luther King, Jr. and the Global Freedom Struggle accessed November 10, 2010, *http://mlk-kpp01.stanford.edu/index.php/encyclopedia/documentsentry/doc_the_drum_major_instinct/* Repeated in Clayborne Carson and Peter Holloran, ed., *A Knock At Midnight: Inspiration from the Great Sermons of Reverend Martin Luther King, Jr.* (New York: Time Warner AudioBooks, 1998)—The Drum Major Instinct.

27 WORDsearch 8. *Preaching Library*. Computer software. WORDsearch Corp., 2008.—Search in NASB for "Jesus" + "life."

also by Joel Patchen

What is the impact of a single life?

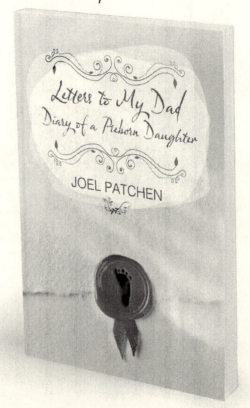

What will the impact of your life be?

Journey with Brooke Anna as she discovers her calling and the purpose for her life. Discover with Brooke the plans God has for each and every life—*the value of every created being.* Share with her the wonders of the womb and the joys of living. Experience how God's place of beginning (the sanctuary of protection we call the womb) is the foundation for everything we are and all we might become. Come with Brooke and discover *life*!

also by Joel Patchen

silence can be deadly...